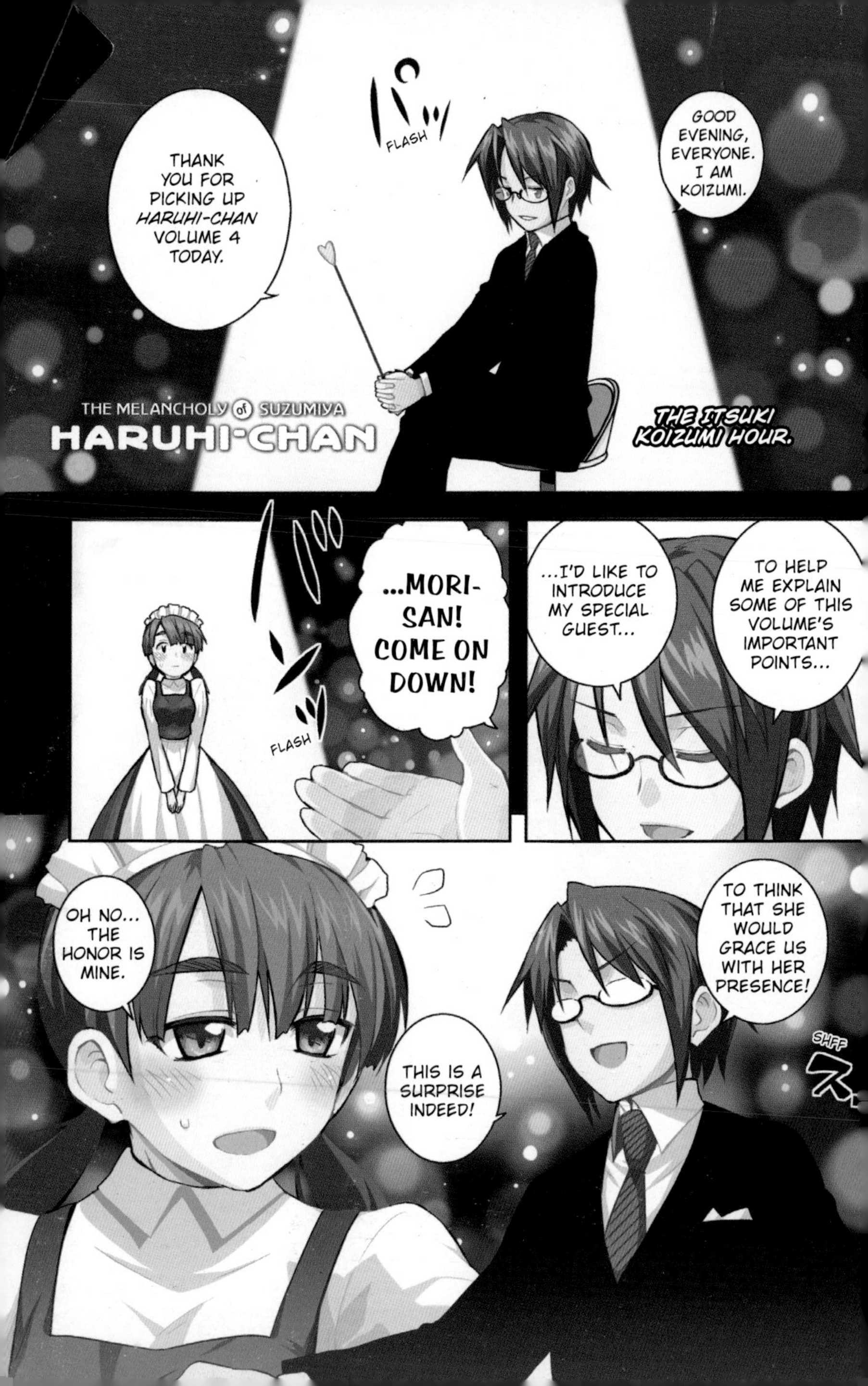
GOOD EVENING, EVERYONE. I AM KOIZUMI.
FLASH
THANK YOU FOR PICKING UP HARUHI-CHAN VOLUME 4 TODAY.
THE ITSUKI KOIZUMI HOUR.
THE MELANCHOLY of SUZUMIYA
HARUHI-CHAN
TO HELP ME EXPLAIN SOME OF THIS VOLUME'S IMPORTANT POINTS...
...I'D LIKE TO INTRODUCE MY SPECIAL GUEST...
...MORI-SAN! COME ON DOWN!
FLASH
TO THINK THAT SHE WOULD GRACE US WITH HER PRESENCE!
SHFF
THIS IS A SURPRISE INDEED!
OH NO... THE HONOR IS MINE.

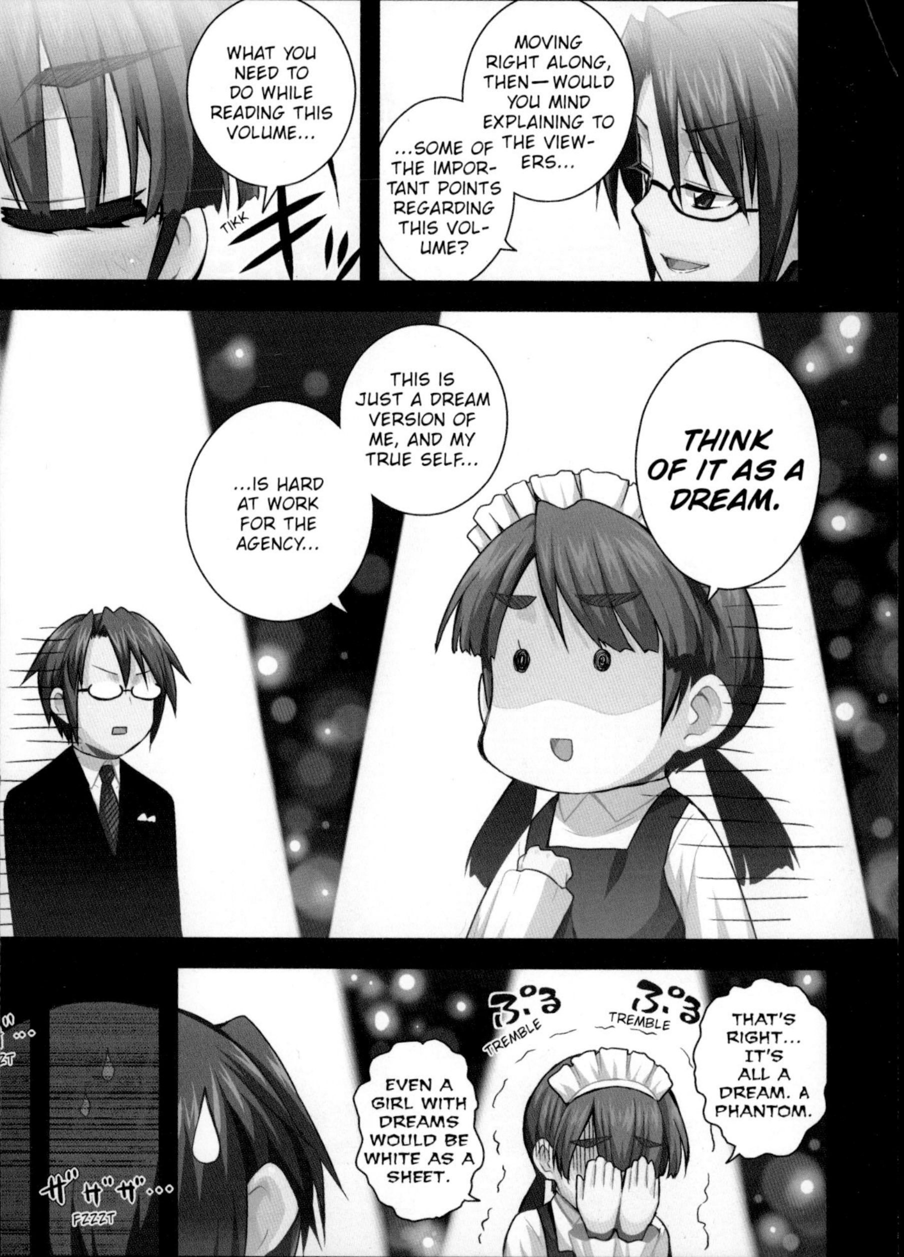
MOVING RIGHT ALONG, THEN—WOULD YOU MIND EXPLAINING TO THE VIEWERS...
...SOME OF THE IMPORTANT POINTS REGARDING THIS VOLUME?
WHAT YOU NEED TO DO WHILE READING THIS VOLUME...
TIKK
THINK OF IT AS A DREAM.
THIS IS JUST A DREAM VERSION OF ME, AND MY TRUE SELF...
...IS HARD AT WORK FOR THE AGENCY...
ぷるぷる
TREMBLE
ぷるぷる
TREMBLE
THAT'S RIGHT... IT'S ALL A DREAM. A PHANTOM.
EVEN A GIRL WITH DREAMS WOULD BE WHITE AS A SHEET.
ザザザ...
FZZZT

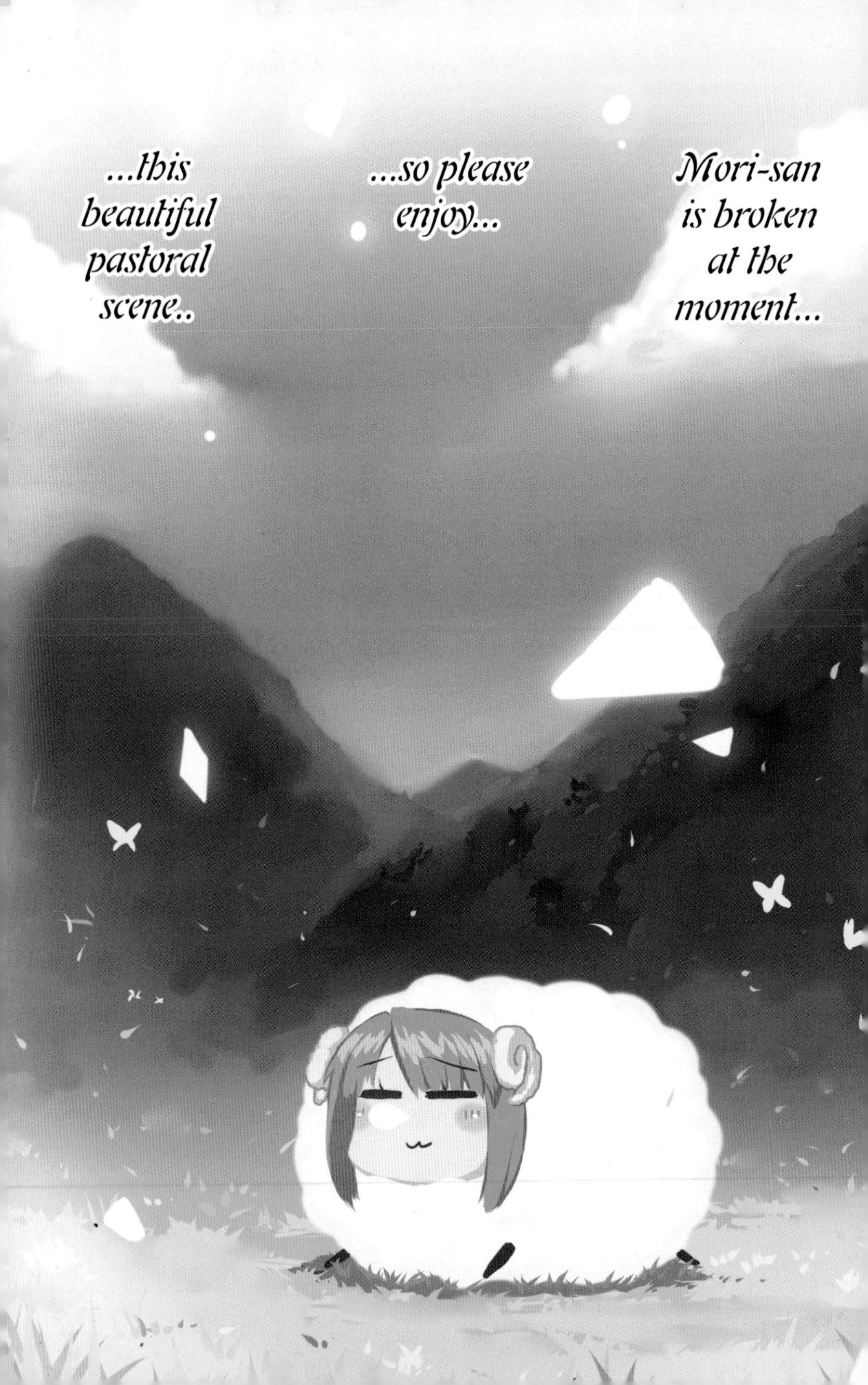
Mori-san is broken at the moment...
...so please enjoy...
...this beautiful pastoral scene..

The Melancholy of Suzumiya Haruhi-chan 04

INDEX

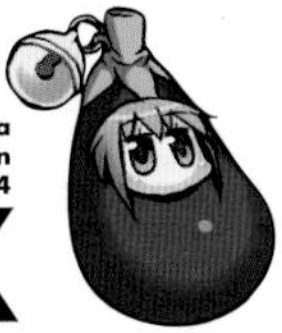

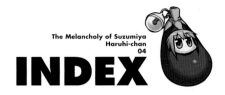

THE MELANCHOLY of SUZUMIYA

HARUHI-CHAN

04

The Untold Adventures of the SOS Brigade

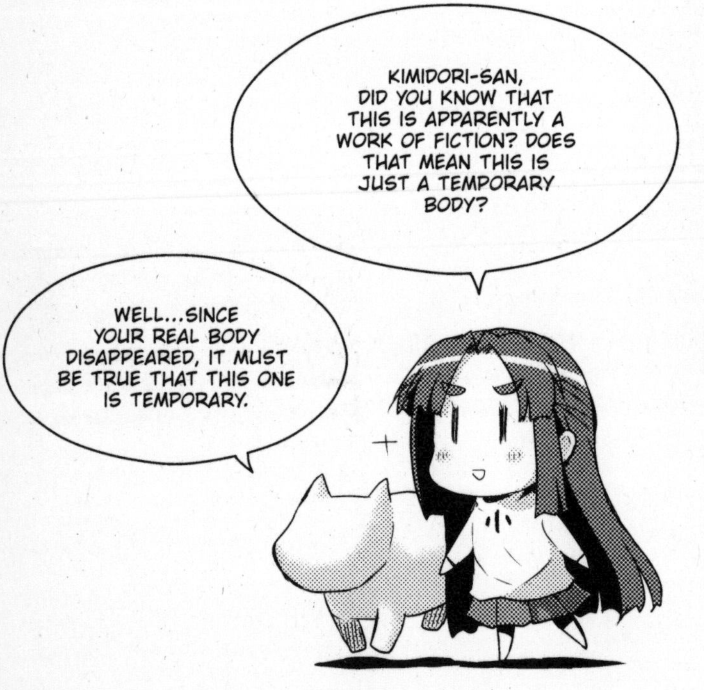
KIMIDORI-SAN, DID YOU KNOW THAT THIS IS APPARENTLY A WORK OF FICTION? DOES THAT MEAN THIS IS JUST A TEMPORARY BODY?
WELL...SINCE YOUR REAL BODY DISAPPEARED, IT MUST BE TRUE THAT THIS ONE IS TEMPORARY.

STORY: **NAGARU TANIGAWA** ART: **PUYO** CHARACTERS: NOIZI ITO

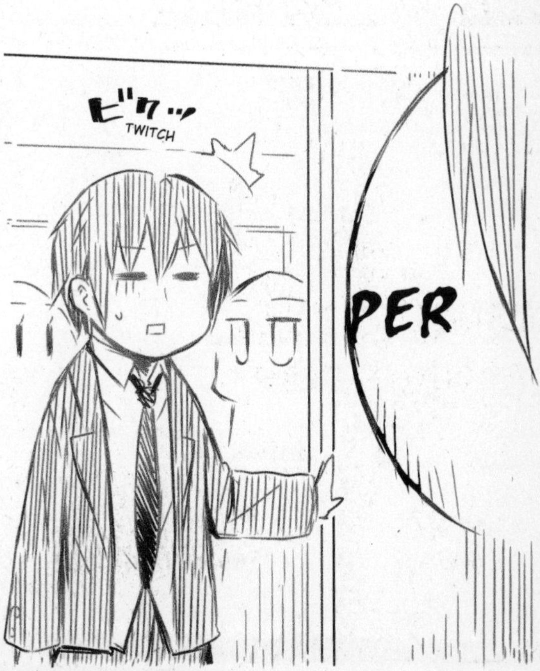
ビクッ
TWITCH
PER

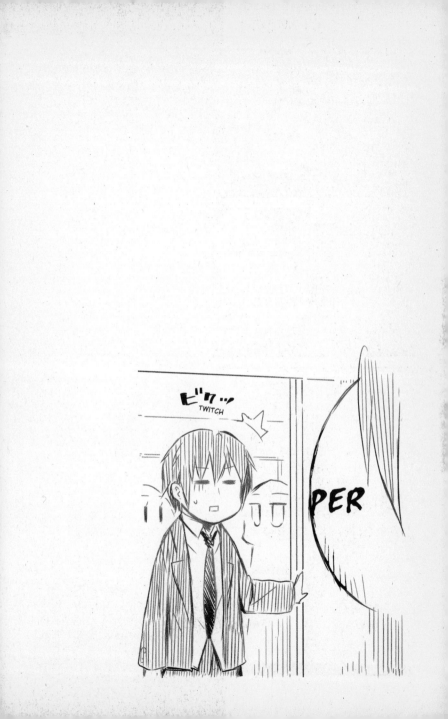

A DAY IN MARCH

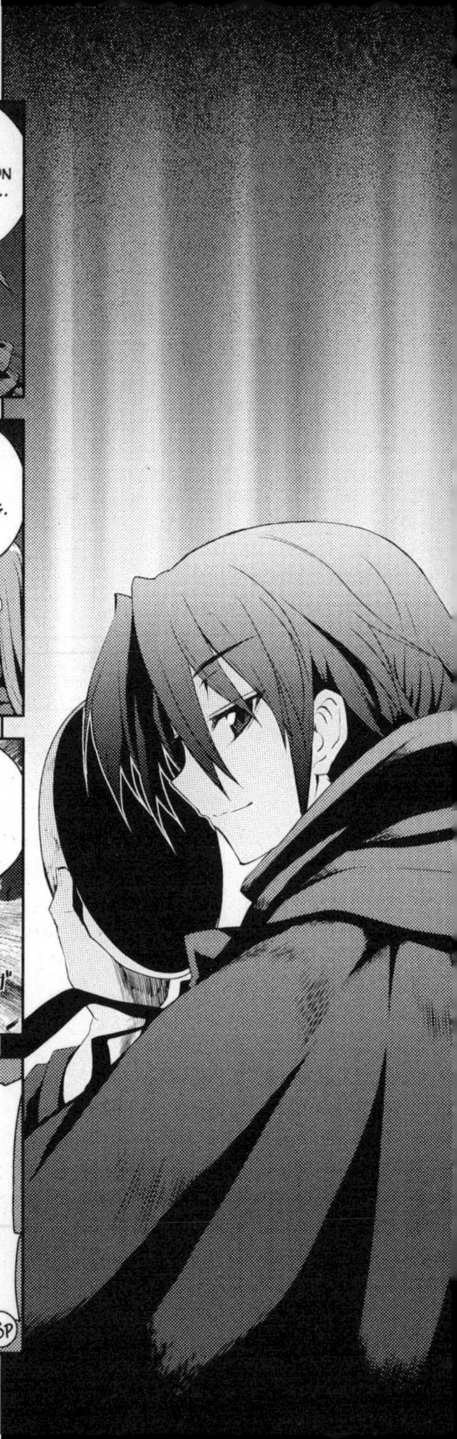

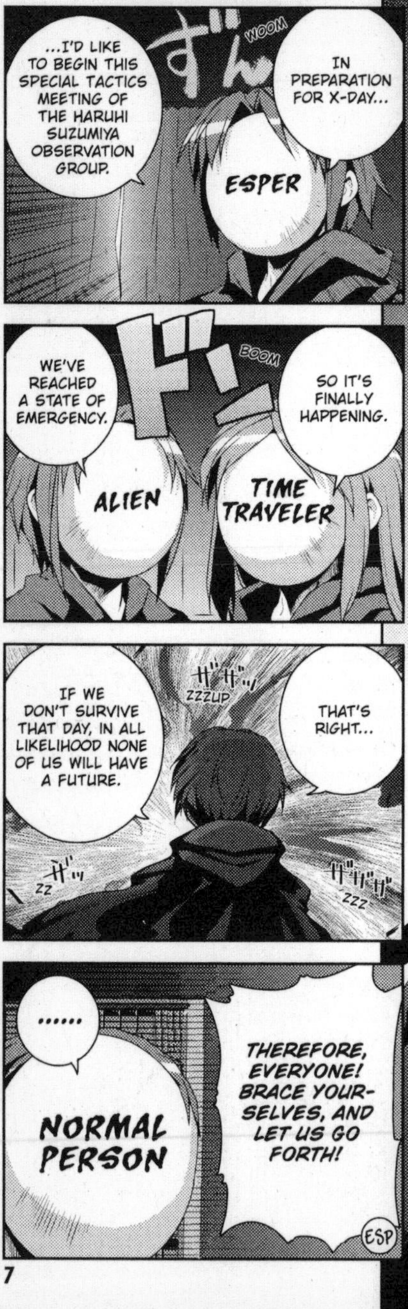
IN PREPARATION FOR X-DAY...
WOOM
...I'D LIKE TO BEGIN THIS SPECIAL TACTICS MEETING OF THE HARUHI SUZUMIYA OBSERVATION GROUP.
ESPER
SO IT'S FINALLY HAPPENING.
BOOM
WE'VE REACHED A STATE OF EMERGENCY.
TIME TRAVELER
ALIEN
THAT'S RIGHT...
ZZZUP
IF WE DON'T SURVIVE THAT DAY, IN ALL LIKELIHOOD NONE OF US WILL HAVE A FUTURE.
ZZZ
ZZ
THEREFORE, EVERYONE! BRACE YOURSELVES, AND LET US GO FORTH!
......
NORMAL PERSON
ESP

STATEMENTS OF OPINION

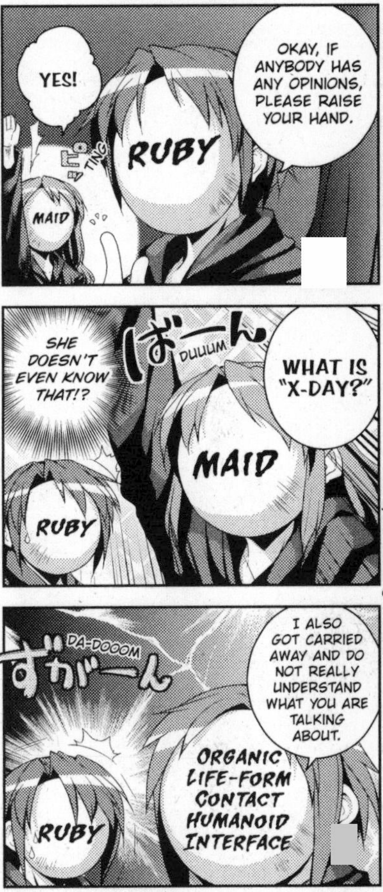
OKAY, IF ANYBODY HAS ANY OPINIONS, PLEASE RAISE YOUR HAND.
YES!
TING
RUBY
MAID
WHAT IS "X-DAY?"
DUUUM
SHE DOESN'T EVEN KNOW THAT!?
MAID
RUBY
I ALSO GOT CARRIED AWAY AND DO NOT REALLY UNDERSTAND WHAT YOU ARE TALKING ABOUT.
DA-DOOOM
ORGANIC LIFE-FORM CONTACT HUMANOID INTERFACE
RUBY
I'M SO GLAD I WASN'T THE ONLY ONE WHO DIDN'T GET IT!
AH HA HA...
BACK TO SQUARE ONE.

IMPORTANT PRESENTATION

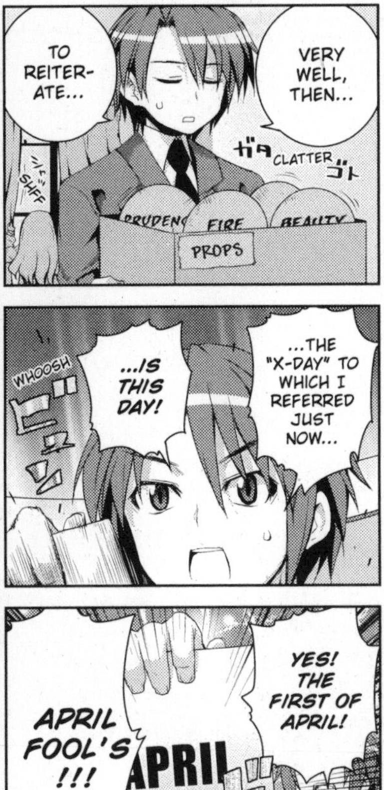
VERY WELL, THEN...
TO REITER-ATE...
CLATTER
SHFF
PRUDENC
FIRE
BEAUTY
PROPS
...THE "X-DAY" TO WHICH I REFERRED JUST NOW...
...IS THIS DAY!
WHOOSH
YES! THE FIRST OF APRIL!
APRIL FOOL'S !!!
APRIL 1ST
WHAM
ALSO KNOWN AS "THE DAY ALL OF SUZUMIYA'S LIES BECOME REALITY"!
EEEEK
THAT'S A WEIGHTY ENOUGH ISSUE, IT MAY JUST CRUSH US ALL!
K

RUBY

•Koizumi •Usually scheming in the background, but today he's front-and-center for once.

•Kyon •The lone normal person in the SOS Brigade. As a straight man, spends his days enduring countless troubles.

•Mikuru-chan •The Brigade's time-traveling mascot, she'll have a more active role in this volume.

REDXXXX-SENSEI

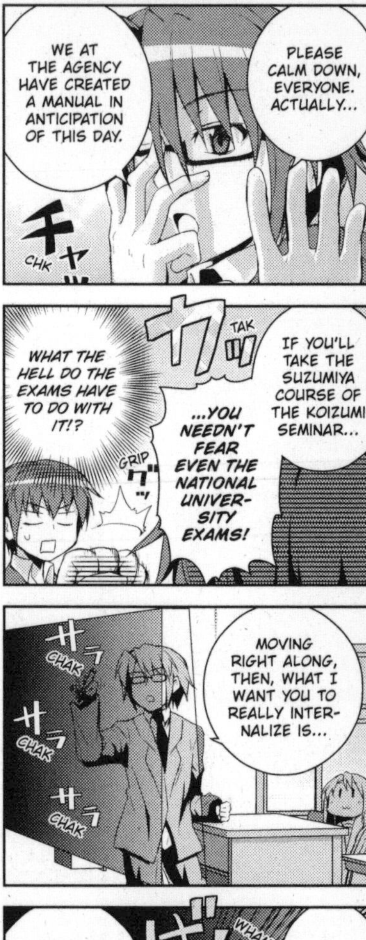
PLEASE CALM DOWN, EVERYONE. ACTUALLY...
WE AT THE AGENCY HAVE CREATED A MANUAL IN ANTICIPATION OF THIS DAY.
CHK
TAK
IF YOU'LL TAKE THE SUZUMIYA COURSE OF THE KOIZUMI SEMINAR...
...YOU NEEDN'T FEAR EVEN THE NATIONAL UNIVERSITY EXAMS!
WHAT THE HELL DO THE EXAMS HAVE TO DO WITH IT!?
GRIP
MOVING RIGHT ALONG, THEN, WHAT I WANT YOU TO REALLY INTERNALIZE IS...
CHAK
CHAK
CHAK
WHAM
...THIS!
Principle #1 Avoid Suzumiya
THAT'S GONNA BE TOUGH IF YOU'RE IN THE SAME CLASS AS HER.

ADVICE

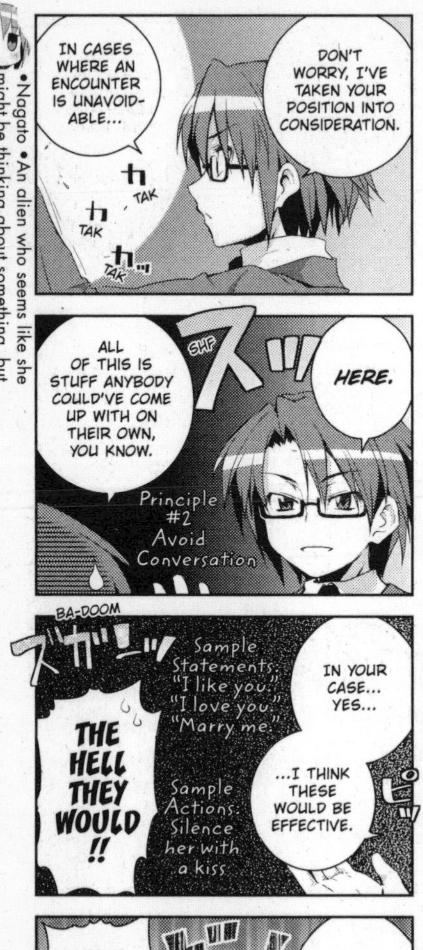
DON'T WORRY, I'VE TAKEN YOUR POSITION INTO CONSIDERATION.
IN CASES WHERE AN ENCOUNTER IS UNAVOIDABLE...
TAK
TAK
TAK
SHF
HERE.
Principle #2 Avoid Conversation
ALL OF THIS IS STUFF ANYBODY COULD'VE COME UP WITH ON THEIR OWN, YOU KNOW.
IN YOUR CASE... YES...
...I THINK THESE WOULD BE EFFECTIVE.
Sample Statements: "I like you." "I love you." "Marry me."
Sample Actions: Silence her with a kiss
BA-DOOM
THE HELL THEY WOULD!!
HOWEVER, WHILE THESE WOULD BE EFFECTIVE...
...IF SHE THOUGHT THEY WERE ONLY APRIL FOOLS' PRANKS, IT WOULD BE A TERRIBLE DISASTER.
DOONG
THAT'S A WHOLE LOT OF DOWNSIDE FOR SUCH A SNEAKY GAMBLER!

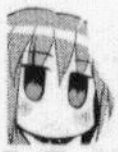

•Nagato •An alien who seems like she might be thinking about something, but might not be thinking about anything.

IMPORTANT POINT

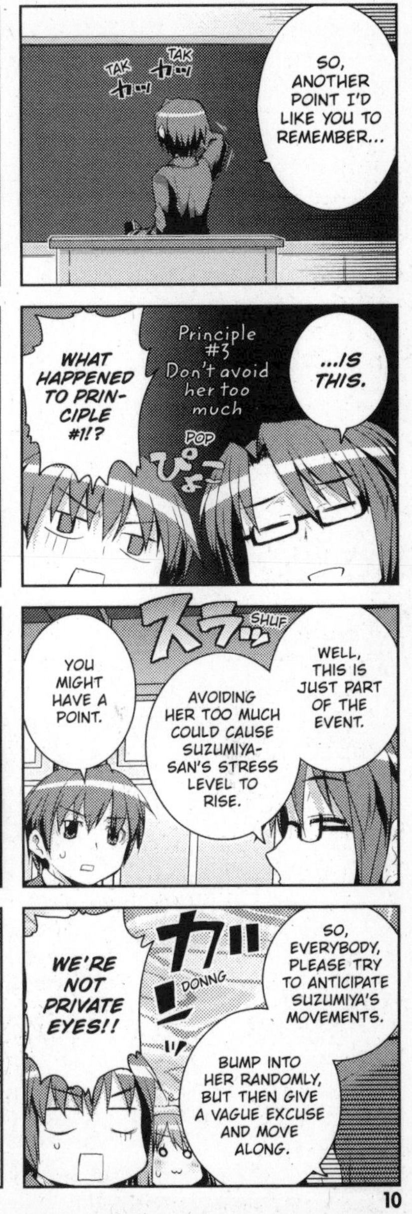
SO, ANOTHER POINT I'D LIKE YOU TO REMEMBER...
TAK
TAK
...IS THIS.
Principle #3 Don't avoid her too much
POP
WHAT HAPPENED TO PRINCIPLE #1!?
WELL, THIS IS JUST PART OF THE EVENT.
SHUF
AVOIDING HER TOO MUCH COULD CAUSE SUZUMIYA-SAN'S STRESS LEVEL TO RISE.
YOU MIGHT HAVE A POINT.
SO, EVERYBODY, PLEASE TRY TO ANTICIPATE SUZUMIYA'S MOVEMENTS.
DONNG
WE'RE NOT PRIVATE EYES!!
BUMP INTO HER RANDOMLY, BUT THEN GIVE A VAGUE EXCUSE AND MOVE ALONG.

CRUCIAL

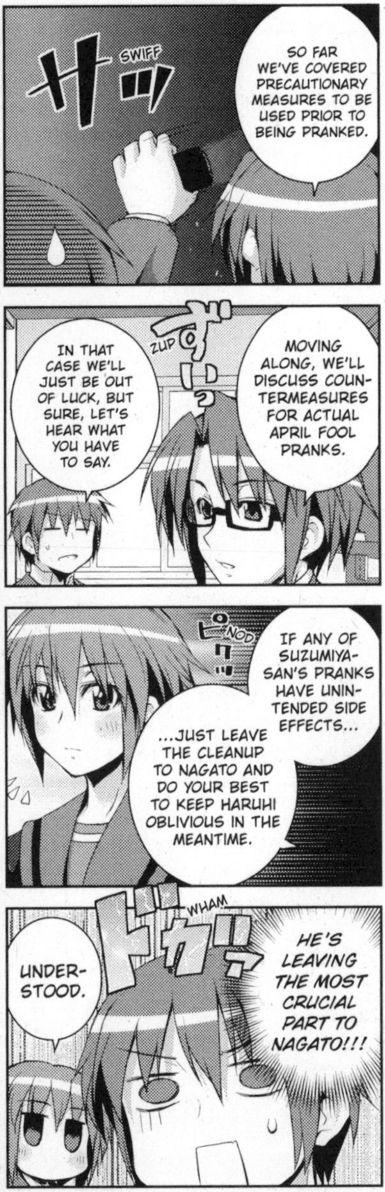
SO FAR WE'VE COVERED PRECAUTIONARY MEASURES TO BE USED PRIOR TO BEING PRANKED.
SWIFF
MOVING ALONG, WE'LL DISCUSS COUNTERMEASURES FOR ACTUAL APRIL FOOL PRANKS.
ZUP
IN THAT CASE WE'LL JUST BE OUT OF LUCK, BUT SURE, LET'S HEAR WHAT YOU HAVE TO SAY.
IF ANY OF SUZUMIYA-SAN'S PRANKS HAVE UNINTENDED SIDE EFFECTS...
NOD
...JUST LEAVE THE CLEANUP TO NAGATO AND DO YOUR BEST TO KEEP HARUHI OBLIVIOUS IN THE MEANTIME.
HE'S LEAVING THE MOST CRUCIAL PART TO NAGATO!!!
WHAM
UNDER-STOOD.

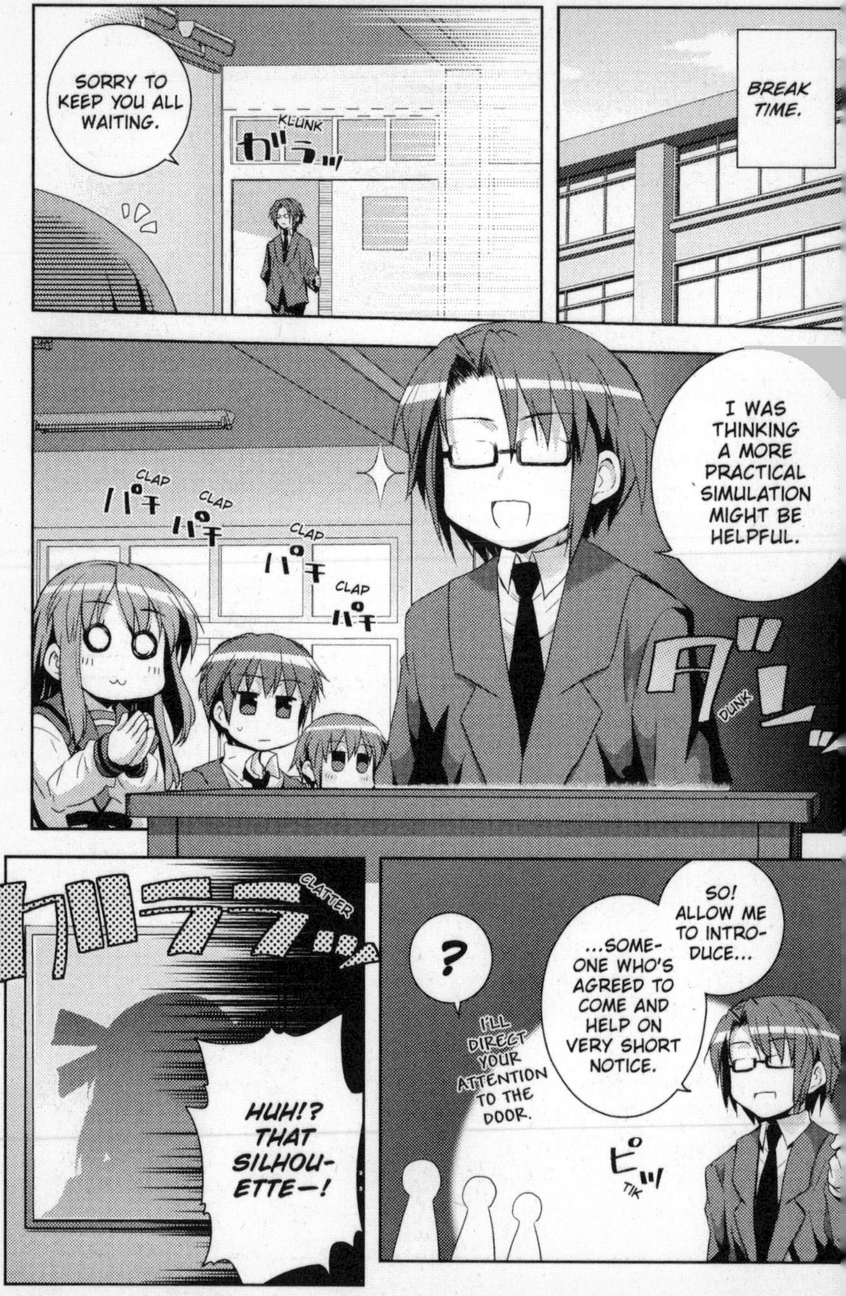
BREAK TIME.
SORRY TO KEEP YOU ALL WAITING.
KLUNK
I WAS THINKING A MORE PRACTICAL SIMULATION MIGHT BE HELPFUL.
DUNK
CLAP
CLAP
CLAP
CLAP
SO! ALLOW ME TO INTRODUCE...
...SOMEONE WHO'S AGREED TO COME AND HELP ON VERY SHORT NOTICE.
?
I'LL DIRECT YOUR ATTENTION TO THE DOOR.
TIK
CLATTER
HUH!? THAT SILHOUETTE—!

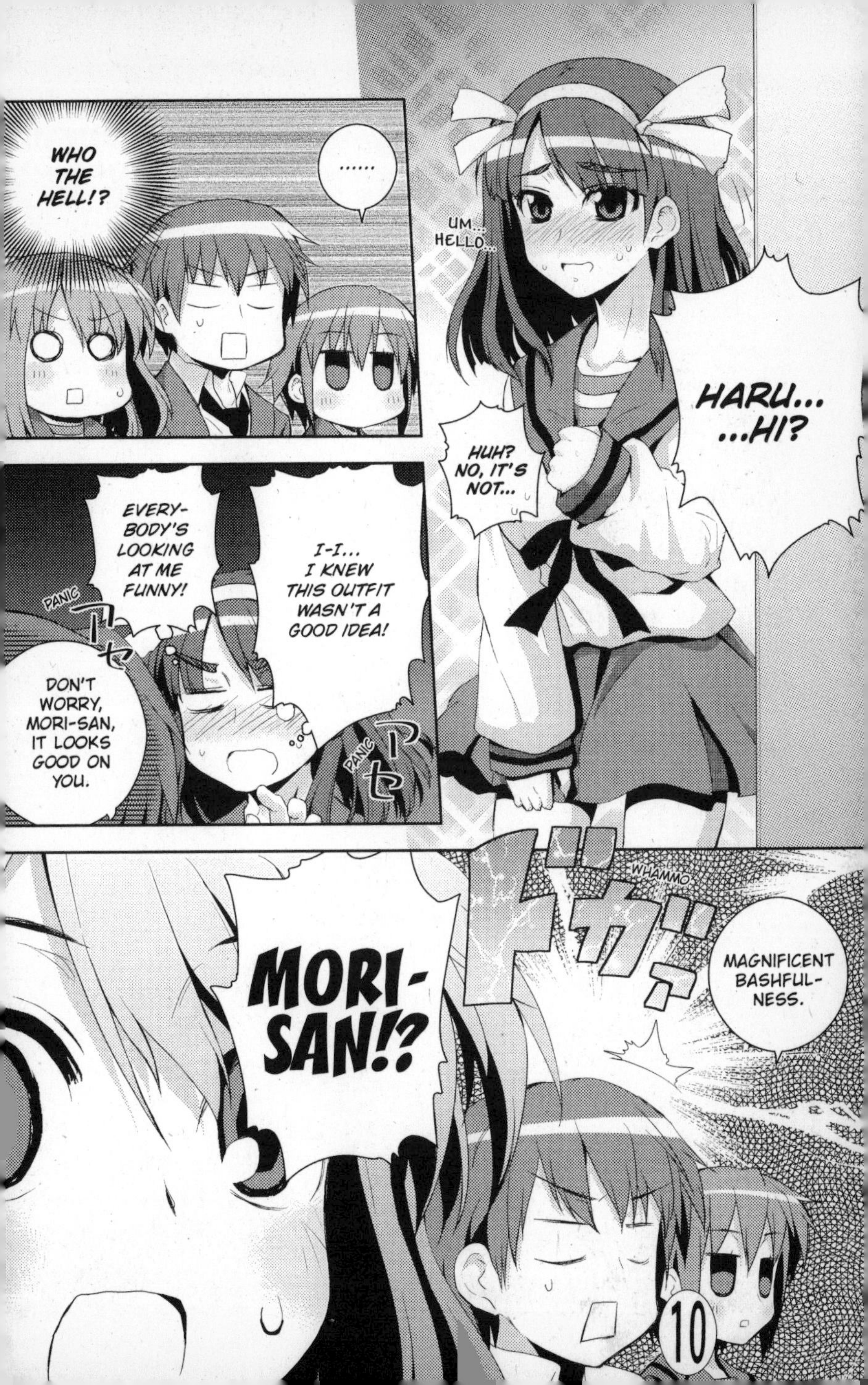
UM... HELLO...
HARU... ...HI?
HUH? NO, IT'S NOT...
WHO THE HELL!?
......
I-I... I KNEW THIS OUTFIT WASN'T A GOOD IDEA!
EVERYBODY'S LOOKING AT ME FUNNY!
PANIC
DON'T WORRY, MORI-SAN, IT LOOKS GOOD ON YOU.
PANIC
WHAMMO
MAGNIFICENT BASHFULNESS.
MORI-SAN!?

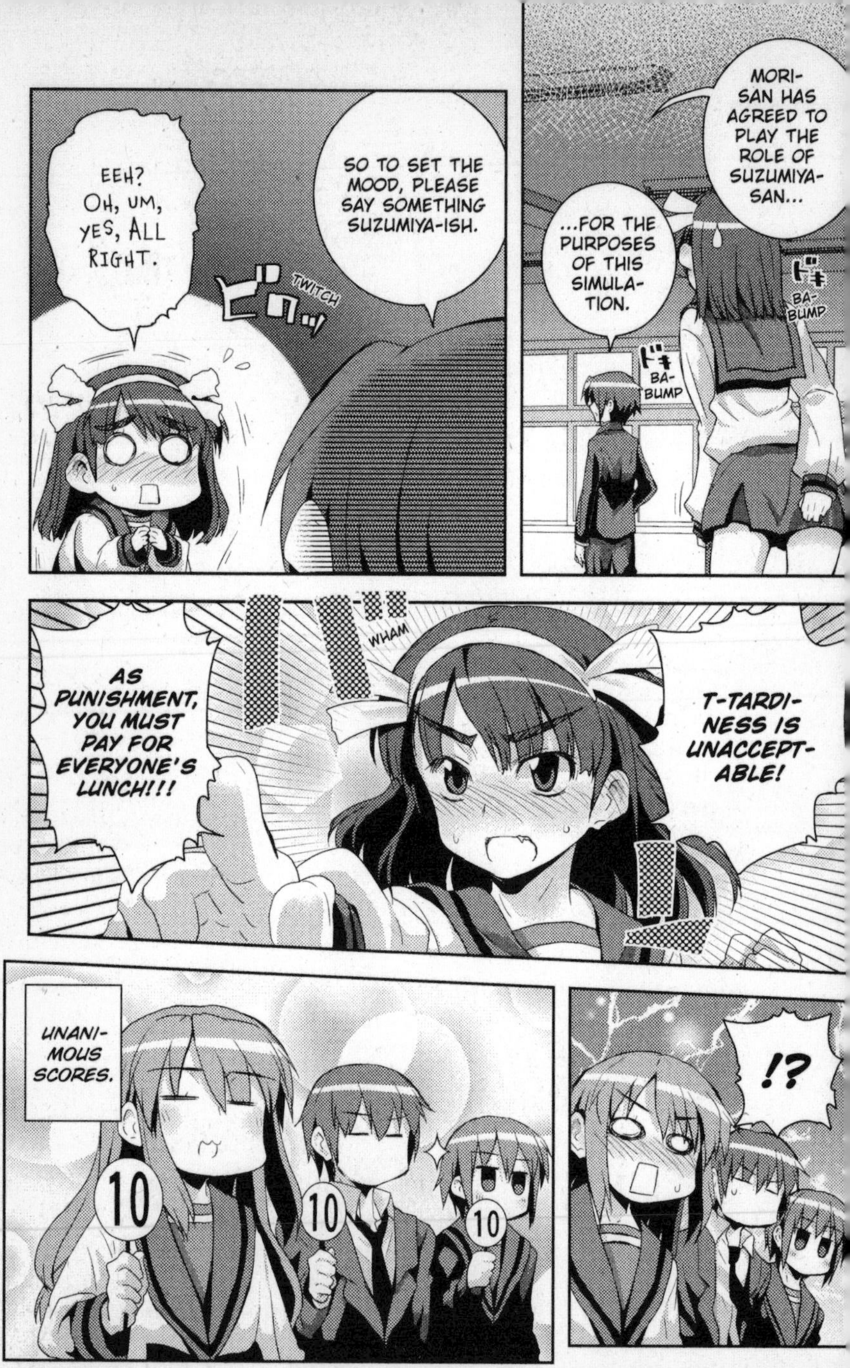

MORI-SAN HAS AGREED TO PLAY THE ROLE OF SUZUMIYA-SAN...
ドキ
BA-BUMP
...FOR THE PURPOSES OF THIS SIMULATION.
ドキ
BA-BUMP
SO TO SET THE MOOD, PLEASE SAY SOMETHING SUZUMIYA-ISH.
TWITCH
EEH? OH, UM, YES, ALL RIGHT.
T-TARDINESS IS UNACCEPTABLE!
WHAM
AS PUNISHMENT, YOU MUST PAY FOR EVERYONE'S LUNCH!!!
!?
UNANIMOUS SCORES.
10
10
10

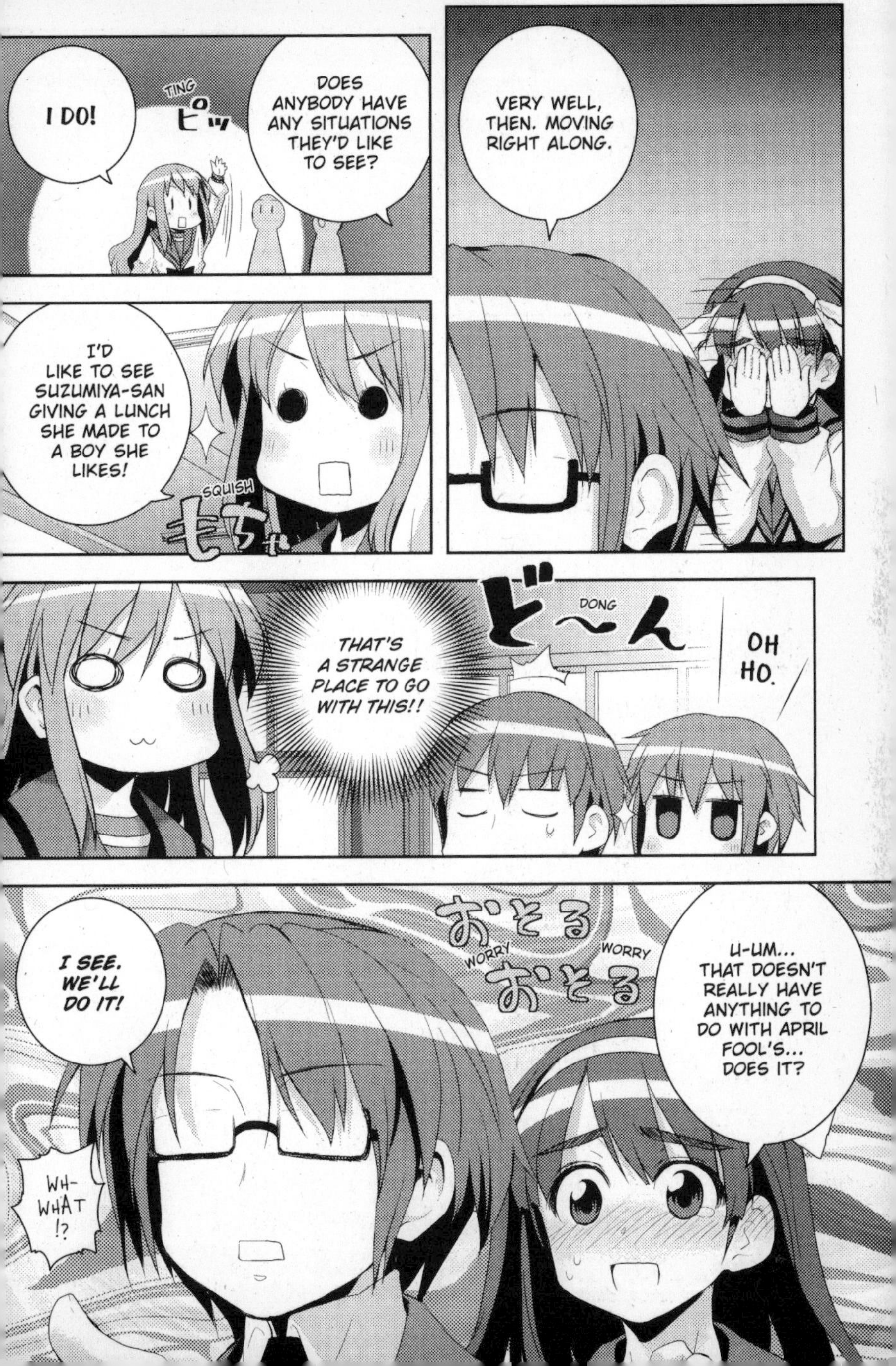
VERY WELL, THEN. MOVING RIGHT ALONG.
DOES ANYBODY HAVE ANY SITUATIONS THEY'D LIKE TO SEE?
TING
ピッ
I DO!
I'D LIKE TO SEE SUZUMIYA-SAN GIVING A LUNCH SHE MADE TO A BOY SHE LIKES!
SQUISH
もちゃ
OH HO.
DONG
ど〜ん
THAT'S A STRANGE PLACE TO GO WITH THIS!!
U-UM... THAT DOESN'T REALLY HAVE ANYTHING TO DO WITH APRIL FOOL'S... DOES IT?
WORRY
おそる
WORRY
おそる
I SEE. WE'LL DO IT!
WH-WHAT!?

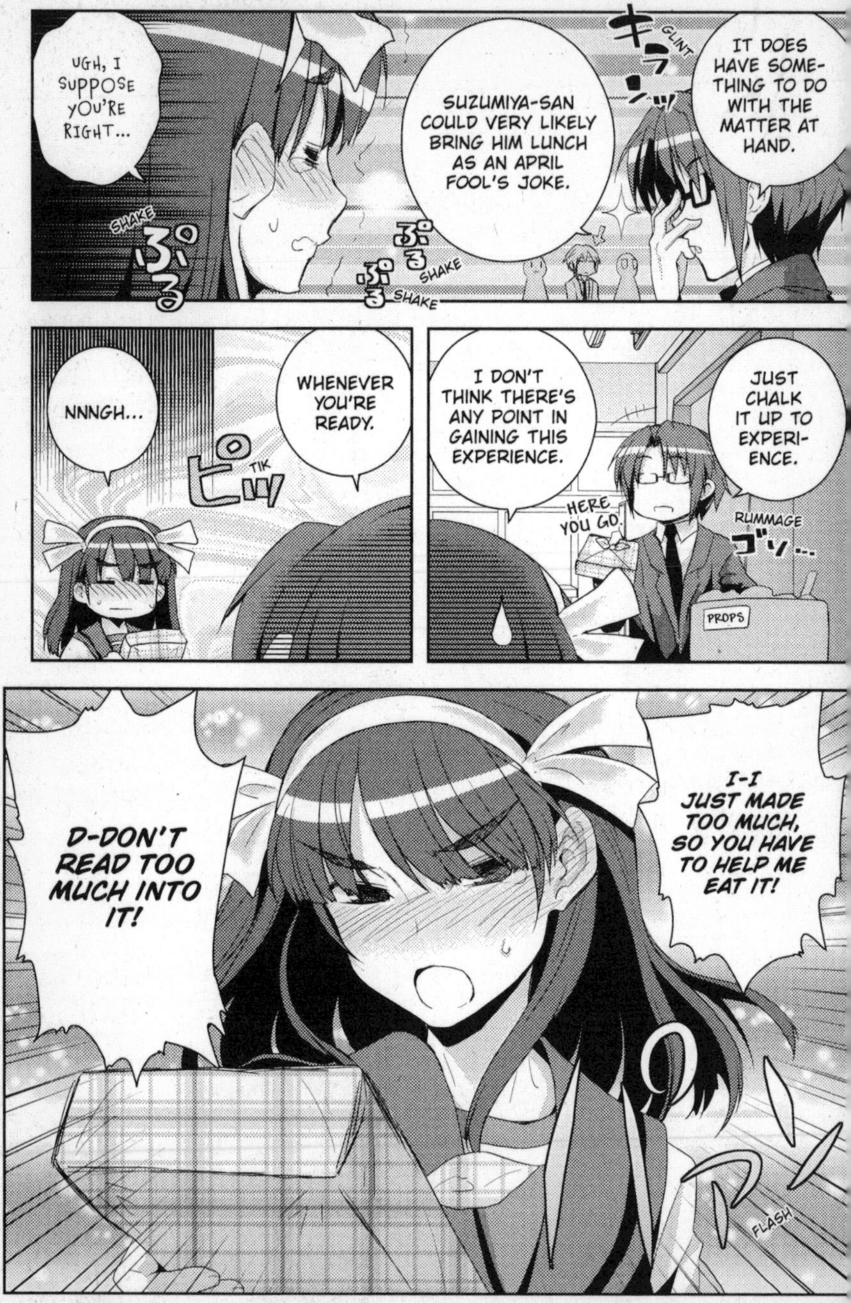
GLINT
IT DOES HAVE SOME-THING TO DO WITH THE MATTER AT HAND.
SUZUMIYA-SAN COULD VERY LIKELY BRING HIM LUNCH AS AN APRIL FOOL'S JOKE.
SHAKE
SHAKE
SHAKE
UGH, I SUPPOSE YOU'RE RIGHT...
JUST CHALK IT UP TO EXPERI-ENCE.
RUMMAGE
PROPS
I DON'T THINK THERE'S ANY POINT IN GAINING THIS EXPERIENCE.
HERE YOU GO.
WHENEVER YOU'RE READY.
TIK
NNNGH...
I-I JUST MADE TOO MUCH, SO YOU HAVE TO HELP ME EAT IT!
D-DON'T READ TOO MUCH INTO IT!
FLASH

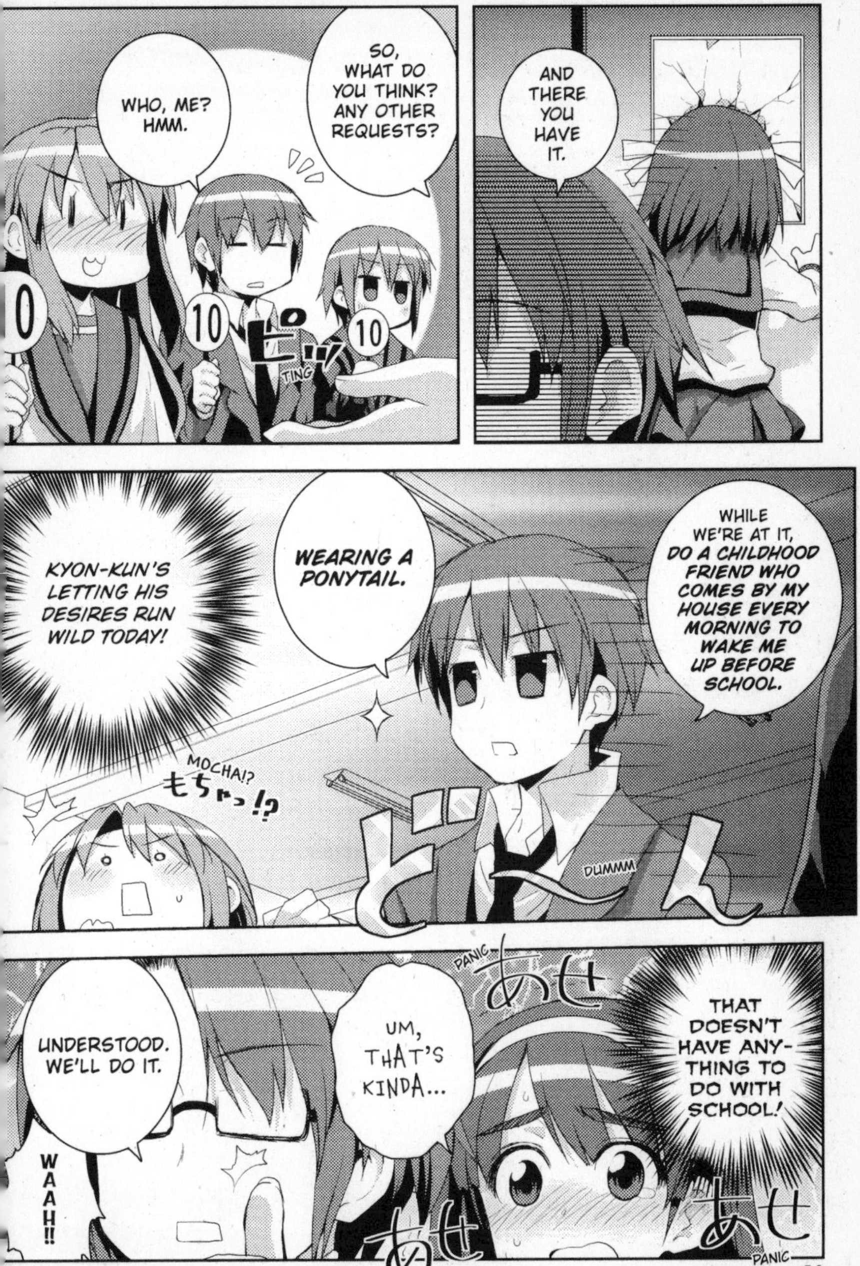
AND THERE YOU HAVE IT.
SO, WHAT DO YOU THINK? ANY OTHER REQUESTS?
WHO, ME? HMM.
10
10
ピッ
TING
10
WHILE WE'RE AT IT, DO A CHILDHOOD FRIEND WHO COMES BY MY HOUSE EVERY MORNING TO WAKE ME UP BEFORE SCHOOL.
WEARING A PONYTAIL.
KYON-KUN'S LETTING HIS DESIRES RUN WILD TODAY!
MOCHA!?
もちゃっ!?
DUMMM
THAT DOESN'T HAVE ANY-THING TO DO WITH SCHOOL!
PANIC
あせ
UM, THAT'S KINDA...
UNDERSTOOD. WE'LL DO IT.
WAAAH!!
あせ
PANIC
あせ
PANIC

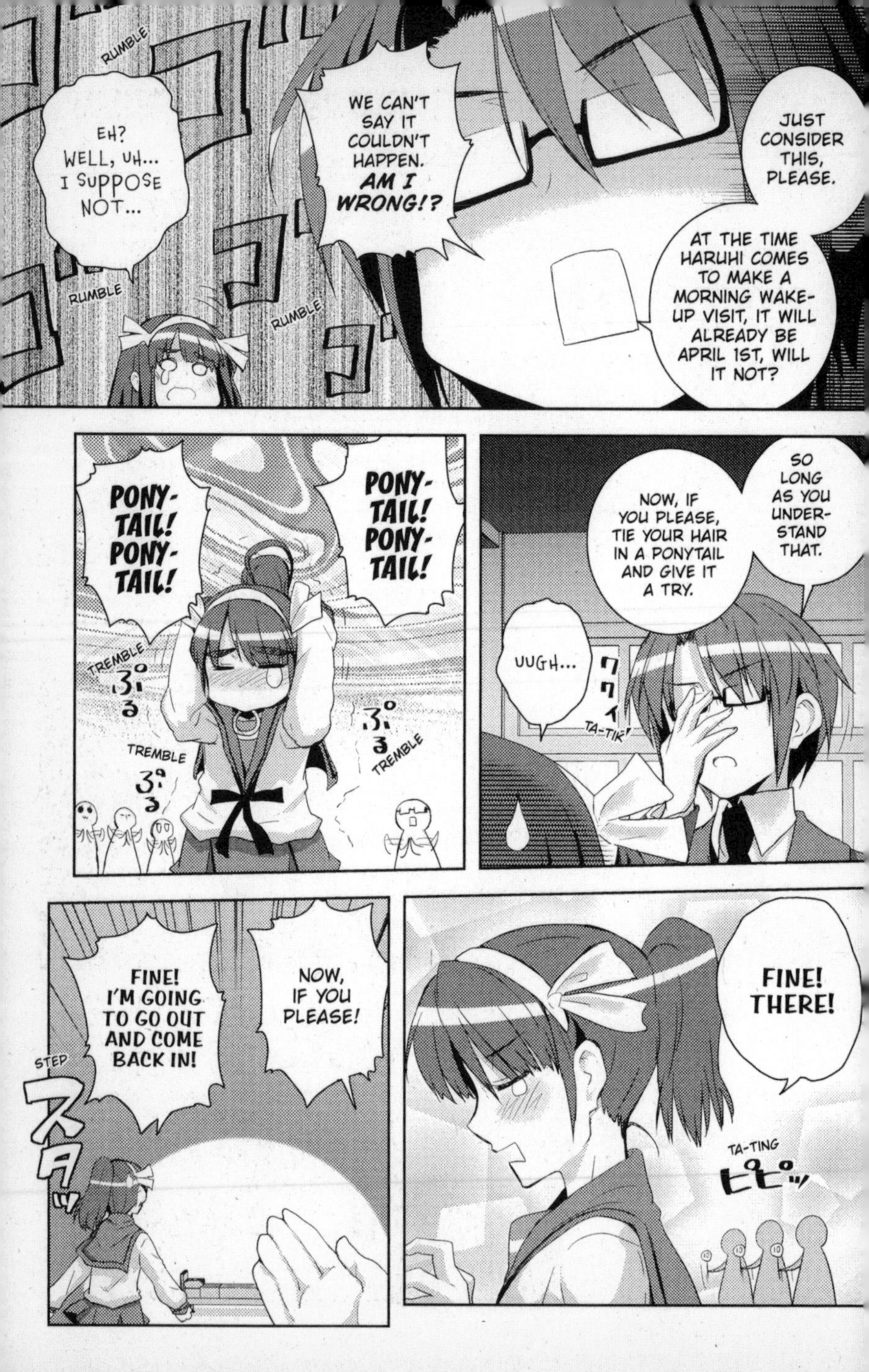
JUST CONSIDER THIS, PLEASE.
AT THE TIME HARUHI COMES TO MAKE A MORNING WAKE-UP VISIT, IT WILL ALREADY BE APRIL 1ST, WILL IT NOT?
WE CAN'T SAY IT COULDN'T HAPPEN. AM I WRONG!?
RUMBLE
EH? WELL, UH... I SUPPOSE NOT...
RUMBLE
RUMBLE
SO LONG AS YOU UNDERSTAND THAT.
NOW, IF YOU PLEASE, TIE YOUR HAIR IN A PONYTAIL AND GIVE IT A TRY.
UUGH...
TA-TIK
PONY-TAIL! PONY-TAIL!
PONY-TAIL! PONY-TAIL!
TREMBLE
ぷる
TREMBLE
ぷる
TREMBLE
ぷる
FINE! THERE!
TA-TING
ピピッ
NOW, IF YOU PLEASE!
FINE! I'M GOING TO GO OUT AND COME BACK IN!
STEP
スタッ

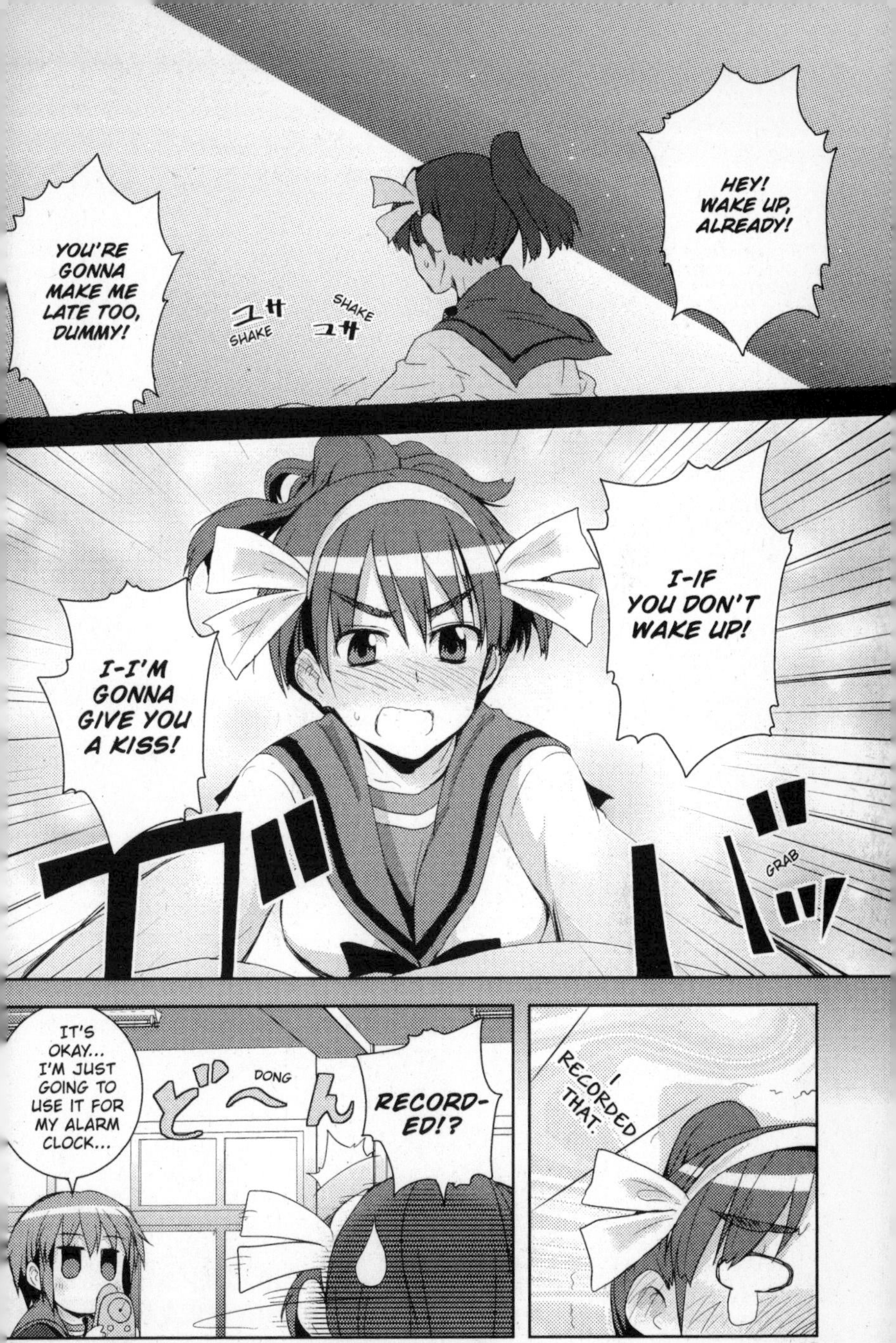
HEY! WAKE UP, ALREADY!
ユサ SHAKE ユサ SHAKE
YOU'RE GONNA MAKE ME LATE TOO, DUMMY!
I-IF YOU DON'T WAKE UP!
I-I'M GONNA GIVE YOU A KISS!
GRAB
I RECORDED THAT.
RECORD-ED!?
DONG
IT'S OKAY... I'M JUST GOING TO USE IT FOR MY ALARM CLOCK...

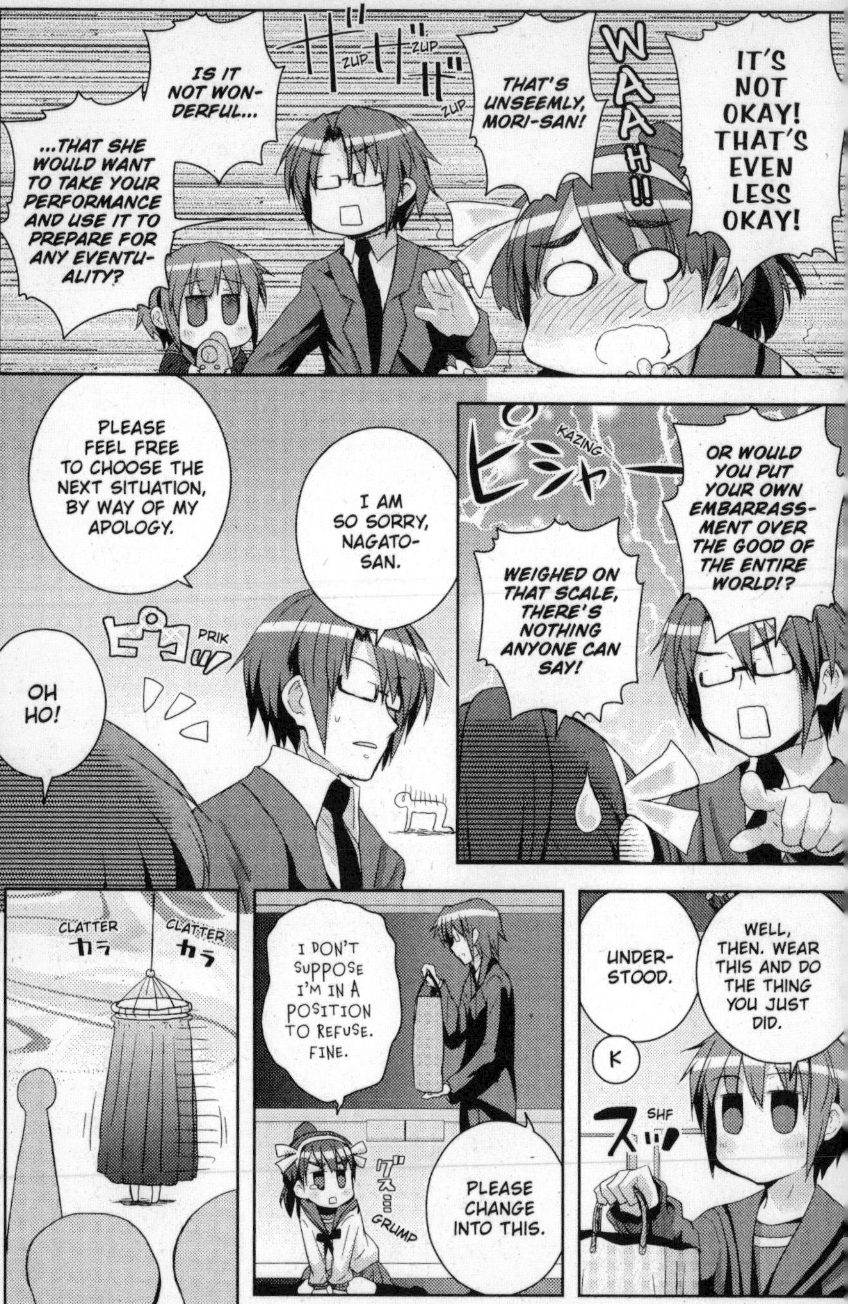
IT'S NOT OKAY! THAT'S EVEN LESS OKAY!
WAAH!!
THAT'S UNSEEMLY, MORI-SAN!
ZUP
ZUP
ZUP
IS IT NOT WONDERFUL...
...THAT SHE WOULD WANT TO TAKE YOUR PERFORMANCE AND USE IT TO PREPARE FOR ANY EVENTUALITY?
OR WOULD YOU PUT YOUR OWN EMBARRASSMENT OVER THE GOOD OF THE ENTIRE WORLD!?
KAZING
WEIGHED ON THAT SCALE, THERE'S NOTHING ANYONE CAN SAY!
I AM SO SORRY, NAGATO-SAN.
PLEASE FEEL FREE TO CHOOSE THE NEXT SITUATION, BY WAY OF MY APOLOGY.
PRIK
OH HO!
WELL, THEN. WEAR THIS AND DO THE THING YOU JUST DID.
UNDERSTOOD.
K
SHF
PLEASE CHANGE INTO THIS.
GRUMP
I DON'T SUPPOSE I'M IN A POSITION TO REFUSE. FINE.
CLATTER
CLATTER

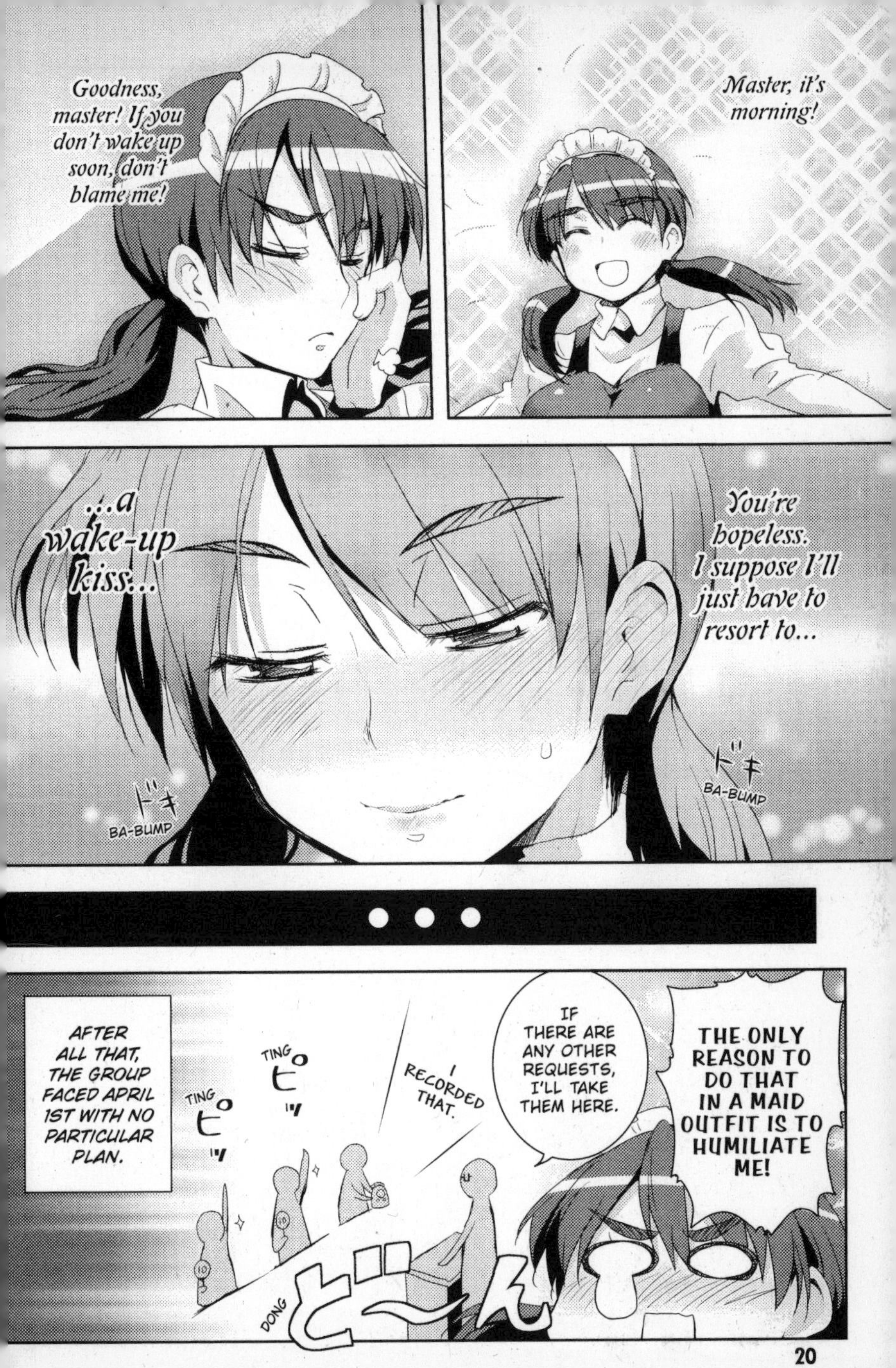
Master, it's morning!
Goodness, master! If you don't wake up soon, don't blame me!
You're hopeless. I suppose I'll just have to resort to...
...a wake-up kiss...
ドキ BA-BUMP
ドキ BA-BUMP
THE ONLY REASON TO DO THAT IN A MAID OUTFIT IS TO HUMILIATE ME!
IF THERE ARE ANY OTHER REQUESTS, I'LL TAKE THEM HERE.
I RECORDED THAT.
TING ピッ
TING ピッ
AFTER ALL THAT, THE GROUP FACED APRIL 1ST WITH NO PARTICULAR PLAN.
DONG どーん

OPENING GAME

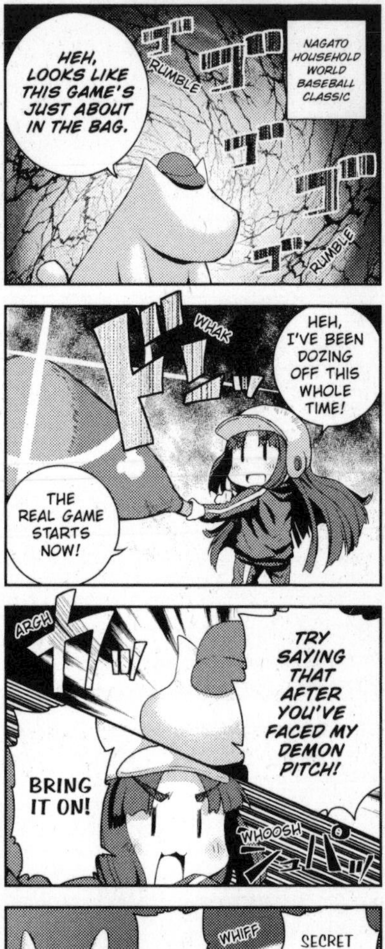
NAGATO HOUSEHOLD WORLD BASEBALL CLASSIC
HEH, LOOKS LIKE THIS GAME'S JUST ABOUT IN THE BAG.
RUMBLE
RUMBLE
WHAK
HEH, I'VE BEEN DOZING OFF THIS WHOLE TIME!
THE REAL GAME STARTS NOW!
TRY SAYING THAT AFTER YOU'VE FACED MY DEMON PITCH!
ARGH
BRING IT ON!
WHOOSH
SECRET CLOSE-SHAVE PITCH!
WHIFF
NYAR!

DEMON PITCH

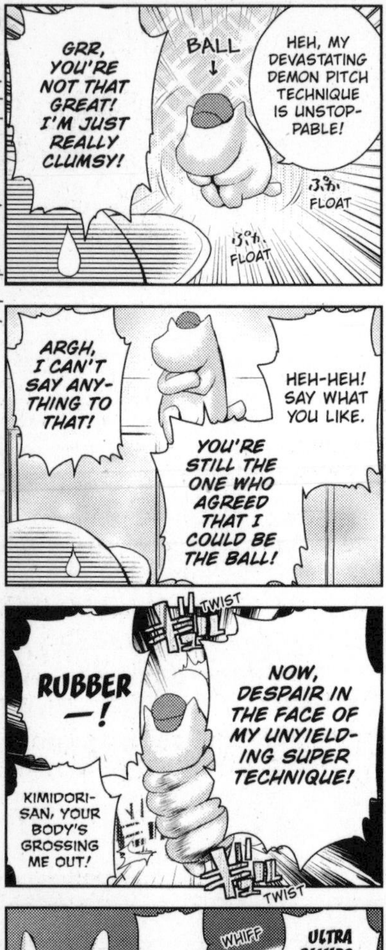
HEH, MY DEVASTATING DEMON PITCH TECHNIQUE IS UNSTOPPABLE!
BALL ↓
GRR, YOU'RE NOT THAT GREAT! I'M JUST REALLY CLUMSY!
ぷか FLOAT
ぷか FLOAT
HEH-HEH! SAY WHAT YOU LIKE.
YOU'RE STILL THE ONE WHO AGREED THAT I COULD BE THE BALL!
ARGH, I CAN'T SAY ANYTHING TO THAT!
TWIST
NOW, DESPAIR IN THE FACE OF MY UNYIELDING SUPER TECHNIQUE!
RUBBER—!
KIMIDORI-SAN, YOUR BODY'S GROSSING ME OUT!
TWIST
ULTRA BLIMPOSAURUS REX PITCH!
WHIFF
NYAR!

•Achakura-san •Apparently she's been watching baseball on TV. Cute and easy to see through.

•Kimidori-san •Ace pitcher of the Nagato household. Victorious in a closely-matched (?) game.

BREAKTHROUGH

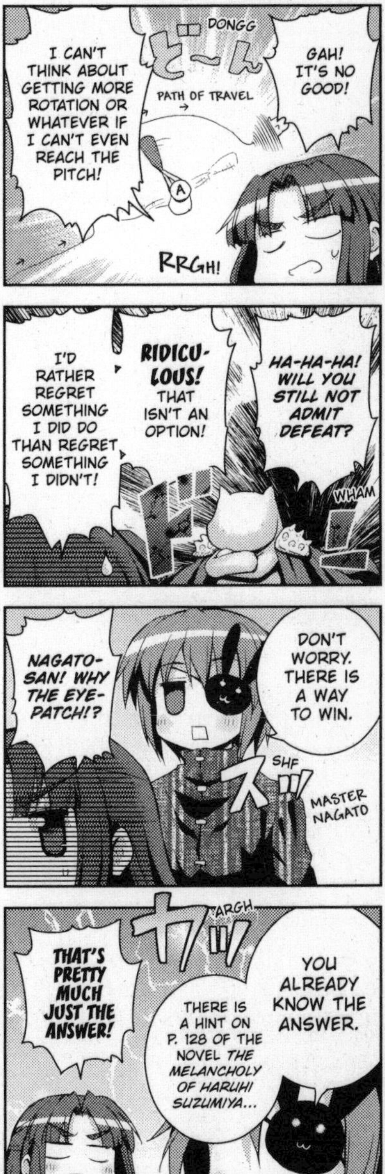
GAH! IT'S NO GOOD!
DONGG
PATH OF TRAVEL
I CAN'T THINK ABOUT GETTING MORE ROTATION OR WHATEVER IF I CAN'T EVEN REACH THE PITCH!
A
RRGH!
HA-HA-HA! WILL YOU STILL NOT ADMIT DEFEAT?
RIDICU-LOUS! THAT ISN'T AN OPTION!
I'D RATHER REGRET SOMETHING I DID DO THAN REGRET SOMETHING I DIDN'T!
WHAM
DON'T WORRY. THERE IS A WAY TO WIN.
NAGATO-SAN! WHY THE EYE-PATCH!?
SHF
MASTER NAGATO
YOU ALREADY KNOW THE ANSWER.
THERE IS A HINT ON P. 128 OF THE NOVEL THE MELANCHOLY OF HARUHI SUZUMIYA...
ARGH
THAT'S PRETTY MUCH JUST THE ANSWER!

FINAL ACT

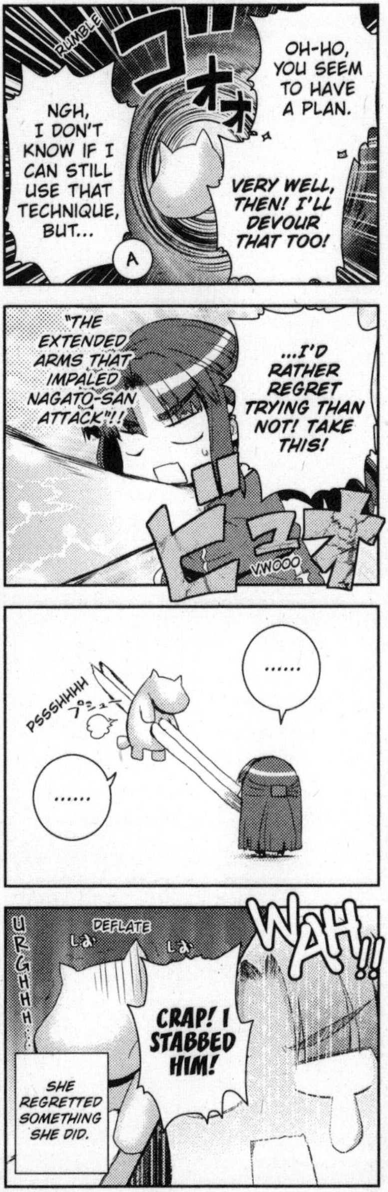
OH-HO, YOU SEEM TO HAVE A PLAN.
RUMBLE
NGH, I DON'T KNOW IF I CAN STILL USE THAT TECHNIQUE, BUT...
VERY WELL, THEN! I'LL DEVOUR THAT TOO!
A
...I'D RATHER REGRET TRYING THAN NOT! TAKE THIS!
"THE EXTENDED ARMS THAT IMPALED NAGATO-SAN ATTACK"!!
VWOOO
......
PSSSHHHH
......
WAH!!
DEFLATE
URGHHH...
CRAP! I STABBED HIM!
SHE REGRETTED SOMETHING SHE DID.

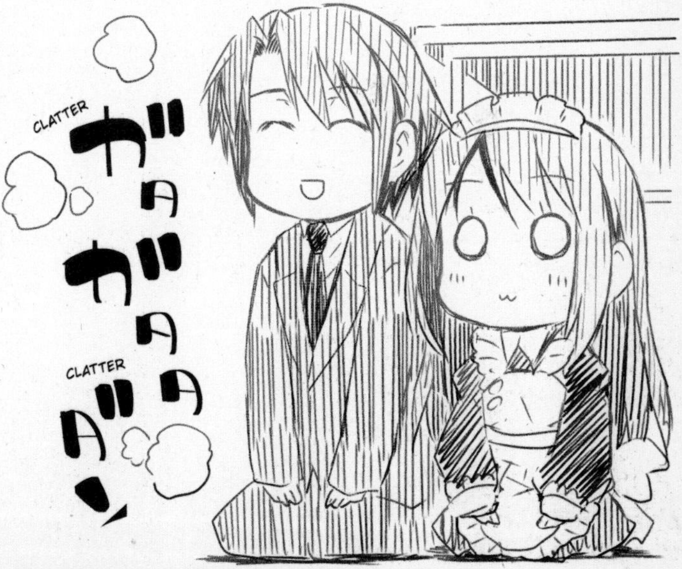
CLATTER
CLATTER
ガタガタタダ!

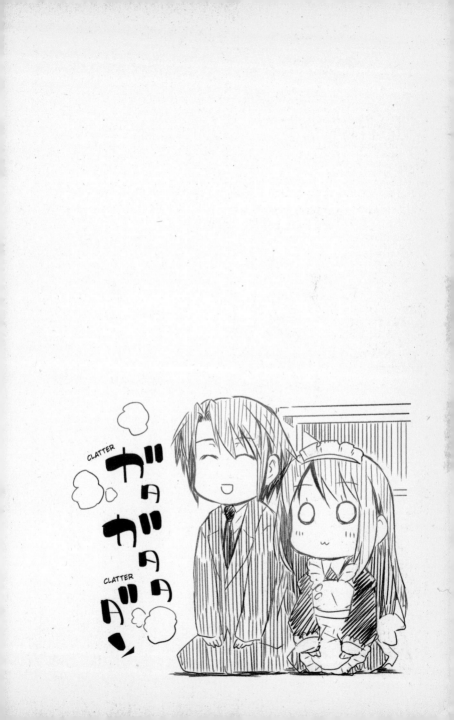

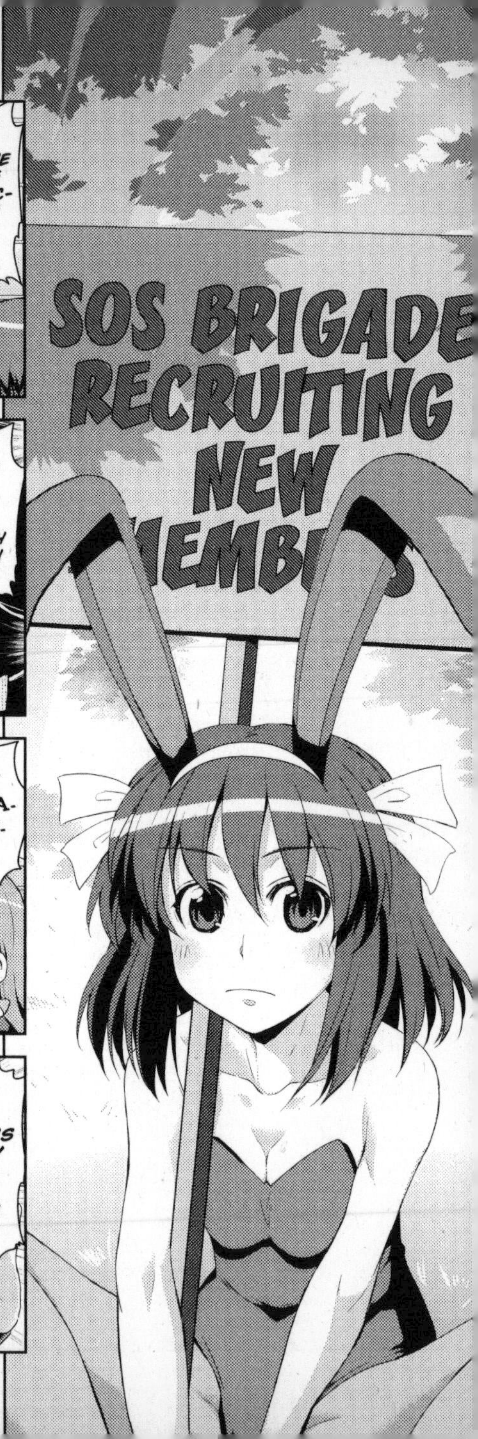
SOS BRIGADE
RECRUITING
NEW

LECTURE

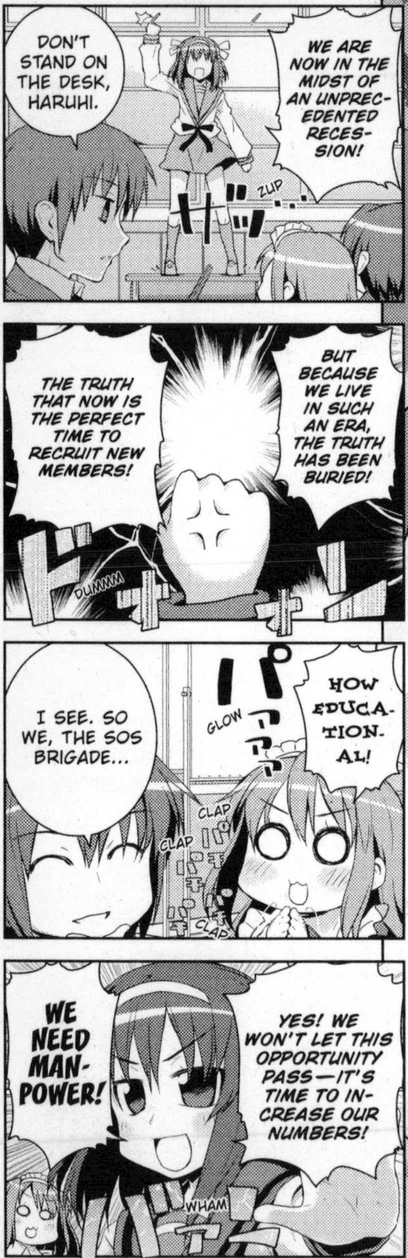
WE ARE NOW IN THE MIDST OF AN UNPRECEDENTED RECESSION!
DON'T STAND ON THE DESK, HARUHI.
ZUP
BUT BECAUSE WE LIVE IN SUCH AN ERA, THE TRUTH HAS BEEN BURIED!
THE TRUTH THAT NOW IS THE PERFECT TIME TO RECRUIT NEW MEMBERS!
DUMMM
HOW EDUCATIONAL!
GLOW
I SEE. SO WE, THE SOS BRIGADE...
CLAP
CLAP
CLAP
YES! WE WON'T LET THIS OPPORTUNITY PASS—IT'S TIME TO INCREASE OUR NUMBERS!
WE NEED MANPOWER!
WHAM

•Haruhi-chan •SOS Brigade brigade chief. Is actually talking sense, for once.

•Kyon •Supposed to be the main character of this story. His hair gets a little messed up when he gets angry.

•Mikuru-chan •Time-traveler. Makes the sound effect "mochi mochi" when she concentrates on writing very carefully.

HARUHI, MASTER PAINTER

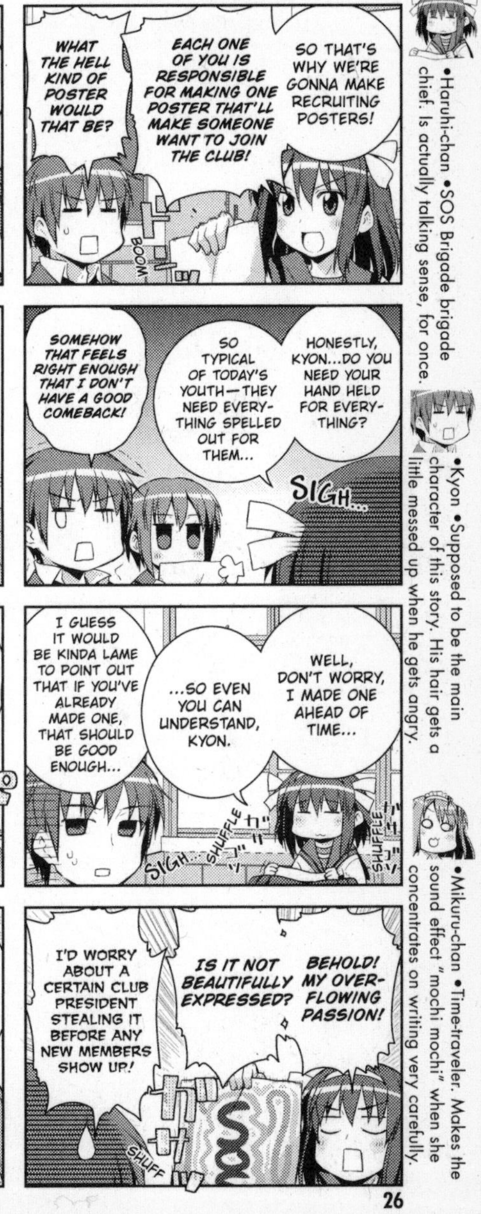
SO THAT'S WHY WE'RE GONNA MAKE RECRUITING POSTERS!
EACH ONE OF YOU IS RESPONSIBLE FOR MAKING ONE POSTER THAT'LL MAKE SOMEONE WANT TO JOIN THE CLUB!
WHAT THE HELL KIND OF POSTER WOULD THAT BE?
BOOM
HONESTLY, KYON...DO YOU NEED YOUR HAND HELD FOR EVERYTHING?
SO TYPICAL OF TODAY'S YOUTH—THEY NEED EVERYTHING SPELLED OUT FOR THEM...
SOMEHOW THAT FEELS RIGHT ENOUGH THAT I DON'T HAVE A GOOD COMEBACK!
SIGH...
WELL, DON'T WORRY, I MADE ONE AHEAD OF TIME...
...SO EVEN YOU CAN UNDERSTAND, KYON.
I GUESS IT WOULD BE KINDA LAME TO POINT OUT THAT IF YOU'VE ALREADY MADE ONE, THAT SHOULD BE GOOD ENOUGH...
SHUFFLE
SHUFFLE
SIGH...
BEHOLD! MY OVERFLOWING PASSION!
IS IT NOT BEAUTIFULLY EXPRESSED?
I'D WORRY ABOUT A CERTAIN CLUB PRESIDENT STEALING IT BEFORE ANY NEW MEMBERS SHOW UP!
SHUFF

THEME

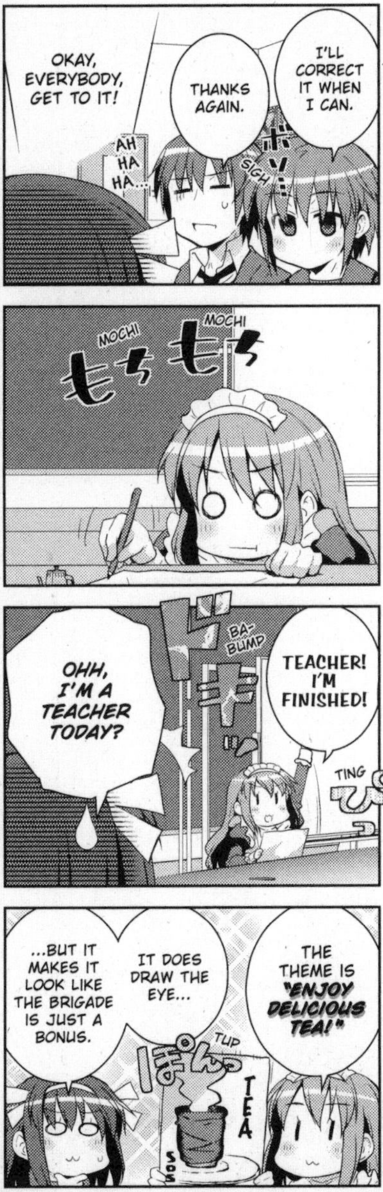
I'LL CORRECT IT WHEN I CAN.
THANKS AGAIN.
OKAY, EVERYBODY, GET TO IT!
SIGH
AH HA HA...
MOCHI
MOCHI
TEACHER! I'M FINISHED!
BA-BUMP
OHH, I'M A TEACHER TODAY?
TING
THE THEME IS "ENJOY DELICIOUS TEA!"
IT DOES DRAW THE EYE...
...BUT IT MAKES IT LOOK LIKE THE BRIGADE IS JUST A BONUS.
TUP
TEA
SOS

SETUP

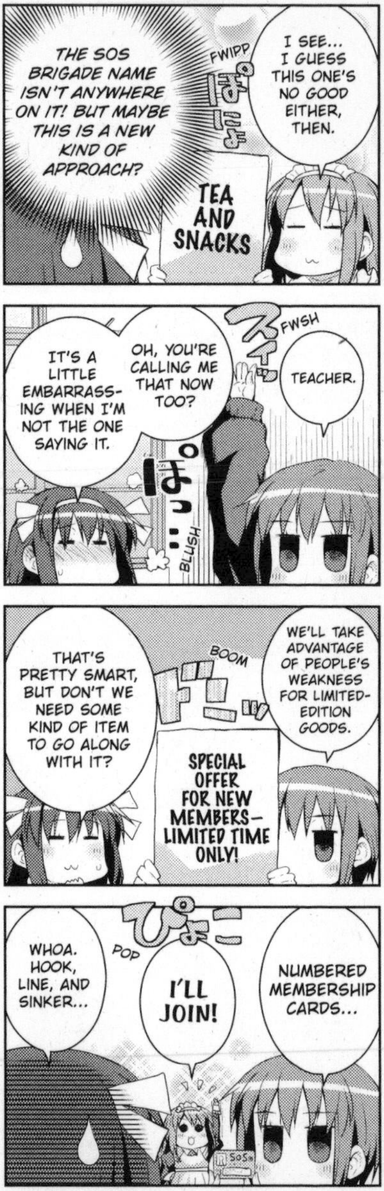

I SEE... I GUESS THIS ONE'S NO GOOD EITHER, THEN.
FWIPP
TEA AND SNACKS
THE SOS BRIGADE NAME ISN'T ANYWHERE ON IT! BUT MAYBE THIS IS A NEW KIND OF APPROACH?
TEACHER.
FWSH
OH, YOU'RE CALLING ME THAT NOW TOO?
IT'S A LITTLE EMBARRASSING WHEN I'M NOT THE ONE SAYING IT.
BLUSH
WE'LL TAKE ADVANTAGE OF PEOPLE'S WEAKNESS FOR LIMITED-EDITION GOODS.
BOOM
SPECIAL OFFER FOR NEW MEMBERS—LIMITED TIME ONLY!
THAT'S PRETTY SMART, BUT DON'T WE NEED SOME KIND OF ITEM TO GO ALONG WITH IT?
NUMBERED MEMBERSHIP CARDS...
POP
I'LL JOIN!
WHOA. HOOK, LINE, AND SINKER...

POSITION

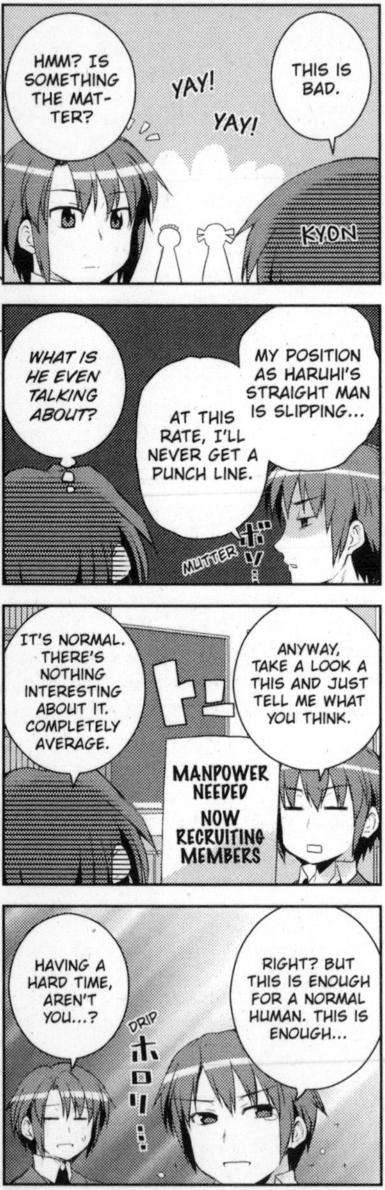

THIS IS BAD.
YAY!
YAY!
KYON
HMM? IS SOMETHING THE MAT-TER?
MY POSITION AS HARUHI'S STRAIGHT MAN IS SLIPPING...
AT THIS RATE, I'LL NEVER GET A PUNCH LINE.
MUTTER
WHAT IS HE EVEN TALKING ABOUT?
ANYWAY, TAKE A LOOK A THIS AND JUST TELL ME WHAT YOU THINK.
MANPOWER NEEDED NOW RECRUITING MEMBERS
IT'S NORMAL. THERE'S NOTHING INTERESTING ABOUT IT. COMPLETELY AVERAGE.
RIGHT? BUT THIS IS ENOUGH FOR A NORMAL HUMAN. THIS IS ENOUGH...
DRIP
HAVING A HARD TIME, AREN'T YOU...?

•Koizumi •Enigmatic transfer student and esper. Apparently secretly wants Kyon and Haruhi to get together.

•Nagato •Alien. The type of person who signs up for something just to get the special offer.

REPRESENTATIVE

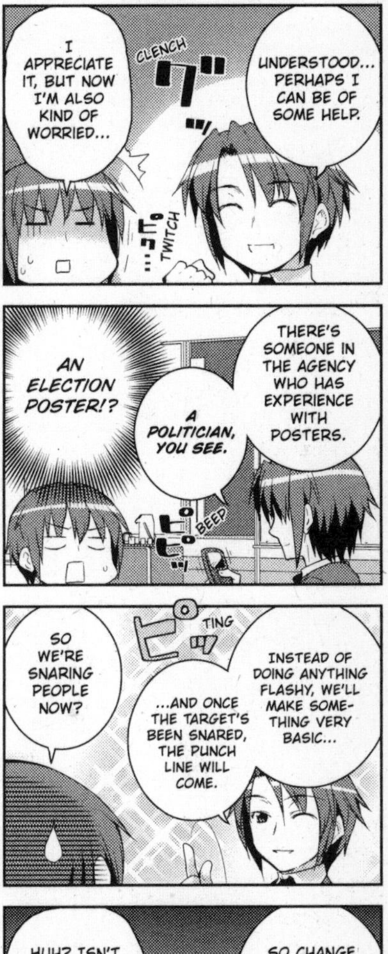
UNDERSTOOD... PERHAPS I CAN BE OF SOME HELP.
CLENCH
I APPRECIATE IT, BUT NOW I'M ALSO KIND OF WORRIED...
TWITCH
THERE'S SOMEONE IN THE AGENCY WHO HAS EXPERIENCE WITH POSTERS.
A POLITICIAN, YOU SEE.
AN ELECTION POSTER!?
BEEP
INSTEAD OF DOING ANYTHING FLASHY, WE'LL MAKE SOME-THING VERY BASIC...
TING
...AND ONCE THE TARGET'S BEEN SNARED, THE PUNCH LINE WILL COME.
SO WE'RE SNARING PEOPLE NOW?
SO CHANGE INTO A SUIT, AND I'LL TAKE YOUR PICTURE.
SHF
HUH? ISN'T THIS GOING TO MAKE IT LOOK LIKE I'M THE SOS BRIGADE REPRESENTA-TIVE?

JUDGING

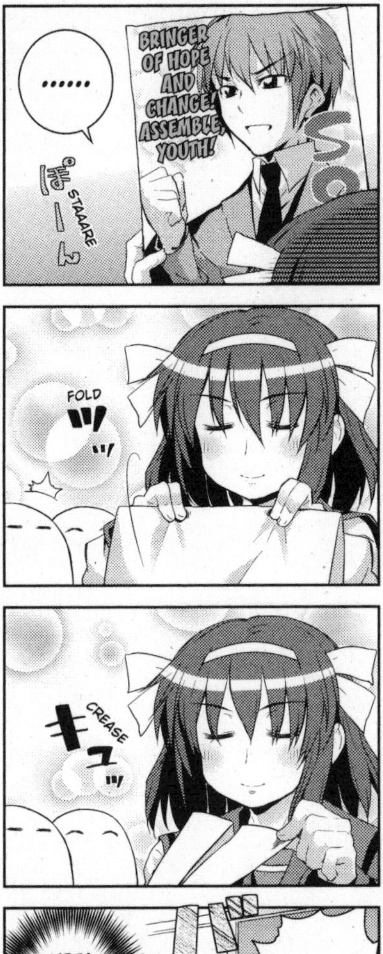
BRINGER OF HOPE AND CHANGE! ASSEMBLE, YOUTH!
......
STAARE
FOLD
CREASE
IDIOTS!
SHOOOO
YES! THE PUNCH LINE!

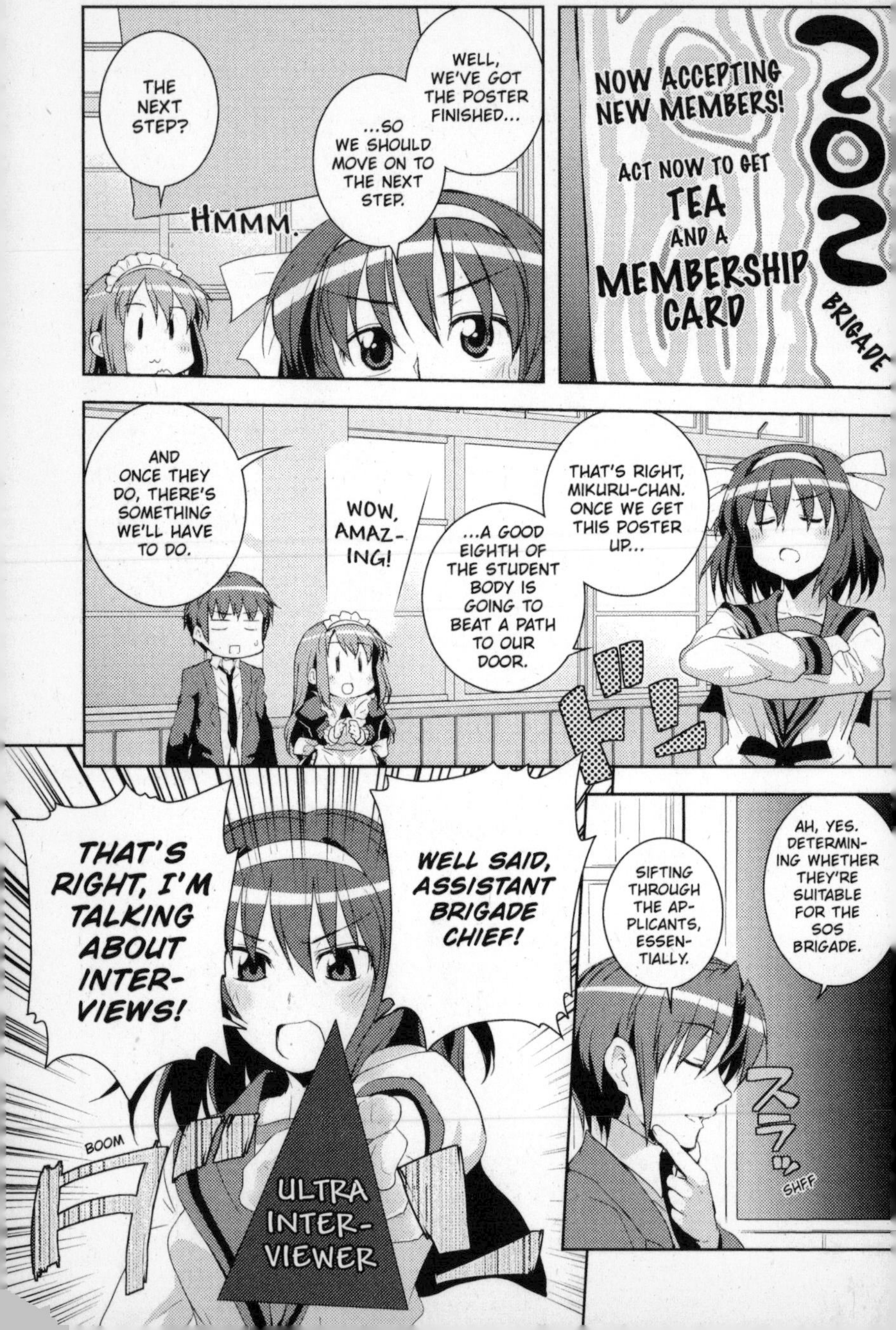
SOS
BRIGADE
NOW ACCEPTING NEW MEMBERS!
ACT NOW TO GET TEA AND A MEMBERSHIP CARD
WELL, WE'VE GOT THE POSTER FINISHED...
...SO WE SHOULD MOVE ON TO THE NEXT STEP.
HMMM.
THE NEXT STEP?
THAT'S RIGHT, MIKURU-CHAN. ONCE WE GET THIS POSTER UP...
...A GOOD EIGHTH OF THE STUDENT BODY IS GOING TO BEAT A PATH TO OUR DOOR.
WOW, AMAZ-ING!
AND ONCE THEY DO, THERE'S SOMETHING WE'LL HAVE TO DO.
AH, YES. DETERMIN-ING WHETHER THEY'RE SUITABLE FOR THE SOS BRIGADE.
SIFTING THROUGH THE AP-PLICANTS, ESSEN-TIALLY.
SHFF
WELL SAID, ASSISTANT BRIGADE CHIEF!
THAT'S RIGHT, I'M TALKING ABOUT INTER-VIEWS!
BOOM
ULTRA INTER-VIEWER

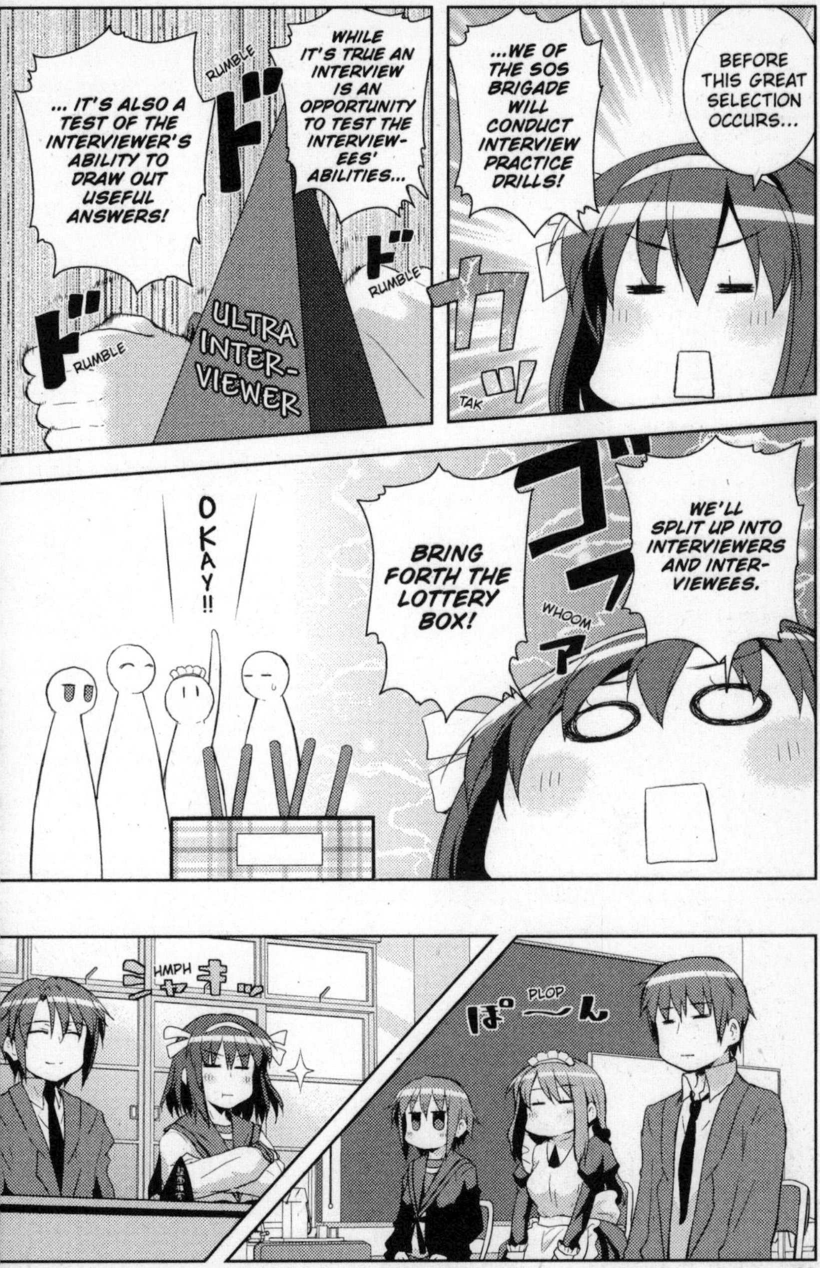
BEFORE THIS GREAT SELECTION OCCURS...
...WE OF THE SOS BRIGADE WILL CONDUCT INTERVIEW PRACTICE DRILLS!
TAK
WHILE IT'S TRUE AN INTERVIEW IS AN OPPORTUNITY TO TEST THE INTERVIEW-EES' ABILITIES...
RUMBLE
RUMBLE
... IT'S ALSO A TEST OF THE INTERVIEWER'S ABILITY TO DRAW OUT USEFUL ANSWERS!
ULTRA INTER-VIEWER
RUMBLE
WE'LL SPLIT UP INTO INTERVIEWERS AND INTER-VIEWEES.
WHOOM
BRING FORTH THE LOTTERY BOX!
OKAY!!
PLOP
HMPH

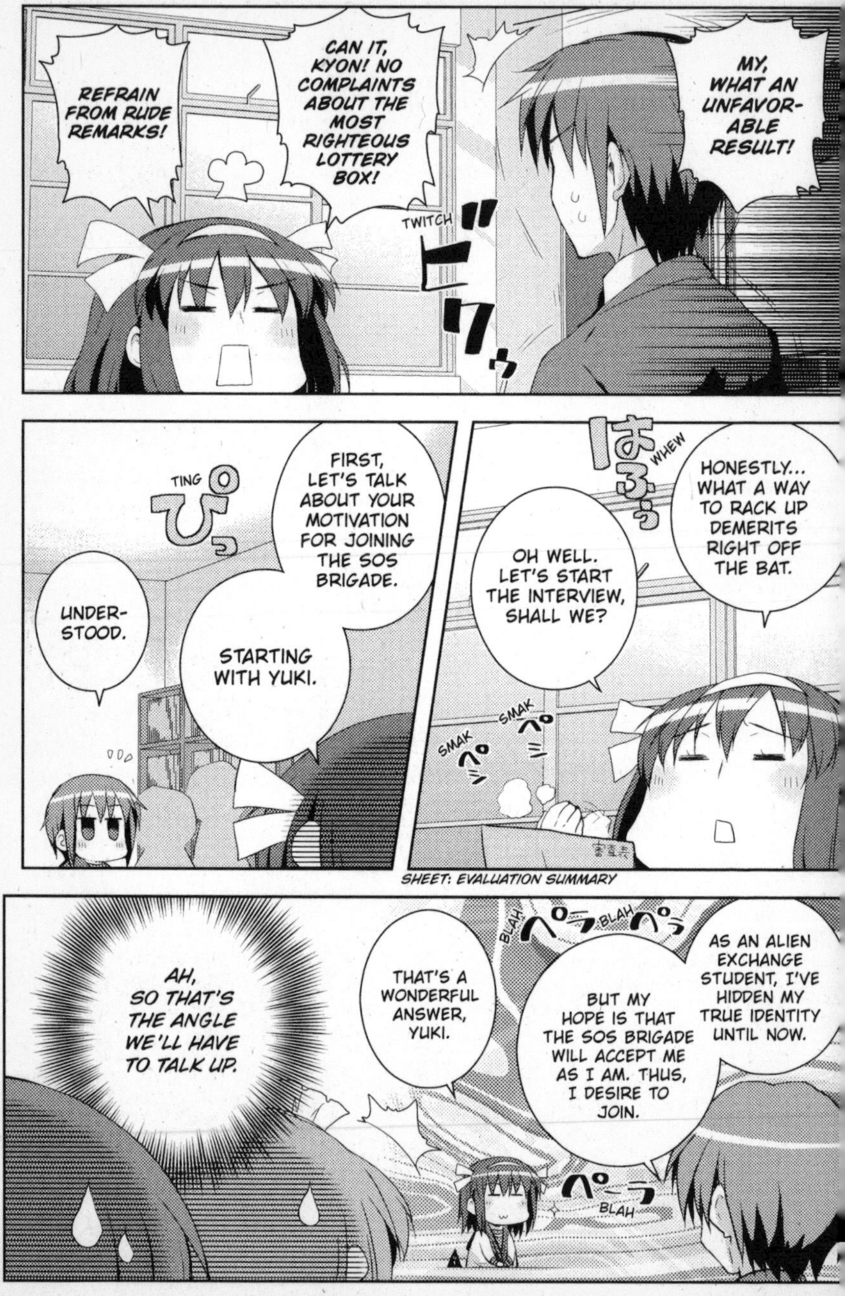
MY, WHAT AN UNFAVORABLE RESULT!
TWITCH
CAN IT, KYON! NO COMPLAINTS ABOUT THE MOST RIGHTEOUS LOTTERY BOX!
REFRAIN FROM RUDE REMARKS!
WHEW
HONESTLY... WHAT A WAY TO RACK UP DEMERITS RIGHT OFF THE BAT.
OH WELL. LET'S START THE INTERVIEW, SHALL WE?
SMAK
SMAK
SHEET: EVALUATION SUMMARY
FIRST, LET'S TALK ABOUT YOUR MOTIVATION FOR JOINING THE SOS BRIGADE.
TING
STARTING WITH YUKI.
UNDERSTOOD.
BLAH
BLAH
AS AN ALIEN EXCHANGE STUDENT, I'VE HIDDEN MY TRUE IDENTITY UNTIL NOW.
BUT MY HOPE IS THAT THE SOS BRIGADE WILL ACCEPT ME AS I AM. THUS, I DESIRE TO JOIN.
BLAH
THAT'S A WONDERFUL ANSWER, YUKI.
AH, SO THAT'S THE ANGLE WE'LL HAVE TO TALK UP.

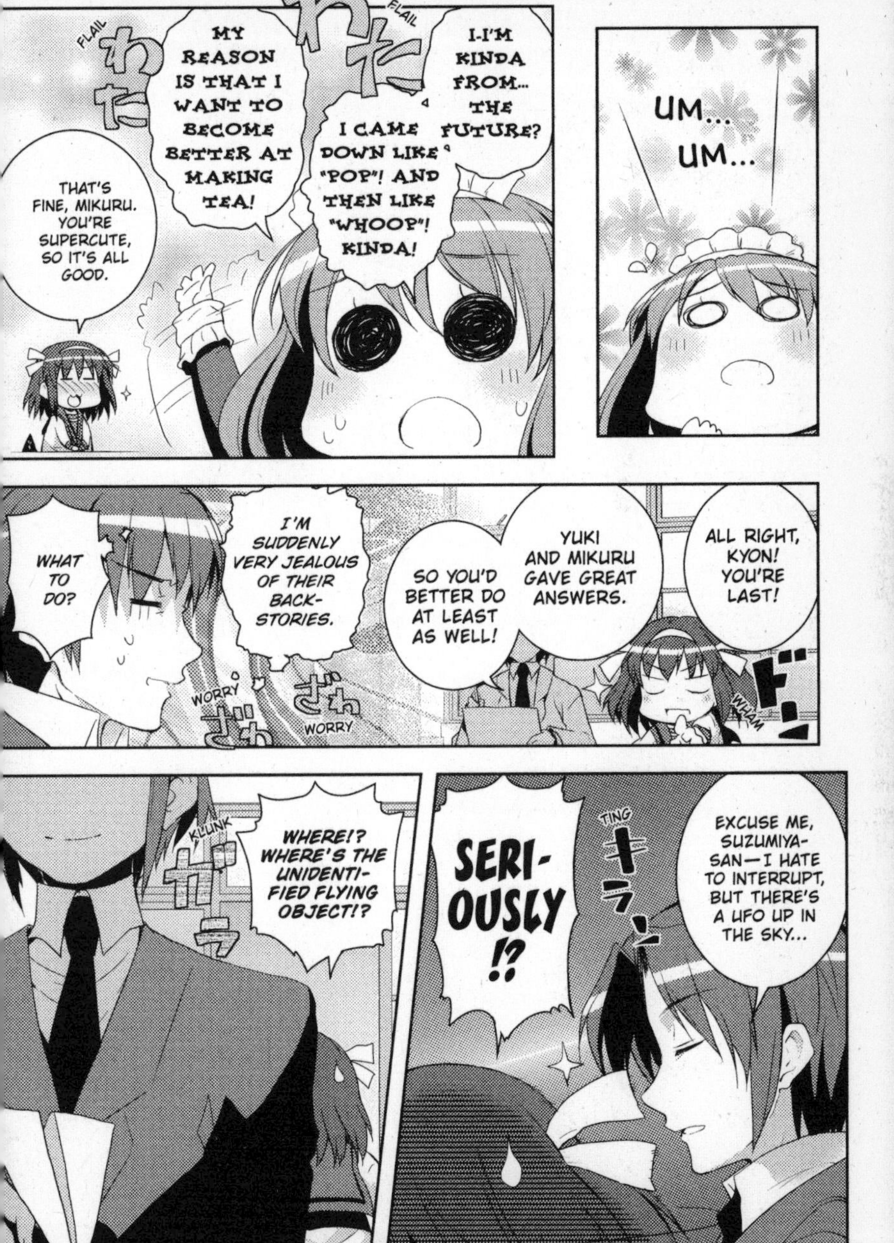
UM... UM...
I-I'M KINDA FROM... THE FUTURE?
FLAIL
I CAME DOWN LIKE "POP"! AND THEN LIKE "WHOOP"! KINDA!
MY REASON IS THAT I WANT TO BECOME BETTER AT MAKING TEA!
FLAIL
THAT'S FINE, MIKURU. YOU'RE SUPERCUTE, SO IT'S ALL GOOD.
ALL RIGHT, KYON! YOU'RE LAST!
WHAM
YUKI AND MIKURU GAVE GREAT ANSWERS.
SO YOU'D BETTER DO AT LEAST AS WELL!
I'M SUDDENLY VERY JEALOUS OF THEIR BACK-STORIES.
WORRY
WORRY
WHAT TO DO?
EXCUSE ME, SUZUMIYA-SAN—I HATE TO INTERRUPT, BUT THERE'S A UFO UP IN THE SKY...
TING
SERI-OUSLY!?
WHERE!? WHERE'S THE UNIDENTI-FIED FLYING OBJECT!?
KLUNK

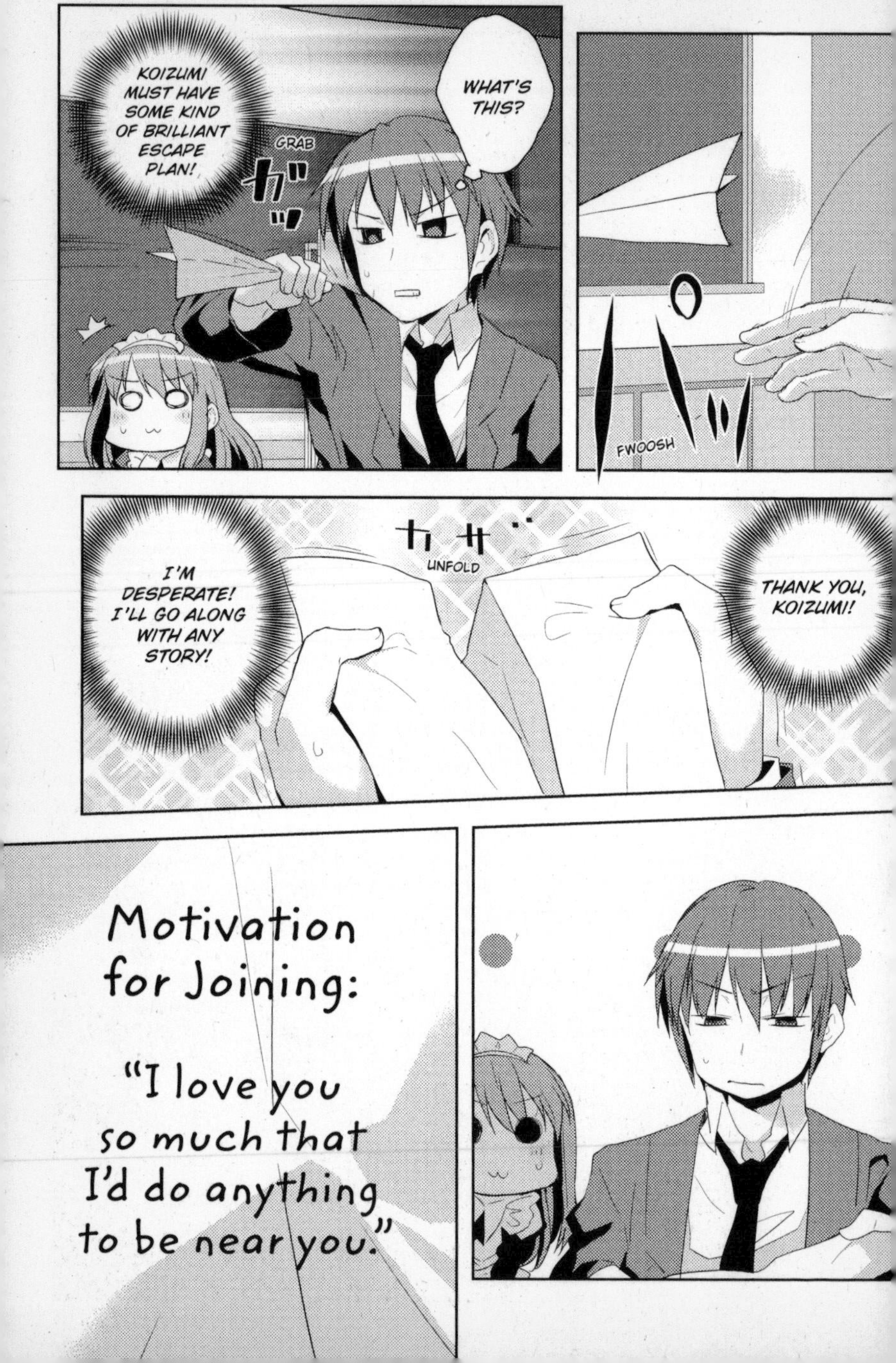
FWOOSH
WHAT'S THIS?
KOIZUMI MUST HAVE SOME KIND OF BRILLIANT ESCAPE PLAN!
GRAB
THANK YOU, KOIZUMI!
UNFOLD
I'M DESPERATE! I'LL GO ALONG WITH ANY STORY!
Motivation for Joining:
"I love you so much that I'd do anything to be near you."

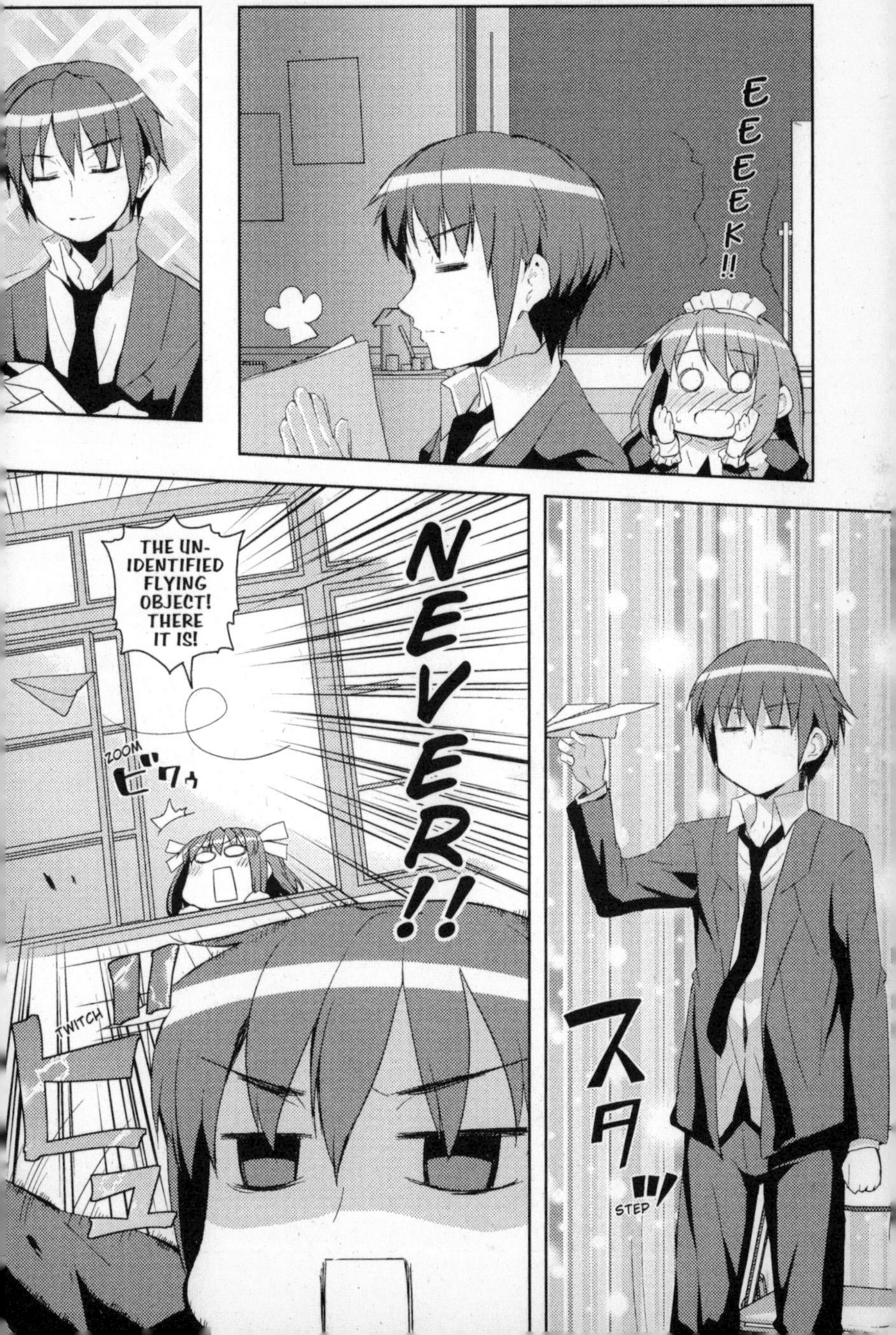
EEEEEK!!
スタ
STEP
THE UN-IDENTIFIED FLYING OBJECT! THERE IT IS!
NEVER!!
ZOOM
ビクゥ
TWITCH

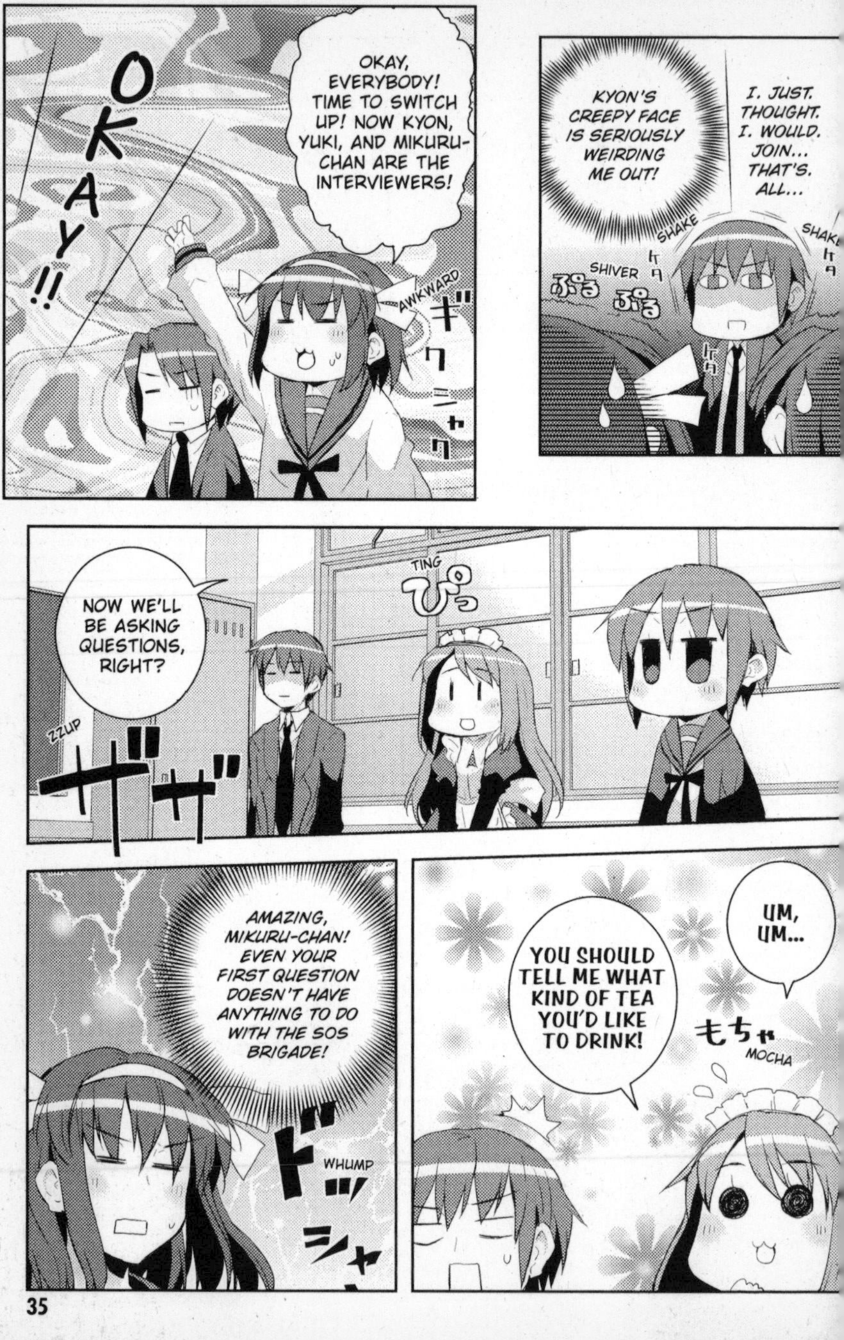
I. JUST. THOUGHT. I. WOULD. JOIN... THAT'S. ALL...
KYON'S CREEPY FACE IS SERIOUSLY WEIRDING ME OUT!
SHAKE
SHAKE
SHIVER
ぷる ぷる
OKAY, EVERYBODY! TIME TO SWITCH UP! NOW KYON, YUKI, AND MIKURU-CHAN ARE THE INTERVIEWERS!
AWKWARD
OKAY!!
TING
ぴっ
NOW WE'LL BE ASKING QUESTIONS, RIGHT?
ZZUP
UM, UM...
YOU SHOULD TELL ME WHAT KIND OF TEA YOU'D LIKE TO DRINK!
もちゃ
MOCHA
AMAZING, MIKURU-CHAN! EVEN YOUR FIRST QUESTION DOESN'T HAVE ANYTHING TO DO WITH THE SOS BRIGADE!
WHUMP

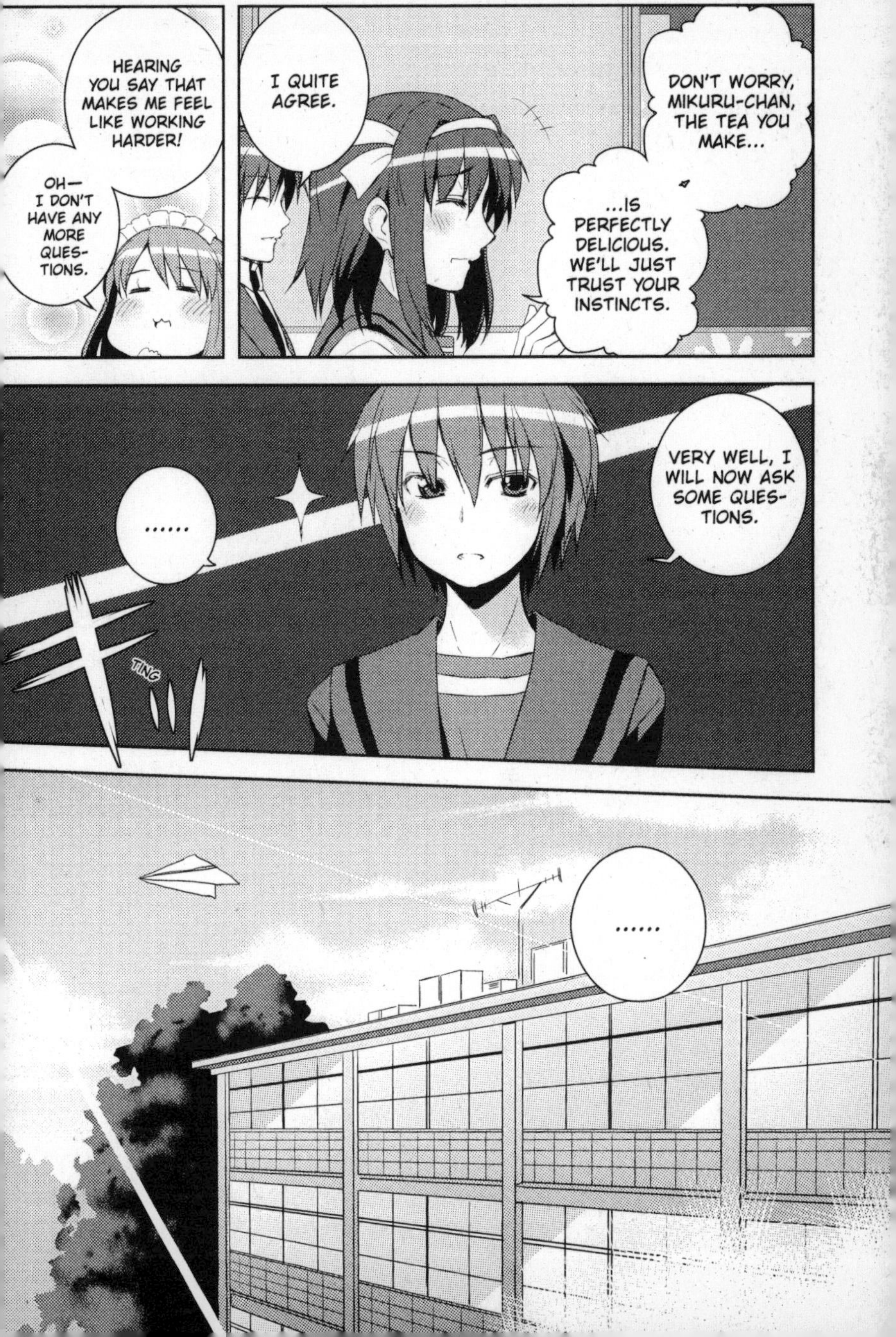
DON'T WORRY, MIKURU-CHAN, THE TEA YOU MAKE...
...IS PERFECTLY DELICIOUS. WE'LL JUST TRUST YOUR INSTINCTS.
I QUITE AGREE.
HEARING YOU SAY THAT MAKES ME FEEL LIKE WORKING HARDER!
OH— I DON'T HAVE ANY MORE QUES-TIONS.
VERY WELL, I WILL NOW ASK SOME QUES-TIONS.
......
TING
......

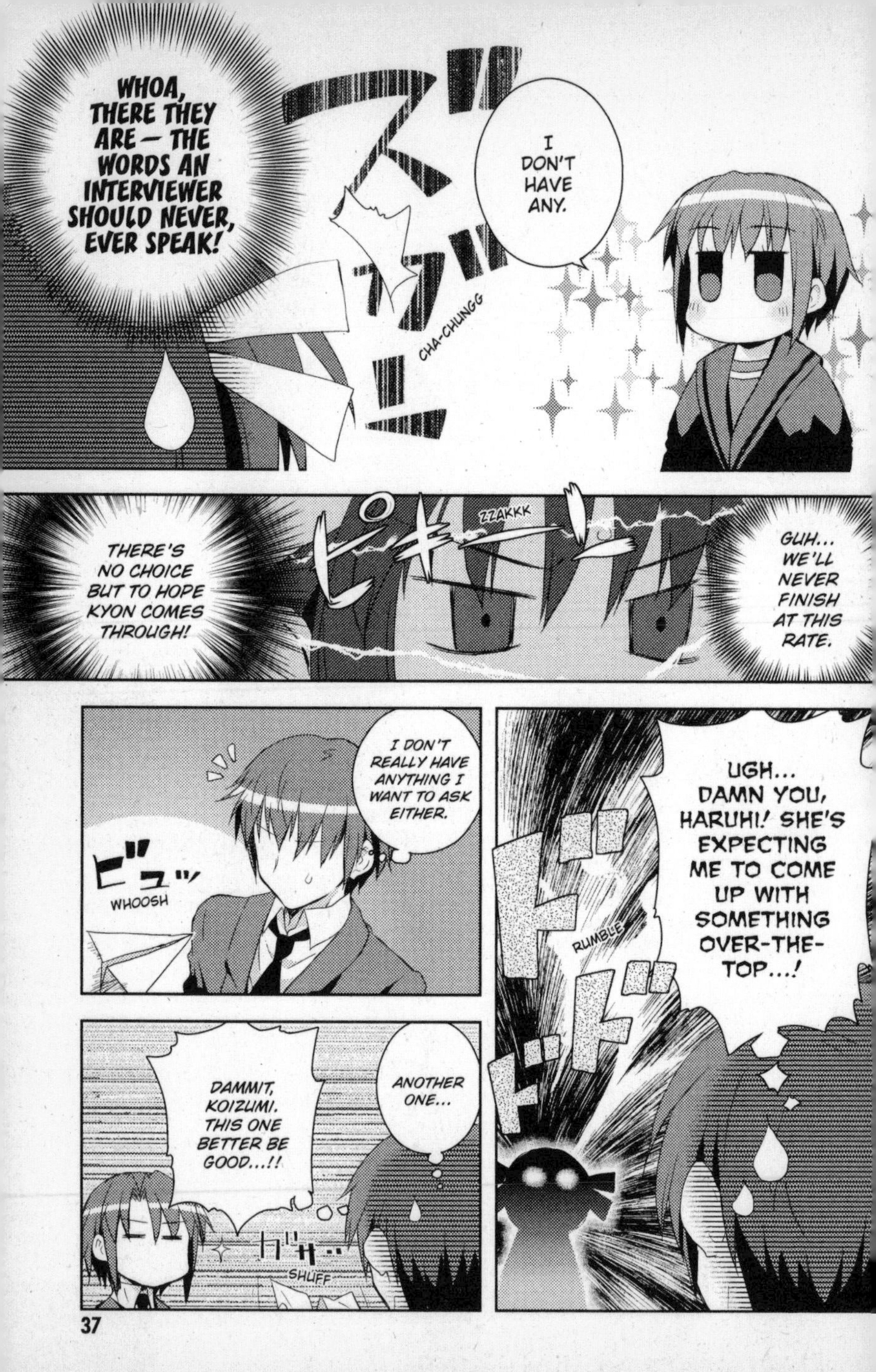
I DON'T HAVE ANY.
WHOA, THERE THEY ARE — THE WORDS AN INTERVIEWER SHOULD NEVER, EVER SPEAK!
CHA-CHUNGG
GUH... WE'LL NEVER FINISH AT THIS RATE.
ZZAKKK
THERE'S NO CHOICE BUT TO HOPE KYON COMES THROUGH!
UGH... DAMN YOU, HARUHI! SHE'S EXPECTING ME TO COME UP WITH SOMETHING OVER-THE-TOP...!
RUMBLE
I DON'T REALLY HAVE ANYTHING I WANT TO ASK EITHER.
WHOOSH
ANOTHER ONE...
DAMMIT, KOIZUMI. THIS ONE BETTER BE GOOD...!!
SHUFF

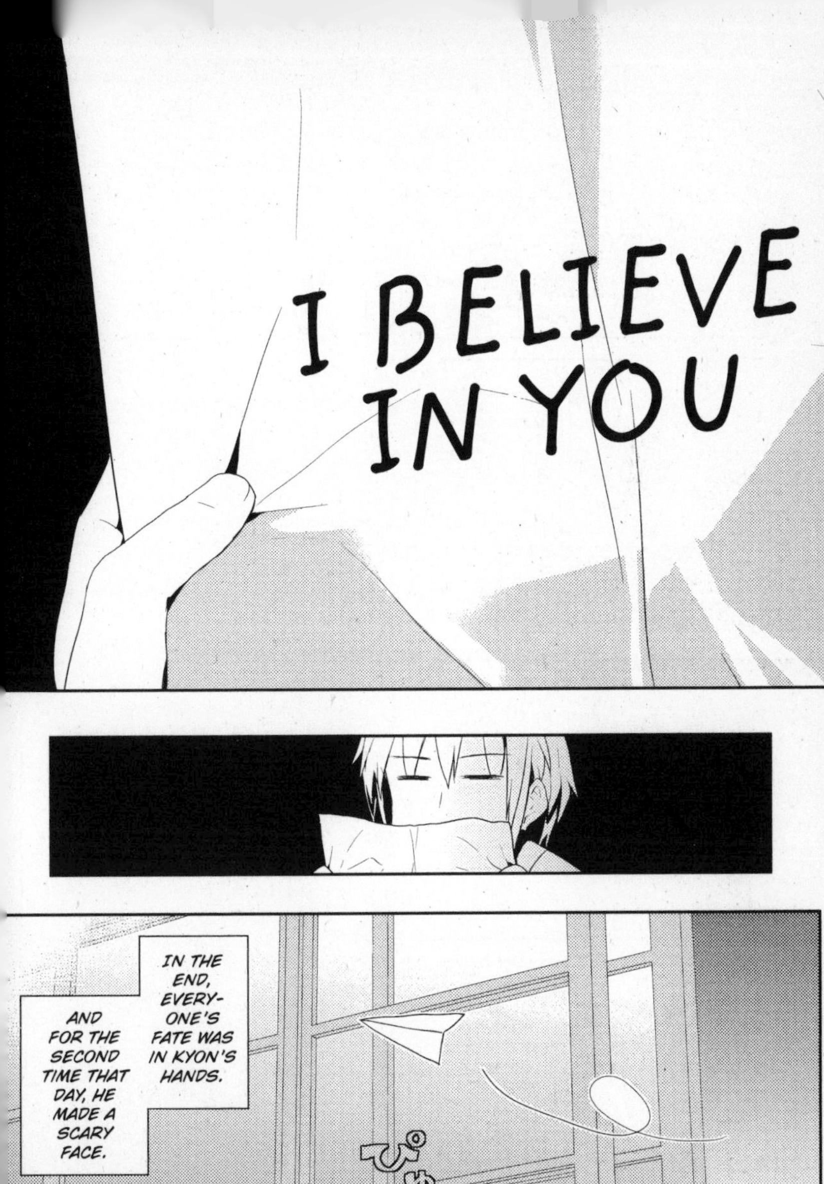
I BELIEVE IN YOU
IN THE END, EVERY-ONE'S FATE WAS IN KYON'S HANDS.
AND FOR THE SECOND TIME THAT DAY, HE MADE A SCARY FACE.
ぴゅ
WHOOSH

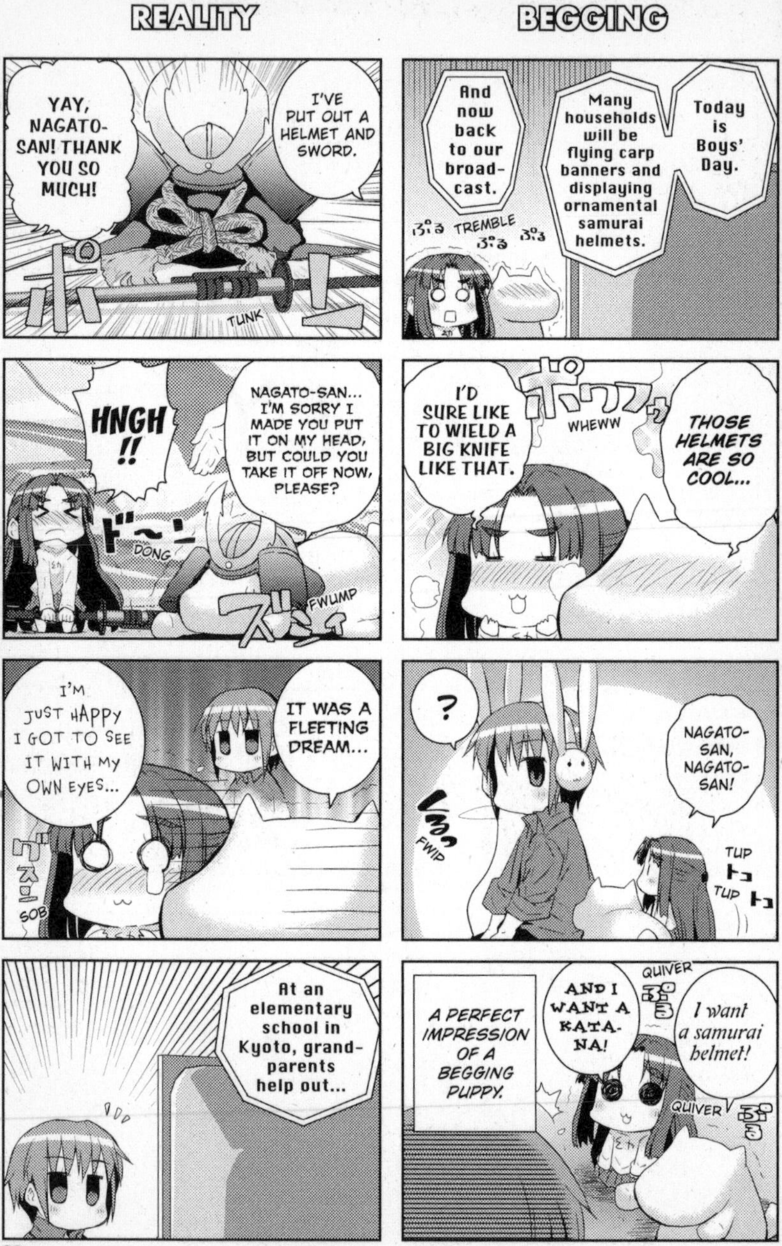
BEGGING
Today is Boys' Day.
Many households will be flying carp banners and displaying ornamental samurai helmets.
And now back to our broadcast.
ぷる TREMBLE ぷる ぷる
THOSE HELMETS ARE SO COOL...
ポワワ WHEWW
I'D SURE LIKE TO WIELD A BIG KNIFE LIKE THAT.
NAGATO-SAN, NAGATO-SAN!
TUP トコ TUP トコ
?
FWIP
QUIVER ぷる
I want a samurai helmet!
AND I WANT A KATA-NA!
QUIVER ぷる
A PERFECT IMPRESSION OF A BEGGING PUPPY.
REALITY
I'VE PUT OUT A HELMET AND SWORD.
YAY, NAGATO-SAN! THANK YOU SO MUCH!
TUNK
NAGATO-SAN... I'M SORRY I MADE YOU PUT IT ON MY HEAD, BUT COULD YOU TAKE IT OFF NOW, PLEASE?
HNGH !!
DONG
FWUMP
IT WAS A FLEETING DREAM...
I'M JUST HAPPY I GOT TO SEE IT WITH MY OWN EYES...
SOB
At an elementary school in Kyoto, grand-parents help out...

•Achakura-san •Loves all blades, perhaps because they remind her of a previous life.

•Kimidori-san •Loves fishing shows like an old man. On the other hand, is obsessed with samurai helmets.

SYMPATHY

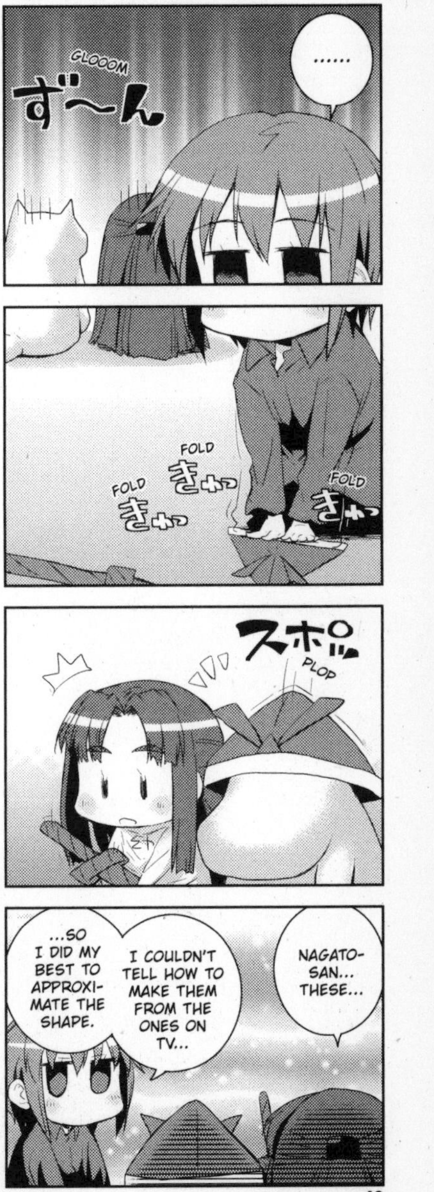
GLOOOM
ず～ん
......
FOLD
きゅっ
FOLD
きゅっ
FOLD
きゅっ
スポッ
PLOP
NAGATO-SAN... THESE...
I COULDN'T TELL HOW TO MAKE THEM FROM THE ONES ON TV...
...SO I DID MY BEST TO APPROXIMATE THE SHAPE.

GRATITUDE

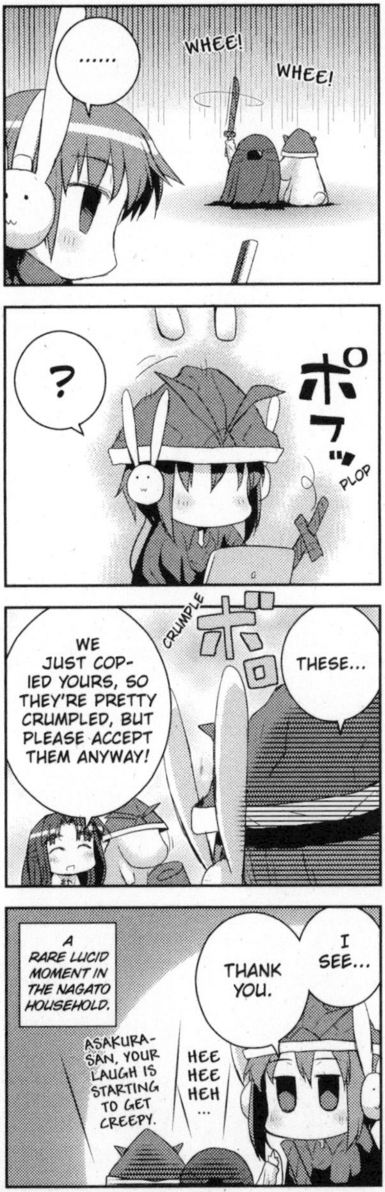
WHEE!
WHEE!
......
ポフッ
PLOP
?
THESE...
ボロ
CRUMPLE
WE JUST COPIED YOURS, SO THEY'RE PRETTY CRUMPLED, BUT PLEASE ACCEPT THEM ANYWAY!
I SEE...
THANK YOU.
HEE HEE HEH ...
ASAKURA-SAN, YOUR LAUGH IS STARTING TO GET CREEPY.
A RARE LUCID MOMENT IN THE NAGATO HOUSEHOLD.

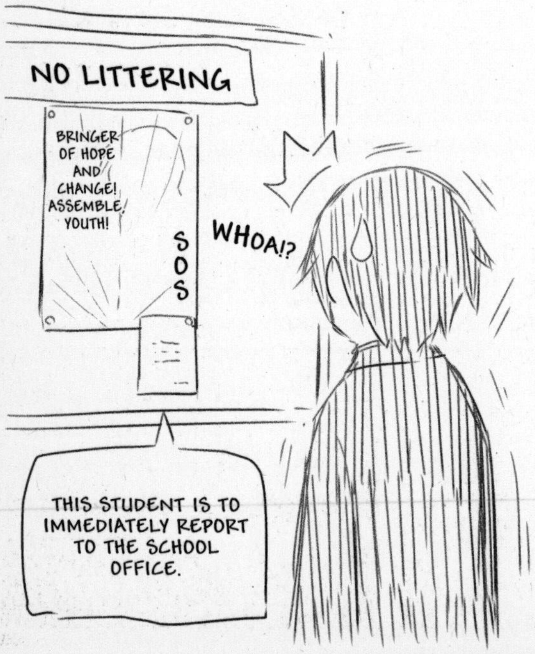
NO LITTERING
BRINGER OF HOPE AND CHANGE! ASSEMBLE YOUTH!
SOS
WHOA!?
THIS STUDENT IS TO IMMEDIATELY REPORT TO THE SCHOOL OFFICE.

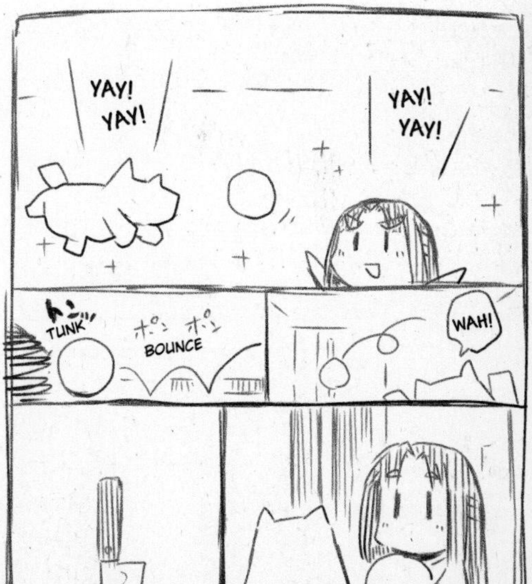
YAY! YAY!
YAY! YAY!
TUNK
BOUNCE
WAH!

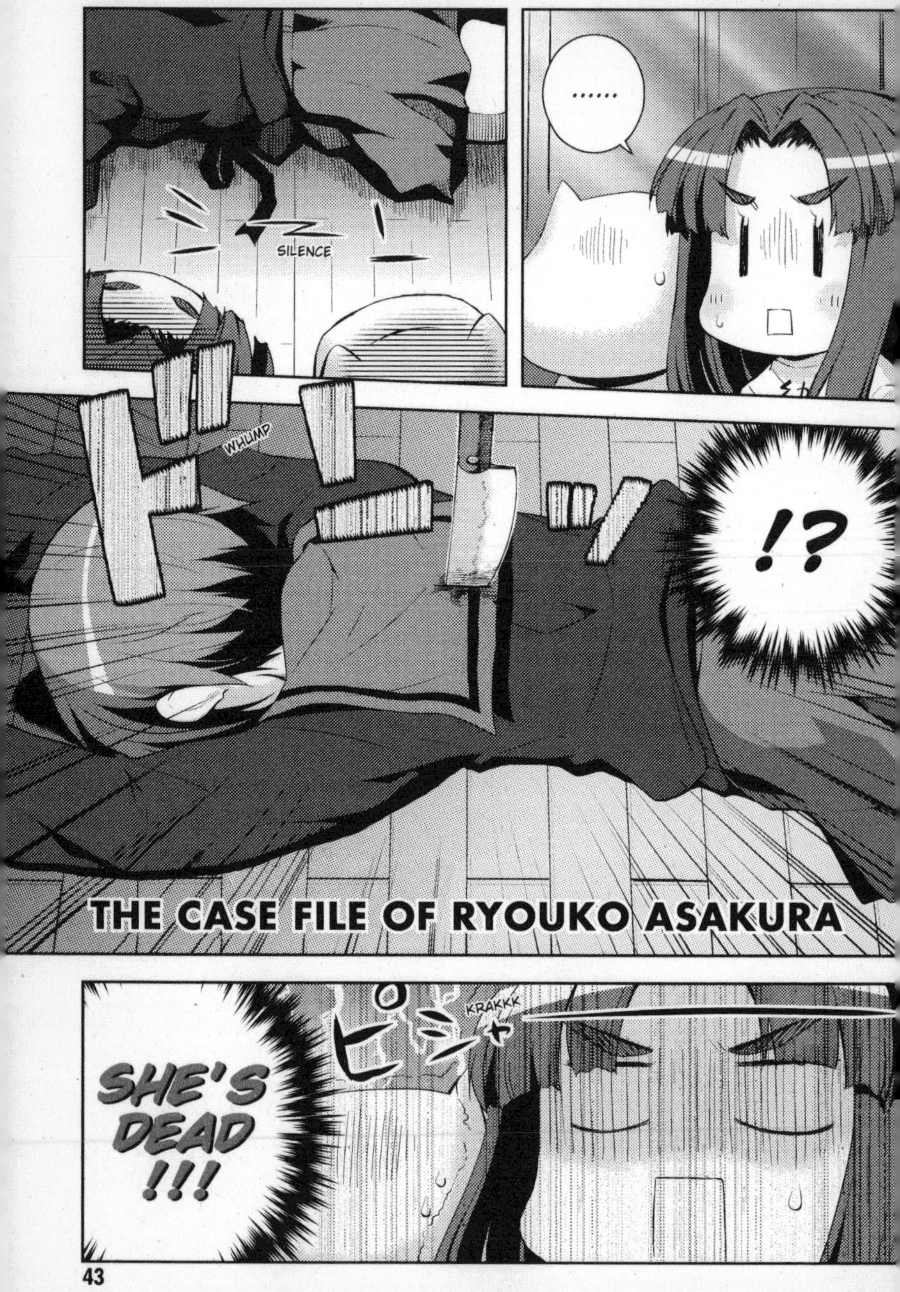
......
SILENCE
WHUMP
!?
THE CASE FILE OF RYOUKO ASAKURA
KRAKKK
SHE'S DEAD !!!

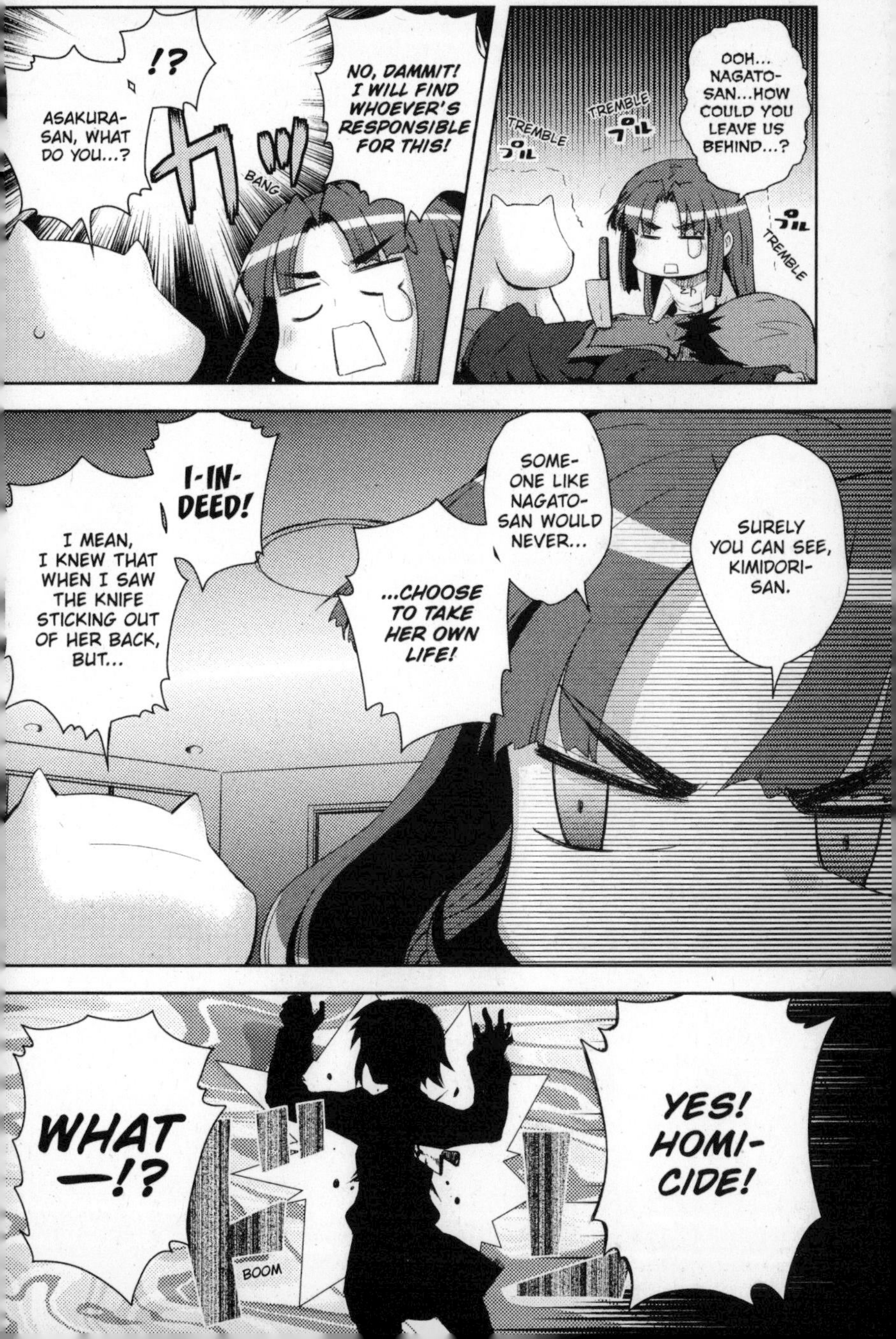
OOH... NAGATO-SAN...HOW COULD YOU LEAVE US BEHIND...?
TREMBLE
TREMBLE
TREMBLE
NO, DAMMIT! I WILL FIND WHOEVER'S RESPONSIBLE FOR THIS!
BANG
!?
ASAKURA-SAN, WHAT DO YOU...?
SURELY YOU CAN SEE, KIMIDORI-SAN.
SOME-ONE LIKE NAGATO-SAN WOULD NEVER...
...CHOOSE TO TAKE HER OWN LIFE!
I-IN-DEED!
I MEAN, I KNEW THAT WHEN I SAW THE KNIFE STICKING OUT OF HER BACK, BUT...
YES! HOMI-CIDE!
BOOM
WHAT—!?

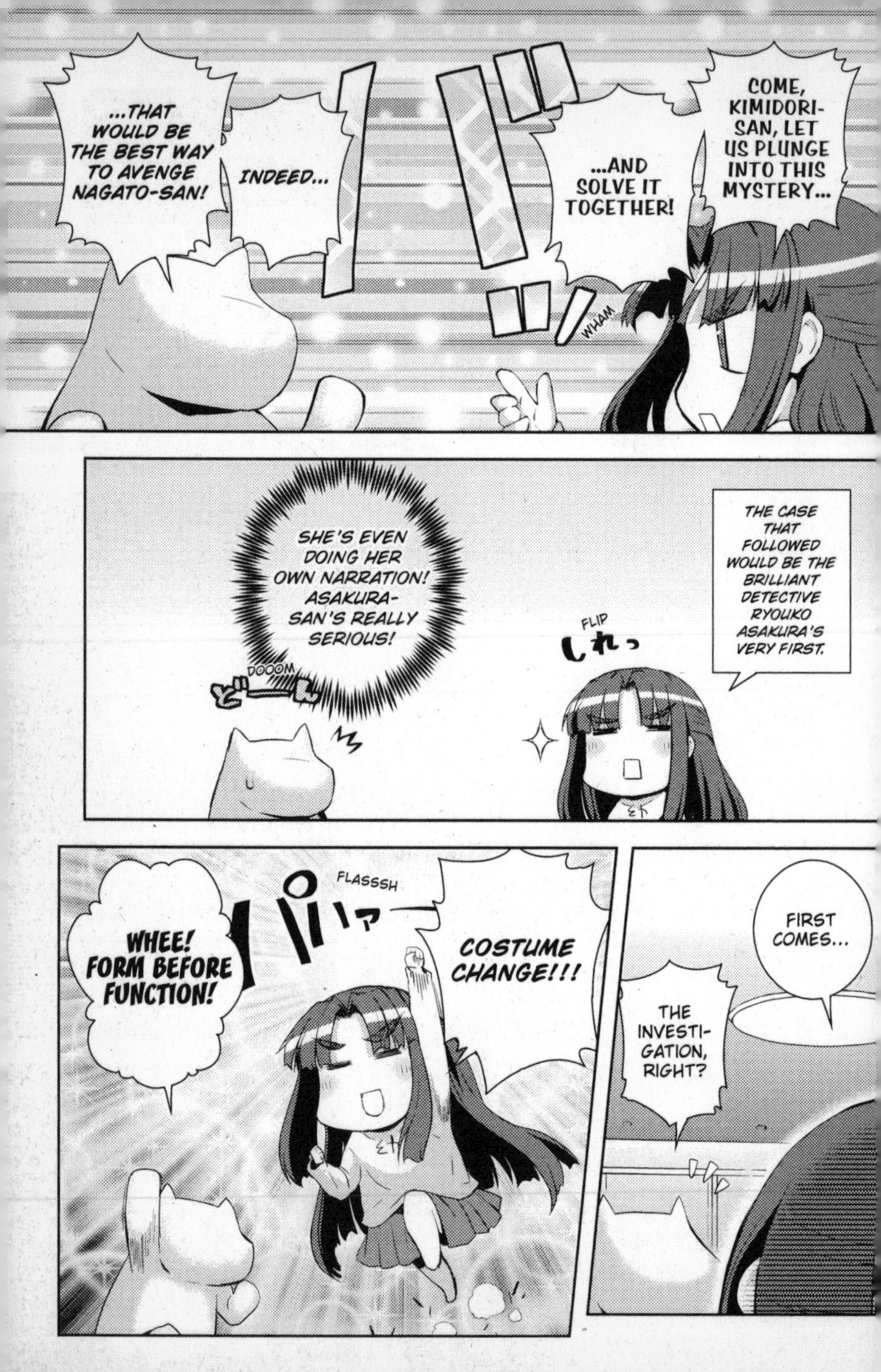
COME, KIMIDORI-SAN, LET US PLUNGE INTO THIS MYSTERY...
...AND SOLVE IT TOGETHER!
WHAM
INDEED...
...THAT WOULD BE THE BEST WAY TO AVENGE NAGATO-SAN!
THE CASE THAT FOLLOWED WOULD BE THE BRILLIANT DETECTIVE RYOUKO ASAKURA'S VERY FIRST.
FLIP
しれっ
SHE'S EVEN DOING HER OWN NARRATION! ASAKURA-SAN'S REALLY SERIOUS!
DOOOM
FIRST COMES...
THE INVESTIGATION, RIGHT?
COSTUME CHANGE!!!
FLASSSH
WHEE! FORM BEFORE FUNCTION!

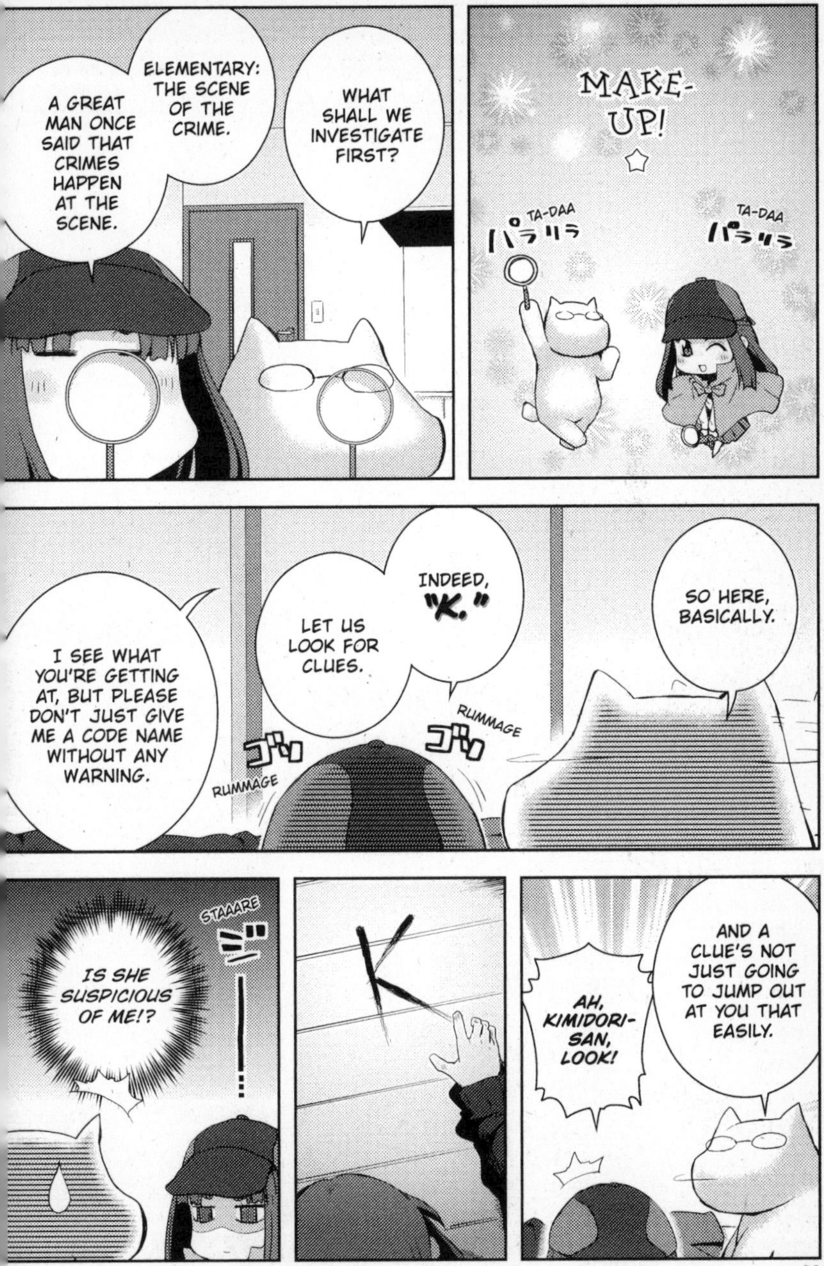
MAKE-UP!
TA-DAA
パラリラ
TA-DAA
パラリラ
WHAT SHALL WE INVESTIGATE FIRST?
ELEMENTARY: THE SCENE OF THE CRIME.
A GREAT MAN ONCE SAID THAT CRIMES HAPPEN AT THE SCENE.
SO HERE, BASICALLY.
INDEED, "K."
LET US LOOK FOR CLUES.
RUMMAGE
ゴソ
ゴソ
RUMMAGE
I SEE WHAT YOU'RE GETTING AT, BUT PLEASE DON'T JUST GIVE ME A CODE NAME WITHOUT ANY WARNING.
AND A CLUE'S NOT JUST GOING TO JUMP OUT AT YOU THAT EASILY.
AH, KIMIDORI-SAN, LOOK!
STAAARE
ジー…
IS SHE SUSPICIOUS OF ME!?

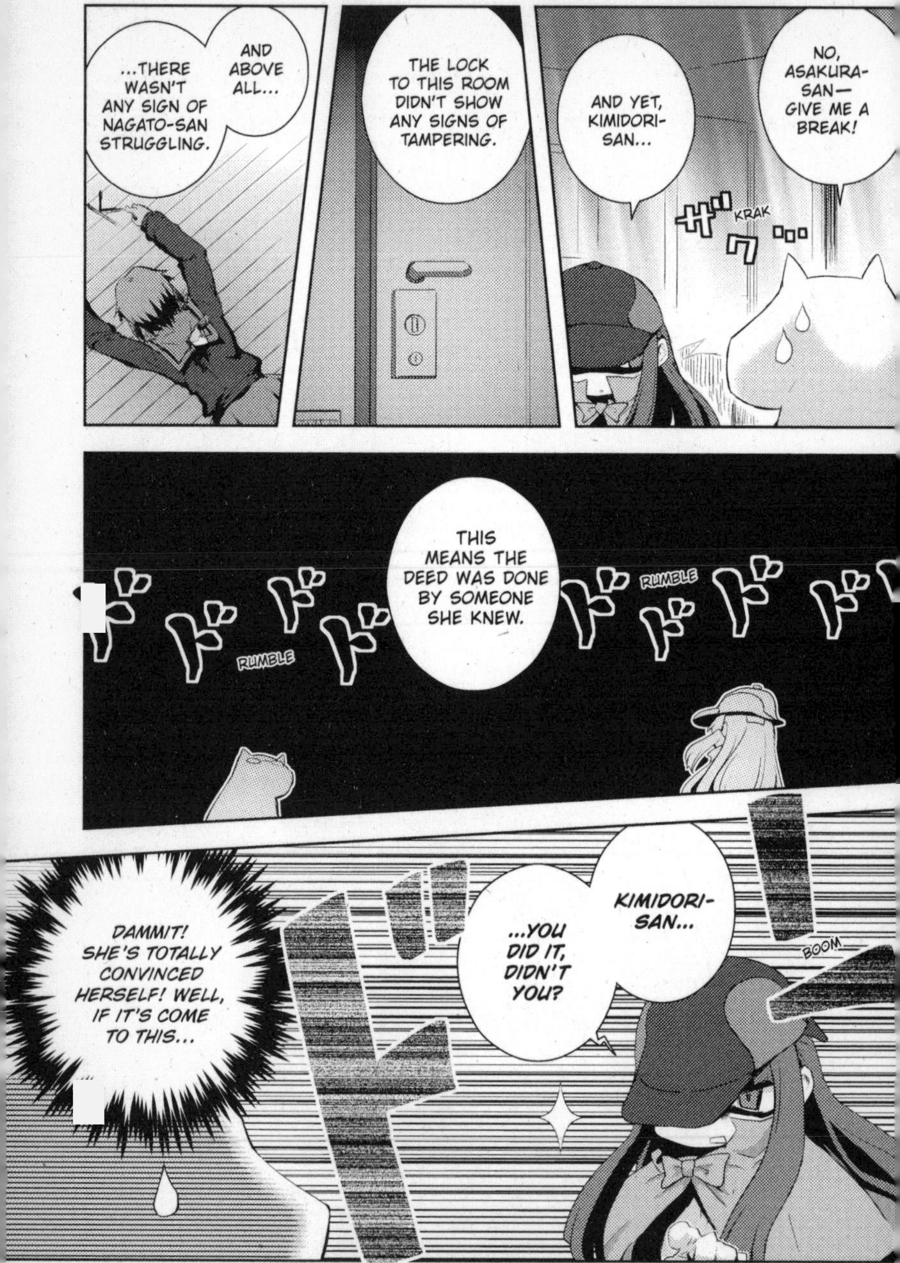

NO, ASAKURA-SAN—GIVE ME A BREAK!
AND YET, KIMIDORI-SAN...
KRAK
THE LOCK TO THIS ROOM DIDN'T SHOW ANY SIGNS OF TAMPERING.
AND ABOVE ALL...
...THERE WASN'T ANY SIGN OF NAGATO-SAN STRUGGLING.
THIS MEANS THE DEED WAS DONE BY SOMEONE SHE KNEW.
RUMBLE
RUMBLE
KIMIDORI-SAN...
BOOM
...YOU DID IT, DIDN'T YOU?
DAMMIT! SHE'S TOTALLY CONVINCED HERSELF! WELL, IF IT'S COME TO THIS...

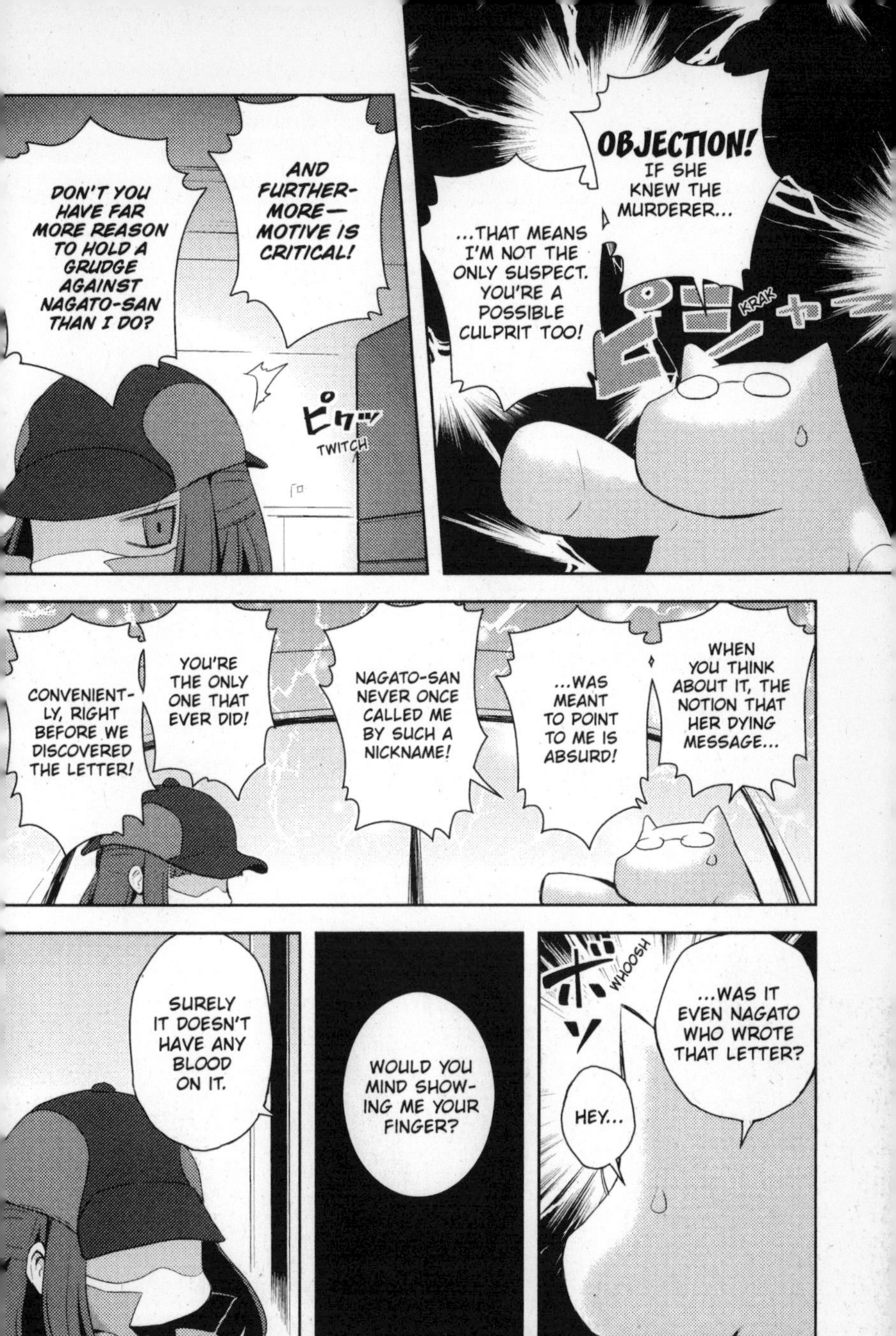
OBJECTION! IF SHE KNEW THE MURDERER...
...THAT MEANS I'M NOT THE ONLY SUSPECT. YOU'RE A POSSIBLE CULPRIT TOO!
KRAK
AND FURTHERMORE— MOTIVE IS CRITICAL!
DON'T YOU HAVE FAR MORE REASON TO HOLD A GRUDGE AGAINST NAGATO-SAN THAN I DO?
TWITCH
WHEN YOU THINK ABOUT IT, THE NOTION THAT HER DYING MESSAGE...
...WAS MEANT TO POINT TO ME IS ABSURD!
NAGATO-SAN NEVER ONCE CALLED ME BY SUCH A NICKNAME!
YOU'RE THE ONLY ONE THAT EVER DID!
CONVENIENTLY, RIGHT BEFORE WE DISCOVERED THE LETTER!
...WAS IT EVEN NAGATO WHO WROTE THAT LETTER?
WHOOSH
HEY...
WOULD YOU MIND SHOWING ME YOUR FINGER?
SURELY IT DOESN'T HAVE ANY BLOOD ON IT.

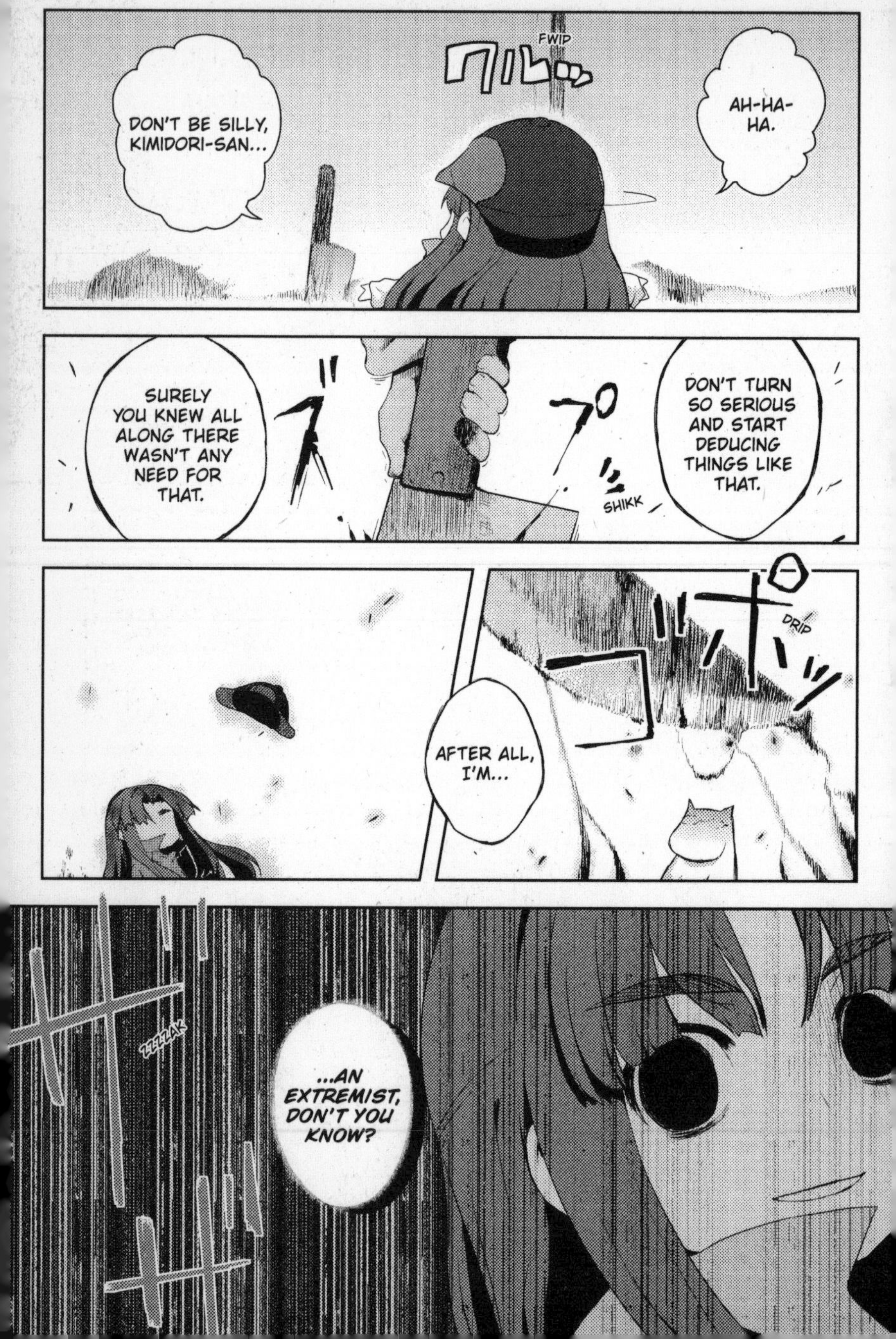
AH-HA-HA.
FWIP
DON'T BE SILLY, KIMIDORI-SAN...
DON'T TURN SO SERIOUS AND START DEDUCING THINGS LIKE THAT.
SHIKK
SURELY YOU KNEW ALL ALONG THERE WASN'T ANY NEED FOR THAT.
DRIP
AFTER ALL, I'M...
...AN EXTREMIST, DON'T YOU KNOW?
ZZZZAK

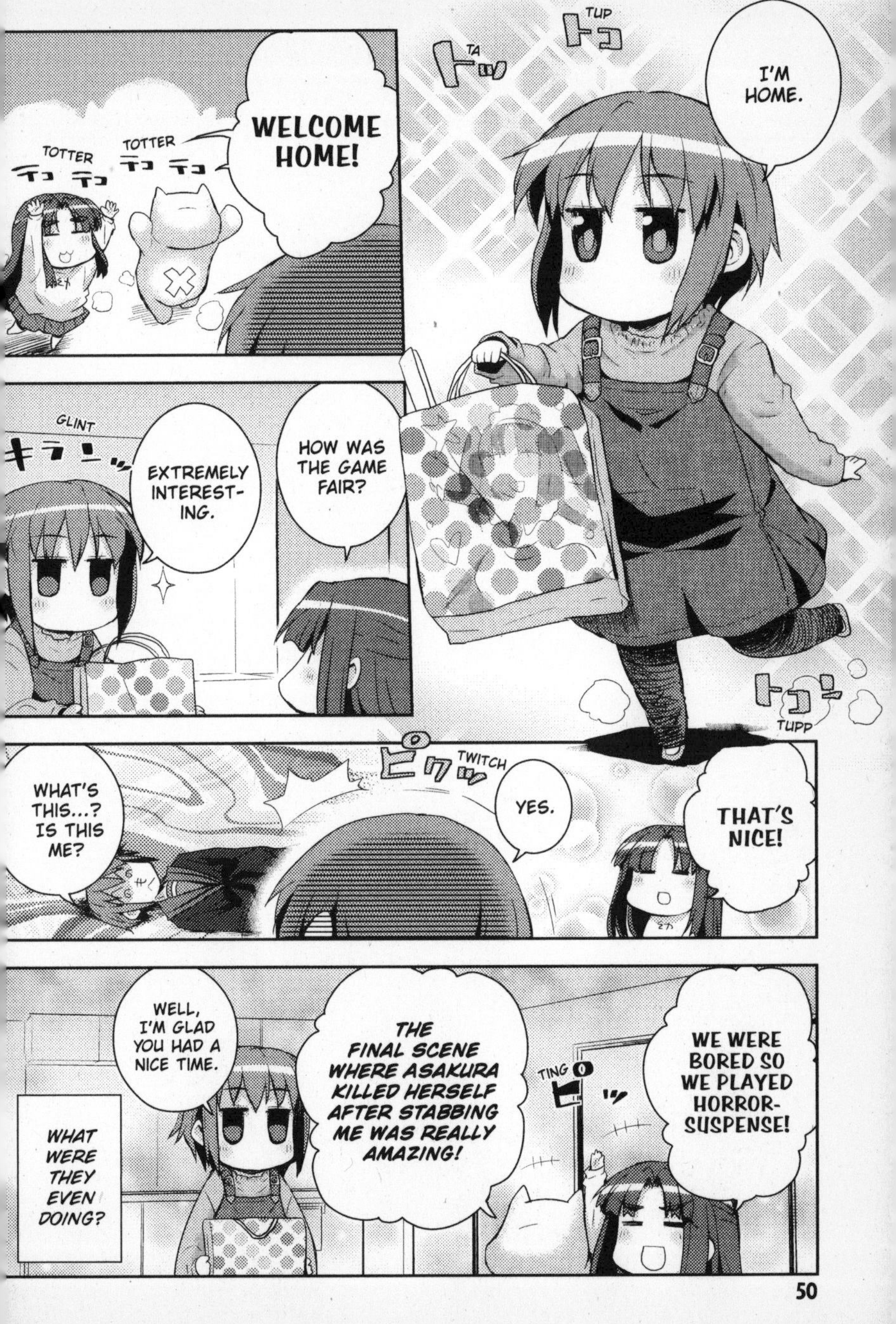
TUP
TA
I'M HOME.
TUPP
WELCOME HOME!
TOTTER
TOTTER
HOW WAS THE GAME FAIR?
EXTREMELY INTERESTING.
GLINT
THAT'S NICE!
YES.
TWITCH
WHAT'S THIS...? IS THIS ME?
WE WERE BORED SO WE PLAYED HORROR-SUSPENSE!
TING
THE FINAL SCENE WHERE ASAKURA KILLED HERSELF AFTER STABBING ME WAS REALLY AMAZING!
WELL, I'M GLAD YOU HAD A NICE TIME.
WHAT WERE THEY EVEN DOING?

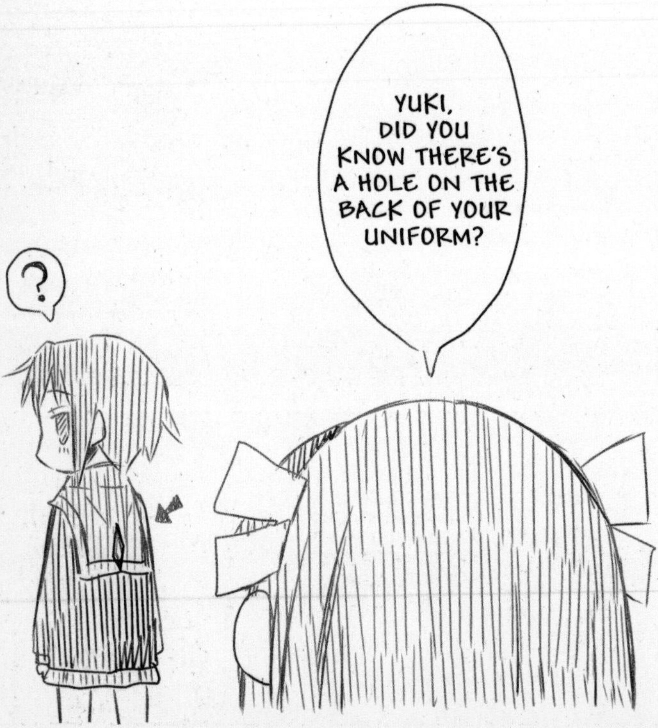
YUKI, DID YOU KNOW THERE'S A HOLE ON THE BACK OF YOUR UNIFORM?
?

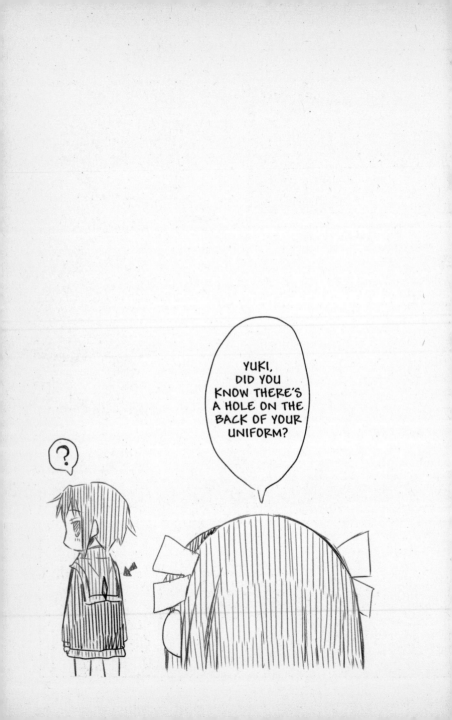

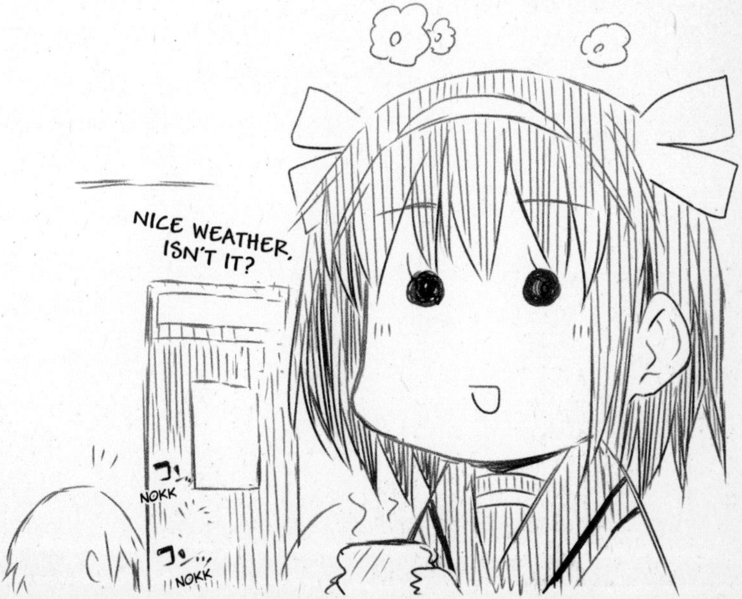
NICE WEATHER, ISN'T IT?
NOKK
NOKK

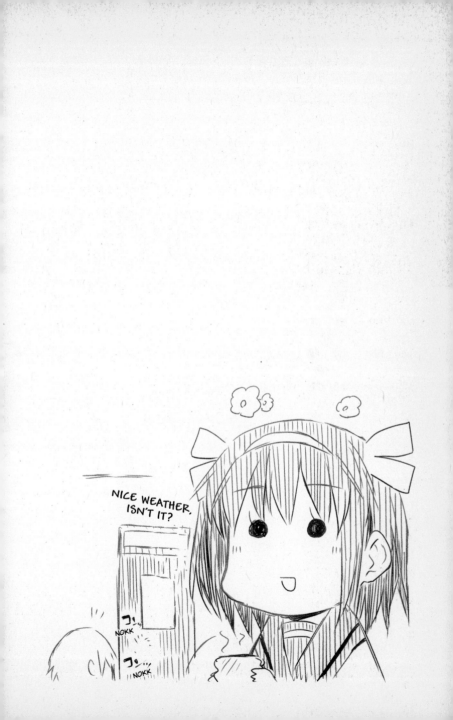

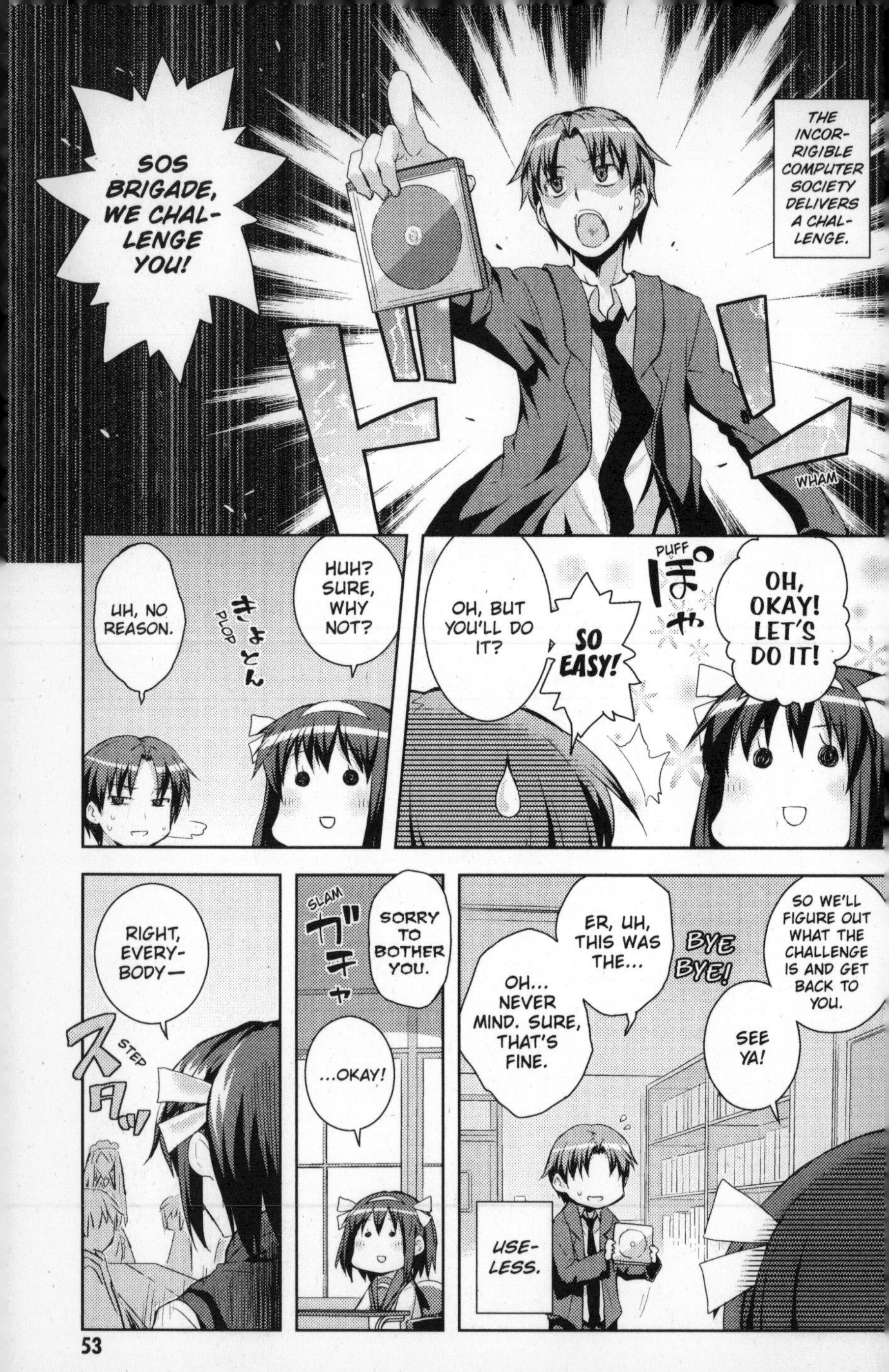
THE INCORRIGIBLE COMPUTER SOCIETY DELIVERS A CHALLENGE.
SOS BRIGADE, WE CHALLENGE YOU!
WHAM
OH, OKAY! LET'S DO IT!
PUFF
SO EASY!
OH, BUT YOU'LL DO IT?
HUH? SURE, WHY NOT?
PLOP
UH, NO REASON.
SO WE'LL FIGURE OUT WHAT THE CHALLENGE IS AND GET BACK TO YOU.
SEE YA!
BYE BYE!
ER, UH, THIS WAS THE...
OH... NEVER MIND. SURE, THAT'S FINE.
USELESS.
SORRY TO BOTHER YOU.
SLAM
...OKAY!
RIGHT, EVERYBODY—
STEP

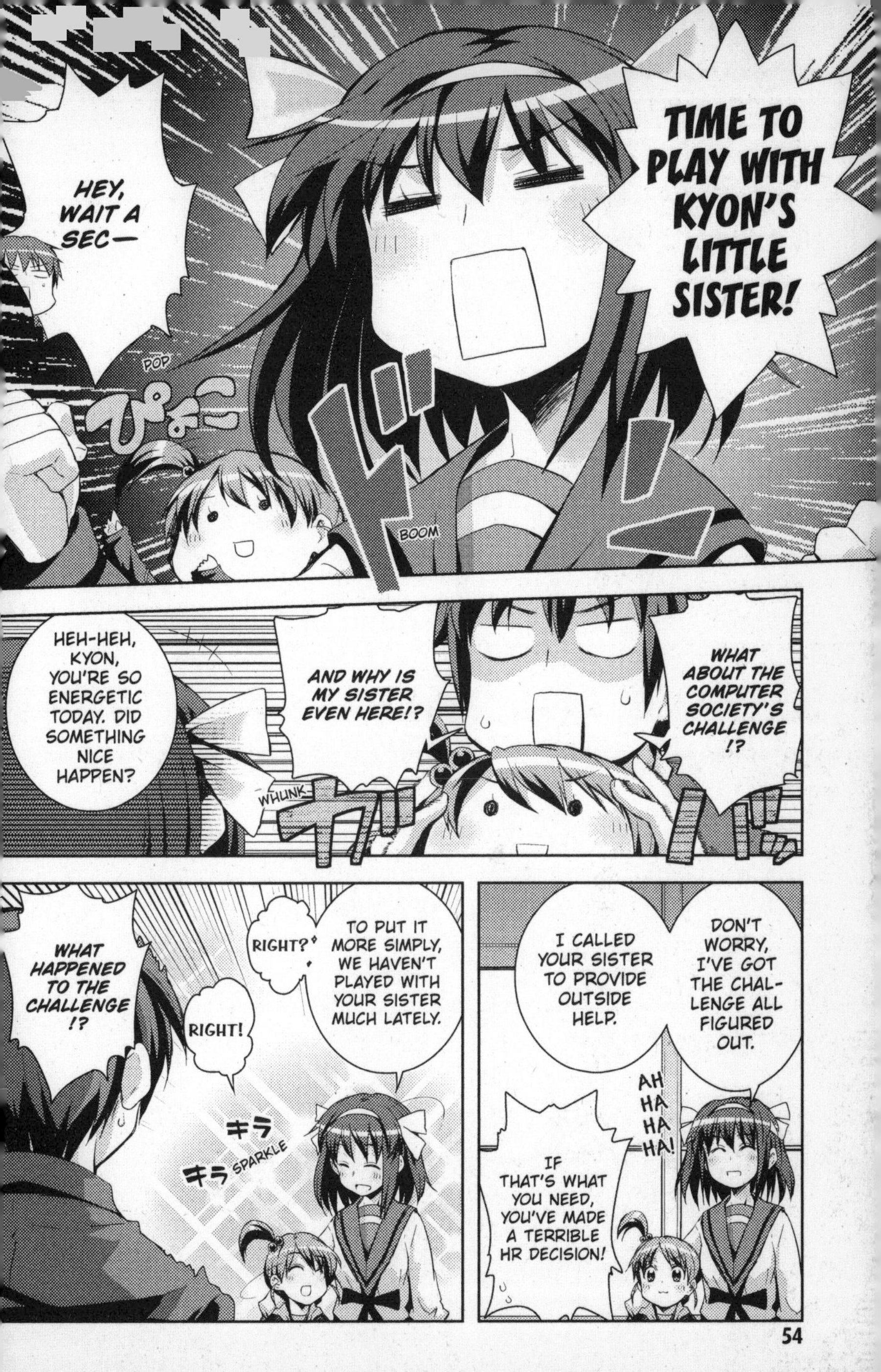
TIME TO PLAY WITH KYON'S LITTLE SISTER!
HEY, WAIT A SEC—
POP
ぴょこ
BOOM
WHAT ABOUT THE COMPUTER SOCIETY'S CHALLENGE !?
AND WHY IS MY SISTER EVEN HERE!?
HEH-HEH, KYON, YOU'RE SO ENERGETIC TODAY. DID SOMETHING NICE HAPPEN?
WHUNK
DON'T WORRY, I'VE GOT THE CHAL-LENGE ALL FIGURED OUT.
I CALLED YOUR SISTER TO PROVIDE OUTSIDE HELP.
AH HA HA HA!
IF THAT'S WHAT YOU NEED, YOU'VE MADE A TERRIBLE HR DECISION!
TO PUT IT MORE SIMPLY, WE HAVEN'T PLAYED WITH YOUR SISTER MUCH LATELY.
RIGHT?
RIGHT!
WHAT HAPPENED TO THE CHALLENGE !?
キラ
キラ SPARKLE

AND ANYWAY, IF MY ULTIMATE GOAL IS TO GET YOUR LITTLE SISTER OR TSURUYA-SAN OR MORI-SAN TO SHOW UP...
...DO I REALLY NEED TO RATIONALIZE THAT...?
HOW THE HELL SHOULD I KNOW!? DON'T ACT LIKE IT'S COMMON KNOWLEDGE!
HEH.
NOW, NOW, KYON-KUN...
AS A MATTER OF FACT, YOU'VE BEEN THE ROOT OF A BUNCH OF PROBLEMS!!
しれっ
SHUP
MY OPINION IS THAT THERE REALLY ISN'T ANY PROBLEM HERE.
ぴょこ
POP
WHO ASKED YOU!?
PAT
HEY, THAT CLOUD LOOKS LIKE KYON'S FACE!
TING
WOW, IT DOES! THAT "SWEPT ALONG BY LIFE" LOOK IS TOTALLY KYON.
FOR A CLOUD.
WOULD YOU GUYS JUST LISTEN TO ME, FOR ONCE!? ALSO, THAT'S NOT EVEN FUNNY!
SNRK!
YOUNGER SISTER CHARACTERS ARE MAGNIFICENT.
WHAT ARE YOU EVEN TALKING ABOUT!?
NAGATO-SAN, CAN WE MAYBE JUST RETHINK YOUR CHARACTER?
ARGH

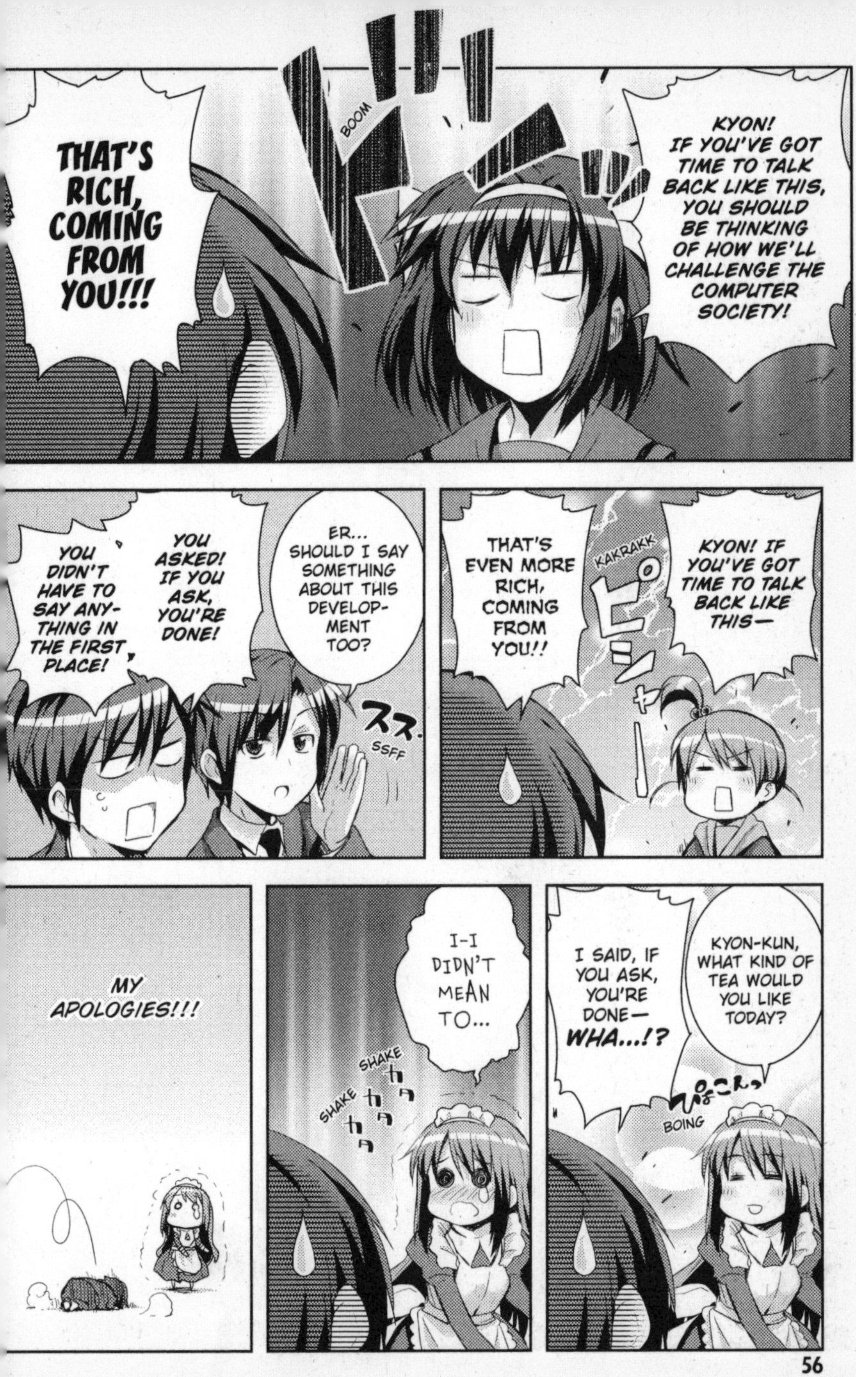
KYON! IF YOU'VE GOT TIME TO TALK BACK LIKE THIS, YOU SHOULD BE THINKING OF HOW WE'LL CHALLENGE THE COMPUTER SOCIETY!
BOOM
THAT'S RICH, COMING FROM YOU!!!
KYON! IF YOU'VE GOT TIME TO TALK BACK LIKE THIS—
KAKRAKK
THAT'S EVEN MORE RICH, COMING FROM YOU!!
ER... SHOULD I SAY SOMETHING ABOUT THIS DEVELOPMENT TOO?
SSFF
YOU ASKED! IF YOU ASK, YOU'RE DONE!
YOU DIDN'T HAVE TO SAY ANYTHING IN THE FIRST PLACE!
KYON-KUN, WHAT KIND OF TEA WOULD YOU LIKE TODAY?
I SAID, IF YOU ASK, YOU'RE DONE— WHA...!?
BOING
I-I DIDN'T MEAN TO...
SHAKE
SHAKE
SHAKE
MY APOLOGIES!!!

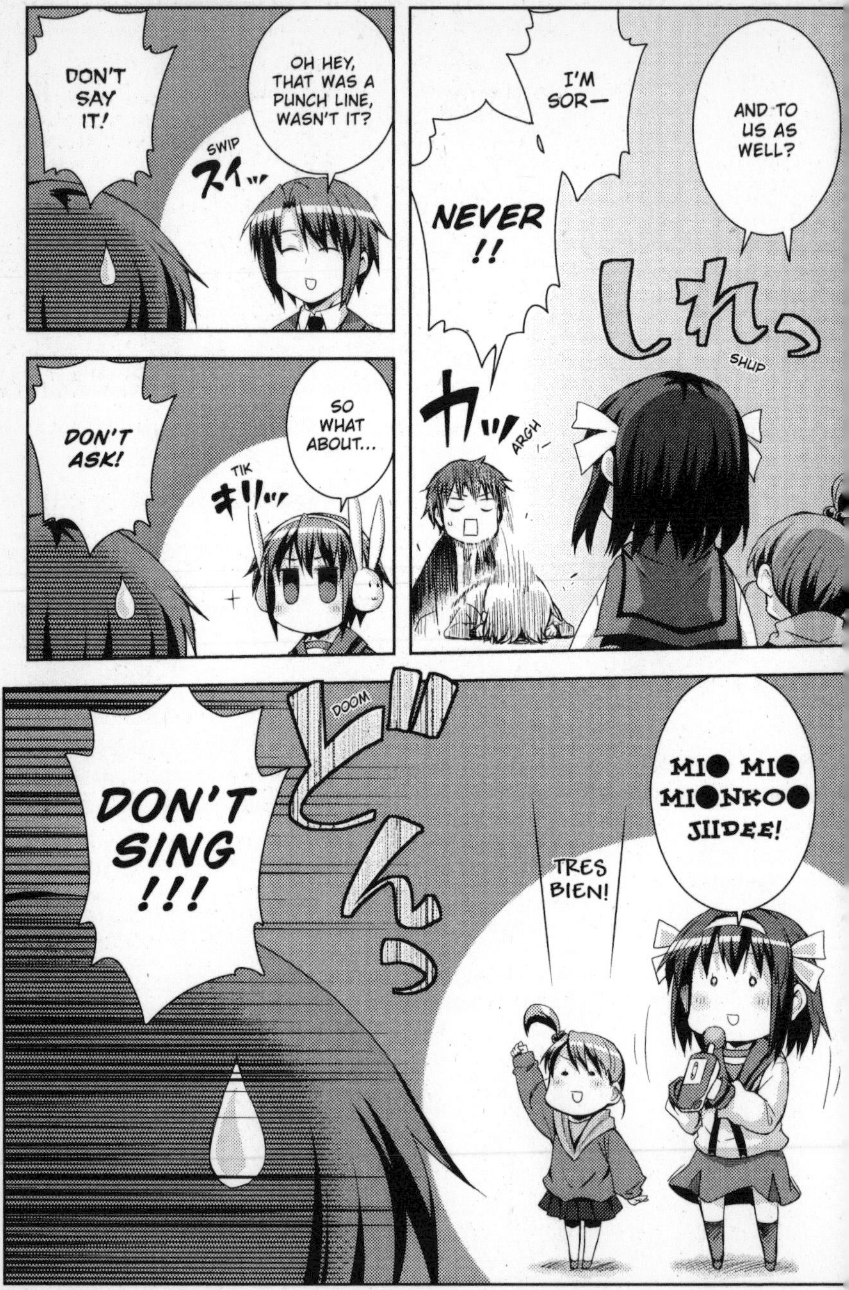
AND TO US AS WELL?
I'M SOR—
NEVER!!
しれっ
SHUP
カッ
ARGH
OH HEY, THAT WAS A PUNCH LINE, WASN'T IT?
DON'T SAY IT!
スィッ
SWIP
SO WHAT ABOUT...
DON'T ASK!
キリッ
TIK
MI● MI● MI●NKO●● JIIDEE!
TRES BIEN!
DOOM
DON'T SING!!!

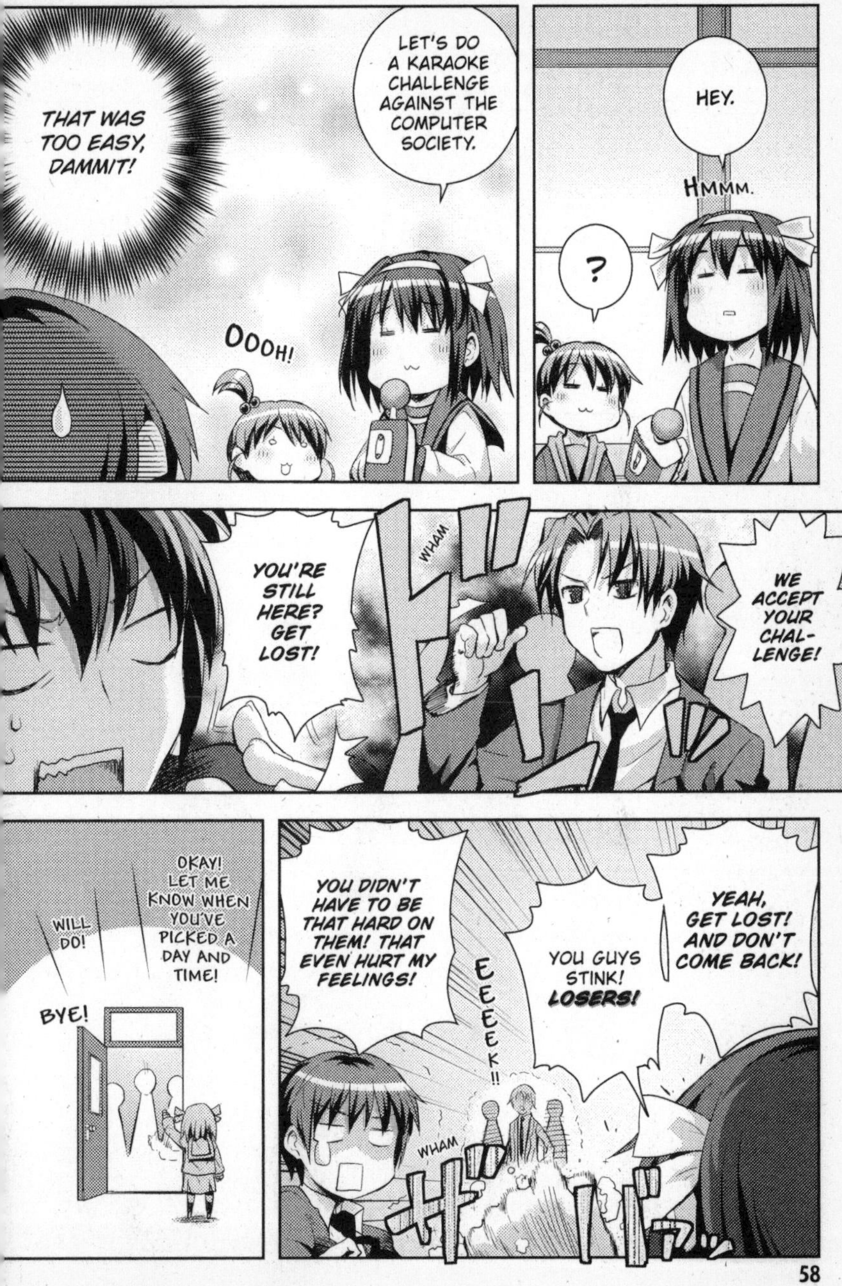
HEY.
HMMM.
?
LET'S DO A KARAOKE CHALLENGE AGAINST THE COMPUTER SOCIETY.
OOOH!
THAT WAS TOO EASY, DAMMIT!
WE ACCEPT YOUR CHAL-LENGE!
WHAM
YOU'RE STILL HERE? GET LOST!
YEAH, GET LOST! AND DON'T COME BACK!
YOU GUYS STINK! LOSERS!
EEEEK!!
WHAM
YOU DIDN'T HAVE TO BE THAT HARD ON THEM! THAT EVEN HURT MY FEELINGS!
OKAY! LET ME KNOW WHEN YOU'VE PICKED A DAY AND TIME!
WILL DO!
BYE!

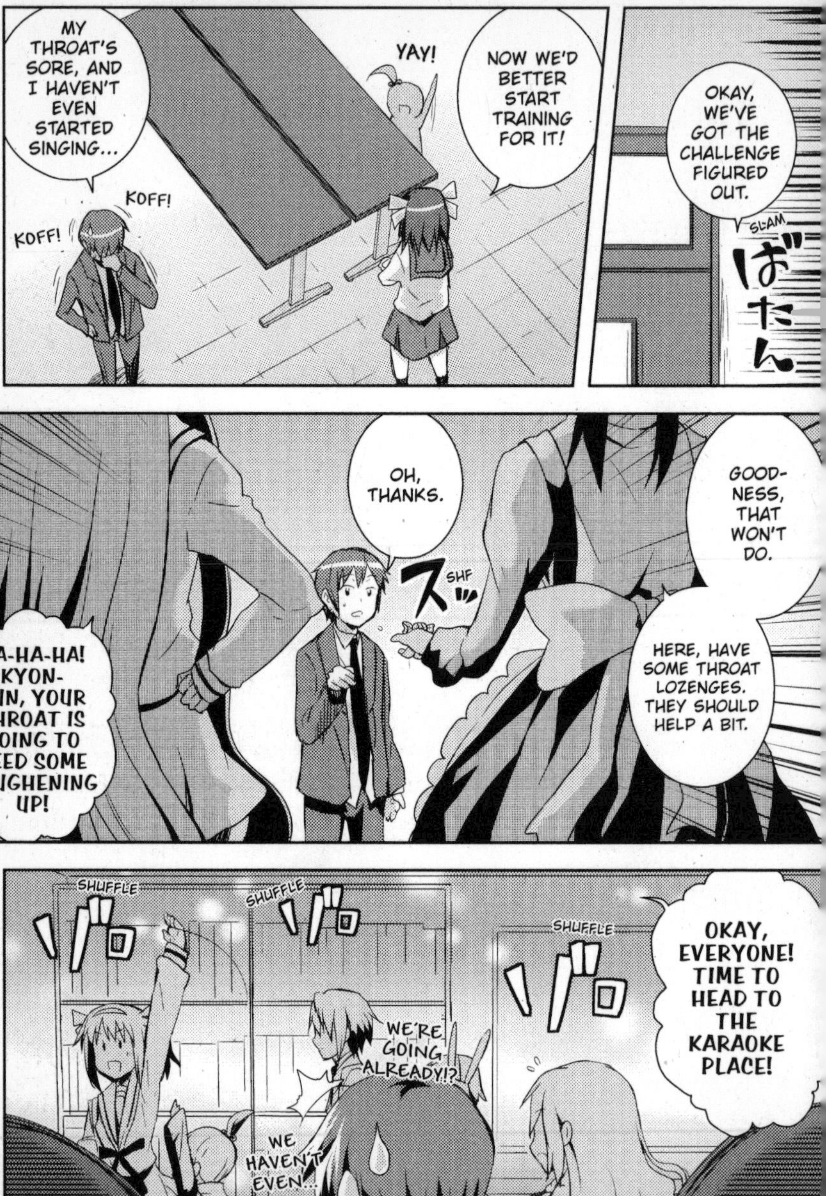
OKAY, WE'VE GOT THE CHALLENGE FIGURED OUT.
SLAM
ばたん
NOW WE'D BETTER START TRAINING FOR IT!
YAY!
MY THROAT'S SORE, AND I HAVEN'T EVEN STARTED SINGING...
KOFF!
KOFF!
GOODNESS, THAT WON'T DO.
HERE, HAVE SOME THROAT LOZENGES. THEY SHOULD HELP A BIT.
SHF
ス
OH, THANKS.
HA-HA-HA! KYON-KUN, YOUR THROAT IS GOING TO NEED SOME TOUGHENING UP!
OKAY, EVERYONE! TIME TO HEAD TO THE KARAOKE PLACE!
SHUFFLE
バロ
WE'RE GOING ALREADY!?
SHUFFLE
バロ
SHUFFLE
バロ
WE HAVEN'T EVEN...

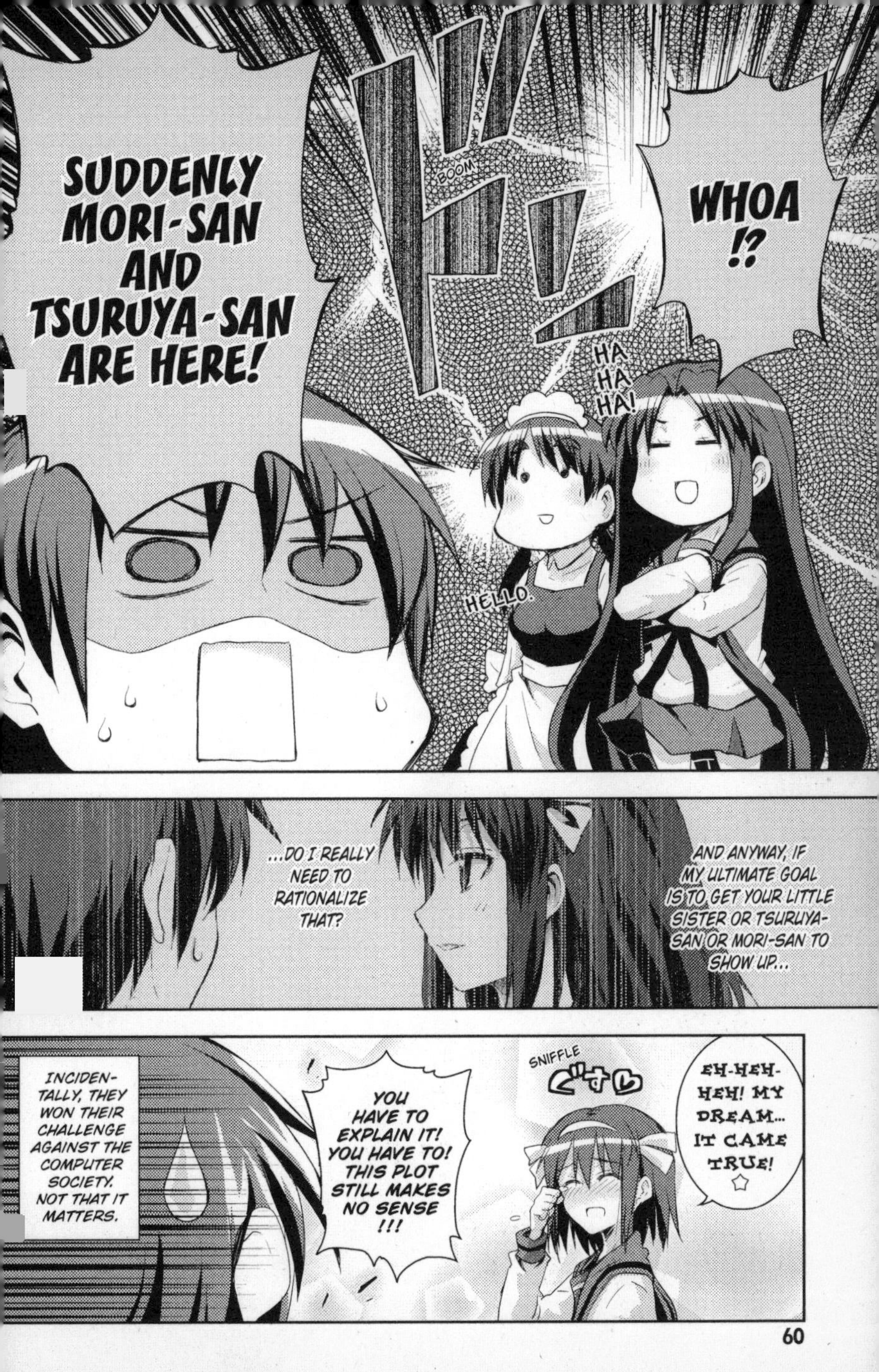
WHOA !?
BOOM
HA HA HA!
HELLO.
SUDDENLY MORI-SAN AND TSURUYA-SAN ARE HERE!
AND ANYWAY, IF MY ULTIMATE GOAL IS TO GET YOUR LITTLE SISTER OR TSURUYA-SAN OR MORI-SAN TO SHOW UP...
...DO I REALLY NEED TO RATIONALIZE THAT?
SNIFFLE
EH-HEH-HEH! MY DREAM... IT CAME TRUE!
YOU HAVE TO EXPLAIN IT! YOU HAVE TO! THIS PLOT STILL MAKES NO SENSE !!!
INCIDENTALLY, THEY WON THEIR CHALLENGE AGAINST THE COMPUTER SOCIETY. NOT THAT IT MATTERS.

KARAOKE

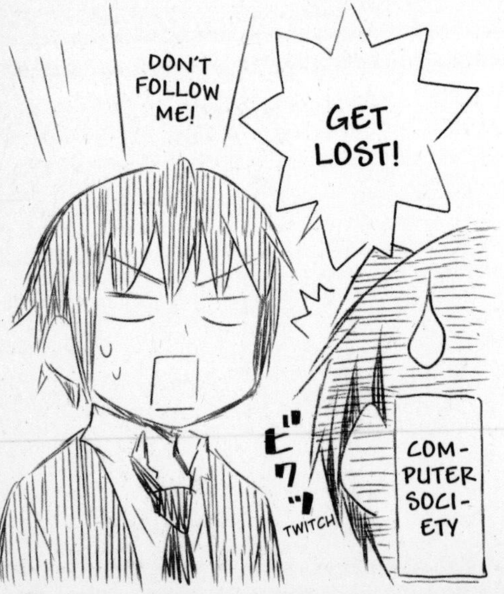
GET LOST!
DON'T FOLLOW ME!
COM- PUTER SOCI- ETY
ビクッ
TWITCH

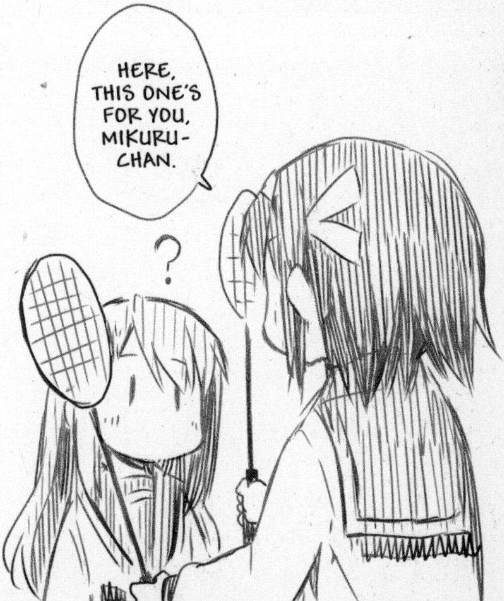
HERE, THIS ONE'S FOR YOU, MIKURU-CHAN.
?

SCATTERSHOT

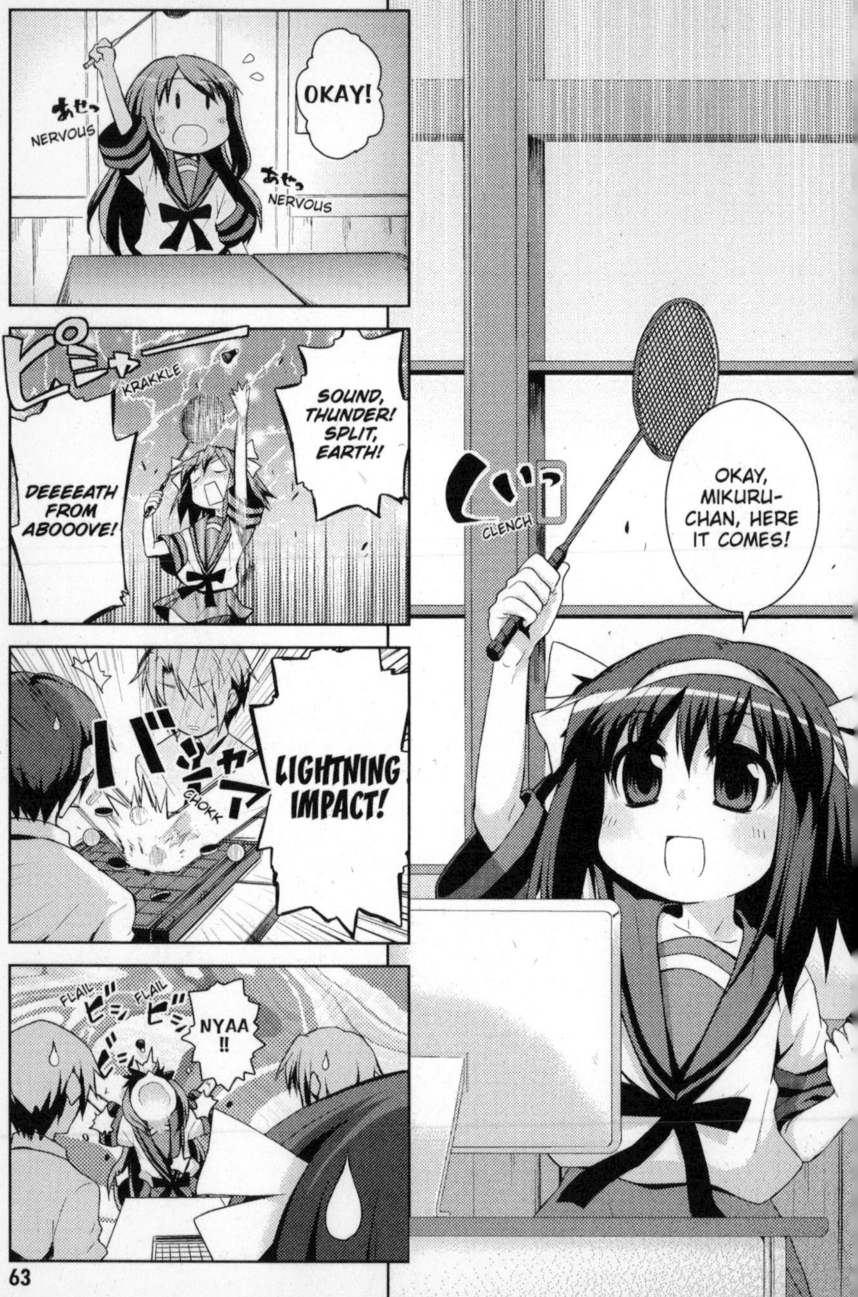
CLENCH
OKAY, MIKURU-CHAN, HERE IT COMES!
OKAY!
あせっ NERVOUS
あせっ NERVOUS
KRAKKLE
SOUND, THUNDER! SPLIT, EARTH!
DEEEEATH FROM ABOOOVE!
CHOKK
LIGHTNING IMPACT!
FLAIL
FLAIL
NYAA!!

•Haruhi-chan •Creates new sports in the midst of her ridiculous fooling around. Pros really are different.

•Mikuru-chan •Forced to play badminton in the clubroom, got hit by a shotgun blast of Othello game pieces.

•Kyon •Supposed to be the main character of this story. The world has been saved countless times by this straight man.

NEW CHALLENGE

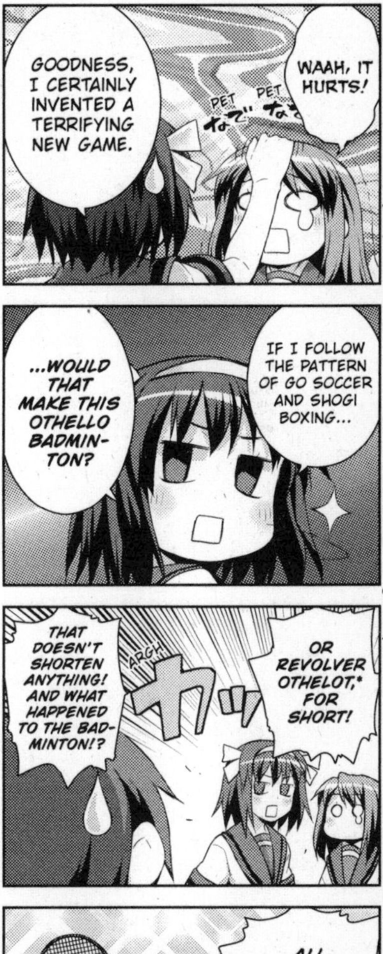
WAAH, IT HURTS!
PET PET
GOODNESS, I CERTAINLY INVENTED A TERRIFYING NEW GAME.
IF I FOLLOW THE PATTERN OF GO SOCCER AND SHOGI BOXING...
...WOULD THAT MAKE THIS OTHELLO BADMINTON?
OR REVOLVER OTHELOT,* FOR SHORT!
ARGH
THAT DOESN'T SHORTEN ANYTHING! AND WHAT HAPPENED TO THE BADMINTON!?
ALL RIGHT! TIME TO START TRAINING FOR THIS NEW GAME!
HUUUH?

COURT

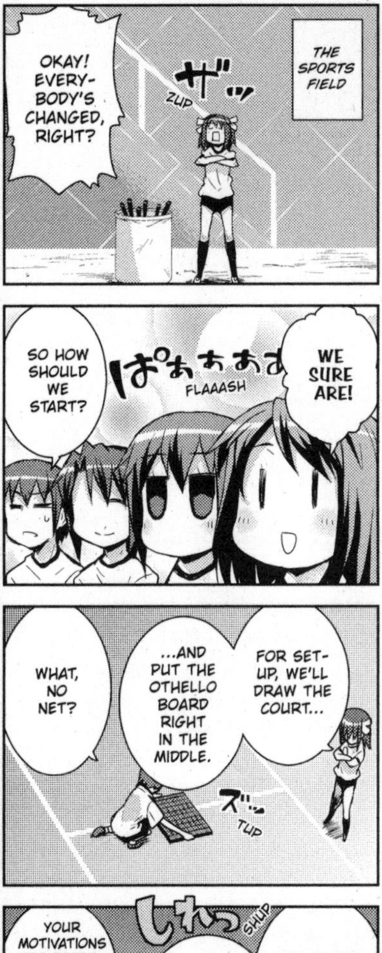
THE SPORTS FIELD
ZUP
OKAY! EVERYBODY'S CHANGED, RIGHT?
WE SURE ARE!
FLAAASH
SO HOW SHOULD WE START?
FOR SET-UP, WE'LL DRAW THE COURT...
...AND PUT THE OTHELLO BOARD RIGHT IN THE MIDDLE.
TUP
WHAT, NO NET?
NO, THAT'D JUST MAKE THINGS TOO CRAZY.
ALSO IT WOULD BE A PAIN TO SET UP AND A PAIN TO DRAW.
SHUP
YOUR MOTIVATIONS ARE BECOMING MORE AND MORE REALISTIC, YOU KNOW.

*REVOLVER OCELOT IS A CHARACTER FROM THE POPULAR METAL GEAR SOLID SERIES OF VIDEO GAMES.

PAIRS

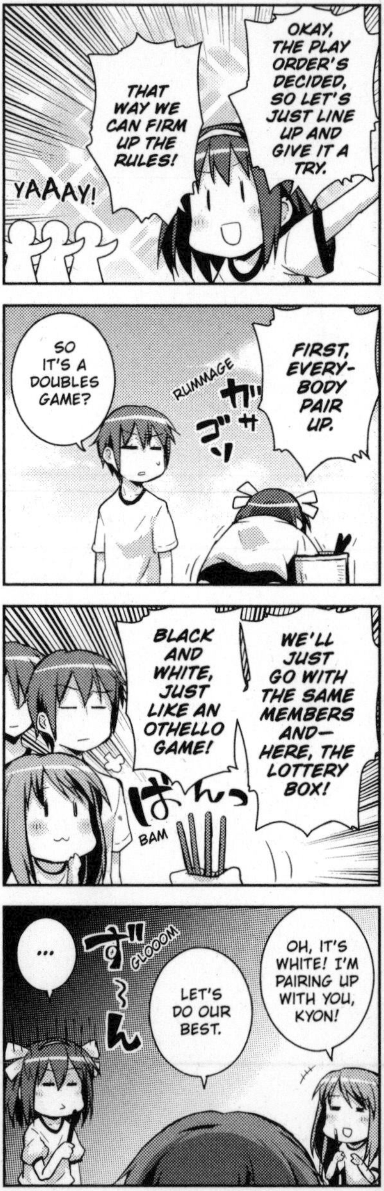
OKAY, THE PLAY ORDER'S DECIDED, SO LET'S JUST LINE UP AND GIVE IT A TRY.
THAT WAY WE CAN FIRM UP THE RULES!
YAAAY!
FIRST, EVERY-BODY PAIR UP.
RUMMAGE
ガサ ゴソ
SO IT'S A DOUBLES GAME?
WE'LL JUST GO WITH THE SAME MEMBERS AND— HERE, THE LOTTERY BOX!
BLACK AND WHITE, JUST LIKE AN OTHELLO GAME!
ばんっ
BAM
OH, IT'S WHITE! I'M PAIRING UP WITH YOU, KYON!
LET'S DO OUR BEST.
ず~ん
GLOOOM
...

FORMATION

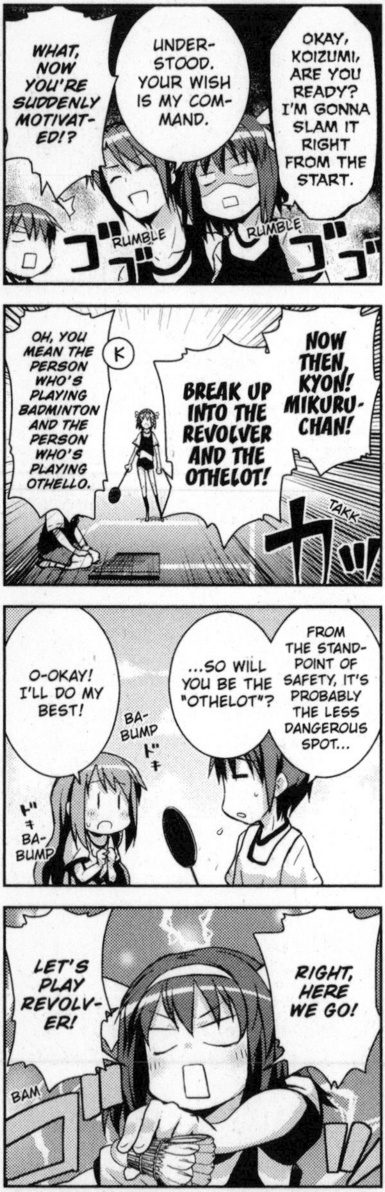
OKAY, KOIZUMI, ARE YOU READY? I'M GONNA SLAM IT RIGHT FROM THE START.
UNDER-STOOD. YOUR WISH IS MY COM-MAND.
WHAT, NOW YOU'RE SUDDENLY MOTIVAT-ED!?
ゴゴ
RUMBLE
ゴゴ
RUMBLE
NOW THEN, KYON! MIKURU-CHAN!
BREAK UP INTO THE REVOLVER AND THE OTHELOT!
カッ!!
TAKK
K
OH, YOU MEAN THE PERSON WHO'S PLAYING BADMINTON AND THE PERSON WHO'S PLAYING OTHELLO.
FROM THE STAND-POINT OF SAFETY, IT'S PROBABLY THE LESS DANGEROUS SPOT...
...SO WILL YOU BE THE "OTHELOT"?
BA-BUMP
ドキ
O-OKAY! I'LL DO MY BEST!
ドキ
BA-BUMP
RIGHT, HERE WE GO!
LET'S PLAY REVOLV-ER!
BAM

*REVOLVER (BADMINTON), OTHELOT (OTHELLO)

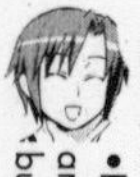

•Koizumi •Mysterious transfer student and esper. He constantly loses every game, but now he'll shine.

PLAY STYLE

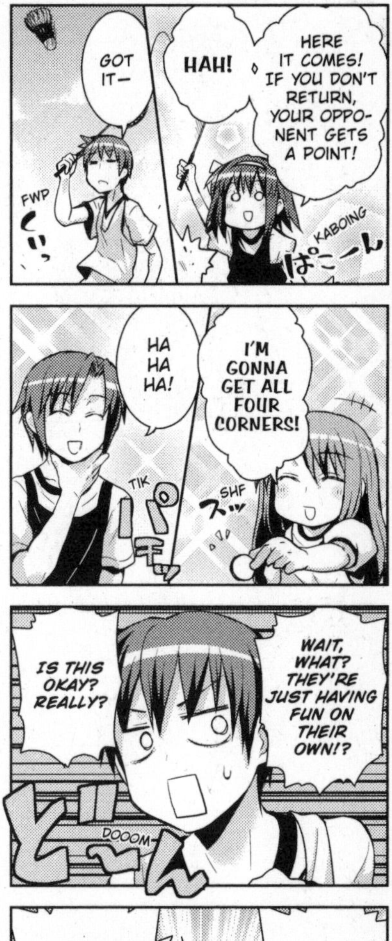
HERE IT COMES! IF YOU DON'T RETURN, YOUR OPPONENT GETS A POINT!
HAH!
GOT IT—
KABOING
FWP
I'M GONNA GET ALL FOUR CORNERS!
HA HA HA!
SHF
TIK
WAIT, WHAT? THEY'RE JUST HAVING FUN ON THEIR OWN!?
IS THIS OKAY? REALLY?
DOOOM
NOW'S YOUR ONLY CHANCE TO SAY THAT, KYON.
YOU'D BETTER GET YOUR MIND ON THE GAME! PLAYING THE STRAIGHT MAN IS GONNA COST YOU YOUR LIFE!
BAM

•Nagato •A completely uncompromising referee. Was ever an alien so perfect a referee as this one is?

LIGHT AND DARKNESS

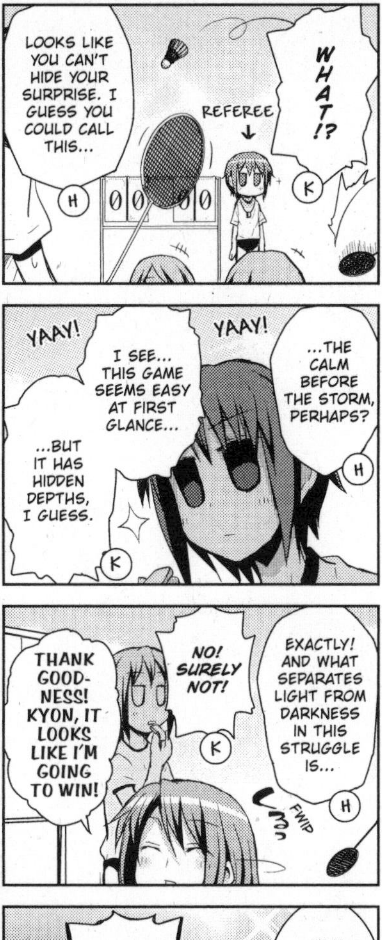
WHAT!?
K
REFEREE ↓
LOOKS LIKE YOU CAN'T HIDE YOUR SURPRISE. I GUESS YOU COULD CALL THIS...
H
YAAY!
...THE CALM BEFORE THE STORM, PERHAPS?
H
YAAY!
I SEE... THIS GAME SEEMS EASY AT FIRST GLANCE...
...BUT IT HAS HIDDEN DEPTHS, I GUESS.
K
EXACTLY! AND WHAT SEPARATES LIGHT FROM DARKNESS IN THIS STRUGGLE IS...
H
FWIP
NO! SURELY NOT!
K
THANK GOODNESS! KYON, IT LOOKS LIKE I'M GOING TO WIN!
IF I PLACE THIS, I SHOULD WIN BY THREE PIECES...
TEE HEE.
ASAHINA-SAN, INCOMING!
TAKK

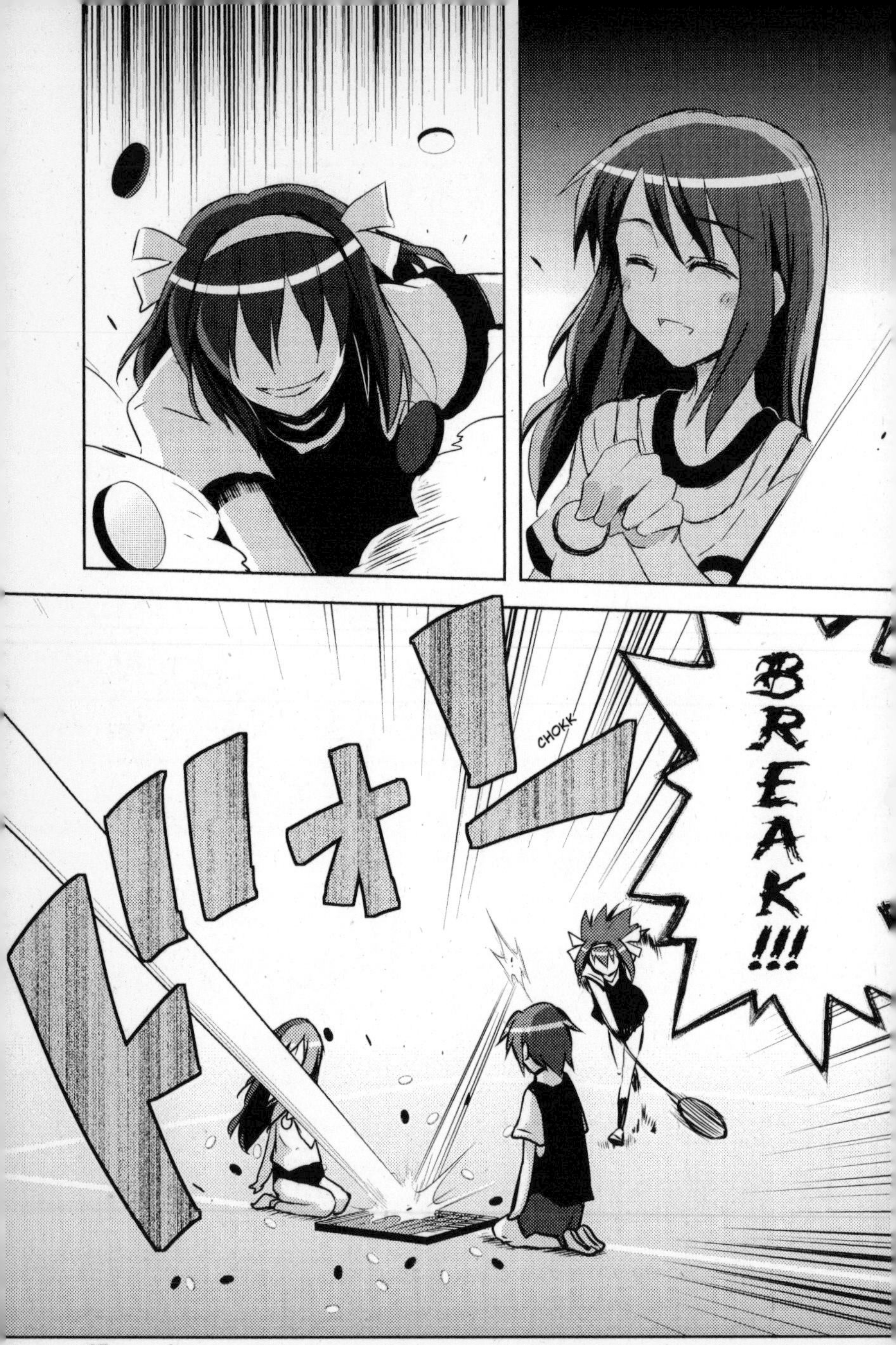
CHOKK
BREAK!!!

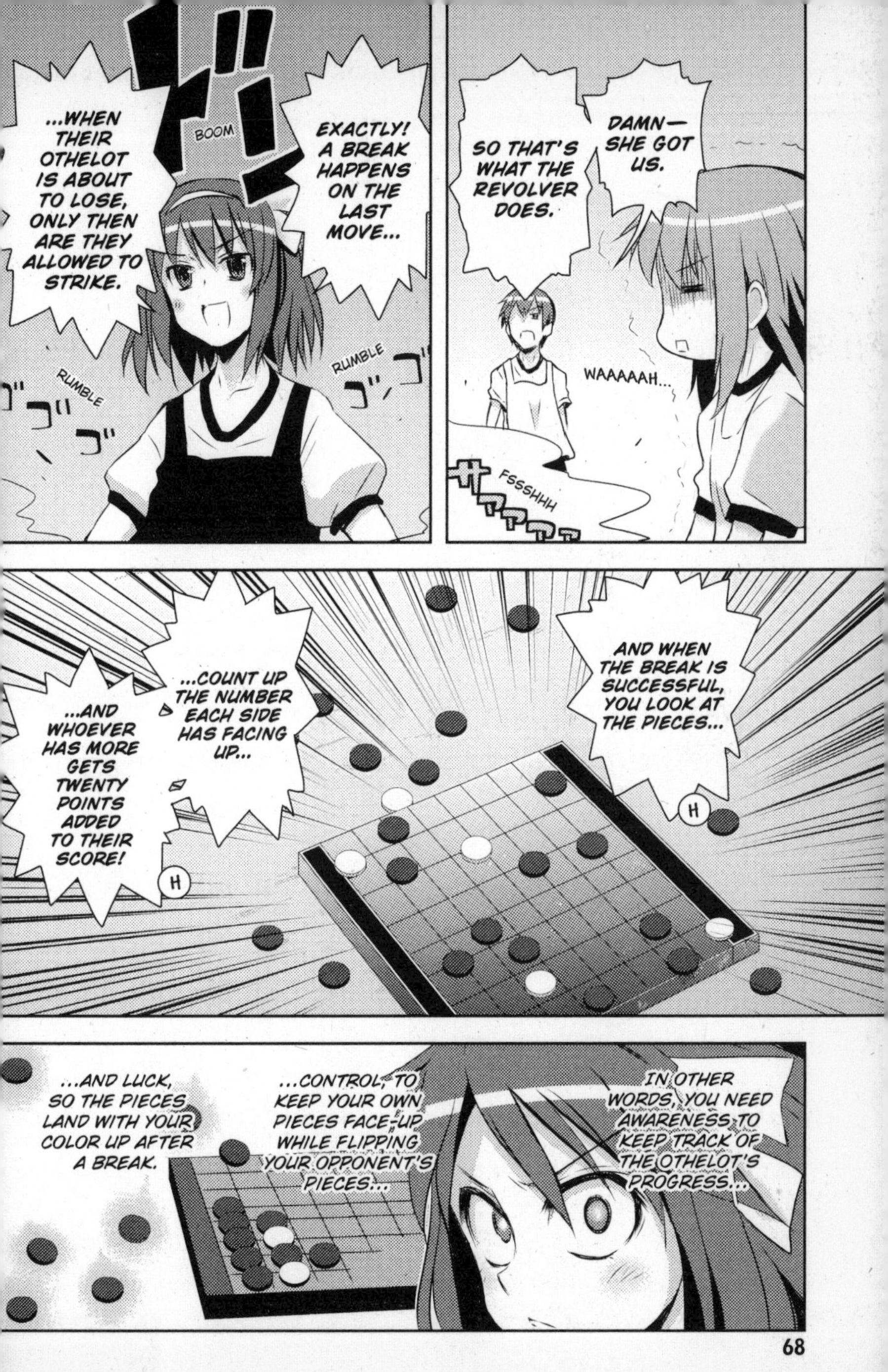
DAMN— SHE GOT US.
SO THAT'S WHAT THE REVOLVER DOES.
WAAAAAH...
FSSSHHH
EXACTLY! A BREAK HAPPENS ON THE LAST MOVE...
BOOM
...WHEN THEIR OTHELOT IS ABOUT TO LOSE, ONLY THEN ARE THEY ALLOWED TO STRIKE.
RUMBLE
RUMBLE
AND WHEN THE BREAK IS SUCCESSFUL, YOU LOOK AT THE PIECES...
...COUNT UP THE NUMBER EACH SIDE HAS FACING UP...
...AND WHOEVER HAS MORE GETS TWENTY POINTS ADDED TO THEIR SCORE!
IN OTHER WORDS, YOU NEED AWARENESS TO KEEP TRACK OF THE OTHELOT'S PROGRESS...
...CONTROL, TO KEEP YOUR OWN PIECES FACE-UP WHILE FLIPPING YOUR OPPONENT'S PIECES...
...AND LUCK, SO THE PIECES LAND WITH YOUR COLOR UP AFTER A BREAK.

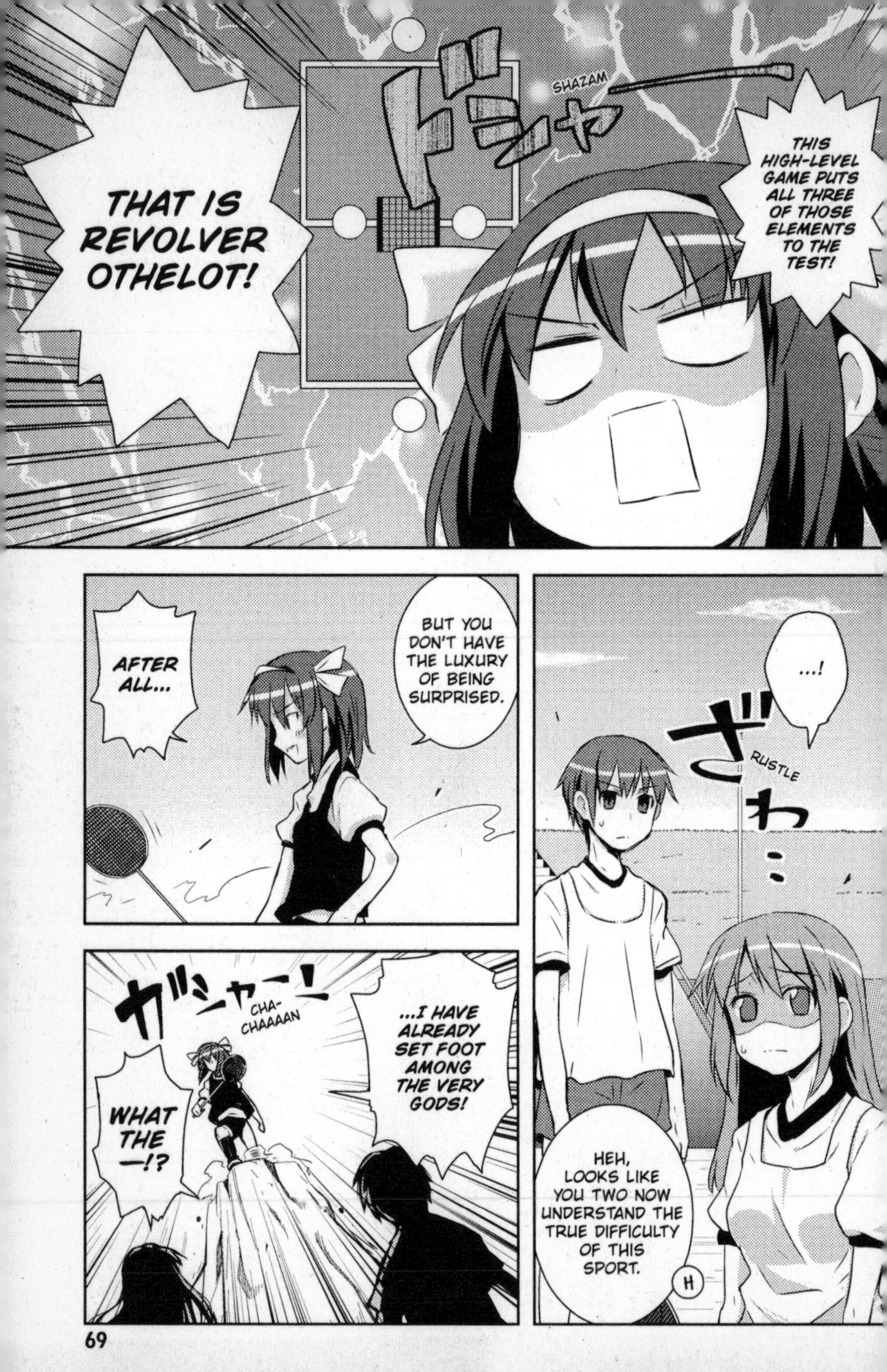
THIS HIGH-LEVEL GAME PUTS ALL THREE OF THOSE ELEMENTS TO THE TEST!
SHAZAM
THAT IS REVOLVER OTHELOT!
...!
RUSTLE
HEH, LOOKS LIKE YOU TWO NOW UNDERSTAND THE TRUE DIFFICULTY OF THIS SPORT.
H
BUT YOU DON'T HAVE THE LUXURY OF BEING SURPRISED.
AFTER ALL...
...I HAVE ALREADY SET FOOT AMONG THE VERY GODS!
CHA-CHAAAAN
WHAT THE—!?

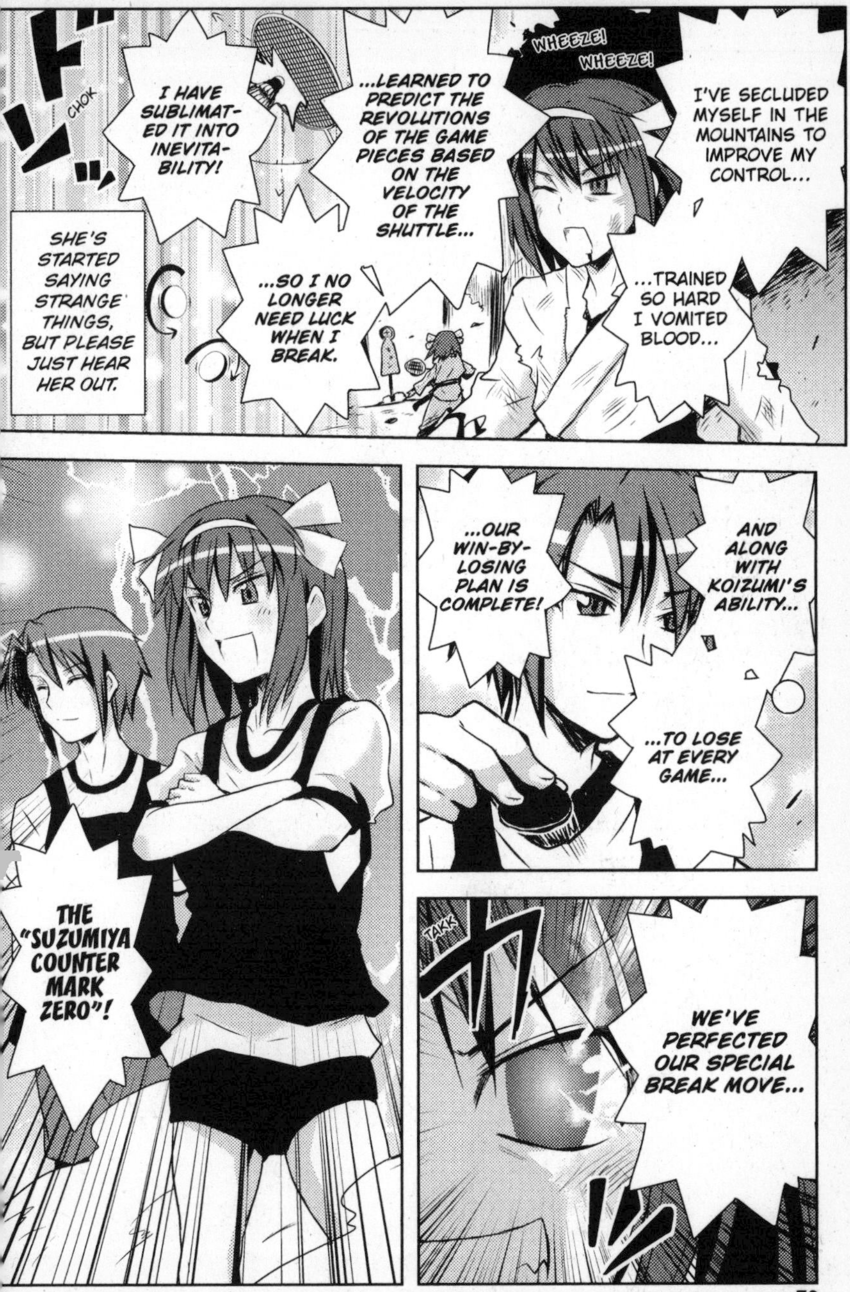
WHEEZE!
WHEEZE!
I'VE SECLUDED MYSELF IN THE MOUNTAINS TO IMPROVE MY CONTROL...
...TRAINED SO HARD I VOMITED BLOOD...
...LEARNED TO PREDICT THE REVOLUTIONS OF THE GAME PIECES BASED ON THE VELOCITY OF THE SHUTTLE...
...SO I NO LONGER NEED LUCK WHEN I BREAK.
I HAVE SUBLIMATED IT INTO INEVITABILITY!
CHOK
SHE'S STARTED SAYING STRANGE THINGS, BUT PLEASE JUST HEAR HER OUT.
AND ALONG WITH KOIZUMI'S ABILITY...
...TO LOSE AT EVERY GAME...
...OUR WIN-BY-LOSING PLAN IS COMPLETE!
TAKK
WE'VE PERFECTED OUR SPECIAL BREAK MOVE...
THE "SUZUMIYA COUNTER MARK ZERO"!

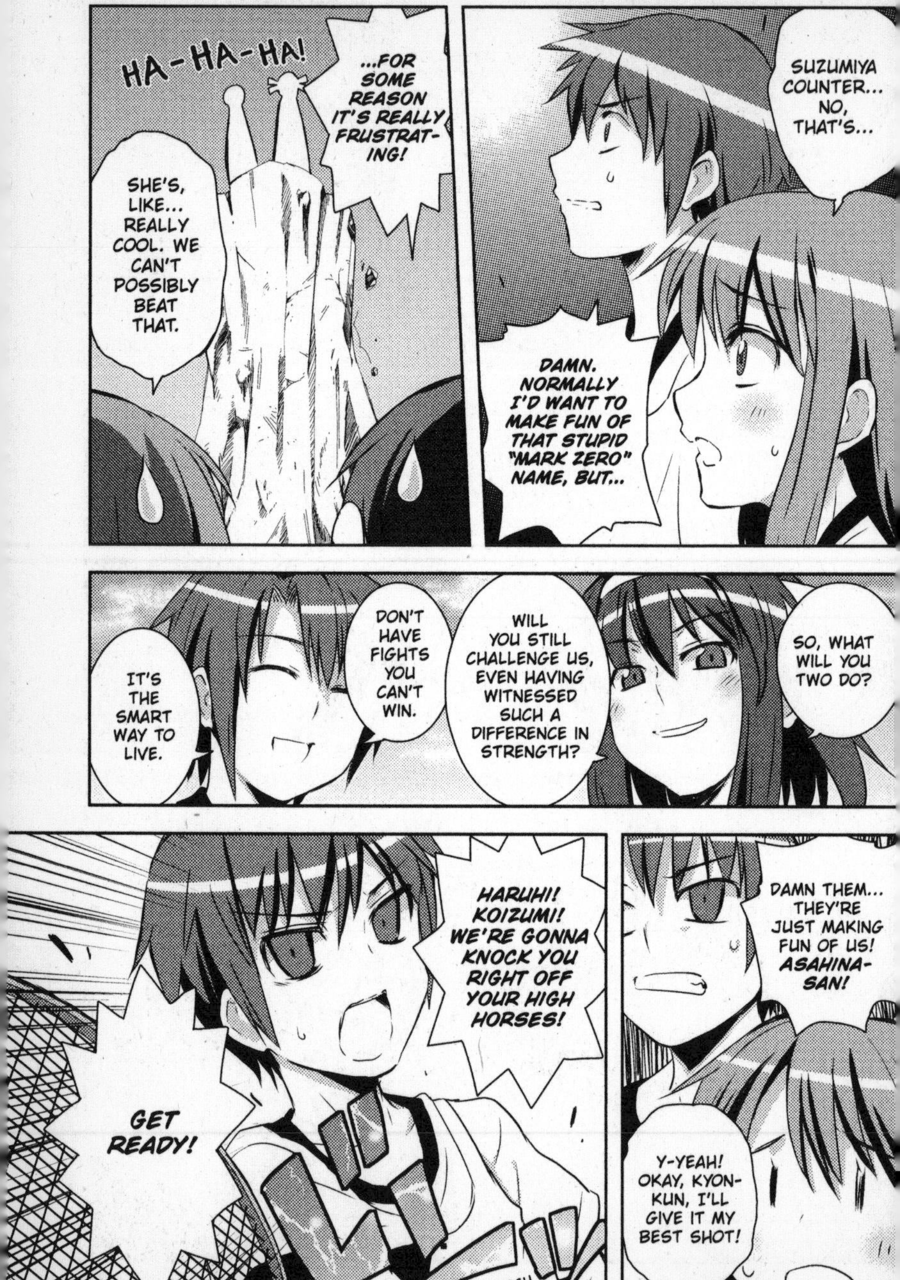
SUZUMIYA COUNTER... NO, THAT'S...
DAMN. NORMALLY I'D WANT TO MAKE FUN OF THAT STUPID "MARK ZERO" NAME, BUT...
...FOR SOME REASON IT'S REALLY FRUSTRATING!
HA-HA-HA!
SHE'S, LIKE... REALLY COOL. WE CAN'T POSSIBLY BEAT THAT.
SO, WHAT WILL YOU TWO DO?
WILL YOU STILL CHALLENGE US, EVEN HAVING WITNESSED SUCH A DIFFERENCE IN STRENGTH?
DON'T HAVE FIGHTS YOU CAN'T WIN.
IT'S THE SMART WAY TO LIVE.
DAMN THEM... THEY'RE JUST MAKING FUN OF US! ASAHINA-SAN!
Y-YEAH! OKAY, KYON-KUN, I'LL GIVE IT MY BEST SHOT!
HARUHI! KOIZUMI! WE'RE GONNA KNOCK YOU RIGHT OFF YOUR HIGH HORSES!
GET READY!
WHOOSH

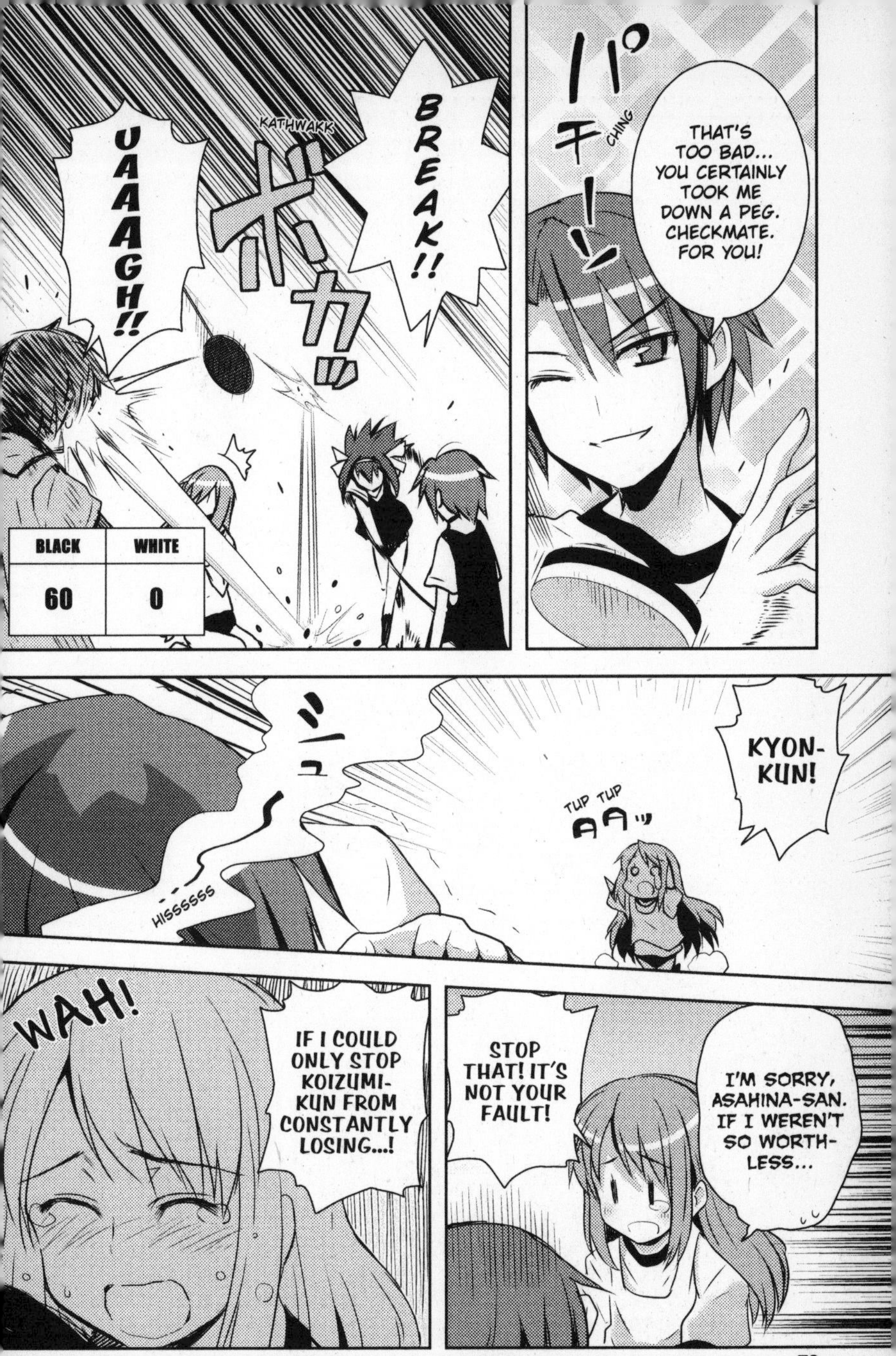
パチーン
CHING
THAT'S TOO BAD... YOU CERTAINLY TOOK ME DOWN A PEG. CHECKMATE. FOR YOU!
BREAK!!
ボカッ
KATHWAKK
UAAAAGH!!
BLACK 60
WHITE 0
KYON-KUN!
タタッ
TUP TUP
シュ〜
HISSSSSS
I'M SORRY, ASAHINA-SAN. IF I WEREN'T SO WORTH-LESS...
STOP THAT! IT'S NOT YOUR FAULT!
IF I COULD ONLY STOP KOIZUMI-KUN FROM CONSTANTLY LOSING...!
WAH!

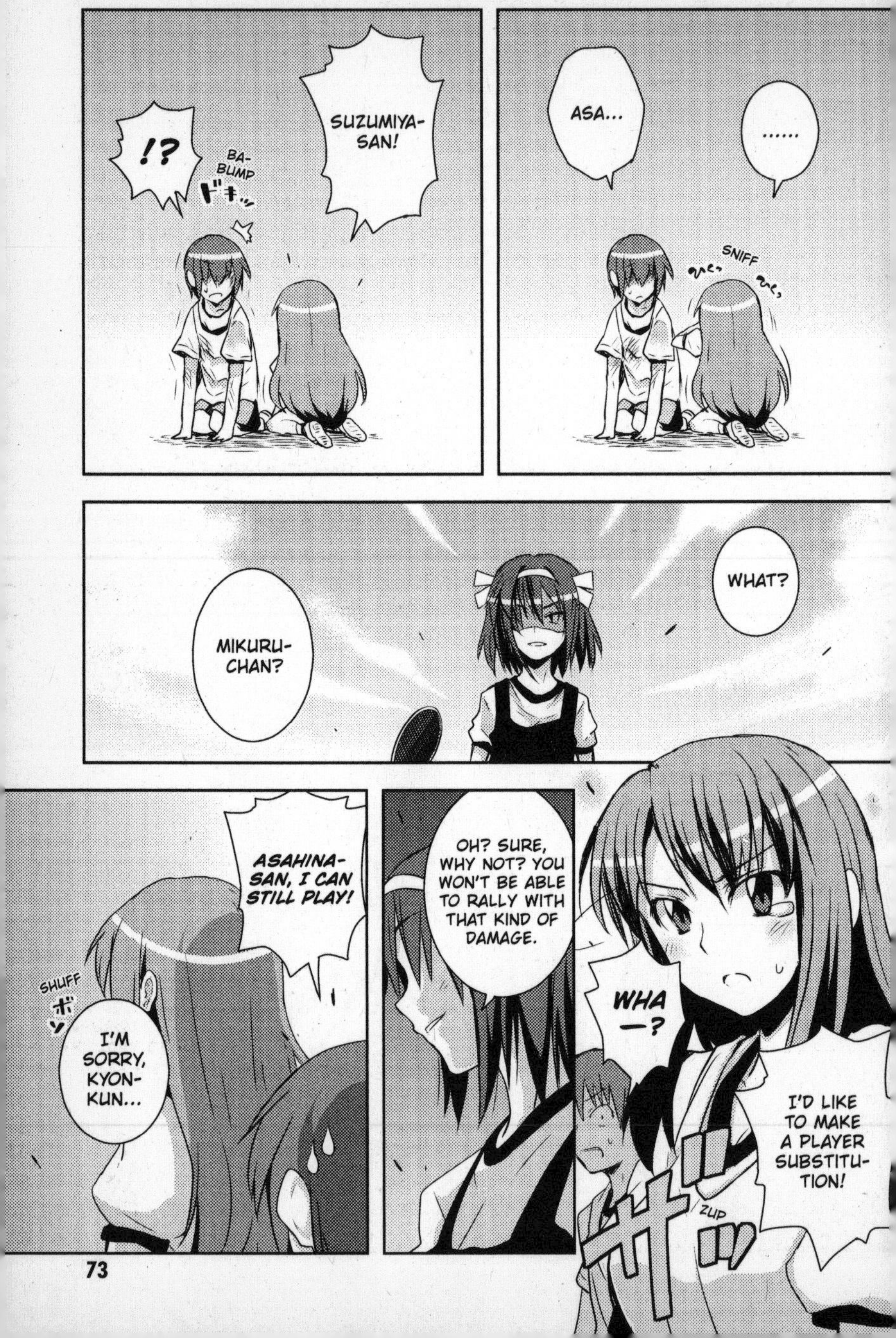
ASA...
......
SNIFF
ひっく ひっく
SUZUMIYA-SAN!
!?
BA-BUMP
ドキッ
WHAT?
MIKURU-CHAN?
WHA—?
I'D LIKE TO MAKE A PLAYER SUBSTITU-TION!
ZUP
ザッ
OH? SURE, WHY NOT? YOU WON'T BE ABLE TO RALLY WITH THAT KIND OF DAMAGE.
ASAHINA-SAN, I CAN STILL PLAY!
SHUFF
ボソ
I'M SORRY, KYON-KUN...

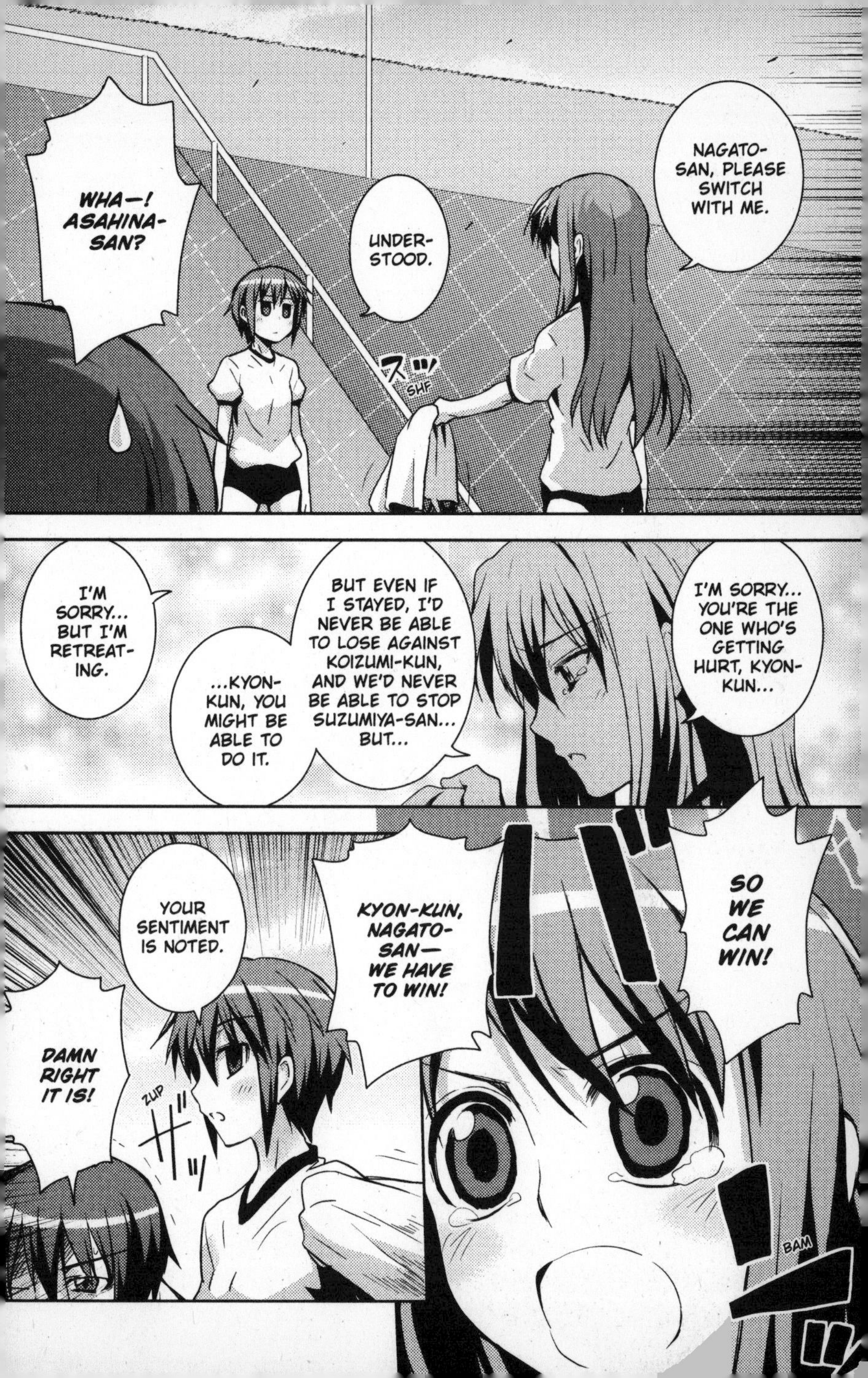
NAGATO-SAN, PLEASE SWITCH WITH ME.
UNDER-STOOD.
スッ
SHF
WHA—! ASAHINA-SAN?
I'M SORRY... YOU'RE THE ONE WHO'S GETTING HURT, KYON-KUN...
BUT EVEN IF I STAYED, I'D NEVER BE ABLE TO LOSE AGAINST KOIZUMI-KUN, AND WE'D NEVER BE ABLE TO STOP SUZUMIYA-SAN... BUT...
...KYON-KUN, YOU MIGHT BE ABLE TO DO IT.
I'M SORRY... BUT I'M RETREAT-ING.
SO WE CAN WIN!
BAM
KYON-KUN, NAGATO-SAN— WE HAVE TO WIN!
YOUR SENTIMENT IS NOTED.
ZUP
DAMN RIGHT IT IS!

NAGATO! YOU GOTTA BE RE-VOLVER.
WOBBLE
よろ
AND DON'T HOLD BACK, OKAY?
WOBBLE
よろ
よろ
WOBBLE
SHF
BUMP
OF COURSE... WE WON'T BE ABLE TO WIN IF I DO.
BUT DO YOU UNDERSTAND YOUR PART?
AS OTHELOT, IF I DON'T LOSE TO HIM...
...SHE CAN'T DO THE BREAK.
YEAH, I UNDERSTAND MY PART.
SO WHAT OF IT?
HUFF
DON'T UNDER-ESTIMATE ME!
HUFF
RIGHT NOW, I'M...
WHITE, 31! BLACK, 33!
...PLENTY WEAK!
I LOSE! NAGATO, NOW!!

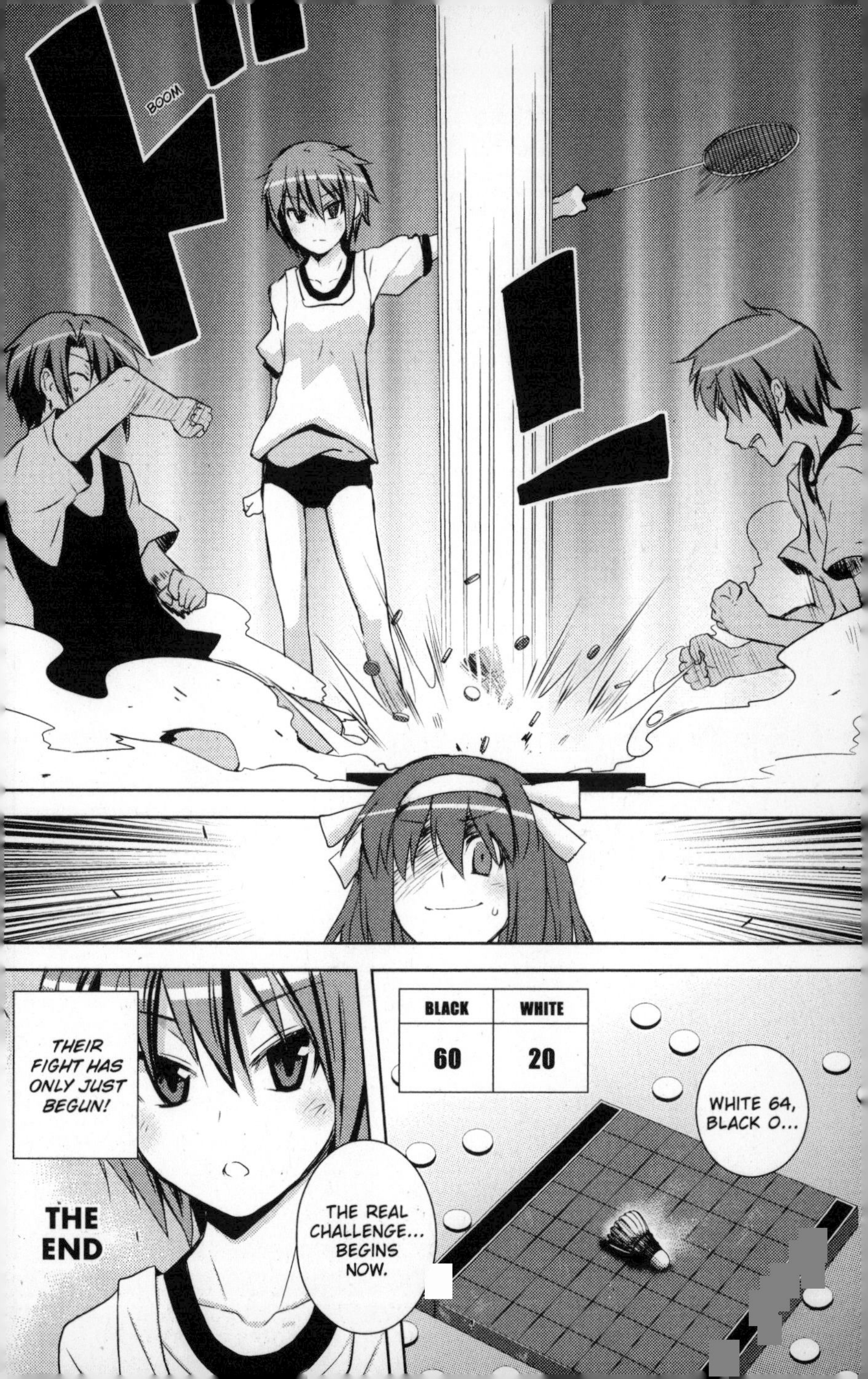
BOOM
BLACK WHITE
60 20
WHITE 64, BLACK 0...
THE REAL CHALLENGE... BEGINS NOW.
THEIR FIGHT HAS ONLY JUST BEGUN!
THE END

ONE HOT DAY

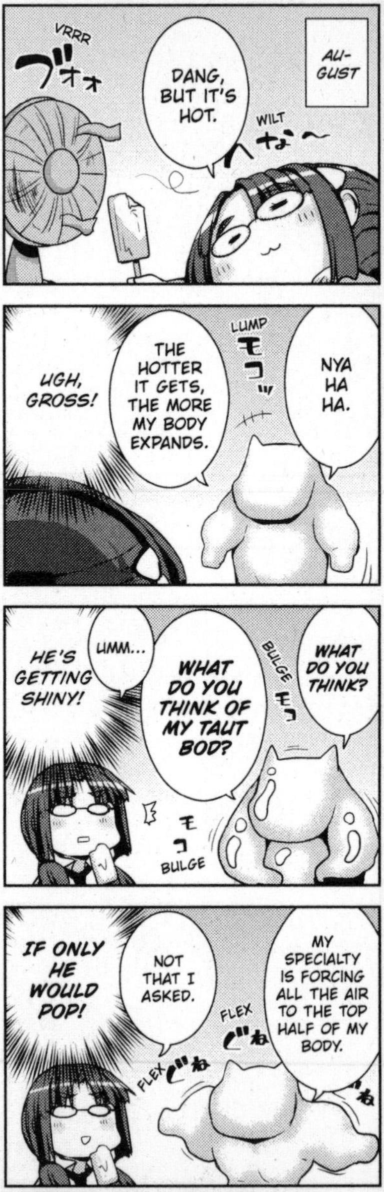
AU-GUST
DANG, BUT IT'S HOT.
WILT
VRRR
NYA HA HA.
LUMP
THE HOTTER IT GETS, THE MORE MY BODY EXPANDS.
UGH, GROSS!
WHAT DO YOU THINK?
BULGE
WHAT DO YOU THINK OF MY TAUT BOD?
UMM...
HE'S GETTING SHINY!
BULGE
MY SPECIALTY IS FORCING ALL THE AIR TO THE TOP HALF OF MY BODY.
FLEX
NOT THAT I ASKED.
IF ONLY HE WOULD POP!
FLEX

ECOLOGY

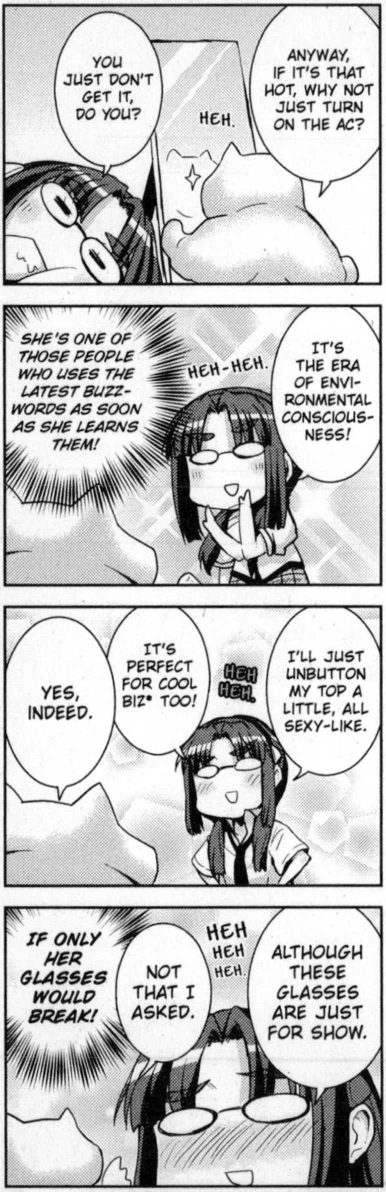
ANYWAY, IF IT'S THAT HOT, WHY NOT JUST TURN ON THE AC?
HEH.
YOU JUST DON'T GET IT, DO YOU?
IT'S THE ERA OF ENVIRONMENTAL CONSCIOUSNESS!
HEH-HEH.
SHE'S ONE OF THOSE PEOPLE WHO USES THE LATEST BUZZWORDS AS SOON AS SHE LEARNS THEM!
I'LL JUST UNBUTTON MY TOP A LITTLE, ALL SEXY-LIKE.
HEH HEH.
IT'S PERFECT FOR COOL BIZ* TOO!
YES, INDEED.
ALTHOUGH THESE GLASSES ARE JUST FOR SHOW.
HEH HEH HEH.
NOT THAT I ASKED.
IF ONLY HER GLASSES WOULD BREAK!

•Kimidori-san •An artificial life-form created by Nagato from a balloon. His ability to change shape is, frankly, disgusting.

•Achakura-san •Having recovered from her annihilation, she moved in with Nagato. Glasses give her an intellectual appeal.

*"COOL BIZ" WAS THE NAME OF A JAPANESE GOVERNMENTAL INITIATIVE THAT TRIED TO GET BUSINESSES TO RELAX THEIR STRICT DRESS CODES, ALLOWING EMPLOYEES TO DRESS FOR WARMER WEATHER AND RUN THE OFFICE AC UNITS LESS, THEREBY SAVING ENERGY.

COLLECTING

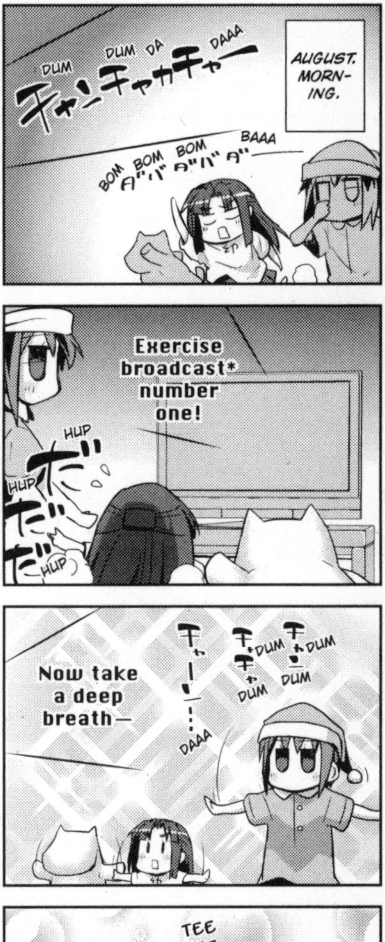
AUGUST. MORNING.
DUM DUM DA DAAA
BOM BOM BOM BAAA
Exercise broadcast* number one!
HUP
HUP
HUP
Now take a deep breath—
DUM
DUM
DUM
DUM
DAAA
TEE HEE HEE HEE HEE.

RESORT

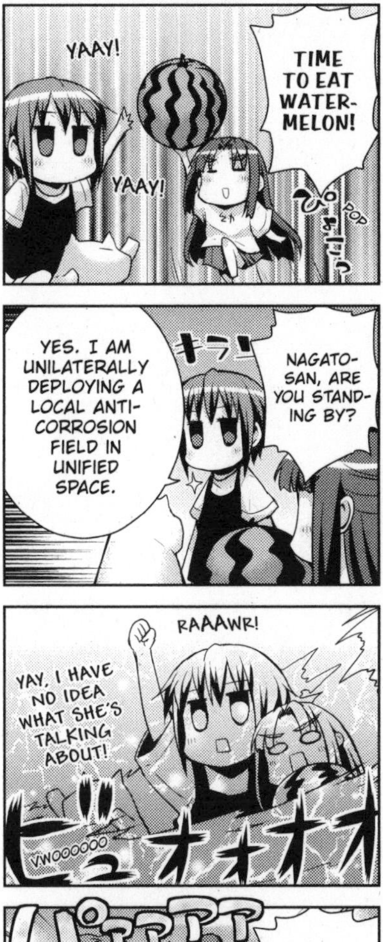
TIME TO EAT WATER-MELON!
YAAY!
YAAY!
POP
NAGATO-SAN, ARE YOU STANDING BY?
YES. I AM UNILATERALLY DEPLOYING A LOCAL ANTI-CORROSION FIELD IN UNIFIED SPACE.
RAAAWR!
YAY, I HAVE NO IDEA WHAT SHE'S TALKING ABOUT!
VWOOOOOO
FLAASH
NOW, TIME TO BREAK IT OPEN!

*WARM-UP CALISTHENICS ARE BROADCAST NATIONALLY ON RADIO AND TELEVISION TO ENCOURAGE HEALTH, WELL-BEING, AND COMMUNITY. SCHOOLCHILDREN MAY BE REWARDED FOR THEIR PARTICIPATION WITH A STAMP ON THEIR STAMP CARD.

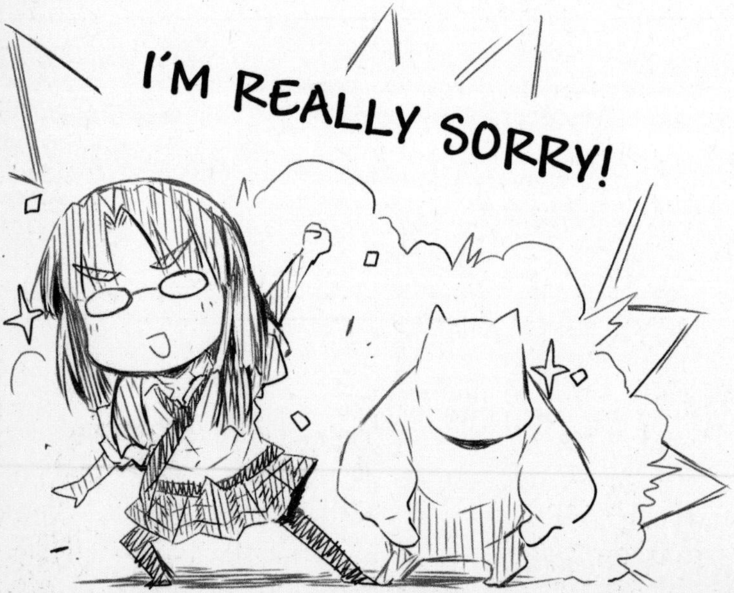
I'M REALLY SORRY!

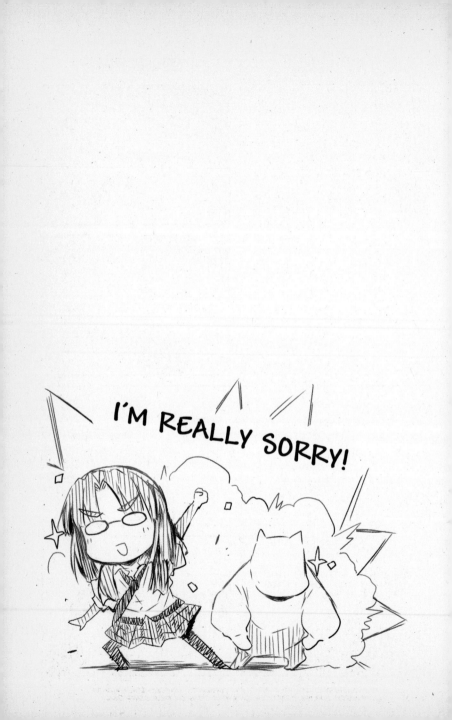

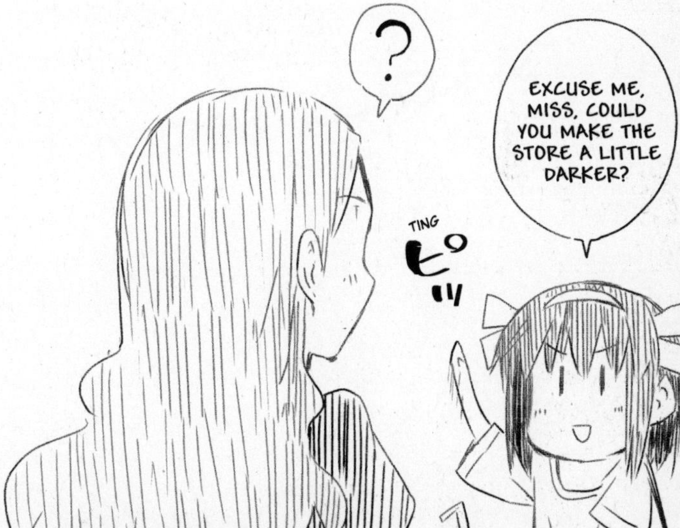
?
EXCUSE ME, MISS, COULD YOU MAKE THE STORE A LITTLE DARKER?
TING
ピッ

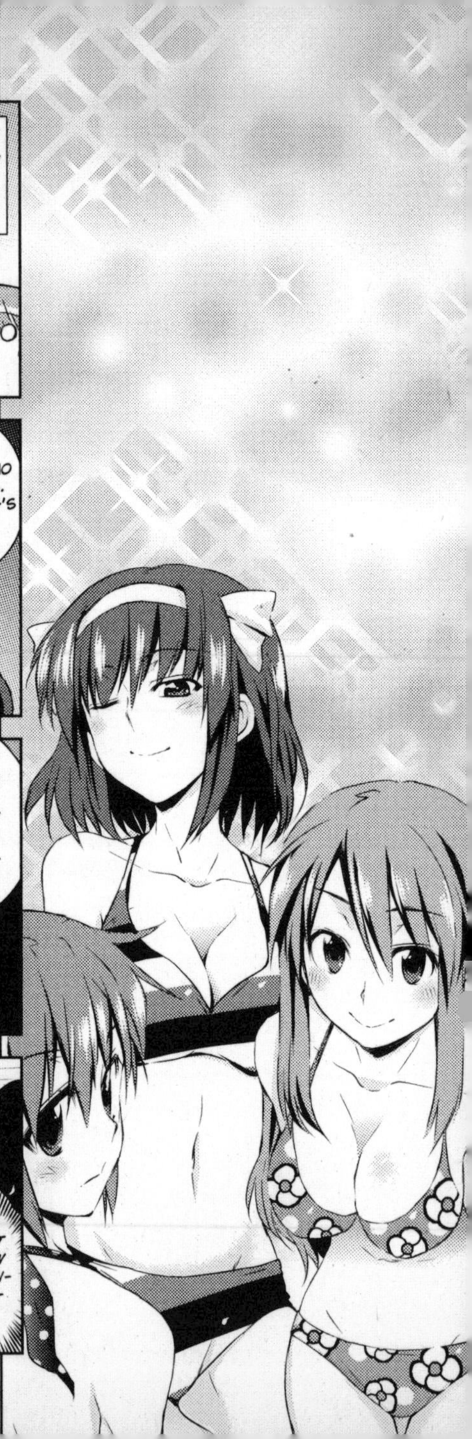

THE PLAN

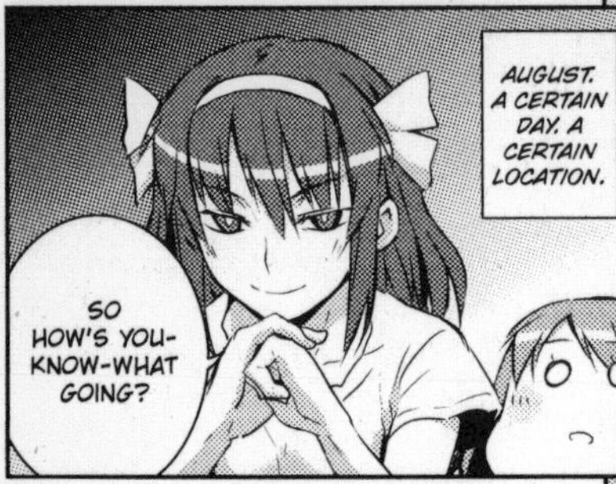
AUGUST. A CERTAIN DAY. A CERTAIN LOCATION.
SO HOW'S YOU-KNOW-WHAT GOING?

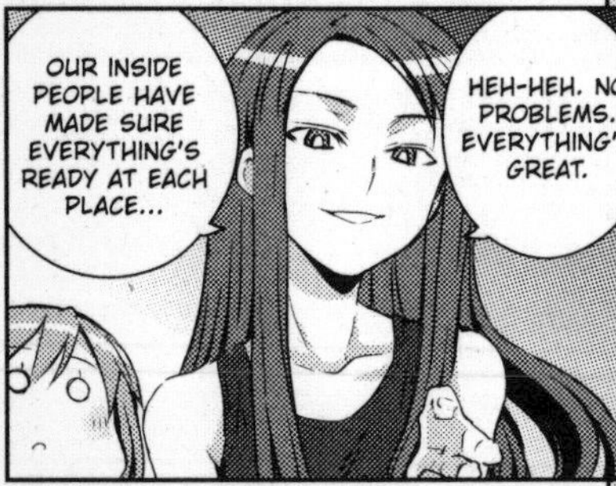
HEH-HEH. NO PROBLEMS. EVERYTHING'S GREAT.
OUR INSIDE PEOPLE HAVE MADE SURE EVERYTHING'S READY AT EACH PLACE...

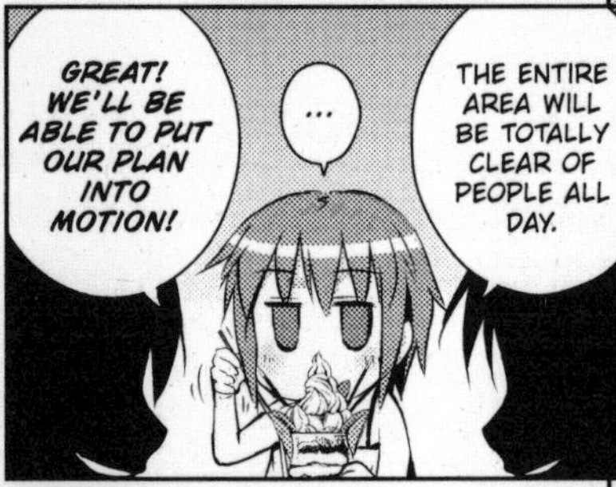
THE ENTIRE AREA WILL BE TOTALLY CLEAR OF PEOPLE ALL DAY.
...
GREAT! WE'LL BE ABLE TO PUT OUR PLAN INTO MOTION!

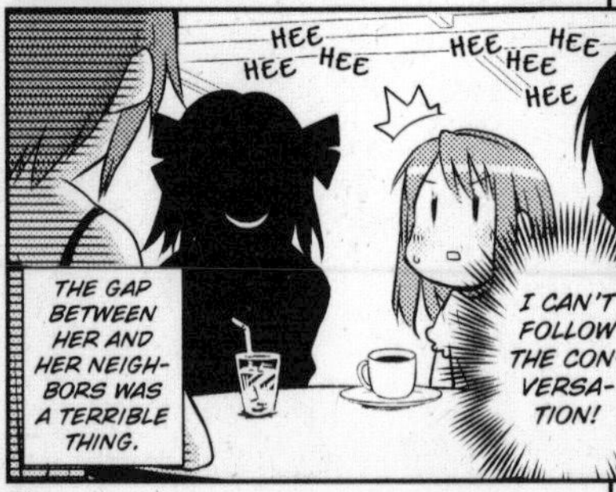
HEE HEE HEE HEE
HEE HEE HEE HEE
I CAN'T FOLLOW THE CON-VERSA-TION!
THE GAP BETWEEN HER AND HER NEIGH-BORS WAS A TERRIBLE THING.

A CERTAIN PLACE

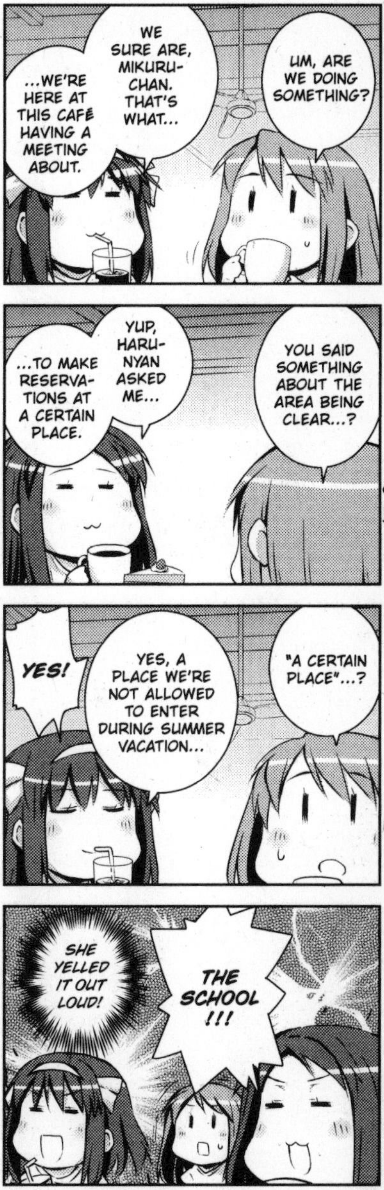
UM, ARE WE DOING SOMETHING?
WE SURE ARE, MIKURU-CHAN. THAT'S WHAT...
...WE'RE HERE AT THIS CAFÉ HAVING A MEETING ABOUT.
YOU SAID SOMETHING ABOUT THE AREA BEING CLEAR...?
YUP, HARUNYAN ASKED ME...
...TO MAKE RESERVATIONS AT A CERTAIN PLACE.
"A CERTAIN PLACE"...?
YES, A PLACE WE'RE NOT ALLOWED TO ENTER DURING SUMMER VACATION...
YES!
THE SCHOOL !!!
SHE YELLED IT OUT LOUD!

PROBLEMS

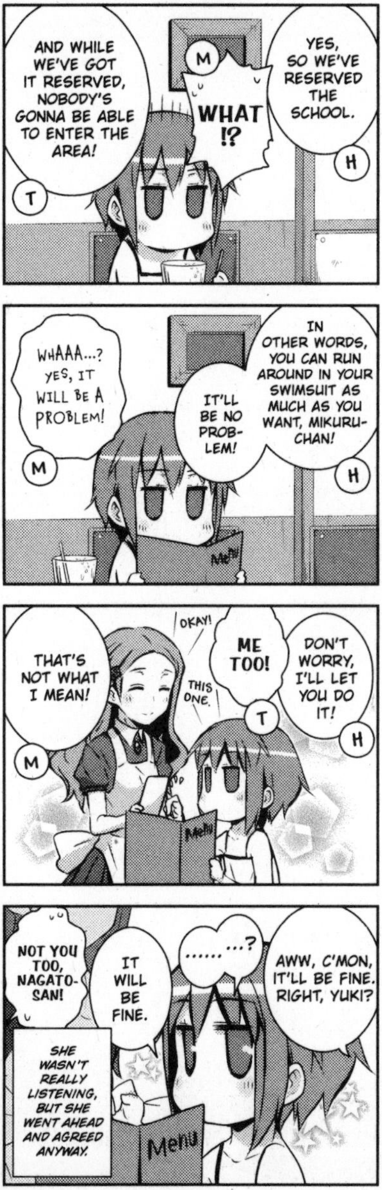
YES, SO WE'VE RESERVED THE SCHOOL.
H
WHAT !?
M
AND WHILE WE'VE GOT IT RESERVED, NOBODY'S GONNA BE ABLE TO ENTER THE AREA!
T
IN OTHER WORDS, YOU CAN RUN AROUND IN YOUR SWIMSUIT AS MUCH AS YOU WANT, MIKURU-CHAN!
IT'LL BE NO PROB-LEM!
H
WHAAA...? YES, IT WILL BE A PROBLEM!
M
Menu
DON'T WORRY, I'LL LET YOU DO IT!
H
ME TOO!
T
OKAY!
THIS ONE.
THAT'S NOT WHAT I MEAN!
M
Menu
AWW, C'MON, IT'LL BE FINE. RIGHT, YUKI?
.........?
IT WILL BE FINE.
NOT YOU TOO, NAGATO-SAN!
SHE WASN'T REALLY LISTENING, BUT SHE WENT AHEAD AND AGREED ANYWAY.
Menu

•Haruhi-chan •SOS Brigade brigade chief. Apparently wants to play around in her swimsuit.

•Mikuru-chan •Time traveler. In charge of being made to do embarrassing things by Haruhi et al.

•Nagato •Alien. According to Haruhi-chan, likes sweet things and has a big appetite.

WHAT TO DO

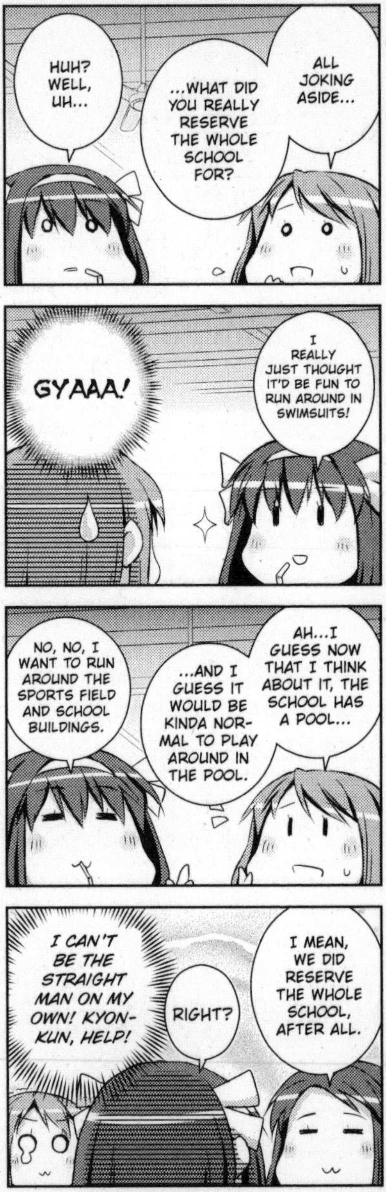
ALL JOKING ASIDE...
...WHAT DID YOU REALLY RESERVE THE WHOLE SCHOOL FOR?
HUH? WELL, UH...
I REALLY JUST THOUGHT IT'D BE FUN TO RUN AROUND IN SWIMSUITS!
GYAAA!
AH...I GUESS NOW THAT I THINK ABOUT IT, THE SCHOOL HAS A POOL...
...AND I GUESS IT WOULD BE KINDA NORMAL TO PLAY AROUND IN THE POOL.
NO, NO, I WANT TO RUN AROUND THE SPORTS FIELD AND SCHOOL BUILDINGS.
I MEAN, WE DID RESERVE THE WHOLE SCHOOL, AFTER ALL.
RIGHT?
I CAN'T BE THE STRAIGHT MAN ON MY OWN! KYON-KUN, HELP!

PROCESS

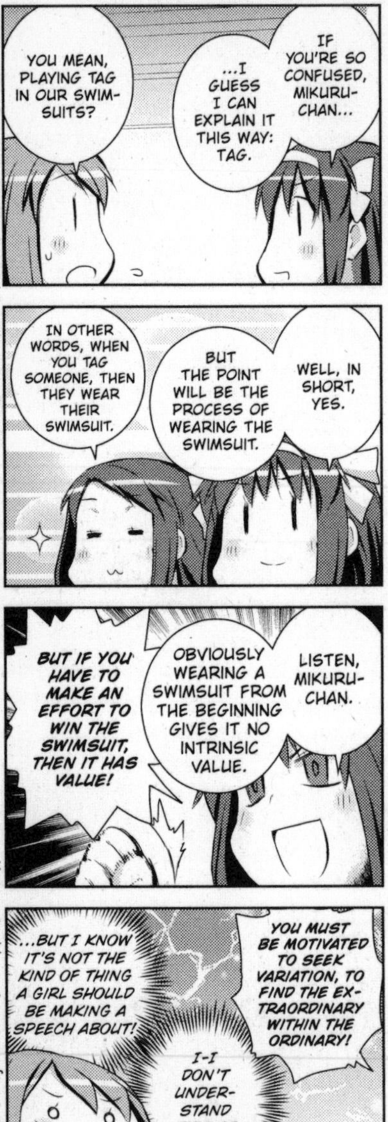
IF YOU'RE SO CONFUSED, MIKURU-CHAN...
...I GUESS I CAN EXPLAIN IT THIS WAY: TAG.
YOU MEAN, PLAYING TAG IN OUR SWIMSUITS?
WELL, IN SHORT, YES.
BUT THE POINT WILL BE THE PROCESS OF WEARING THE SWIMSUIT.
IN OTHER WORDS, WHEN YOU TAG SOMEONE, THEN THEY WEAR THEIR SWIMSUIT.
LISTEN, MIKURU-CHAN.
OBVIOUSLY WEARING A SWIMSUIT FROM THE BEGINNING GIVES IT NO INTRINSIC VALUE.
BUT IF YOU HAVE TO MAKE AN EFFORT TO WIN THE SWIMSUIT, THEN IT HAS VALUE!
YOU MUST BE MOTIVATED TO SEEK VARIATION, TO FIND THE EXTRAORDINARY WITHIN THE ORDINARY!
...BUT I KNOW IT'S NOT THE KIND OF THING A GIRL SHOULD BE MAKING A SPEECH ABOUT!
I-I DON'T UNDERSTAND THIS AT ALL...

•Tsuruya-san •An extremely dangerous individual, capable of putting Haruhi's whims into action.

•Kyon •The main character. Doesn't show up much in this chapter.

•Koizumi •Mysterious transfer student and esper. Doesn't show much in this volume either. Mostly just laughs to himself in the background.

RULES

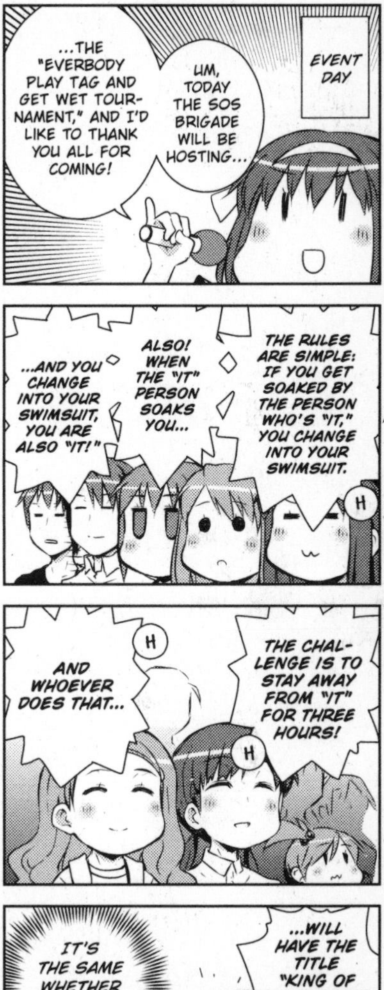

EVENT DAY
UM, TODAY THE SOS BRIGADE WILL BE HOSTING...
...THE "EVERBODY PLAY TAG AND GET WET TOURNAMENT," AND I'D LIKE TO THANK YOU ALL FOR COMING!
THE RULES ARE SIMPLE: IF YOU GET SOAKED BY THE PERSON WHO'S "IT," YOU CHANGE INTO YOUR SWIMSUIT.
ALSO! WHEN THE "IT" PERSON SOAKS YOU...
...AND YOU CHANGE INTO YOUR SWIMSUIT, YOU ARE ALSO "IT!"
H
THE CHALLENGE IS TO STAY AWAY FROM "IT" FOR THREE HOURS!
H
AND WHOEVER DOES THAT...
H
...WILL HAVE THE TITLE "KING OF SWIMSUITS" BESTOWED ON THEM FOR THE DAY!
IT'S THE SAME WHETHER YOU WIN OR LOSE!

BOYS & GIRLS

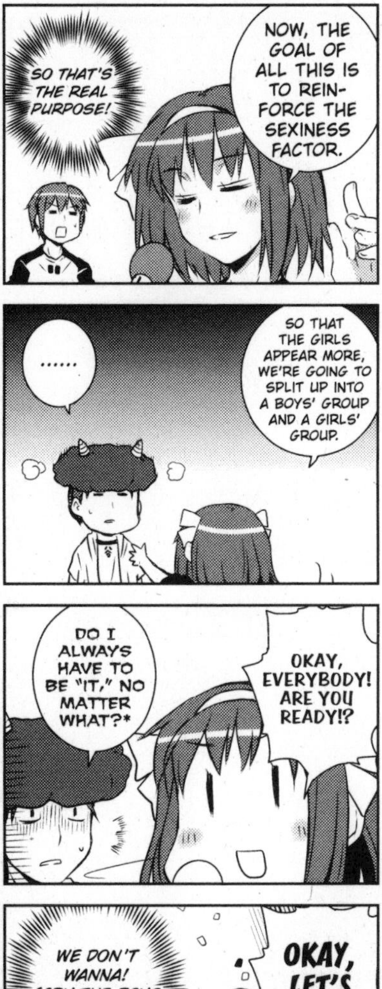

NOW, THE GOAL OF ALL THIS IS TO REINFORCE THE SEXINESS FACTOR.
SO THAT'S THE REAL PURPOSE!
SO THAT THE GIRLS APPEAR MORE, WE'RE GOING TO SPLIT UP INTO A BOYS' GROUP AND A GIRLS' GROUP.
......
OKAY, EVERYBODY! ARE YOU READY!?
DO I ALWAYS HAVE TO BE "IT," NO MATTER WHAT?*
OKAY, LET'S START!
WE DON'T WANNA! (CRY THE BOYS TO THEMSELVES.)

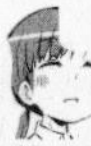

•Mori-san •Is often called to participate in SOS Brigade activities and has rendered distinguished service many times.

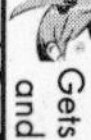

•Little Sister •Kyon's younger sister. Gets along well with Haruhi-chan and has similar tendencies.

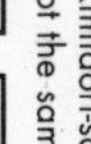

•Kimidori-san •This is her third appearance. Not the same Kimidori as the balloon animal.

*IN JAPAN, THE PERSON WHO IS "IT" IN A GAME OF TAG IS CALLED THE DEMON.

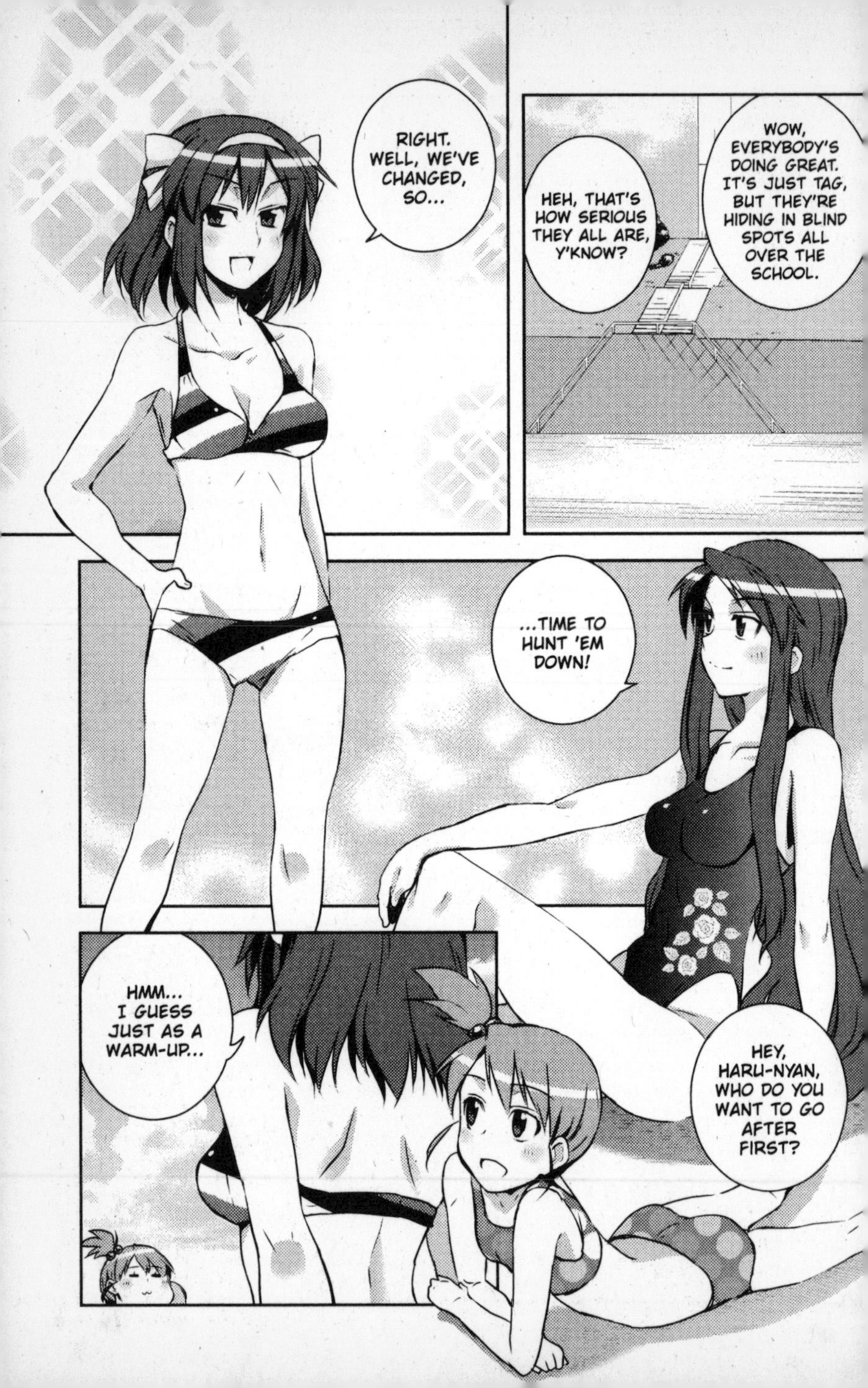

WOW, EVERYBODY'S DOING GREAT. IT'S JUST TAG, BUT THEY'RE HIDING IN BLIND SPOTS ALL OVER THE SCHOOL.
HEH, THAT'S HOW SERIOUS THEY ALL ARE, Y'KNOW?
RIGHT. WELL, WE'VE CHANGED, SO...
...TIME TO HUNT 'EM DOWN!
HEY, HARU-NYAN, WHO DO YOU WANT TO GO AFTER FIRST?
HMM... I GUESS JUST AS A WARM-UP...

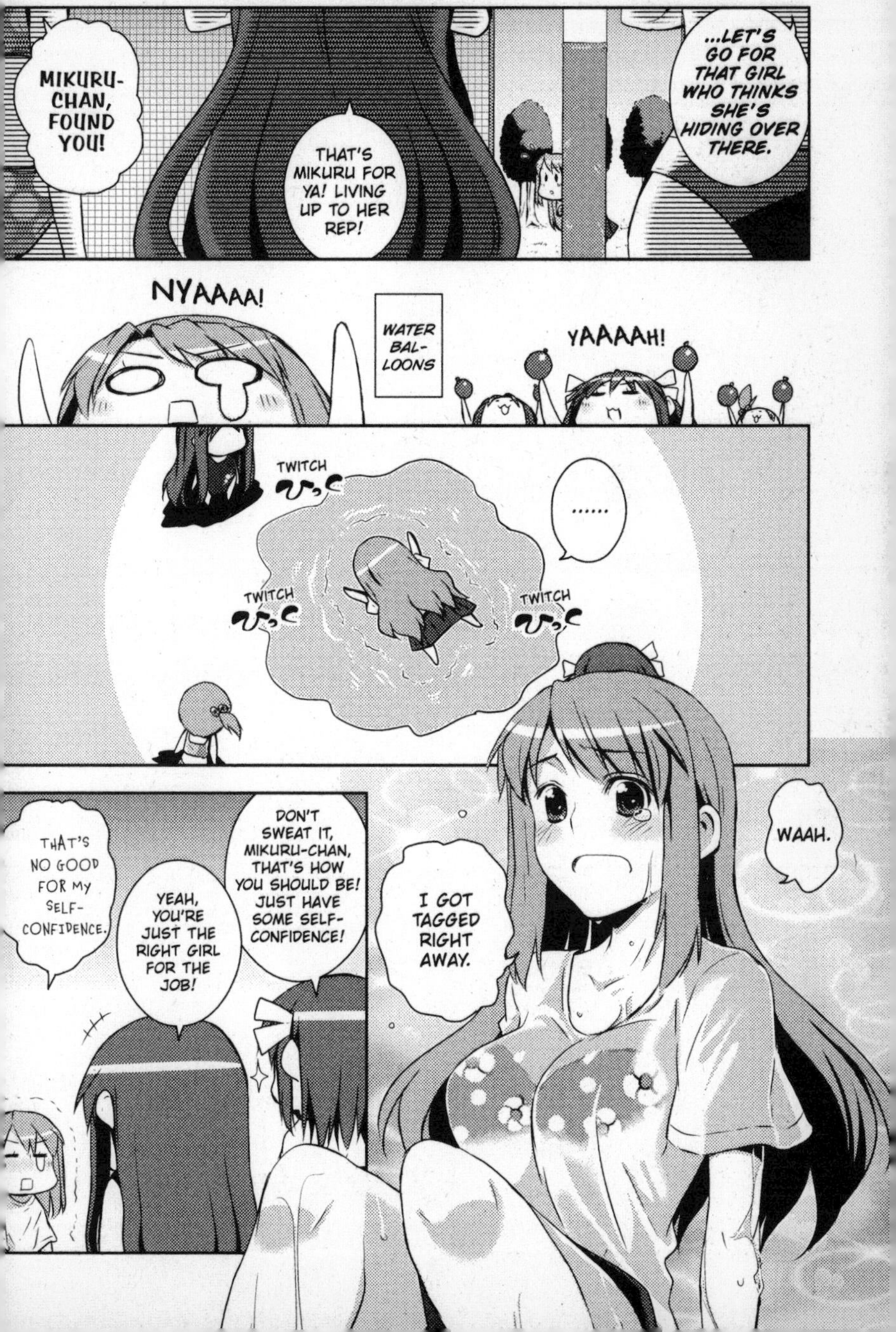
...LET'S GO FOR THAT GIRL WHO THINKS SHE'S HIDING OVER THERE.
MIKURU-CHAN, FOUND YOU!
THAT'S MIKURU FOR YA! LIVING UP TO HER REP!
YAAAAH!
WATER BALLOONS
NYAAAA!
......
TWITCH
TWITCH
TWITCH
WAAH.
I GOT TAGGED RIGHT AWAY.
DON'T SWEAT IT, MIKURU-CHAN, THAT'S HOW YOU SHOULD BE! JUST HAVE SOME SELF-CONFIDENCE!
YEAH, YOU'RE JUST THE RIGHT GIRL FOR THE JOB!
THAT'S NO GOOD FOR MY SELF-CONFIDENCE.

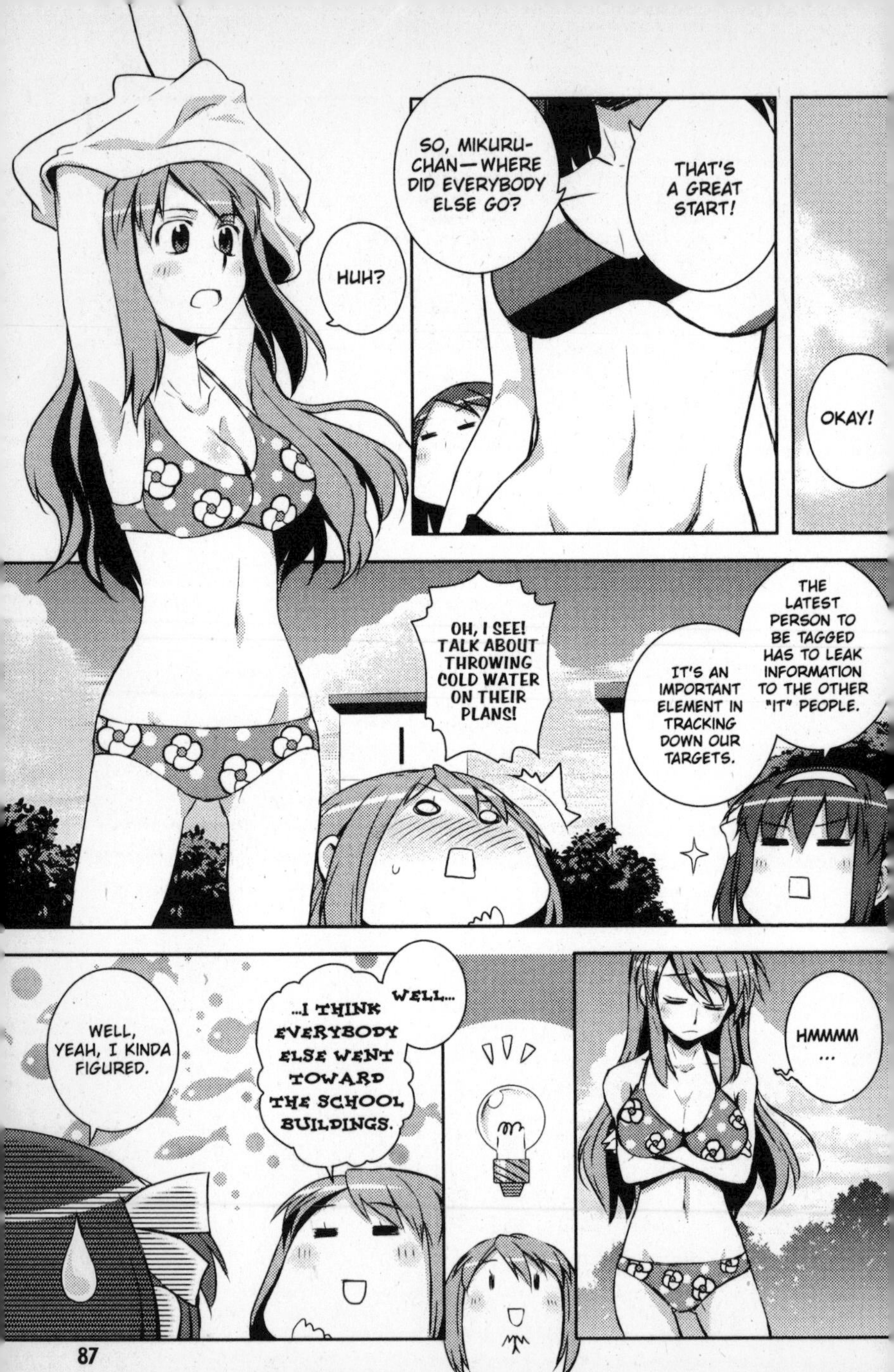
OKAY!
THAT'S A GREAT START!
SO, MIKURU-CHAN—WHERE DID EVERYBODY ELSE GO?
HUH?
THE LATEST PERSON TO BE TAGGED HAS TO LEAK INFORMATION TO THE OTHER "IT" PEOPLE.
IT'S AN IMPORTANT ELEMENT IN TRACKING DOWN OUR TARGETS.
OH, I SEE! TALK ABOUT THROWING COLD WATER ON THEIR PLANS!
HMMMM...
WELL...
...I THINK EVERYBODY ELSE WENT TOWARD THE SCHOOL BUILDINGS.
WELL, YEAH, I KINDA FIGURED.

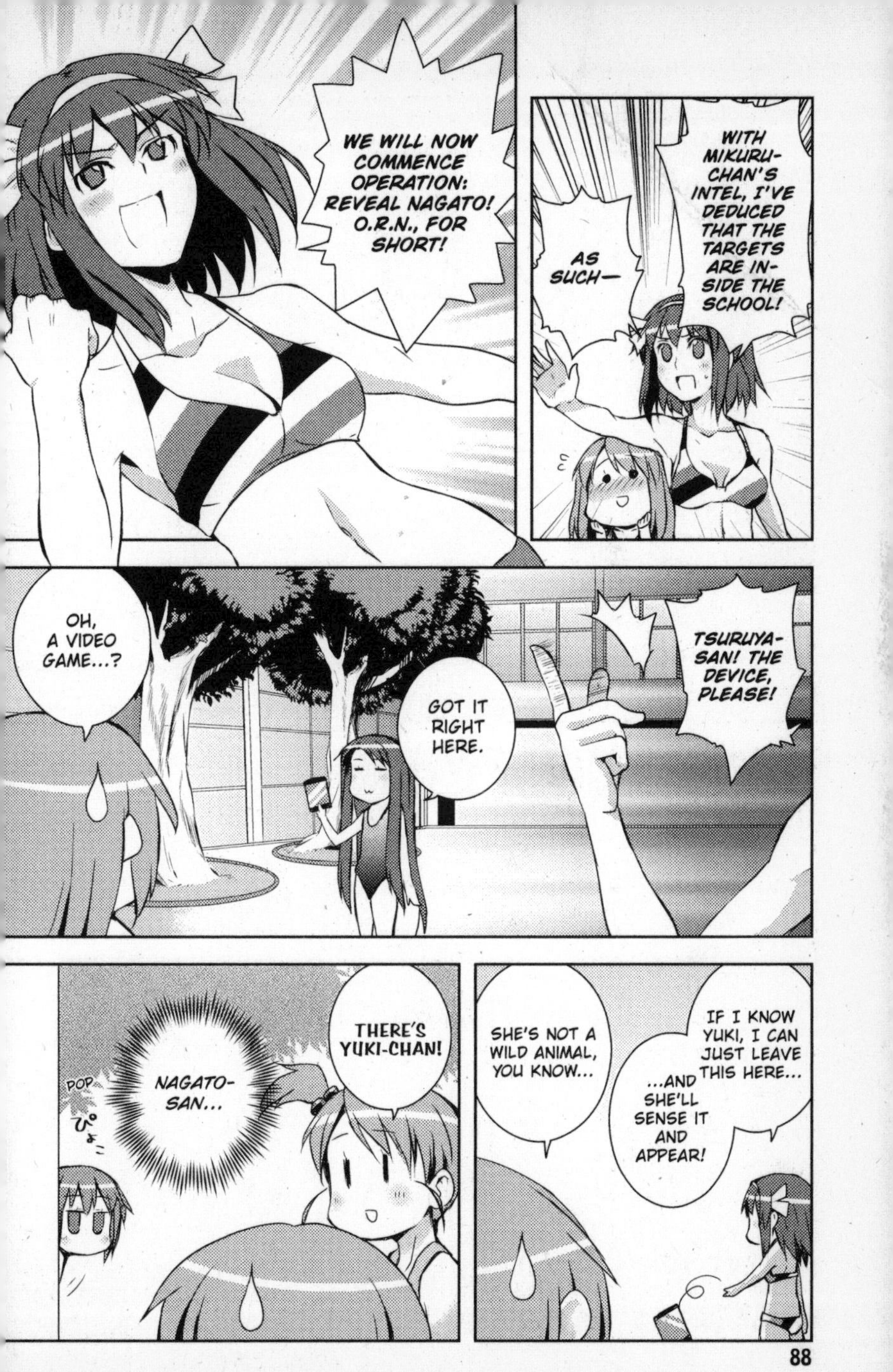
WITH MIKURU-CHAN'S INTEL, I'VE DEDUCED THAT THE TARGETS ARE INSIDE THE SCHOOL!
AS SUCH—
WE WILL NOW COMMENCE OPERATION: REVEAL NAGATO! O.R.N., FOR SHORT!
TSURUYA-SAN! THE DEVICE, PLEASE!
GOT IT RIGHT HERE.
OH, A VIDEO GAME...?
IF I KNOW YUKI, I CAN JUST LEAVE THIS HERE...
...AND SHE'LL SENSE IT AND APPEAR!
SHE'S NOT A WILD ANIMAL, YOU KNOW...
THERE'S YUKI-CHAN!
NAGATO-SAN...
POP
ぴょこ

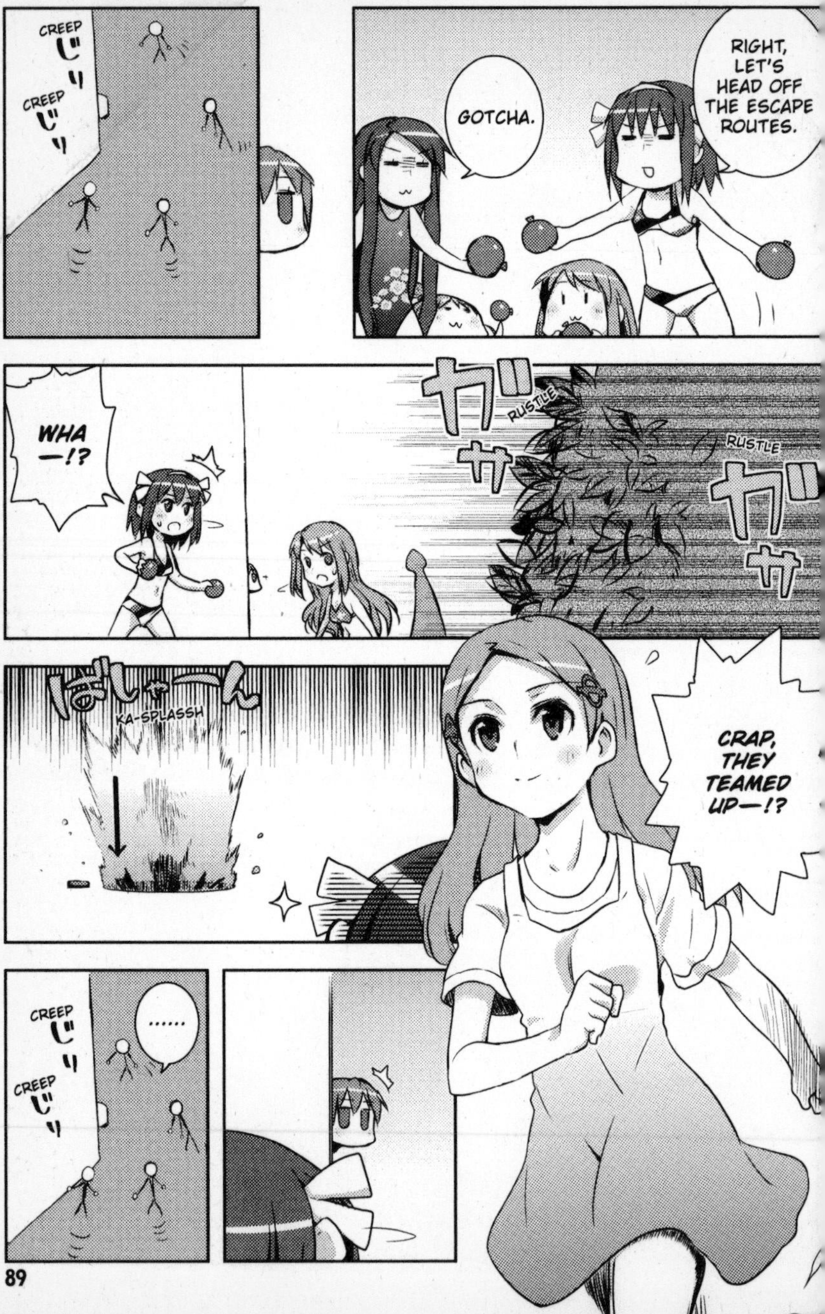
RIGHT, LET'S HEAD OFF THE ESCAPE ROUTES.
GOTCHA.
CREEP じり
CREEP じり
ザッ RUSTLE
ザッ RUSTLE
WHA—!?
CRAP, THEY TEAMED UP—!?
ぱしゃーん KA-SPLASSH
CREEP じり
CREEP じり
......

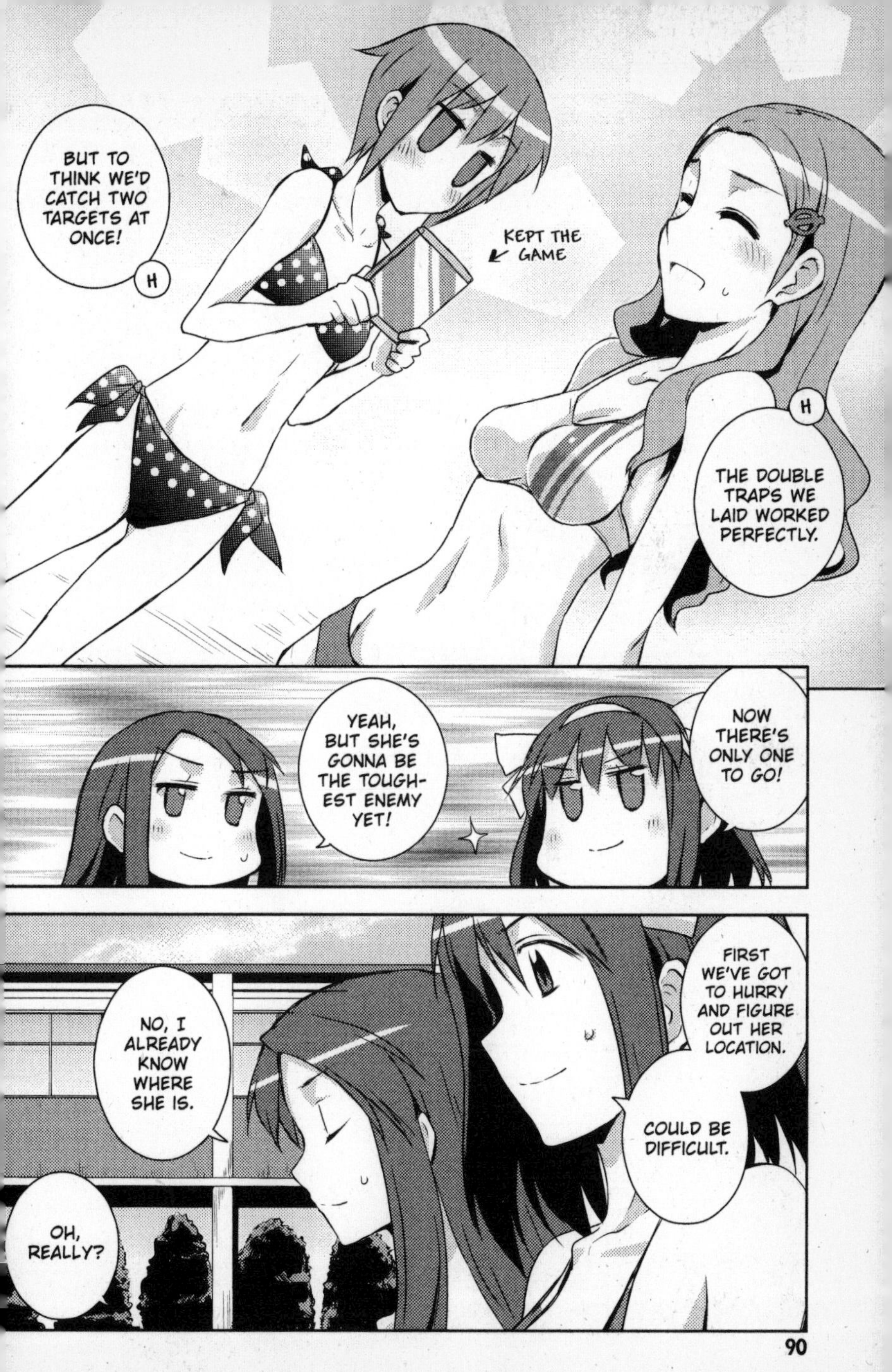
THE DOUBLE TRAPS WE LAID WORKED PERFECTLY.
KEPT THE GAME
BUT TO THINK WE'D CATCH TWO TARGETS AT ONCE!
NOW THERE'S ONLY ONE TO GO!
YEAH, BUT SHE'S GONNA BE THE TOUGHEST ENEMY YET!
FIRST WE'VE GOT TO HURRY AND FIGURE OUT HER LOCATION.
COULD BE DIFFICULT.
NO, I ALREADY KNOW WHERE SHE IS.
OH, REALLY?

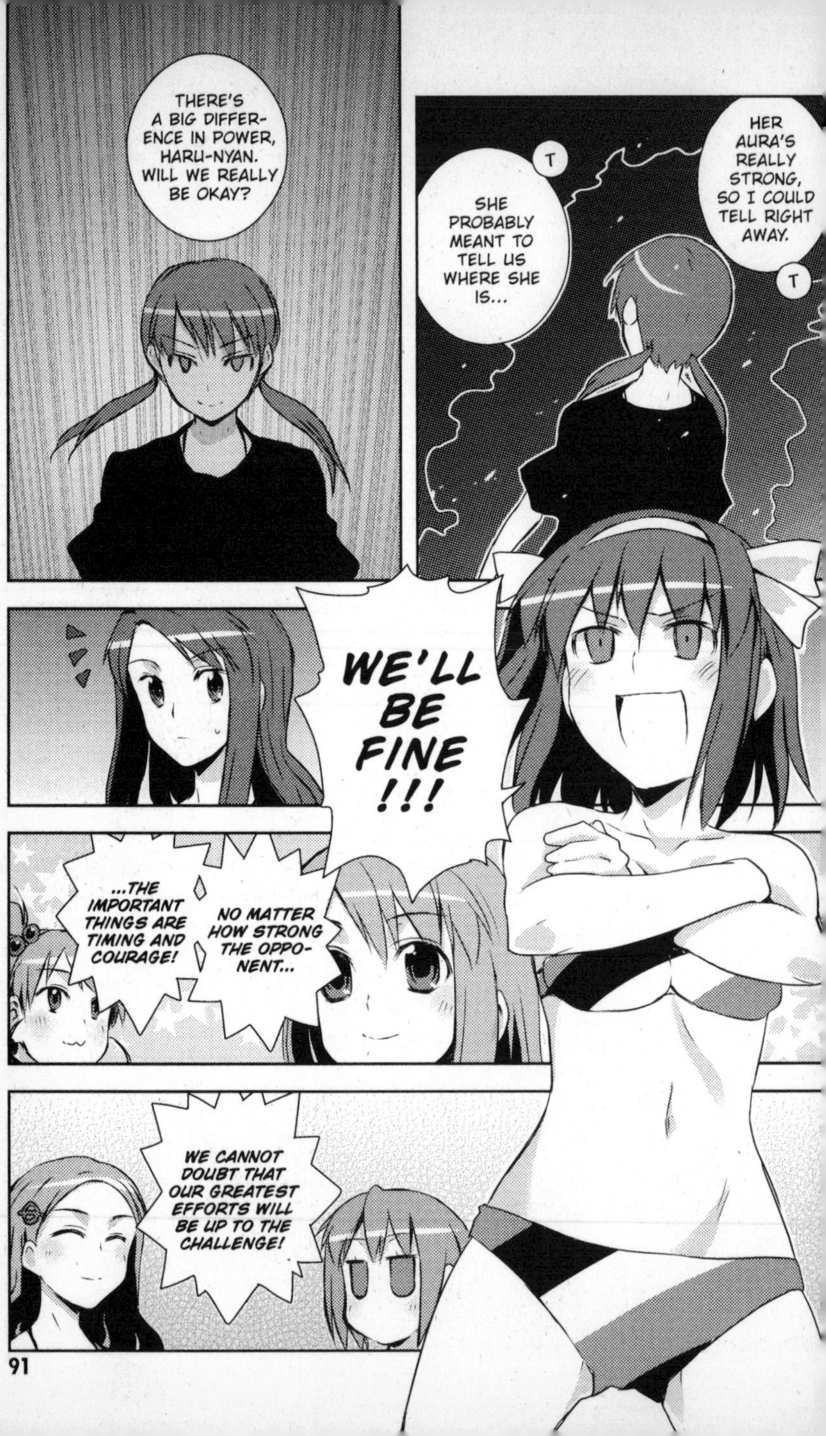
HER AURA'S REALLY STRONG, SO I COULD TELL RIGHT AWAY.
T
SHE PROBABLY MEANT TO TELL US WHERE SHE IS...
T
THERE'S A BIG DIFFERENCE IN POWER, HARU-NYAN. WILL WE REALLY BE OKAY?
WE'LL BE FINE!!!
NO MATTER HOW STRONG THE OPPONENT...
...THE IMPORTANT THINGS ARE TIMING AND COURAGE!
WE CANNOT DOUBT THAT OUR GREATEST EFFORTS WILL BE UP TO THE CHALLENGE!

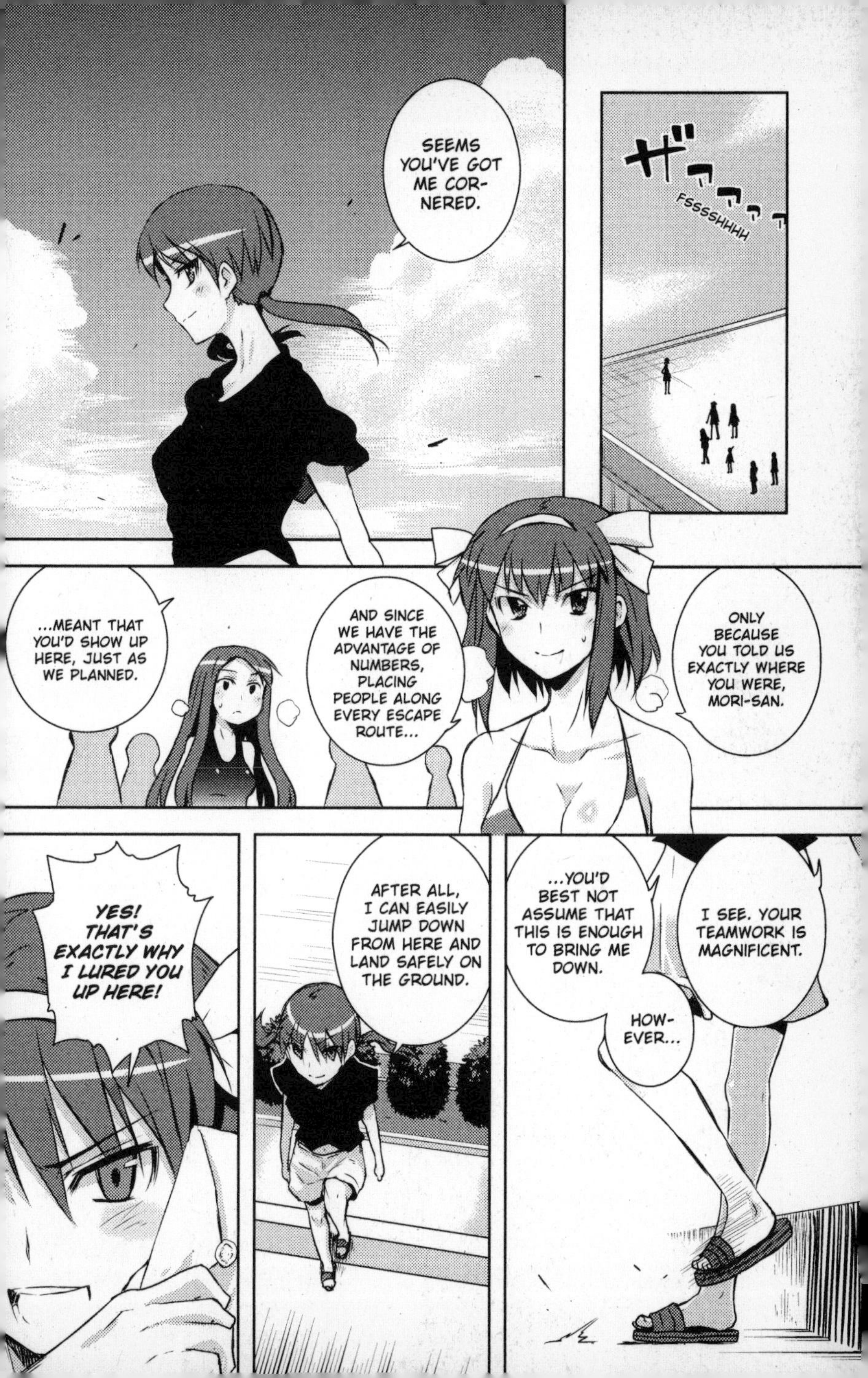
ザァァァァ
FSSSSHHHH
SEEMS YOU'VE GOT ME COR-NERED.
ONLY BECAUSE YOU TOLD US EXACTLY WHERE YOU WERE, MORI-SAN.
AND SINCE WE HAVE THE ADVANTAGE OF NUMBERS, PLACING PEOPLE ALONG EVERY ESCAPE ROUTE...
...MEANT THAT YOU'D SHOW UP HERE, JUST AS WE PLANNED.
I SEE. YOUR TEAMWORK IS MAGNIFICENT.
HOW-EVER...
...YOU'D BEST NOT ASSUME THAT THIS IS ENOUGH TO BRING ME DOWN.
AFTER ALL, I CAN EASILY JUMP DOWN FROM HERE AND LAND SAFELY ON THE GROUND.
YES! THAT'S EXACTLY WHY I LURED YOU UP HERE!

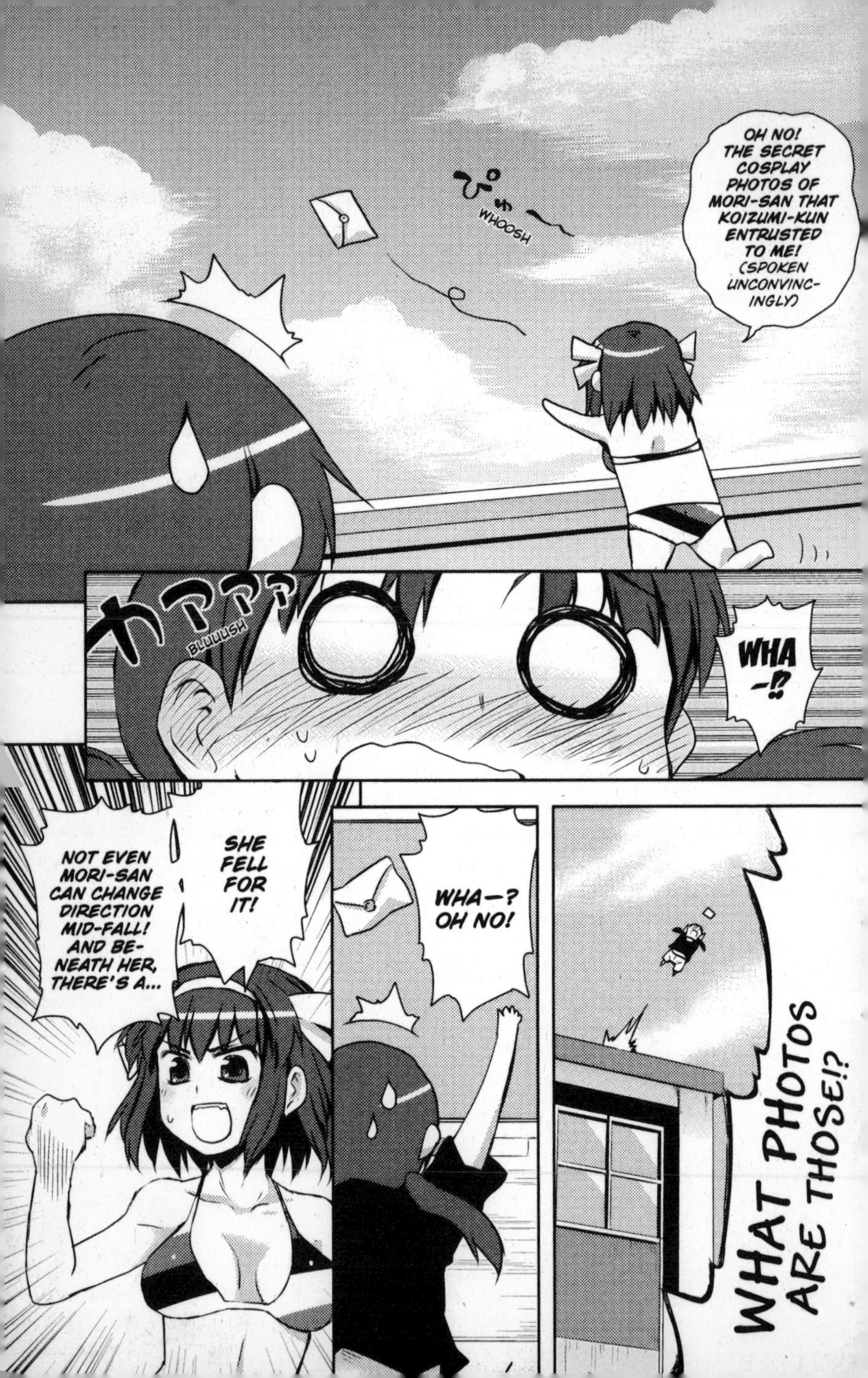
OH NO! THE SECRET COSPLAY PHOTOS OF MORI-SAN THAT KOIZUMI-KUN ENTRUSTED TO ME! (SPOKEN UNCONVINC-INGLY)
ぴゅ～
WHOOSH
WHA—!?
カァァァ
BLUUUSH
WHAT PHOTOS ARE THOSE!?
WHA—? OH NO!
SHE FELL FOR IT!
NOT EVEN MORI-SAN CAN CHANGE DIRECTION MID-FALL! AND BE-NEATH HER, THERE'S A...

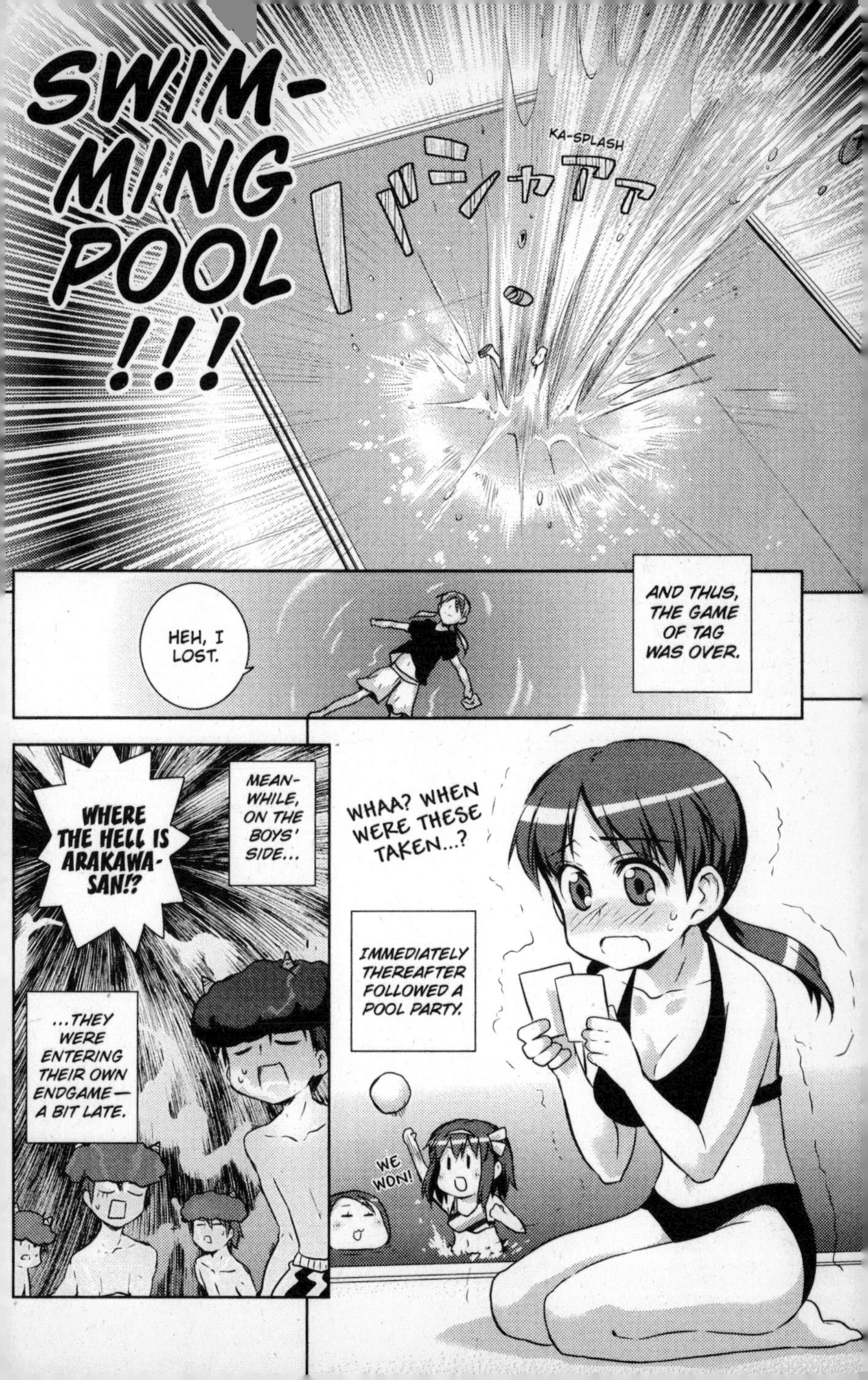
KA-SPLASH
バシャアア
SWIM-MING POOL!!!
AND THUS, THE GAME OF TAG WAS OVER.
HEH, I LOST.
WHAA? WHEN WERE THESE TAKEN...?
IMMEDIATELY THEREAFTER FOLLOWED A POOL PARTY.
WE WON!
MEAN-WHILE, ON THE BOYS' SIDE...
WHERE THE HELL IS ARAKAWA-SAN!?
...THEY WERE ENTERING THEIR OWN ENDGAME—A BIT LATE.

SUMMER HOUSE

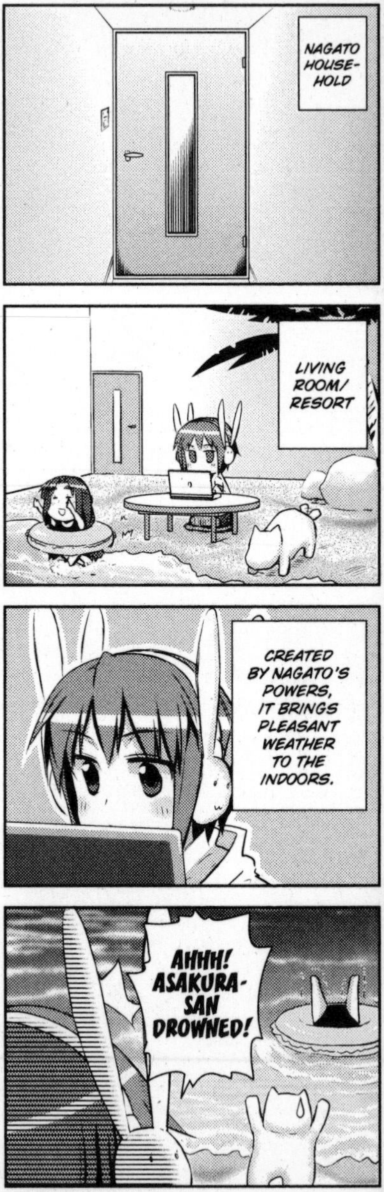
NAGATO HOUSE-HOLD
LIVING ROOM/ RESORT
CREATED BY NAGATO'S POWERS, IT BRINGS PLEASANT WEATHER TO THE INDOORS.
AHHH! ASAKURA-SAN DROWNED!

WAVES

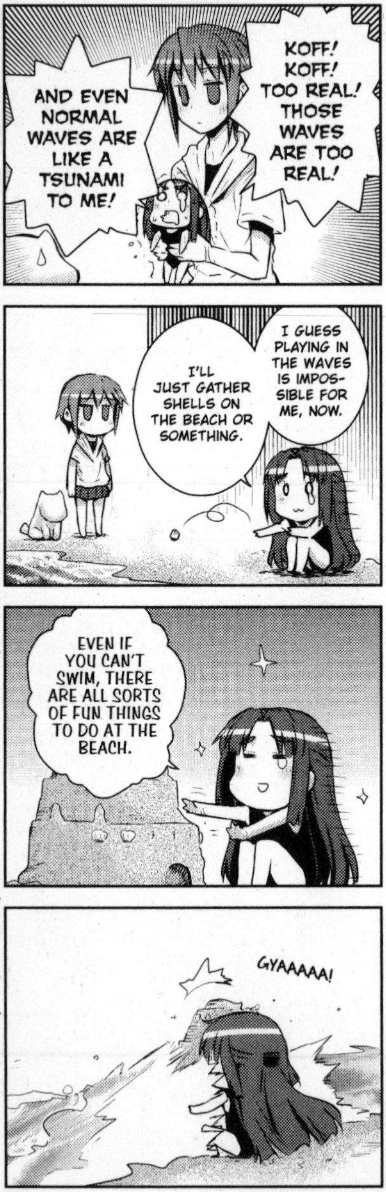
KOFF! KOFF! TOO REAL! THOSE WAVES ARE TOO REAL!
AND EVEN NORMAL WAVES ARE LIKE A TSUNAMI TO ME!
I GUESS PLAYING IN THE WAVES IS IMPOS-SIBLE FOR ME, NOW.
I'LL JUST GATHER SHELLS ON THE BEACH OR SOMETHING.
EVEN IF YOU CAN'T SWIM, THERE ARE ALL SORTS OF FUN THINGS TO DO AT THE BEACH.
GYAAAAA!

•Taniguchi •If someone's "it," it's gotta be Taniguchi. Since this chapter focused on the girls, he didn't appear much.

•Achakura-san •Currently continuing last chapter's episode, wherein Nagato turned her living room into a resort.

•Kimidori-san •Good at swimming, on account of being a balloon animal. His new ability appears on the very next page!?

BREAKTHROUGH

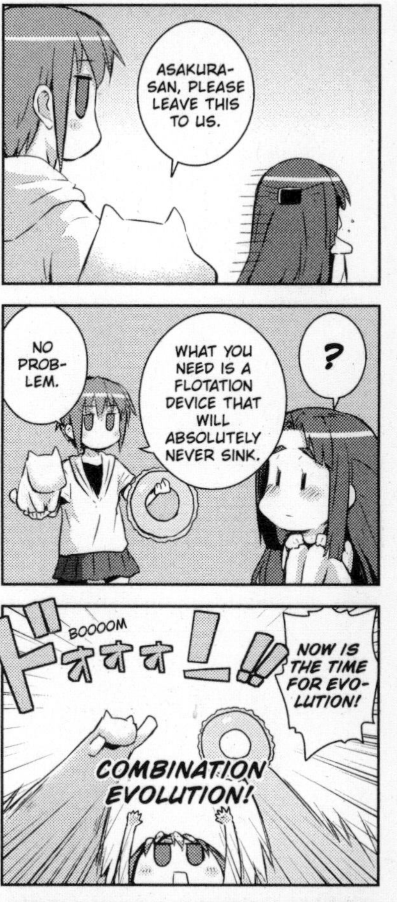

ASAKURA-SAN, PLEASE LEAVE THIS TO US.
?
WHAT YOU NEED IS A FLOTATION DEVICE THAT WILL ABSOLUTELY NEVER SINK.
NO PROB-LEM.
NOW IS THE TIME FOR EVO-LUTION!
ドォォォ!!
BOOOOM
COMBINATION EVOLUTION!
ぱかぱ～ん
TA DAAAA
ALL-PURPOSE DOG-FORM WATER SURFACE FLOTATION DEVICE
SS KIMIDORI, LAUNCH!

TOWARD THE HORIZON

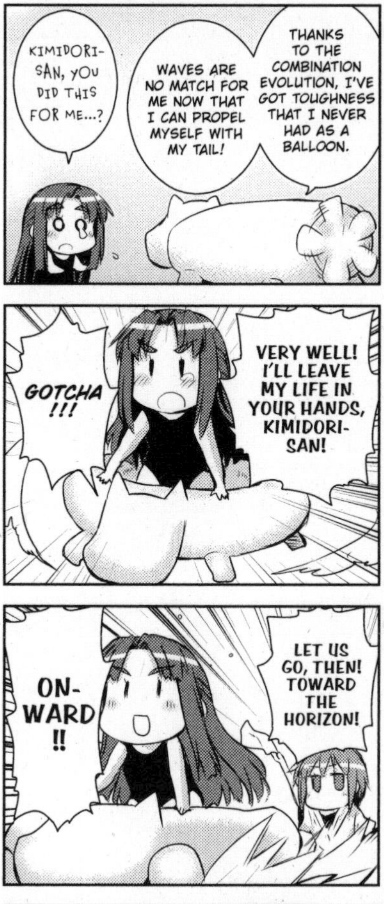

THANKS TO THE COMBINATION EVOLUTION, I'VE GOT TOUGHNESS THAT I NEVER HAD AS A BALLOON.
WAVES ARE NO MATCH FOR ME NOW THAT I CAN PROPEL MYSELF WITH MY TAIL!
KIMIDORI-SAN, YOU DID THIS FOR ME...?
VERY WELL! I'LL LEAVE MY LIFE IN YOUR HANDS, KIMIDORI-SAN!
GOTCHA!!!
LET US GO, THEN! TOWARD THE HORIZON!
ON-WARD!!
WHEE!

THE BOSS UPSTAIRS (AKA THE DATA INTEGRATION THOUGHT ENTITY) NIXED DNA DIGIVOLUTION.
MAYBE IT WAS TOO HARD TO UNDERSTAND...
?

I'M A LITTLE
EARLY...

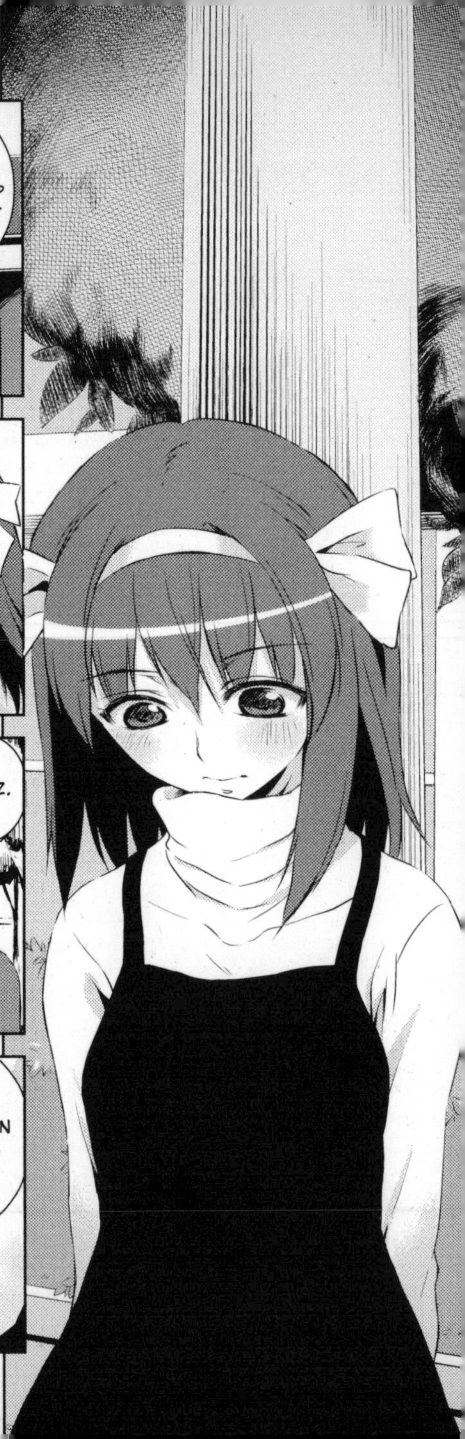

RENDEZVOUS

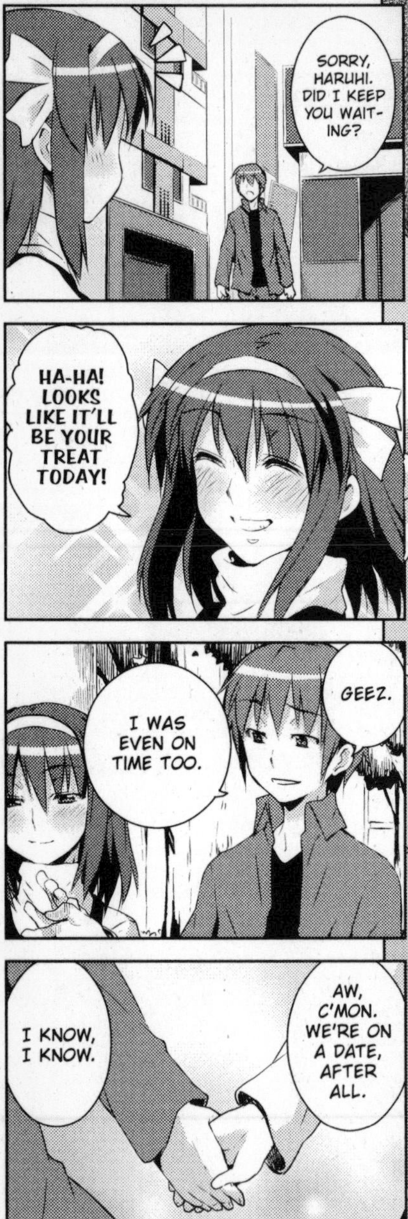
SORRY, HARUHI. DID I KEEP YOU WAIT-ING?
HA-HA! LOOKS LIKE IT'LL BE YOUR TREAT TODAY!
GEEZ.
I WAS EVEN ON TIME TOO.
AW, C'MON. WE'RE ON A DATE, AFTER ALL.
I KNOW, I KNOW.

POWER CUT

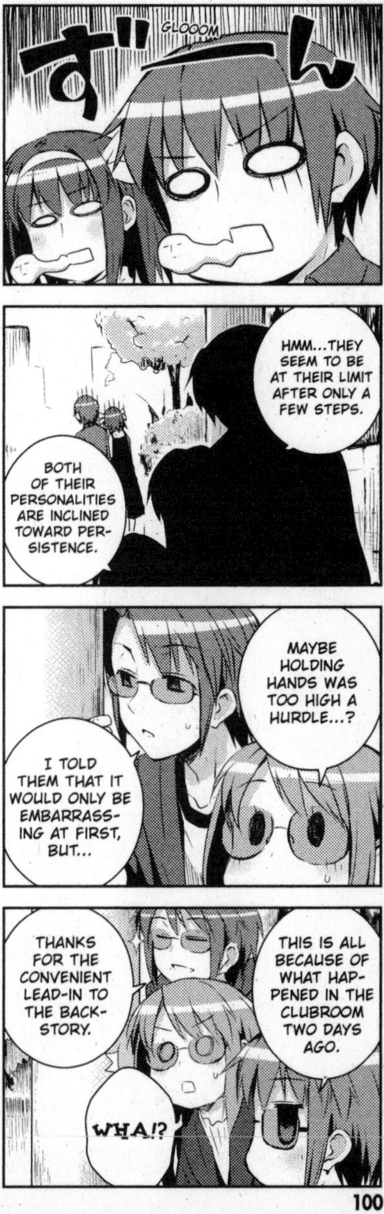

GLOOOM
ずーん
HMM...THEY SEEM TO BE AT THEIR LIMIT AFTER ONLY A FEW STEPS.
BOTH OF THEIR PERSONALITIES ARE INCLINED TOWARD PERSISTENCE.
MAYBE HOLDING HANDS WAS TOO HIGH A HURDLE...?
I TOLD THEM THAT IT WOULD ONLY BE EMBARRASSING AT FIRST, BUT...
THIS IS ALL BECAUSE OF WHAT HAPPENED IN THE CLUBROOM TWO DAYS AGO.
THANKS FOR THE CONVENIENT LEAD-IN TO THE BACKSTORY.
WHA!?

•Kyon •The protagonist of this story. We'll be seeing a manlier side of him this episode — enjoy it!

•Haruhi-chan •SOS Brigade Chief. She only fell asleep on her desk, so how does she end up like this...?

•Nagato •Alien. Actively provides otaku-style explanations of ongoing events.

BORED

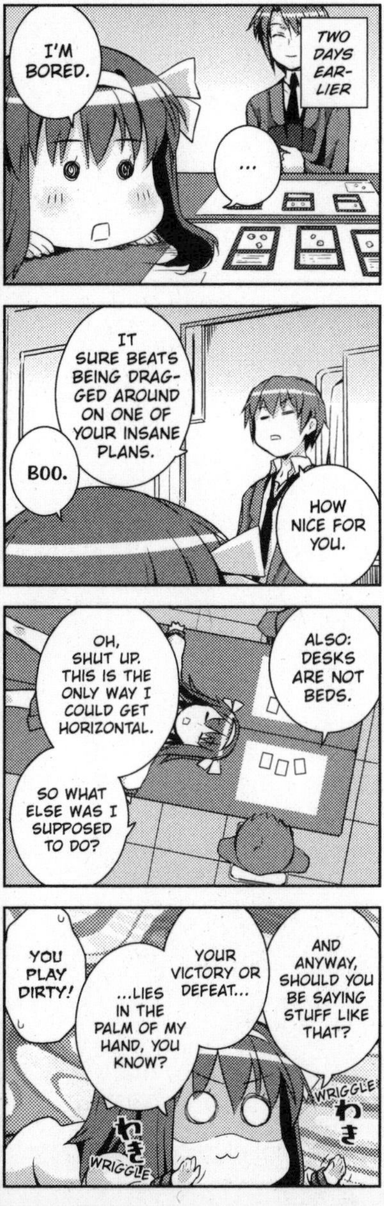

TWO DAYS EARLIER
I'M BORED.
...
IT SURE BEATS BEING DRAGGED AROUND ON ONE OF YOUR INSANE PLANS.
BOO.
HOW NICE FOR YOU.
ALSO: DESKS ARE NOT BEDS.
OH, SHUT UP. THIS IS THE ONLY WAY I COULD GET HORIZONTAL.
SO WHAT ELSE WAS I SUPPOSED TO DO?
AND ANYWAY, SHOULD YOU BE SAYING STUFF LIKE THAT?
YOUR VICTORY OR DEFEAT...
...LIES IN THE PALM OF MY HAND, YOU KNOW?
YOU PLAY DIRTY!
WRIGGLE
わき
わき
WRIGGLE

SACRIFICES

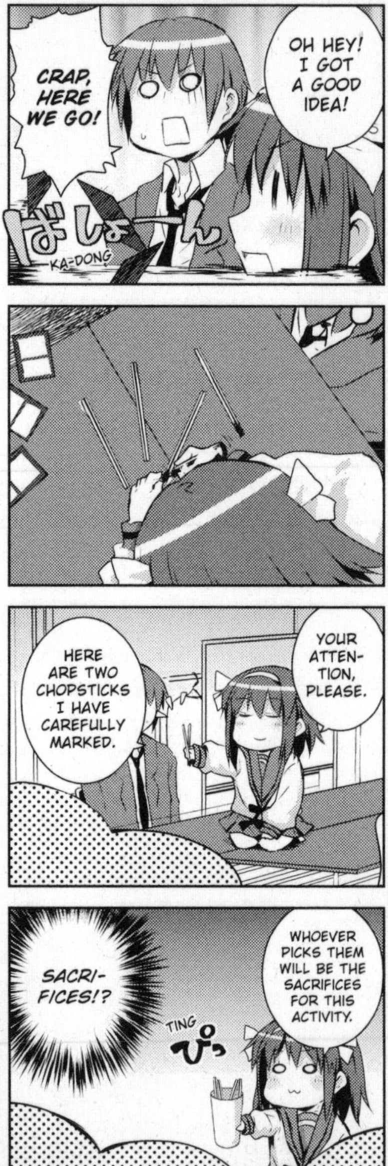
OH HEY! I GOT A GOOD IDEA!
CRAP, HERE WE GO!
ばしょーん
KA-DONG
YOUR ATTENTION, PLEASE.
HERE ARE TWO CHOPSTICKS I HAVE CAREFULLY MARKED.
WHOEVER PICKS THEM WILL BE THE SACRIFICES FOR THIS ACTIVITY.
SACRIFICES!?
TING
ぴっ

PLAYING DIRTY

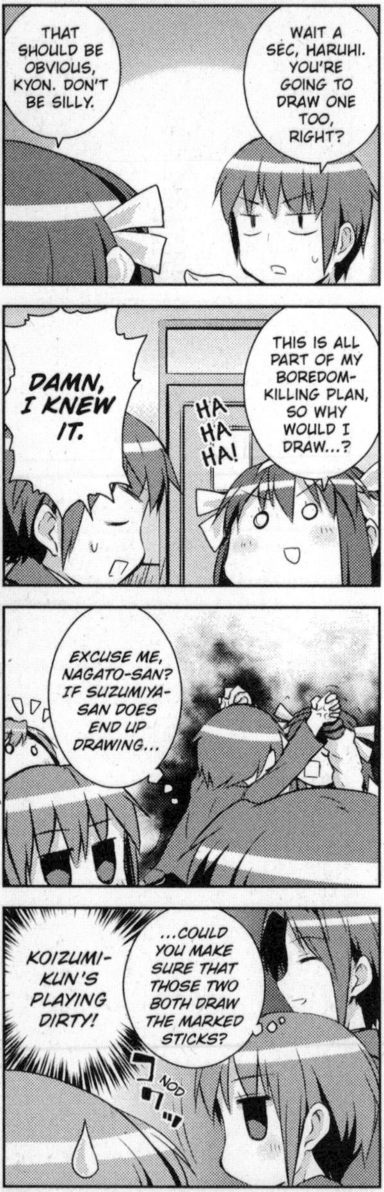
WAIT A SEC, HARUHI. YOU'RE GOING TO DRAW ONE TOO, RIGHT?
THAT SHOULD BE OBVIOUS, KYON. DON'T BE SILLY.
THIS IS ALL PART OF MY BOREDOM-KILLING PLAN, SO WHY WOULD I DRAW...?
HA HA HA!
DAMN, I KNEW IT.
EXCUSE ME, NAGATO-SAN? IF SUZUMIYA-SAN DOES END UP DRAWING...
...COULD YOU MAKE SURE THAT THOSE TWO BOTH DRAW THE MARKED STICKS?
KOIZUMI-KUN'S PLAYING DIRTY!
NOD

•Mikuru-chan •Time traveler. In this chapter, for once, she's just an observer, and isn't getting messed with.

•Koizumi •Enigmatic transfer student and esper. A bad person who conspires with Nagato to rig the outcome.

DICTATORSHIP

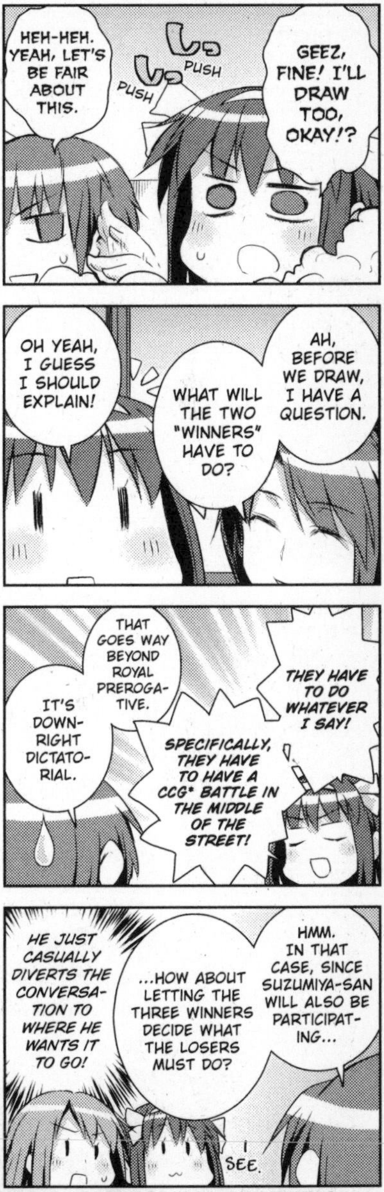
GEEZ, FINE! I'LL DRAW TOO, OKAY!?
PUSH
PUSH
HEH-HEH. YEAH, LET'S BE FAIR ABOUT THIS.
AH, BEFORE WE DRAW, I HAVE A QUESTION.
WHAT WILL THE TWO "WINNERS" HAVE TO DO?
OH YEAH, I GUESS I SHOULD EXPLAIN!
THEY HAVE TO DO WHATEVER I SAY!
SPECIFICALLY, THEY HAVE TO HAVE A CCG* BATTLE IN THE MIDDLE OF THE STREET!
THAT GOES WAY BEYOND ROYAL PREROGA-TIVE.
IT'S DOWN-RIGHT DICTATO-RIAL.
HMM. IN THAT CASE, SINCE SUZUMIYA-SAN WILL ALSO BE PARTICIPAT-ING...
...HOW ABOUT LETTING THE THREE WINNERS DECIDE WHAT THE LOSERS MUST DO?
HE JUST CASUALLY DIVERTS THE CONVERSA-TION TO WHERE HE WANTS IT TO GO!
I SEE.

EQUALITY

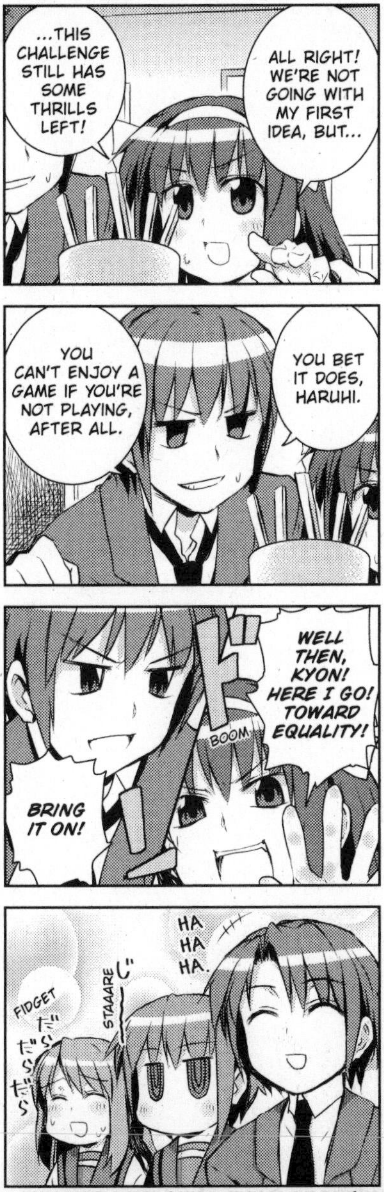
ALL RIGHT! WE'RE NOT GOING WITH MY FIRST IDEA, BUT...
...THIS CHALLENGE STILL HAS SOME THRILLS LEFT!
YOU BET IT DOES, HARUHI.
YOU CAN'T ENJOY A GAME IF YOU'RE NOT PLAYING, AFTER ALL.
WELL THEN, KYON! HERE I GO! TOWARD EQUALITY!
BOOM
BRING IT ON!
HA HA HA.
STAAARE
FIDGET

*COLLECTIBLE CARD GAMES, SUCH AS THE POKÉMON TRADING CARD GAME OR MAGIC: THE GATHERING. KYON AND KOIZUMI CAN BE SEEN PLAYING SUCH A GAME ON THE PREVIOUS SPREAD.

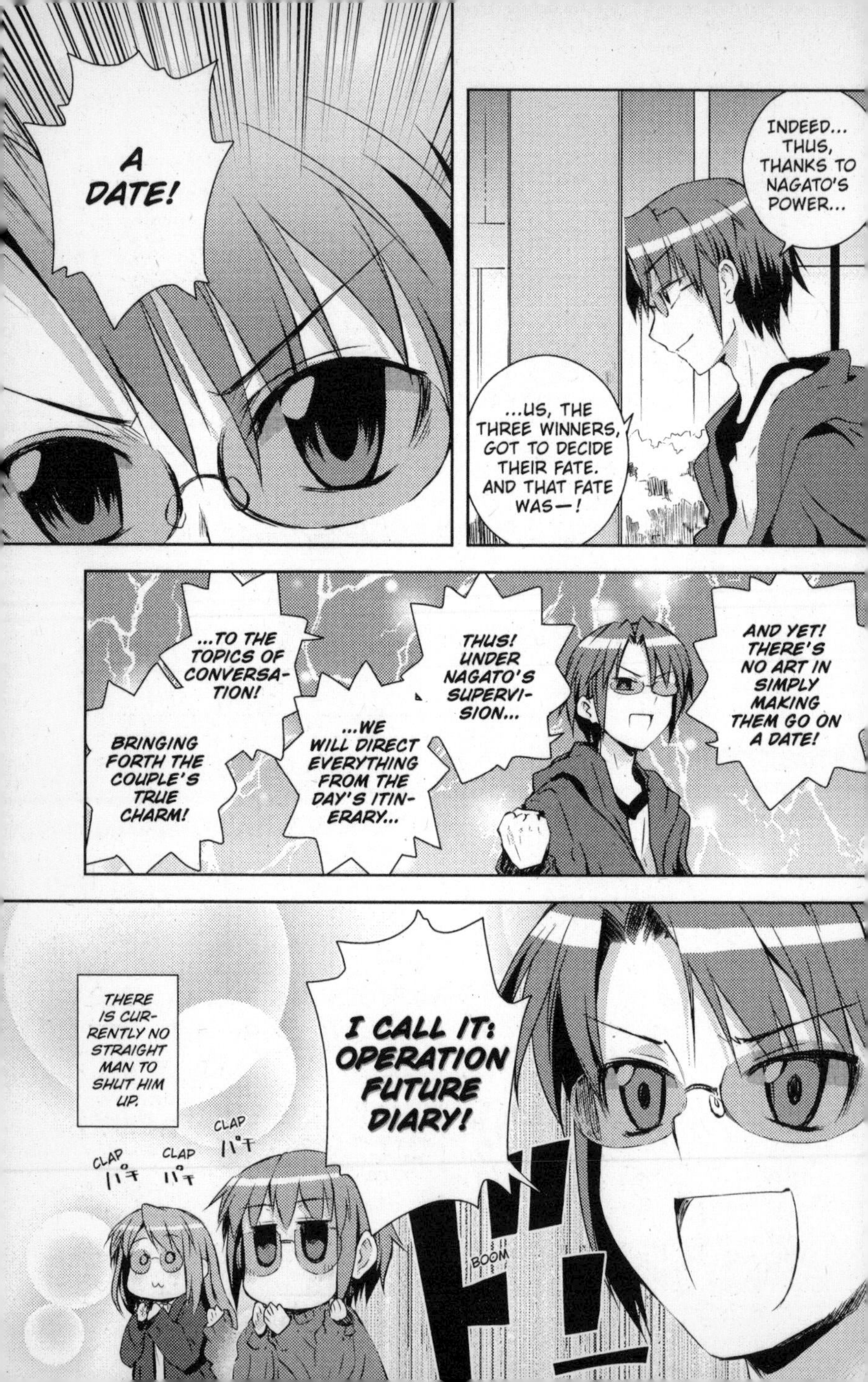
INDEED... THUS, THANKS TO NAGATO'S POWER...
...US, THE THREE WINNERS, GOT TO DECIDE THEIR FATE. AND THAT FATE WAS—!
A DATE!
AND YET! THERE'S NO ART IN SIMPLY MAKING THEM GO ON A DATE!
THUS! UNDER NAGATO'S SUPERVISION...
...WE WILL DIRECT EVERYTHING FROM THE DAY'S ITINERARY...
...TO THE TOPICS OF CONVERSATION!
BRINGING FORTH THE COUPLE'S TRUE CHARM!
I CALL IT: OPERATION FUTURE DIARY!
BOOM
THERE IS CURRENTLY NO STRAIGHT MAN TO SHUT HIM UP.
CLAP
パチ
CLAP
パチ
CLAP
パチ

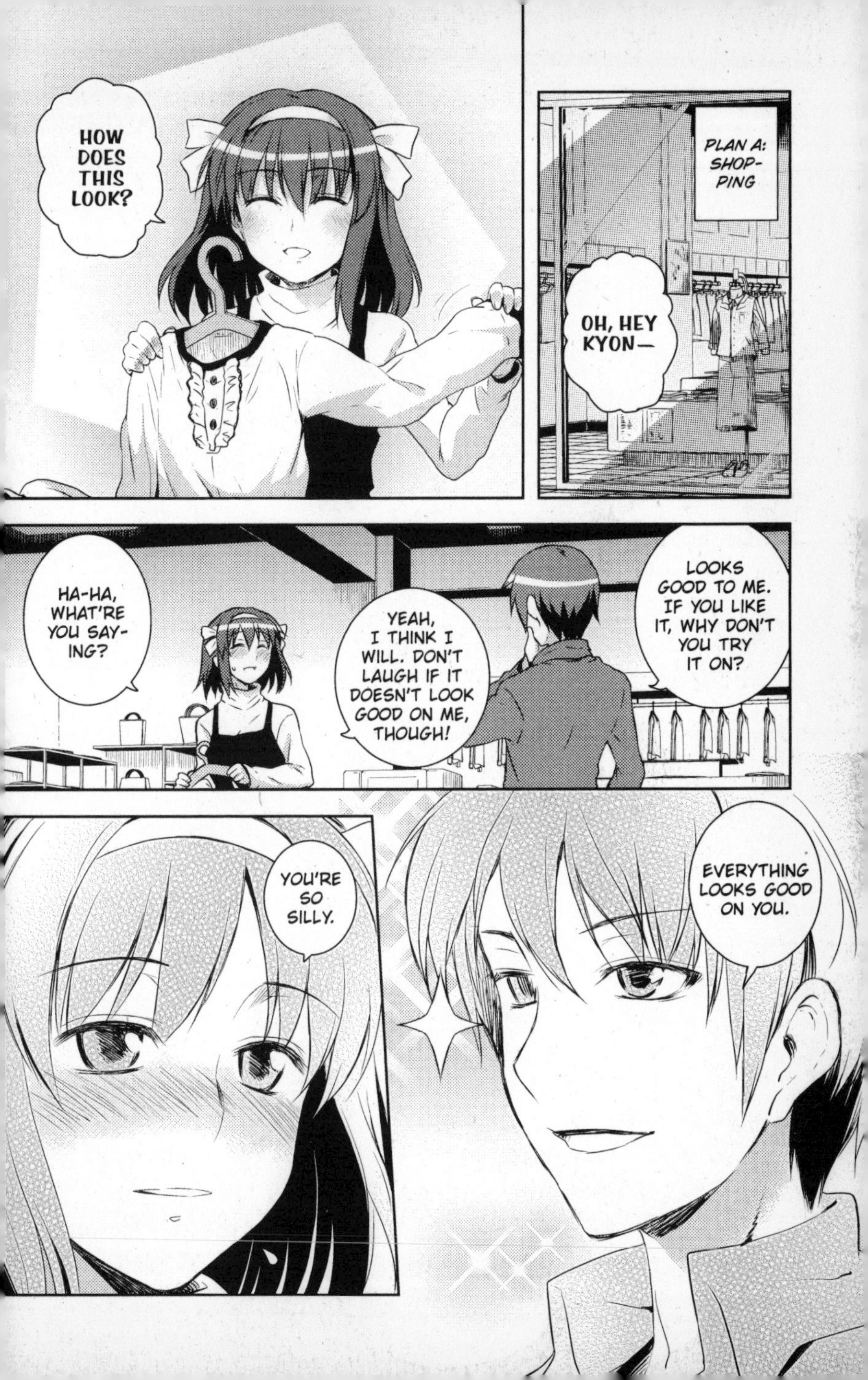
PLAN A: SHOP-PING
OH, HEY KYON—
HOW DOES THIS LOOK?
LOOKS GOOD TO ME. IF YOU LIKE IT, WHY DON'T YOU TRY IT ON?
YEAH, I THINK I WILL. DON'T LAUGH IF IT DOESN'T LOOK GOOD ON ME, THOUGH!
HA-HA, WHAT'RE YOU SAY-ING?
EVERYTHING LOOKS GOOD ON YOU.
YOU'RE SO SILLY.

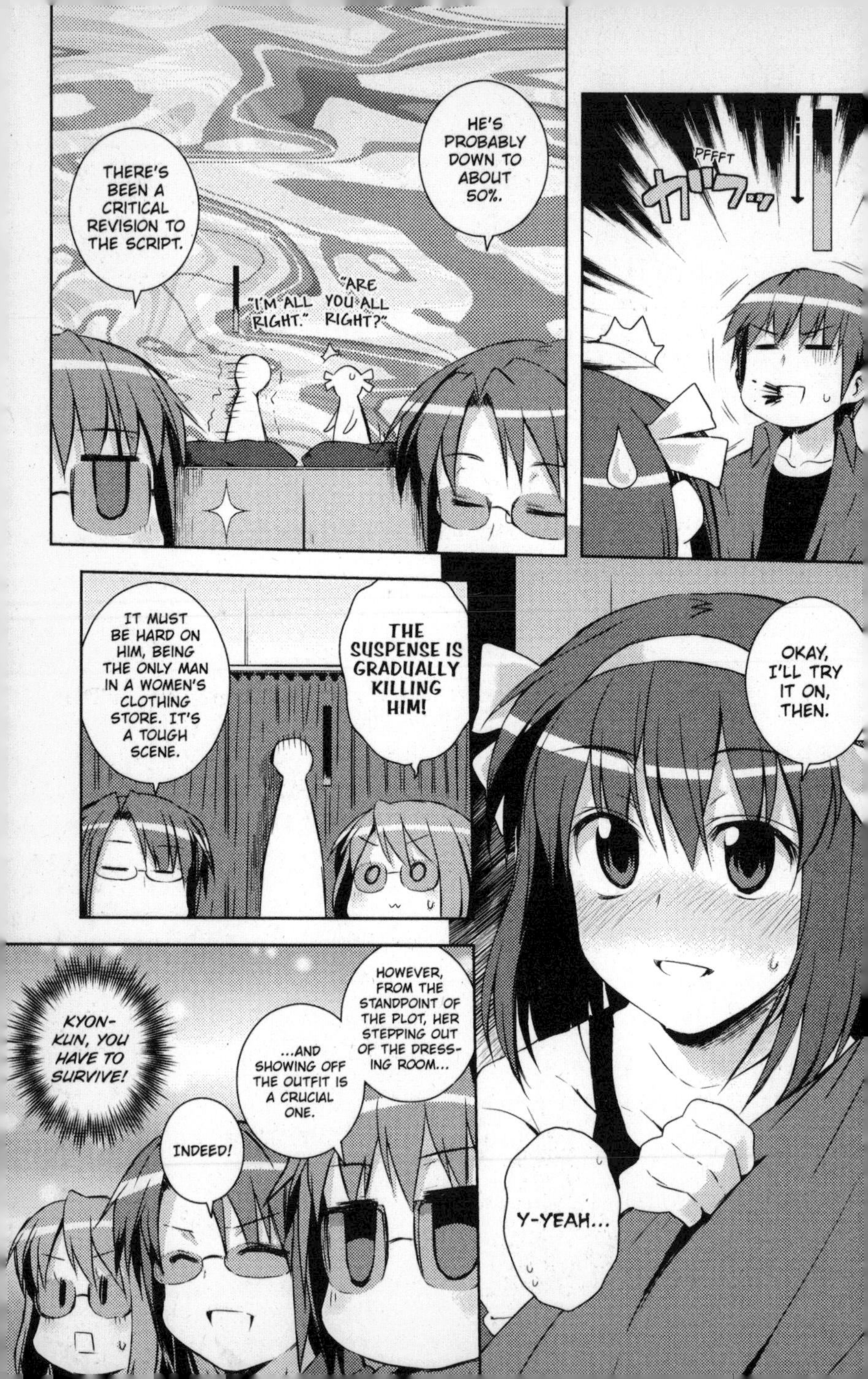
PFFFT
HE'S PROBABLY DOWN TO ABOUT 50%.
THERE'S BEEN A CRITICAL REVISION TO THE SCRIPT.
"ARE YOU ALL RIGHT?"
"I'M ALL RIGHT."
OKAY, I'LL TRY IT ON, THEN.
Y-YEAH...
THE SUSPENSE IS GRADUALLY KILLING HIM!
IT MUST BE HARD ON HIM, BEING THE ONLY MAN IN A WOMEN'S CLOTHING STORE. IT'S A TOUGH SCENE.
HOWEVER, FROM THE STANDPOINT OF THE PLOT, HER STEPPING OUT OF THE DRESSING ROOM...
...AND SHOWING OFF THE OUTFIT IS A CRUCIAL ONE.
KYON-KUN, YOU HAVE TO SURVIVE!
INDEED!

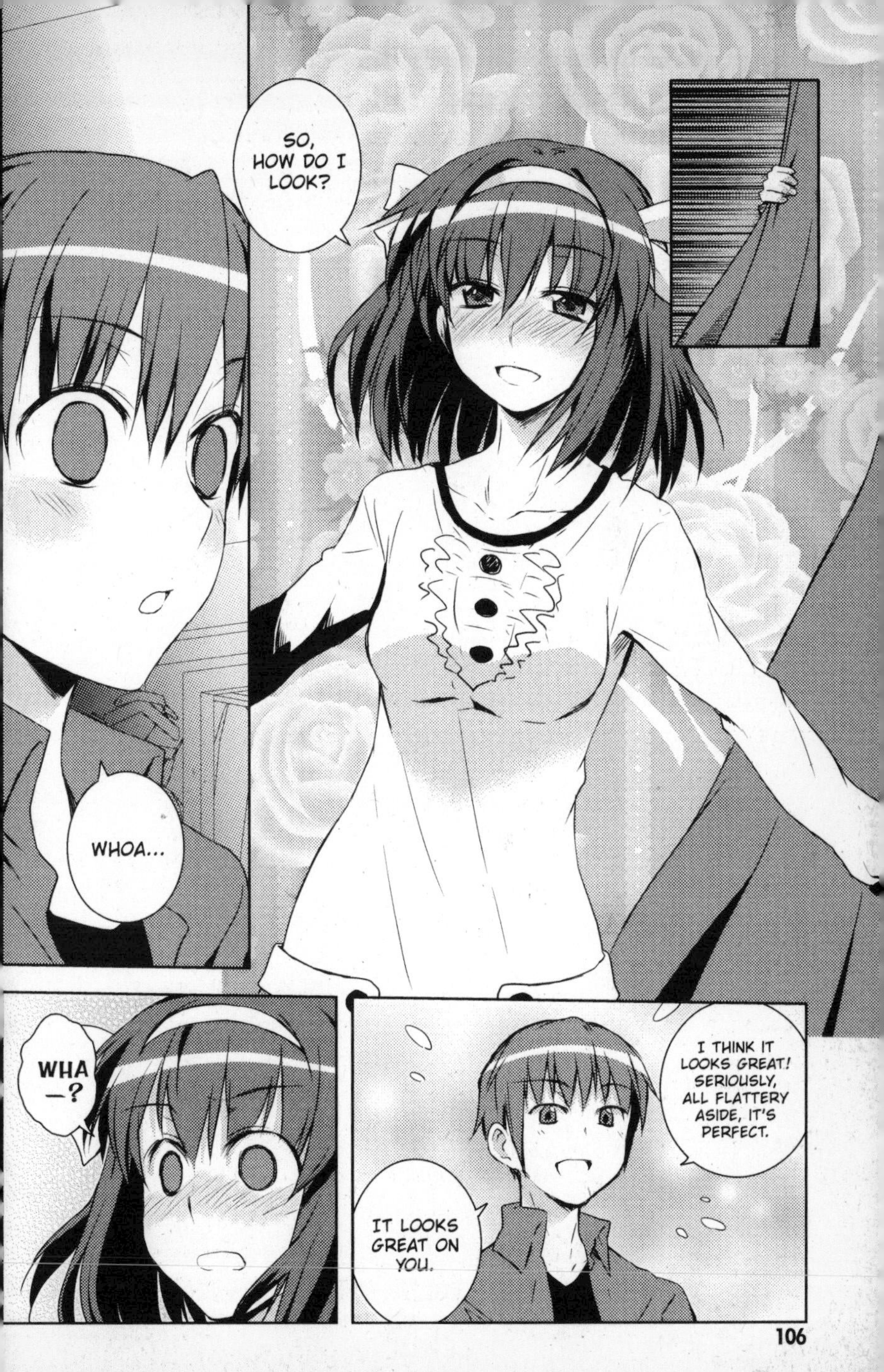
SO, HOW DO I LOOK?
WHOA...
I THINK IT LOOKS GREAT! SERIOUSLY, ALL FLATTERY ASIDE, IT'S PERFECT.
IT LOOKS GREAT ON YOU.
WHA—?

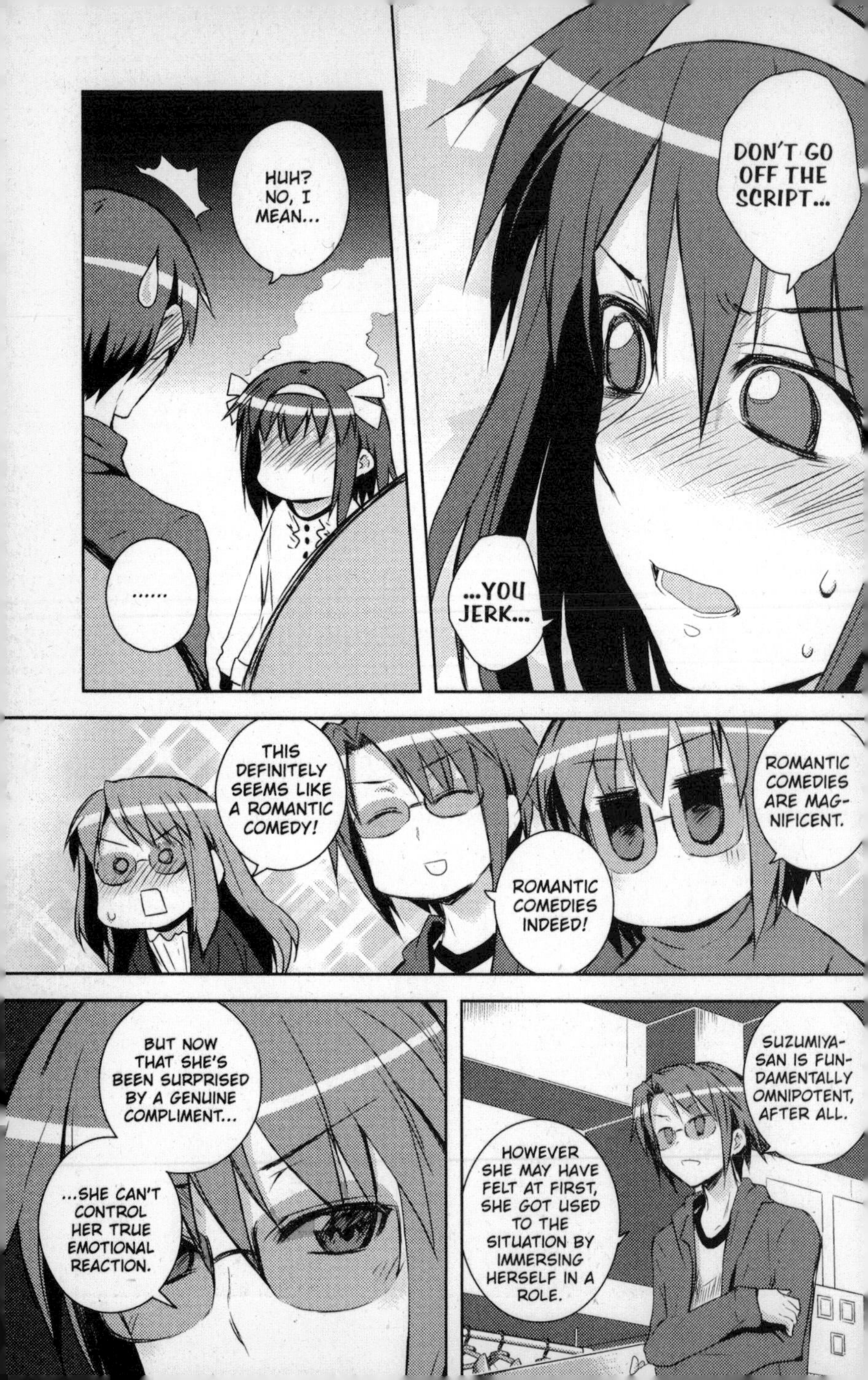
DON'T GO OFF THE SCRIPT...
...YOU JERK...
HUH? NO, I MEAN...
......
ROMANTIC COMEDIES ARE MAGNIFICENT.
THIS DEFINITELY SEEMS LIKE A ROMANTIC COMEDY!
ROMANTIC COMEDIES INDEED!
SUZUMIYA-SAN IS FUNDAMENTALLY OMNIPOTENT, AFTER ALL.
HOWEVER SHE MAY HAVE FELT AT FIRST, SHE GOT USED TO THE SITUATION BY IMMERSING HERSELF IN A ROLE.
BUT NOW THAT SHE'S BEEN SURPRISED BY A GENUINE COMPLIMENT...
...SHE CAN'T CONTROL HER TRUE EMOTIONAL REACTION.

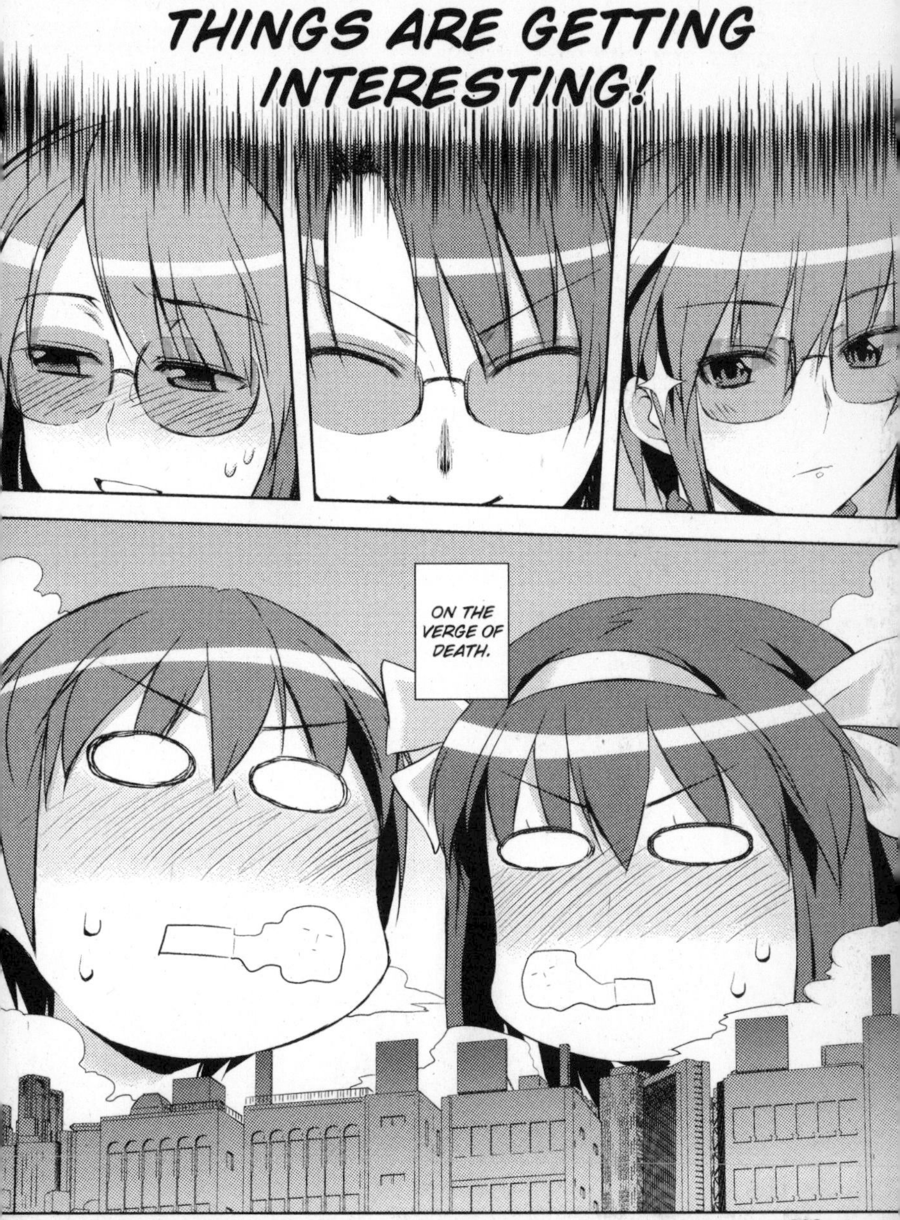
THINGS ARE GETTING INTERESTING!
ON THE VERGE OF DEATH.

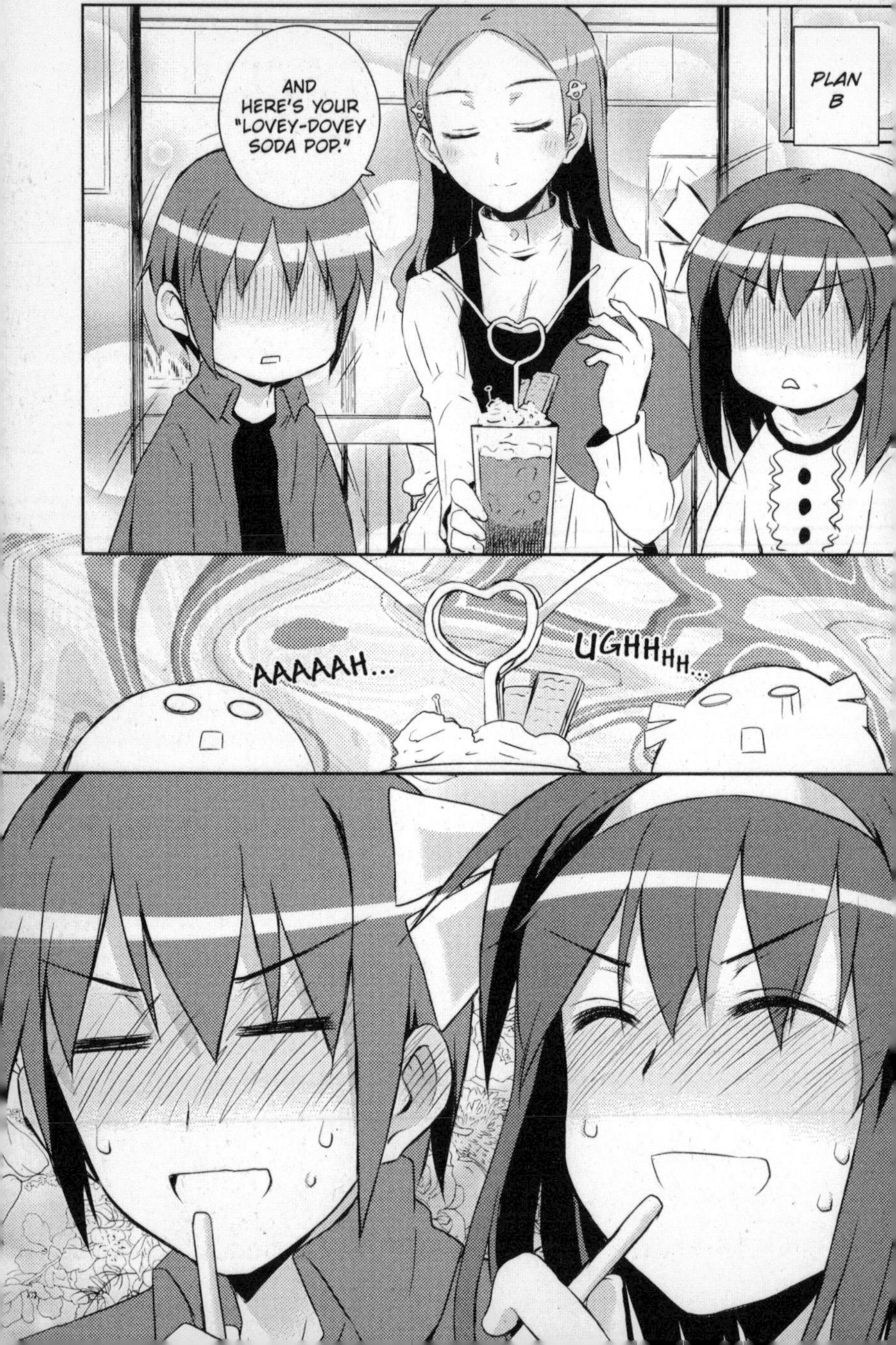
PLAN B
AND HERE'S YOUR "LOVEY-DOVEY SODA POP."
UGHHhh...
AAAAAH...

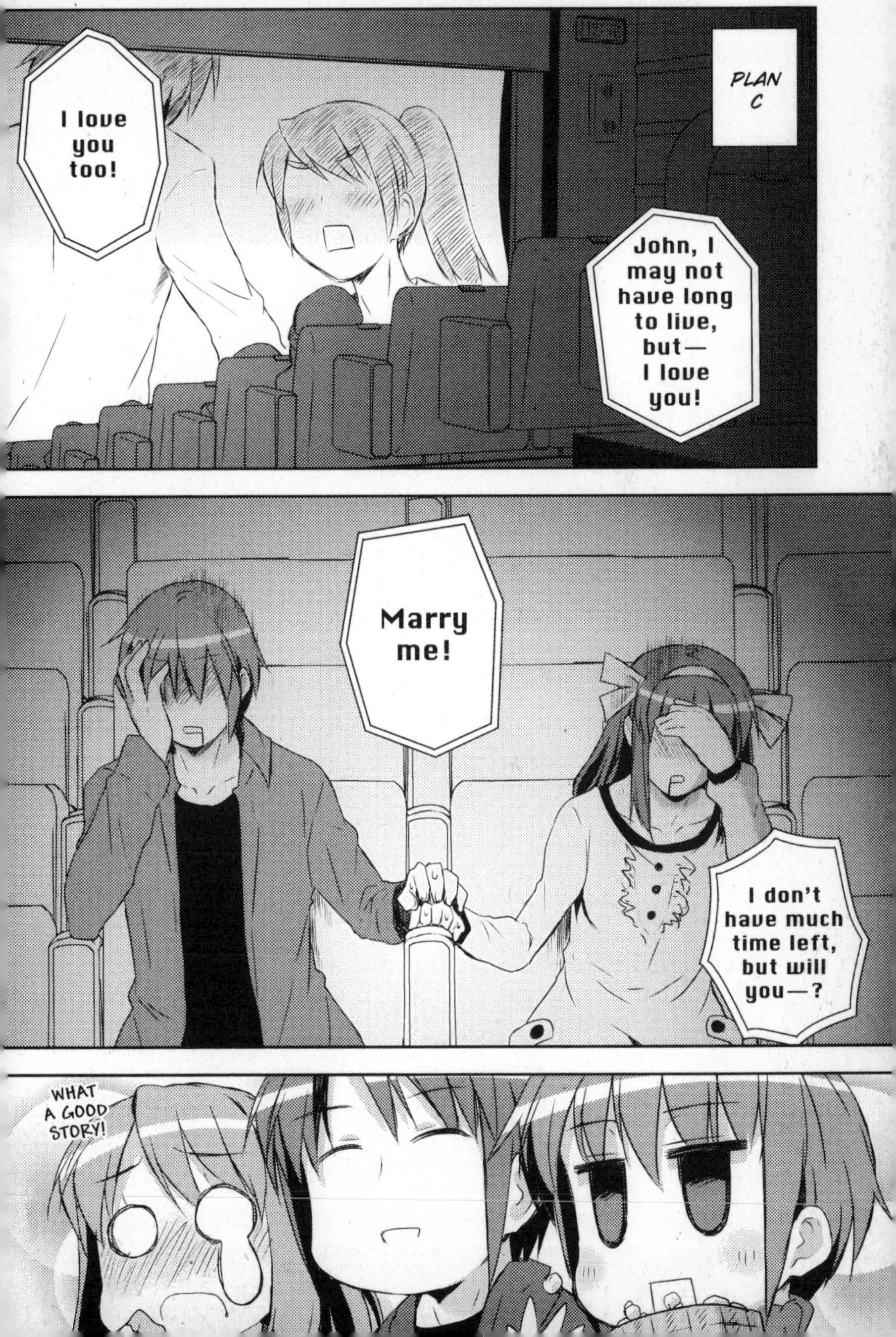
PLAN C
John, I may not have long to live, but— I love you!
I love you too!
I don't have much time left, but will you—?
Marry me!
WHAT A GOOD STORY!

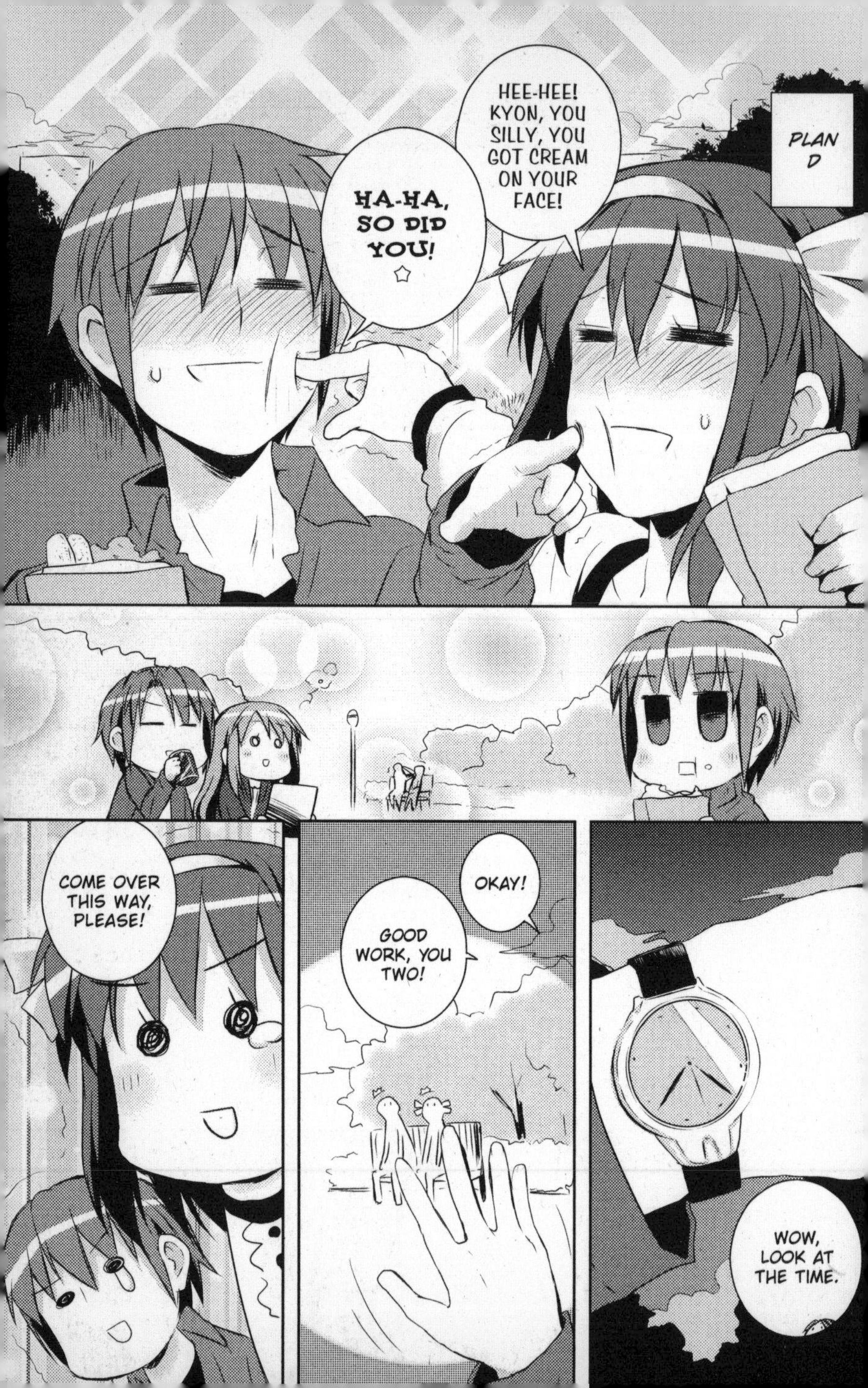
PLAN D
HEE-HEE! KYON, YOU SILLY, YOU GOT CREAM ON YOUR FACE!
HA-HA, SO DID YOU! ☆
WOW, LOOK AT THE TIME.
OKAY!
GOOD WORK, YOU TWO!
COME OVER THIS WAY, PLEASE!

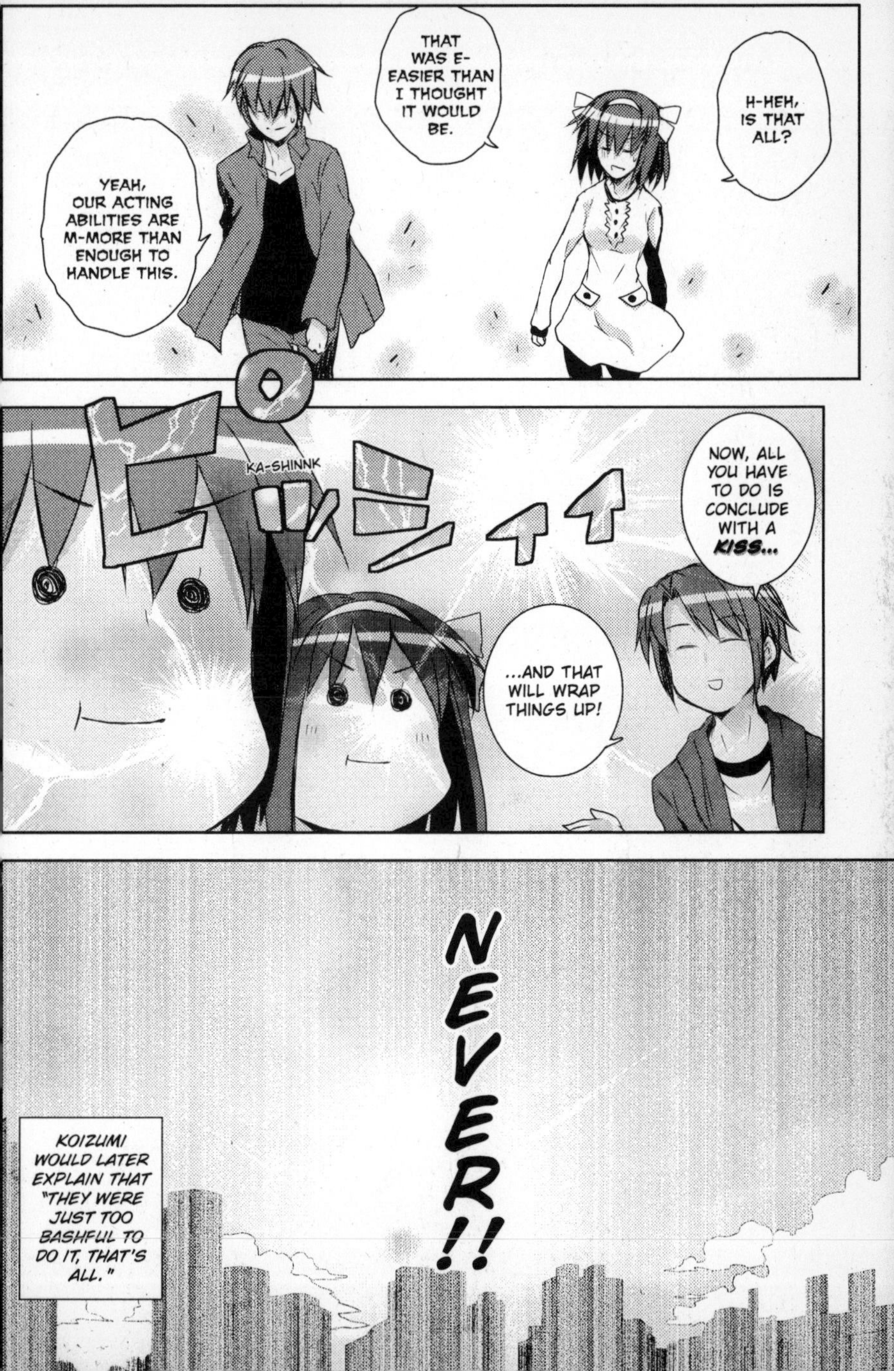
H-HEH, IS THAT ALL?
THAT WAS E-EASIER THAN I THOUGHT IT WOULD BE.
YEAH, OUR ACTING ABILITIES ARE M-MORE THAN ENOUGH TO HANDLE THIS.
NOW, ALL YOU HAVE TO DO IS CONCLUDE WITH A KISS...
...AND THAT WILL WRAP THINGS UP!
KA-SHINNK
NEVER!!
KOIZUMI WOULD LATER EXPLAIN THAT "THEY WERE JUST TOO BASHFUL TO DO IT, THAT'S ALL."

A NEW GAME

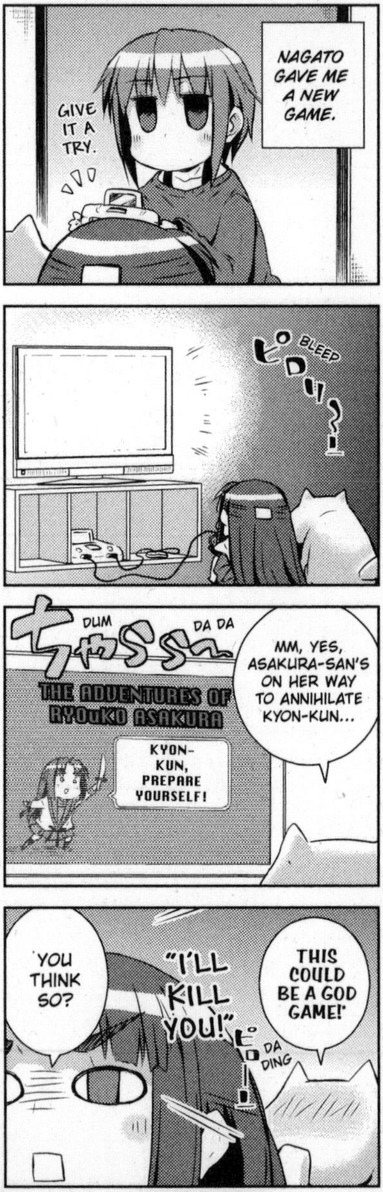
NAGATO GAVE ME A NEW GAME.
GIVE IT A TRY.
BLEEP
DUM
DA DA
THE ADVENTURES OF RYOuKO ASAKURA
MM, YES, ASAKURA-SAN'S ON HER WAY TO ANNIHILATE KYON-KUN...
KYON-KUN, PREPARE YOURSELF!
THIS COULD BE A GOD GAME!'
"I'LL KILL YOU!"
DA DING
'YOU THINK SO?

SHOOTING

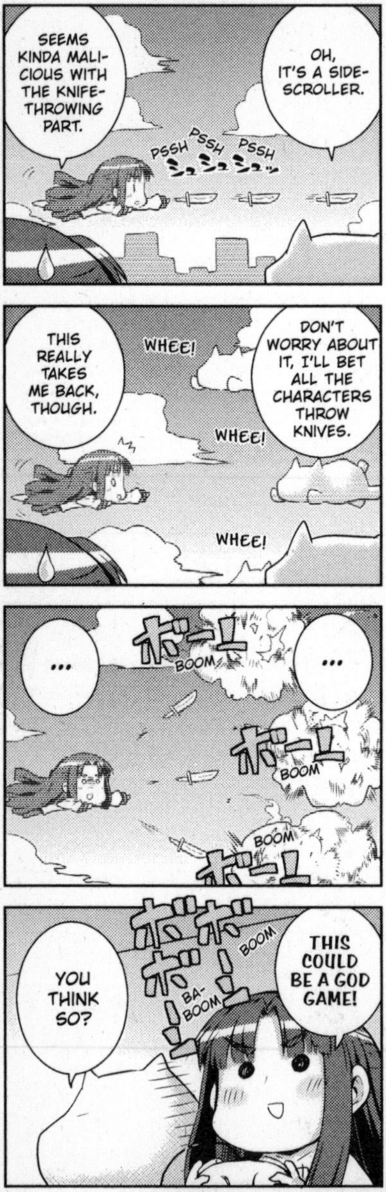
OH, IT'S A SIDE-SCROLLER.
SEEMS KINDA MALICIOUS WITH THE KNIFE-THROWING PART.
PSSH PSSH PSSH
DON'T WORRY ABOUT IT, I'LL BET ALL THE CHARACTERS THROW KNIVES.
WHEE!
WHEE!
WHEE!
THIS REALLY TAKES ME BACK, THOUGH.
...
BOOM
BOOM
BOOM
...
THIS COULD BE A GOD GAME!
BOOM
BA-BOOM
YOU THINK SO?

•Achakura-chan •The controller seems to be a bit large for her, but she's used to it.

•Kimidori-san •It's a mystery how he uses a controller with front paws like that.

*A GOD GAME IS A GAME THAT ALLOWS THE PLAYER TO USE THE CHARACTER'S SUPERNATURAL ABILITIES TO INDIRECTLY CONTROL A GROUP OF "WORSHIPPERS."

LEVEL-ONE BOSS

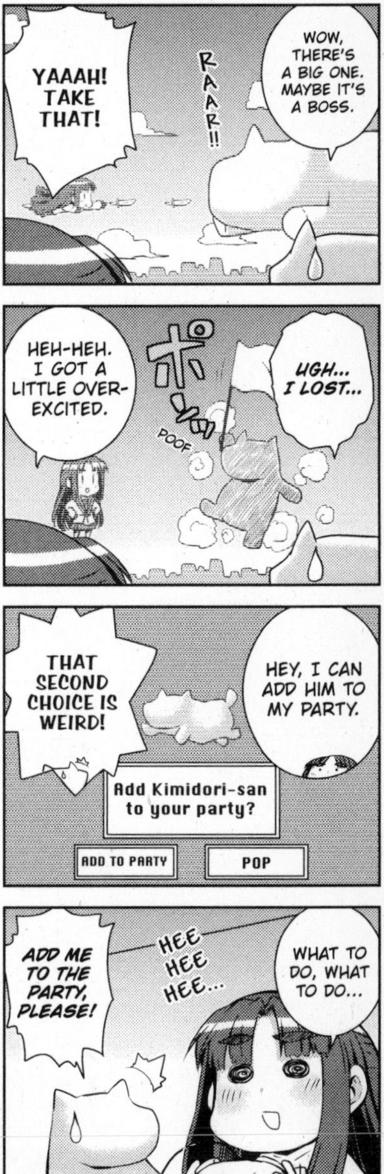
WOW, THERE'S A BIG ONE. MAYBE IT'S A BOSS.
RAAAR!!
YAAAH! TAKE THAT!
UGH... I LOST...
POOF
HEH-HEH. I GOT A LITTLE OVER-EXCITED.
HEY, I CAN ADD HIM TO MY PARTY.
THAT SECOND CHOICE IS WEIRD!
Add Kimidori-san to your party?
ADD TO PARTY
POP
WHAT TO DO, WHAT TO DO...
HEE HEE HEE...
ADD ME TO THE PARTY, PLEASE!

LEVEL-TWO BOSS

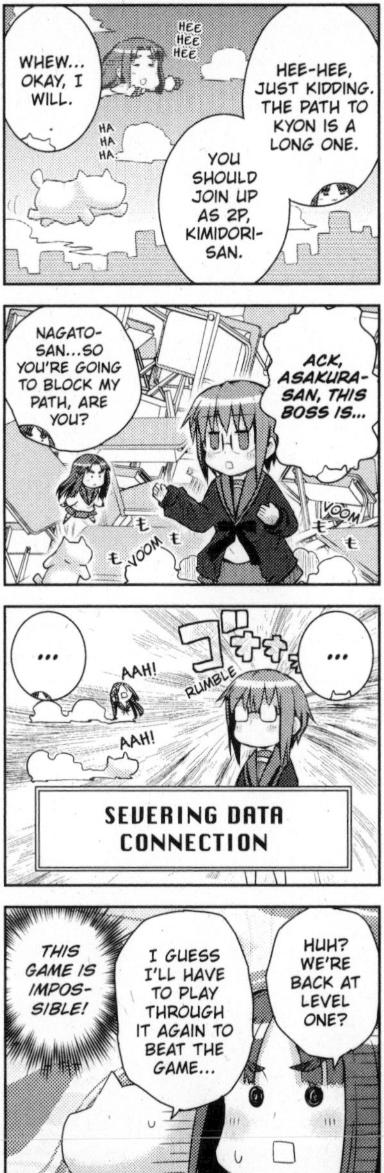
HEE-HEE, JUST KIDDING. THE PATH TO KYON IS A LONG ONE.
HEE HEE HEE
YOU SHOULD JOIN UP AS 2P, KIMIDORI-SAN.
WHEW... OKAY, I WILL.
HA HA HA
ACK, ASAKURA-SAN, THIS BOSS IS...
NAGATO-SAN...SO YOU'RE GOING TO BLOCK MY PATH, ARE YOU?
VOOM
VOOM
...
RUMBLE
...
AAH!
AAH!
SEVERING DATA CONNECTION
HUH? WE'RE BACK AT LEVEL ONE?
I GUESS I'LL HAVE TO PLAY THROUGH IT AGAIN TO BEAT THE GAME...
THIS GAME IS IMPOSSIBLE!

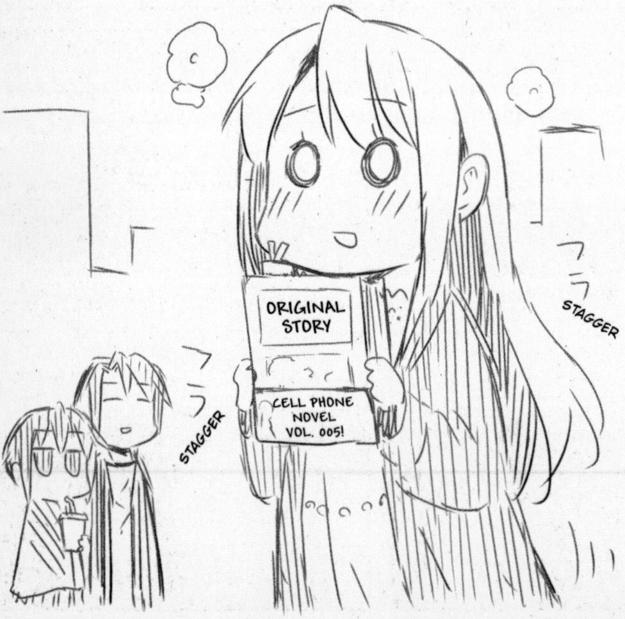
フラ
STAGGER
ORIGINAL STORY
CELL PHONE NOVEL VOL. 005!
フラ
STAGGER

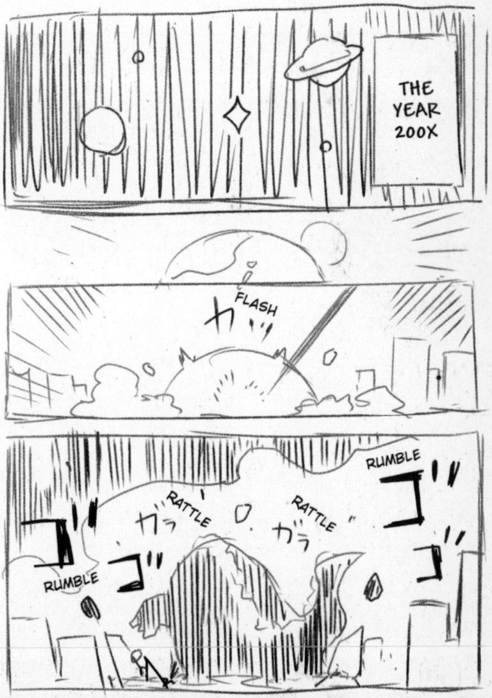
THE YEAR 200X
FLASH
RUMBLE
RATTLE
RATTLE
RUMBLE

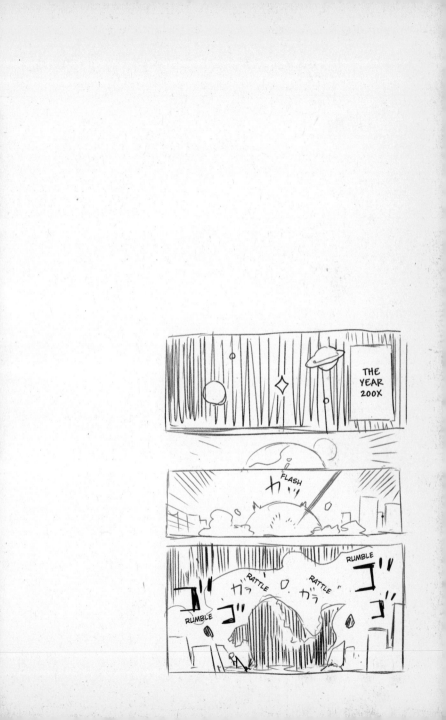

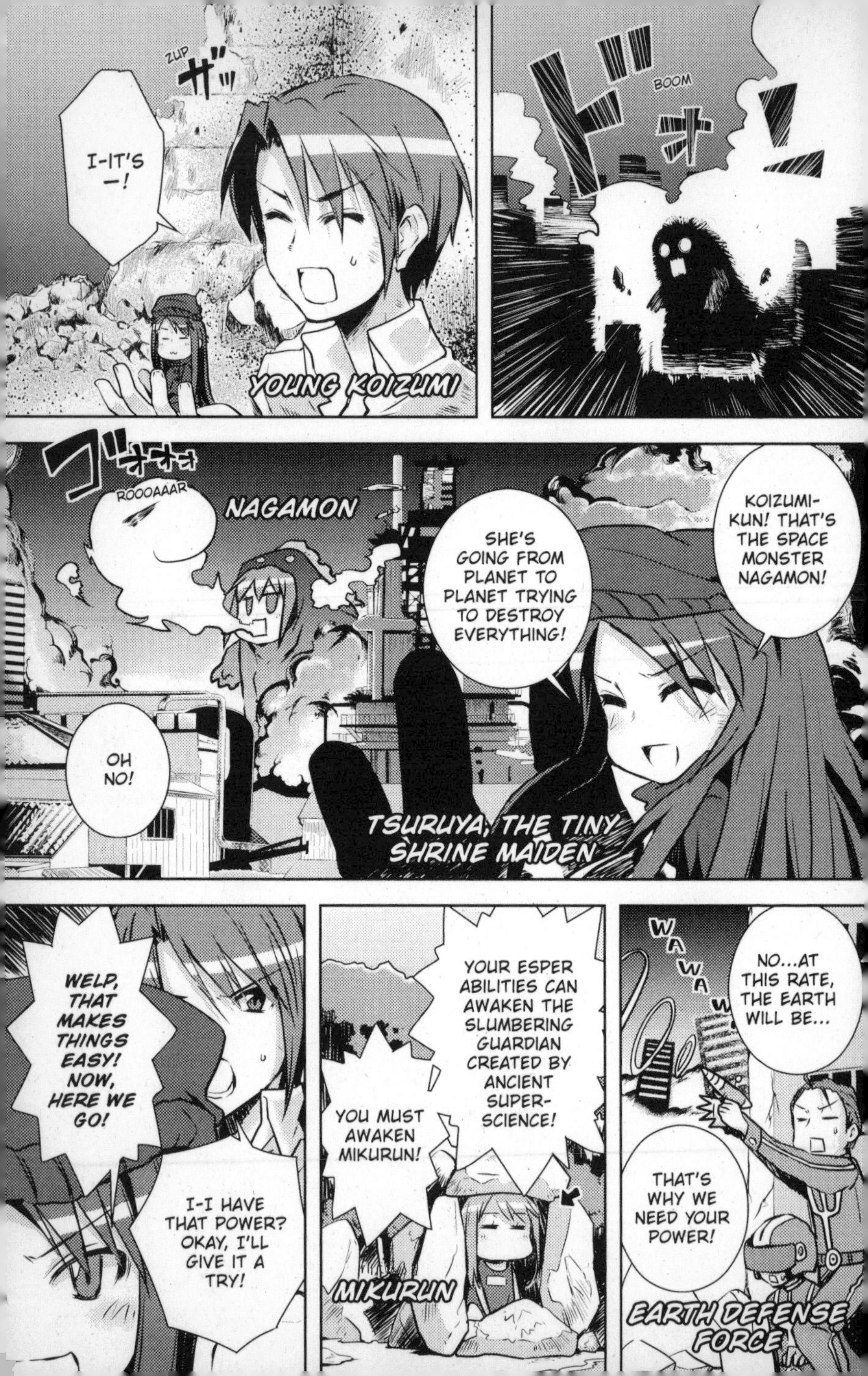
BOOM
ZUP
I-IT'S —!
YOUNG KOIZUMI
KOIZUMI-KUN! THAT'S THE SPACE MONSTER NAGAMON!
SHE'S GOING FROM PLANET TO PLANET TRYING TO DESTROY EVERYTHING!
TSURUYA, THE TINY SHRINE MAIDEN
NAGAMON
ROOOAAAR
OH NO!
WAWAWA
NO...AT THIS RATE, THE EARTH WILL BE...
THAT'S WHY WE NEED YOUR POWER!
EARTH DEFENSE FORCE
YOUR ESPER ABILITIES CAN AWAKEN THE SLUMBERING GUARDIAN CREATED BY ANCIENT SUPER-SCIENCE!
YOU MUST AWAKEN MIKURUN!
MIKURUN
WELP, THAT MAKES THINGS EASY! NOW, HERE WE GO!
I-I HAVE THAT POWER? OKAY, I'LL GIVE IT A TRY!

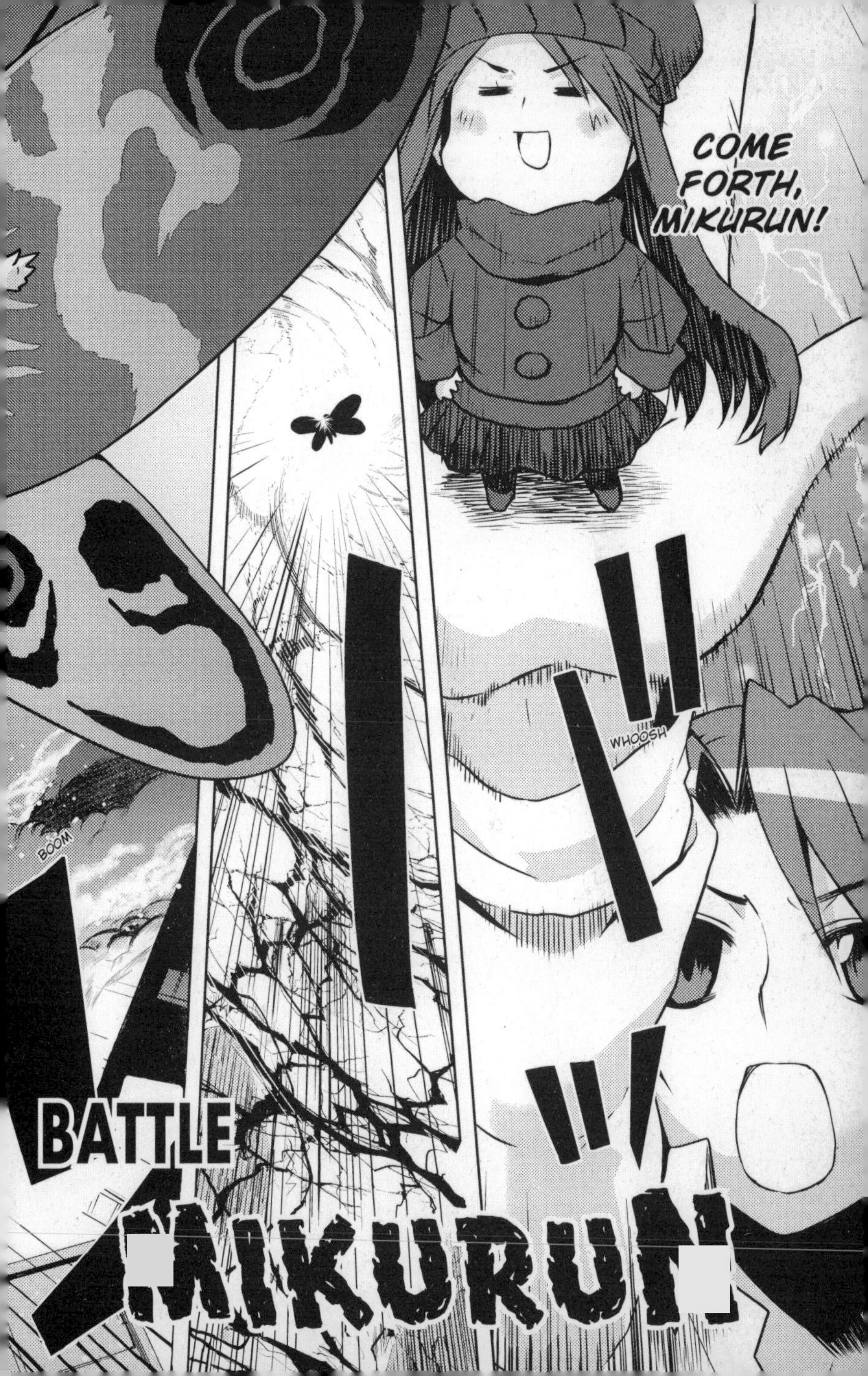
COME FORTH, MIKURUN!
WHOOSH
BOOM
BATTLE
MIKURUN

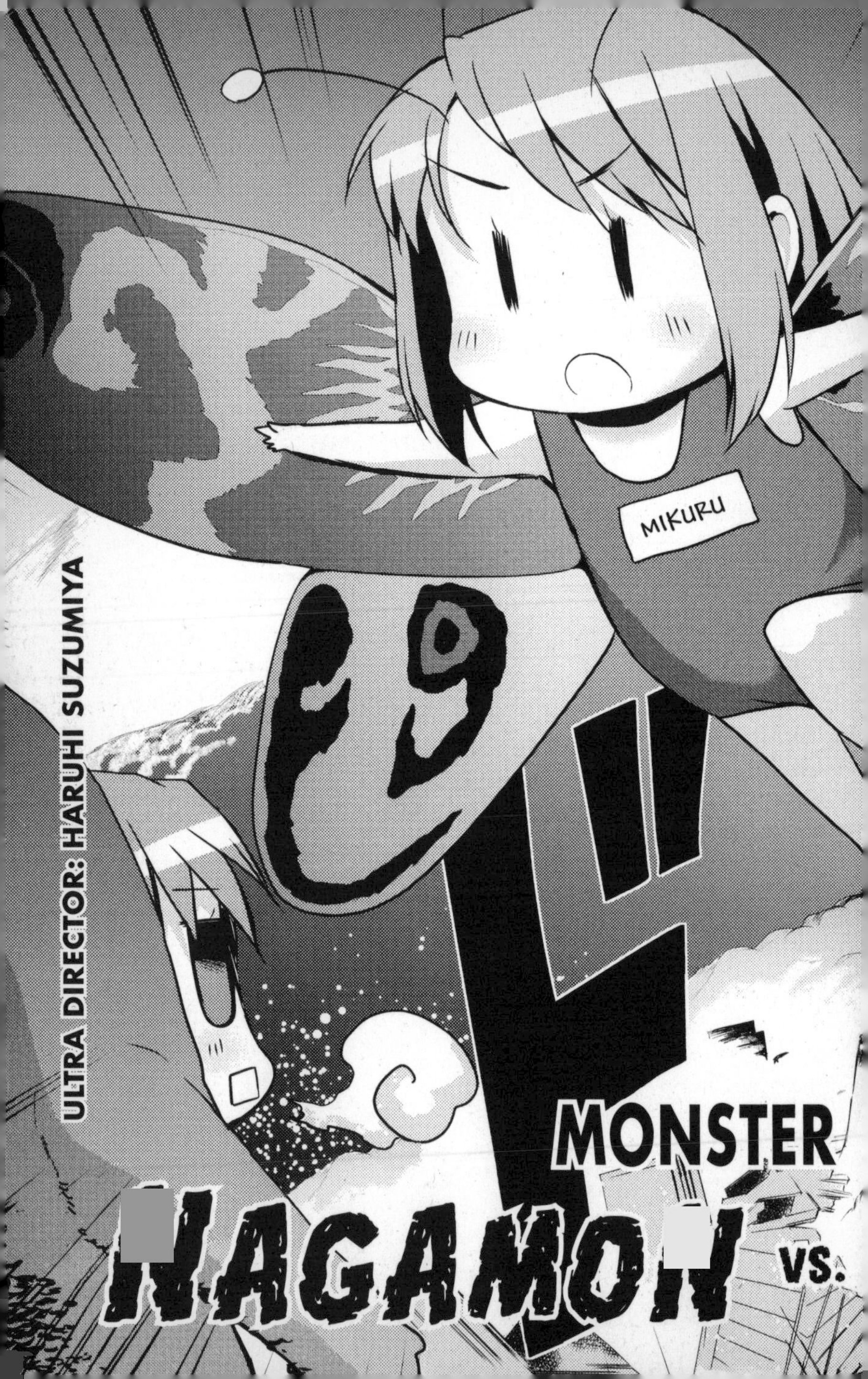
MIKURU
ULTRA DIRECTOR: HARUHI SUZUMIYA
MONSTER
NAGAMON
VS.

CUT HERE

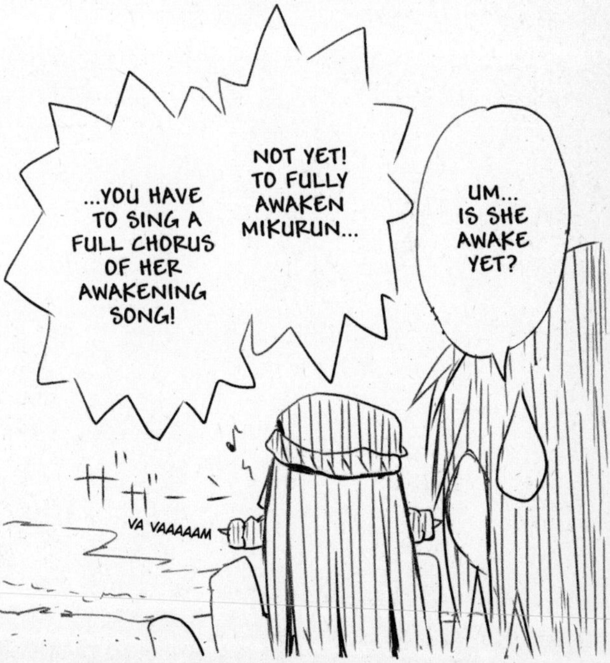
UM... IS SHE AWAKE YET?
NOT YET! TO FULLY AWAKEN MIKURUN...
...YOU HAVE TO SING A FULL CHORUS OF HER AWAKENING SONG!
VA VAAAAAM

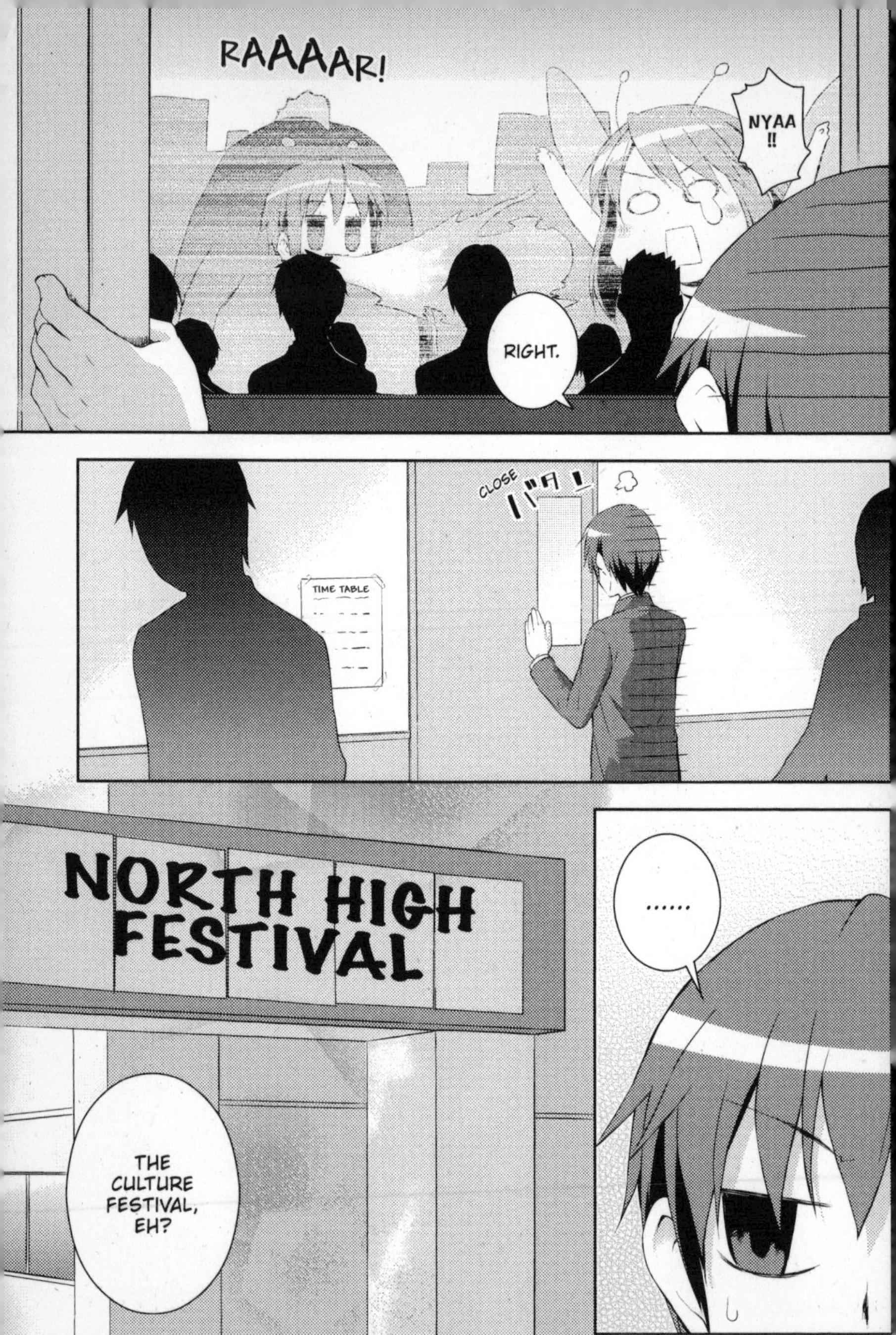
NYAA !!
RAAAAR!
RIGHT.
CLOSE
バタン
TIME TABLE
......
NORTH HIGH FESTIVAL
THE CULTURE FESTIVAL, EH?

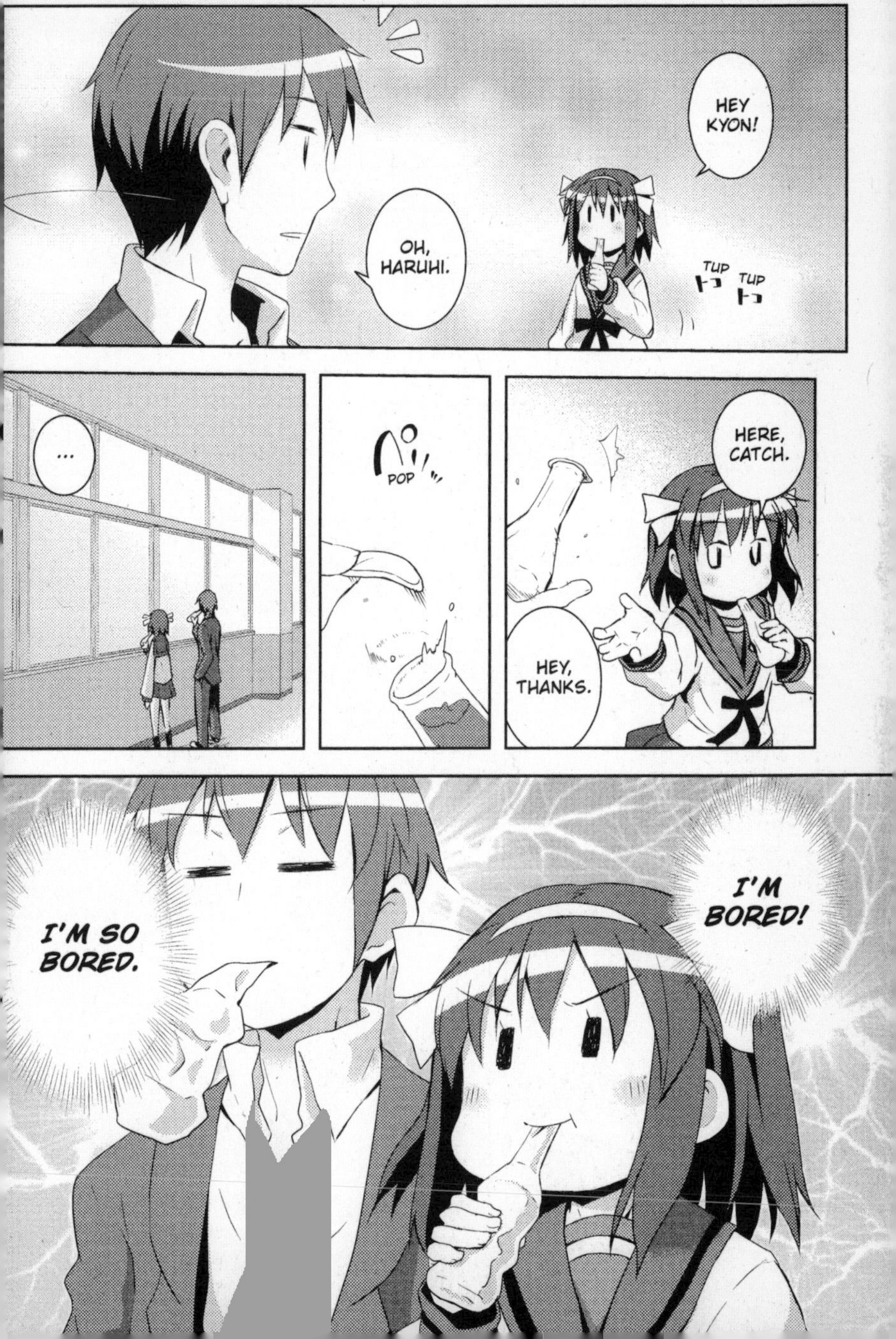
HEY KYON!
OH, HARUHI.
TUP トコ
TUP トコ
HERE, CATCH.
HEY, THANKS.
POP
...
I'M BORED!
I'M SO BORED.

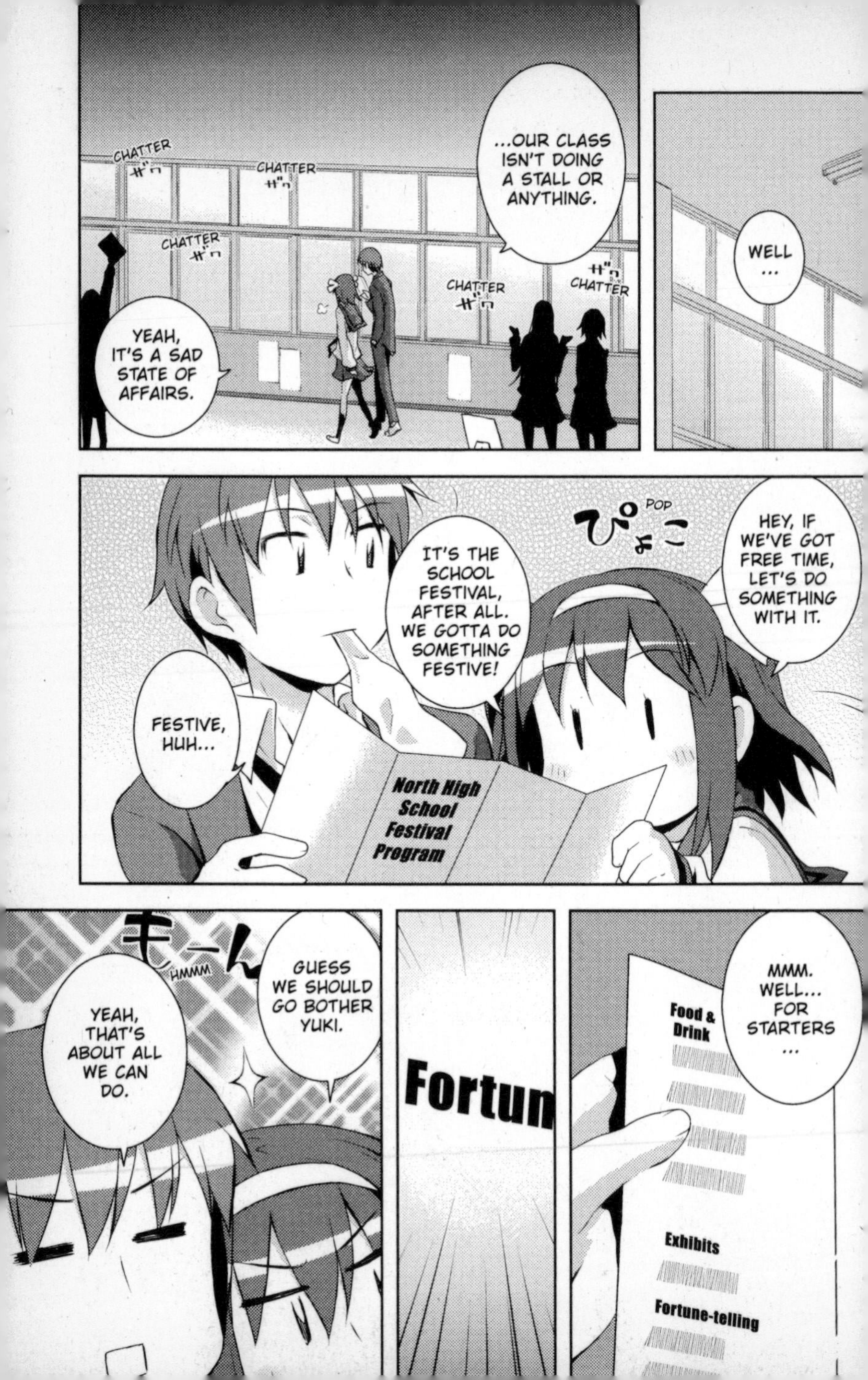
WELL ...
...OUR CLASS ISN'T DOING A STALL OR ANYTHING.
CHATTER
CHATTER
CHATTER
CHATTER
CHATTER
YEAH, IT'S A SAD STATE OF AFFAIRS.
POP
HEY, IF WE'VE GOT FREE TIME, LET'S DO SOMETHING WITH IT.
IT'S THE SCHOOL FESTIVAL, AFTER ALL. WE GOTTA DO SOMETHING FESTIVE!
FESTIVE, HUH...
North High School Festival Program
MMM. WELL... FOR STARTERS ...
Food & Drink
Exhibits
Fortune-telling
Fortun
HMMM
GUESS WE SHOULD GO BOTHER YUKI.
YEAH, THAT'S ABOUT ALL WE CAN DO.

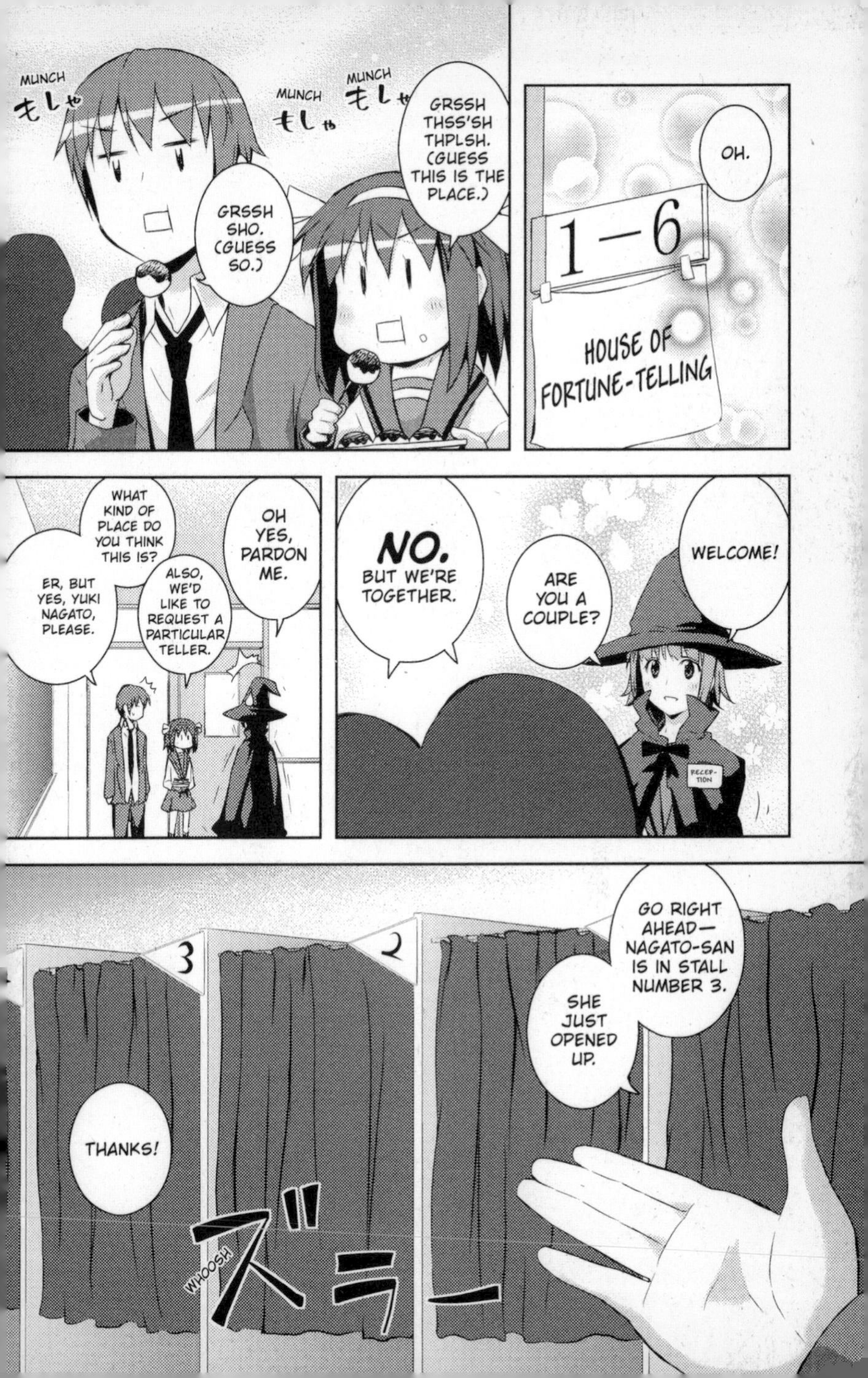
OH.
1—6
HOUSE OF FORTUNE-TELLING
GRSSH THSS'SH THPLSH. (GUESS THIS IS THE PLACE.)
MUNCH もしゃ
MUNCH もしゃ
GRSSH SHO. (GUESS SO.)
MUNCH もしゃ
WELCOME!
ARE YOU A COUPLE?
RECEPTION
NO. BUT WE'RE TOGETHER.
WHAT KIND OF PLACE DO YOU THINK THIS IS?
OH YES, PARDON ME.
ALSO, WE'D LIKE TO REQUEST A PARTICULAR TELLER.
ER, BUT YES, YUKI NAGATO, PLEASE.
GO RIGHT AHEAD—NAGATO-SAN IS IN STALL NUMBER 3.
SHE JUST OPENED UP.
2
3
THANKS!
WHOOSH ズラー

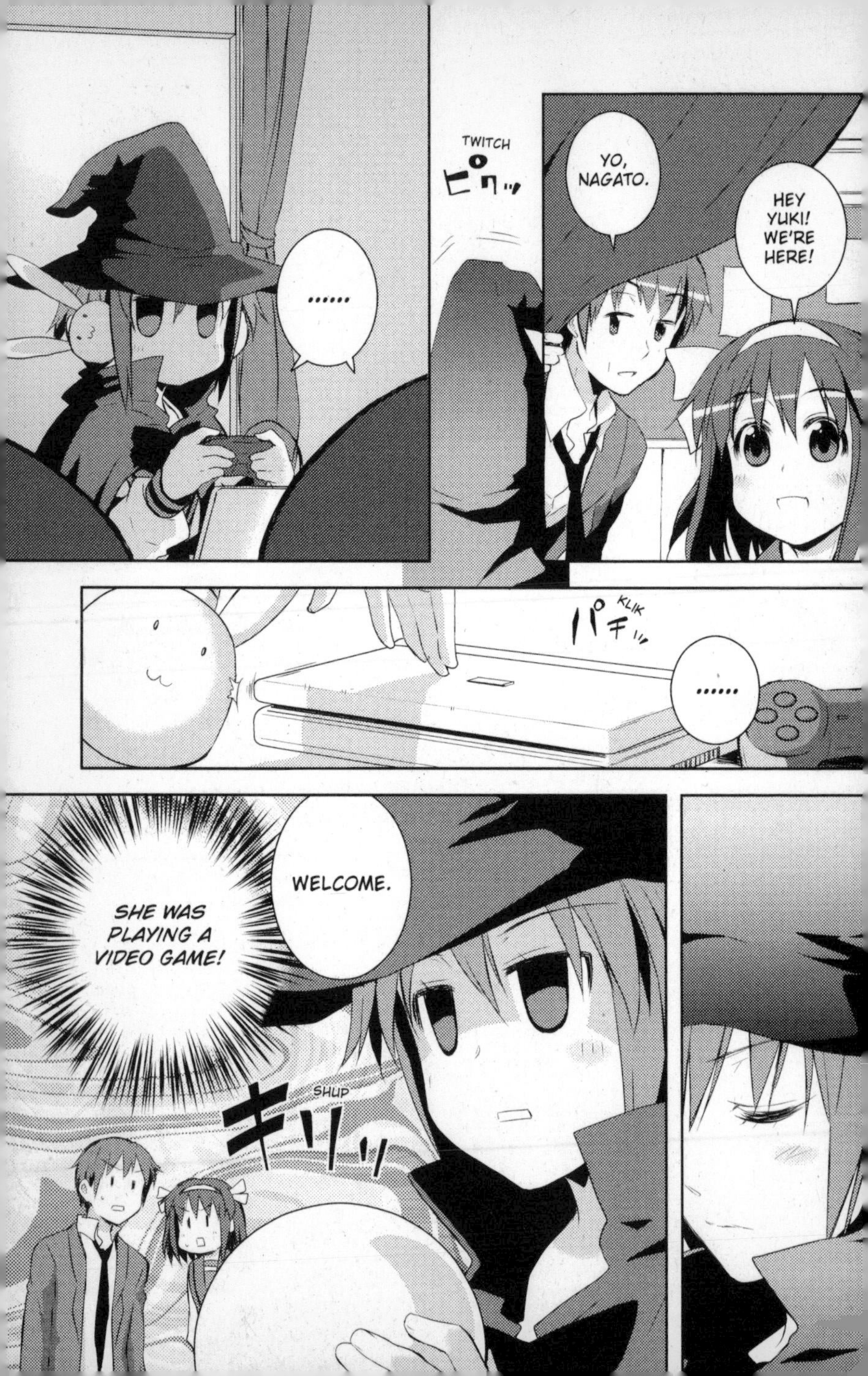
HEY YUKI! WE'RE HERE!
YO, NAGATO.
TWITCH
ピクッ
......
KLIK
パチッ
......
WELCOME.
SHE WAS PLAYING A VIDEO GAME!
SHUP
キリッ

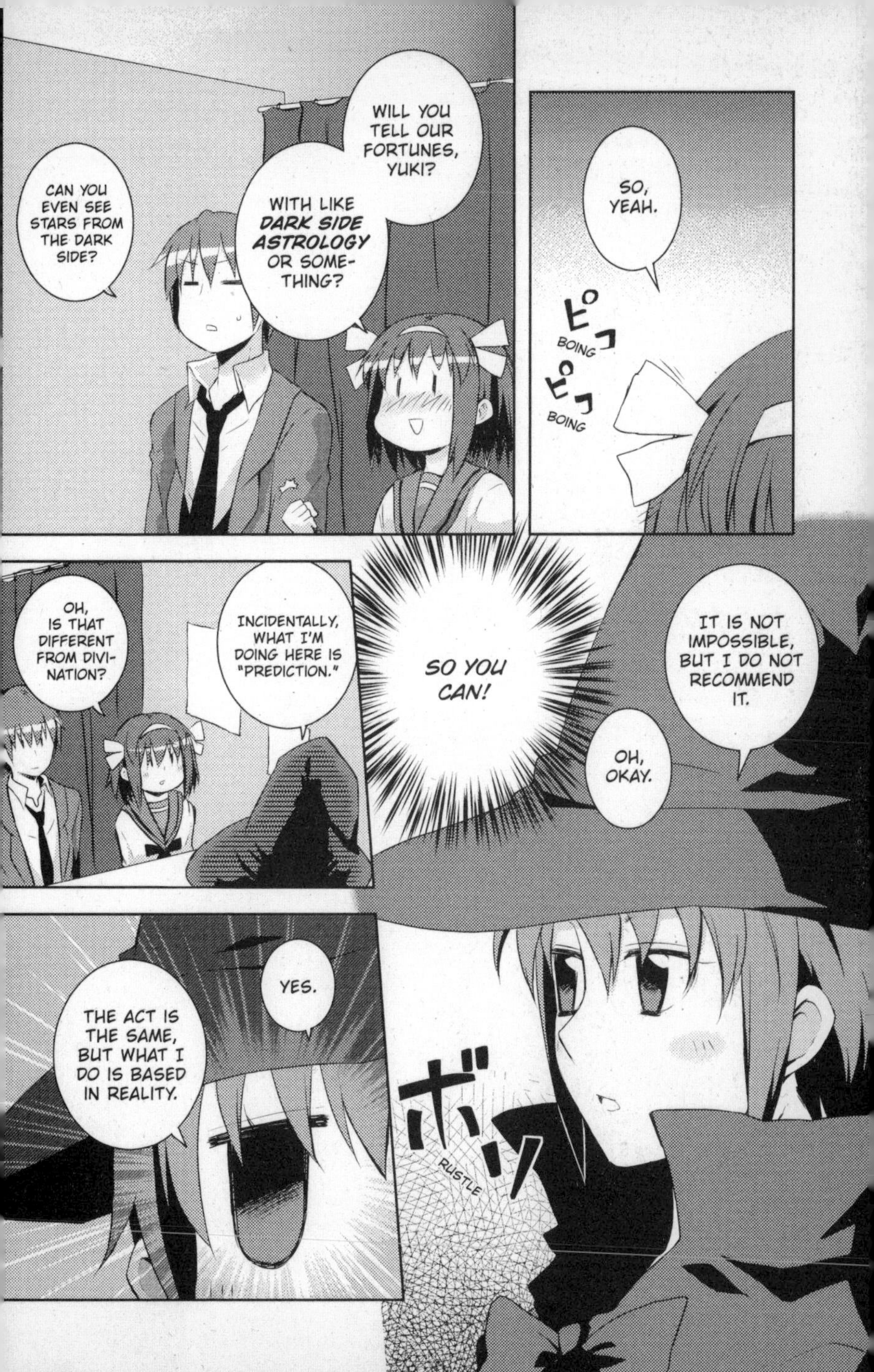
SO, YEAH.
ピコ
BOING
ピコ
BOING
WILL YOU TELL OUR FORTUNES, YUKI?
WITH LIKE *DARK SIDE ASTROLOGY* OR SOME-THING?
CAN YOU EVEN SEE STARS FROM THE DARK SIDE?
IT IS NOT IMPOSSIBLE, BUT I DO NOT RECOMMEND IT.
SO YOU CAN!
OH, OKAY.
INCIDENTALLY, WHAT I'M DOING HERE IS "PREDICTION."
OH, IS THAT DIFFERENT FROM DIVI-NATION?
ガッ
RUSTLE
YES.
THE ACT IS THE SAME, BUT WHAT I DO IS BASED IN REALITY.

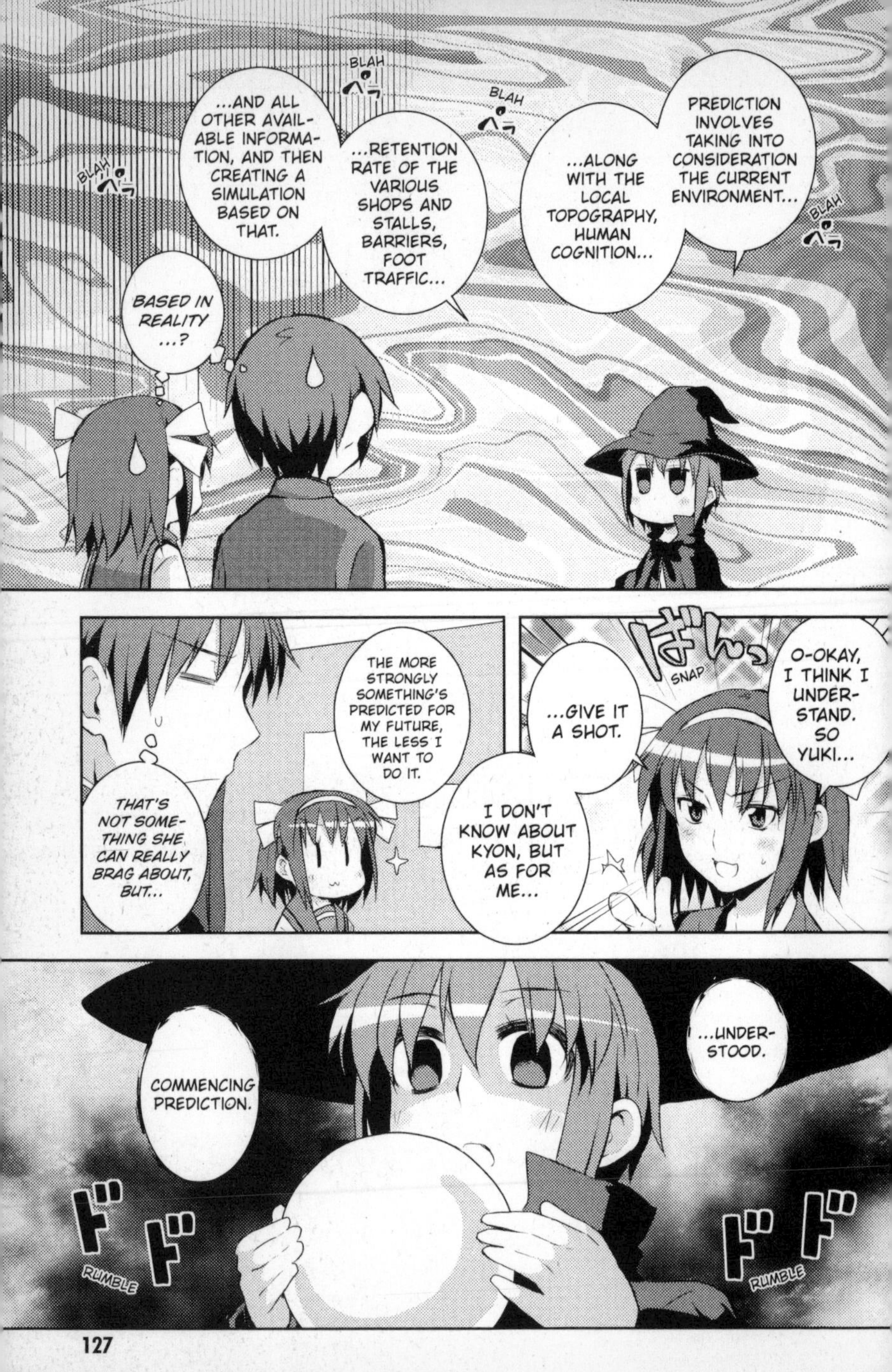
BLAH
PREDICTION INVOLVES TAKING INTO CONSIDERATION THE CURRENT ENVIRONMENT...
...ALONG WITH THE LOCAL TOPOGRAPHY, HUMAN COGNITION...
BLAH
...RETENTION RATE OF THE VARIOUS SHOPS AND STALLS, BARRIERS, FOOT TRAFFIC...
BLAH
...AND ALL OTHER AVAIL-ABLE INFORMA-TION, AND THEN CREATING A SIMULATION BASED ON THAT.
BLAH
BASED IN REALITY ...?
ばんっ
SNAP
O-OKAY, I THINK I UNDER-STAND. SO YUKI...
...GIVE IT A SHOT.
I DON'T KNOW ABOUT KYON, BUT AS FOR ME...
THE MORE STRONGLY SOMETHING'S PREDICTED FOR MY FUTURE, THE LESS I WANT TO DO IT.
THAT'S NOT SOME-THING SHE CAN REALLY BRAG ABOUT, BUT...
...UNDER-STOOD.
COMMENCING PREDICTION.
ドド
RUMBLE
ドド
RUMBLE

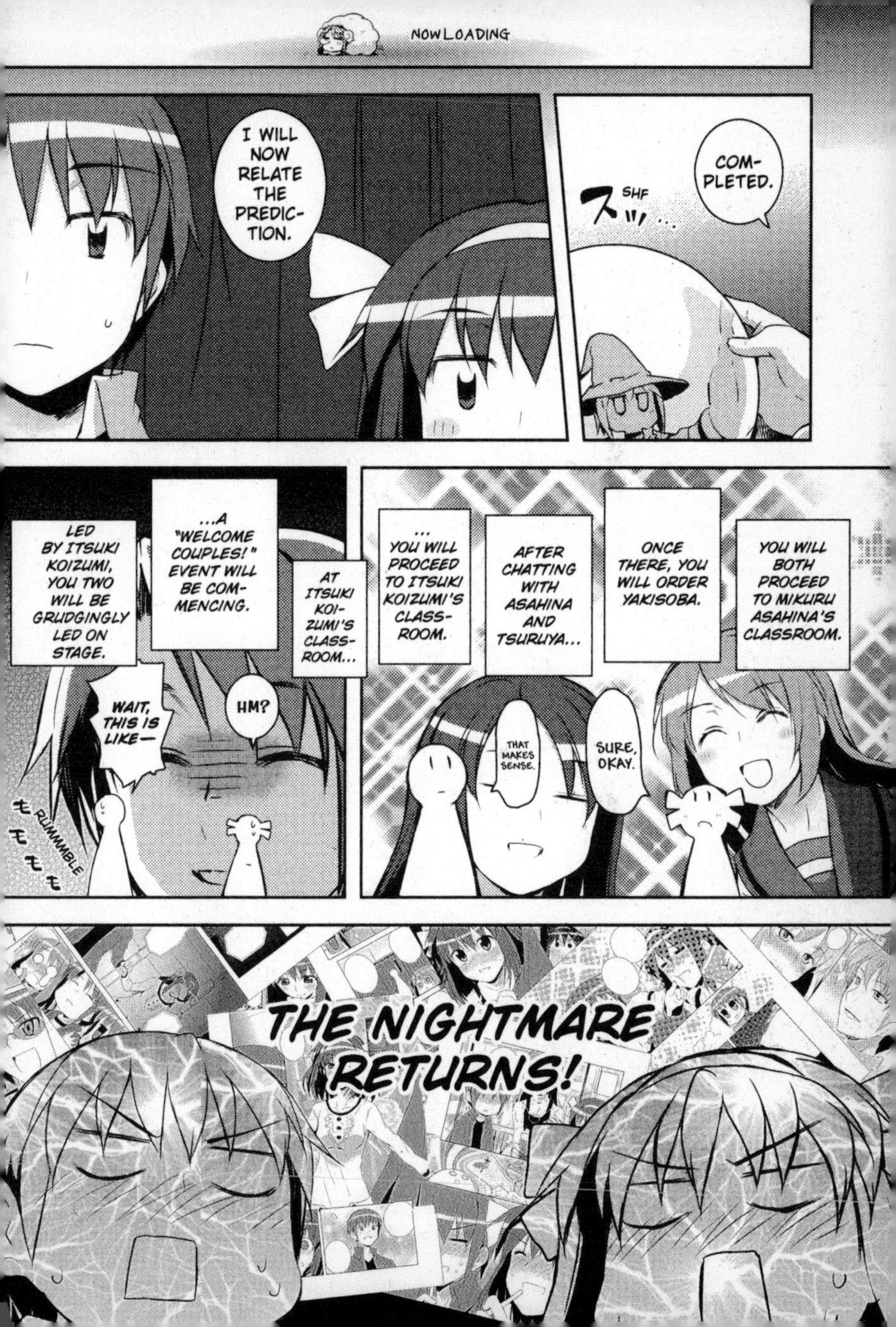
NOW LOADING
COM-PLETED.
SHF
I WILL NOW RELATE THE PREDICTION.
YOU WILL BOTH PROCEED TO MIKURU ASAHINA'S CLASSROOM.
ONCE THERE, YOU WILL ORDER YAKISOBA.
AFTER CHATTING WITH ASAHINA AND TSURUYA...
...YOU WILL PROCEED TO ITSUKI KOIZUMI'S CLASSROOM.
SURE, OKAY.
THAT MAKES SENSE.
AT ITSUKI KOIZUMI'S CLASSROOM...
...A "WELCOME COUPLES!" EVENT WILL BE COM-MENCING.
LED BY ITSUKI KOIZUMI, YOU TWO WILL BE GRUDGINGLY LED ON STAGE.
HM?
WAIT, THIS IS LIKE—
RUMMMBLE
THE NIGHTMARE RETURNS!

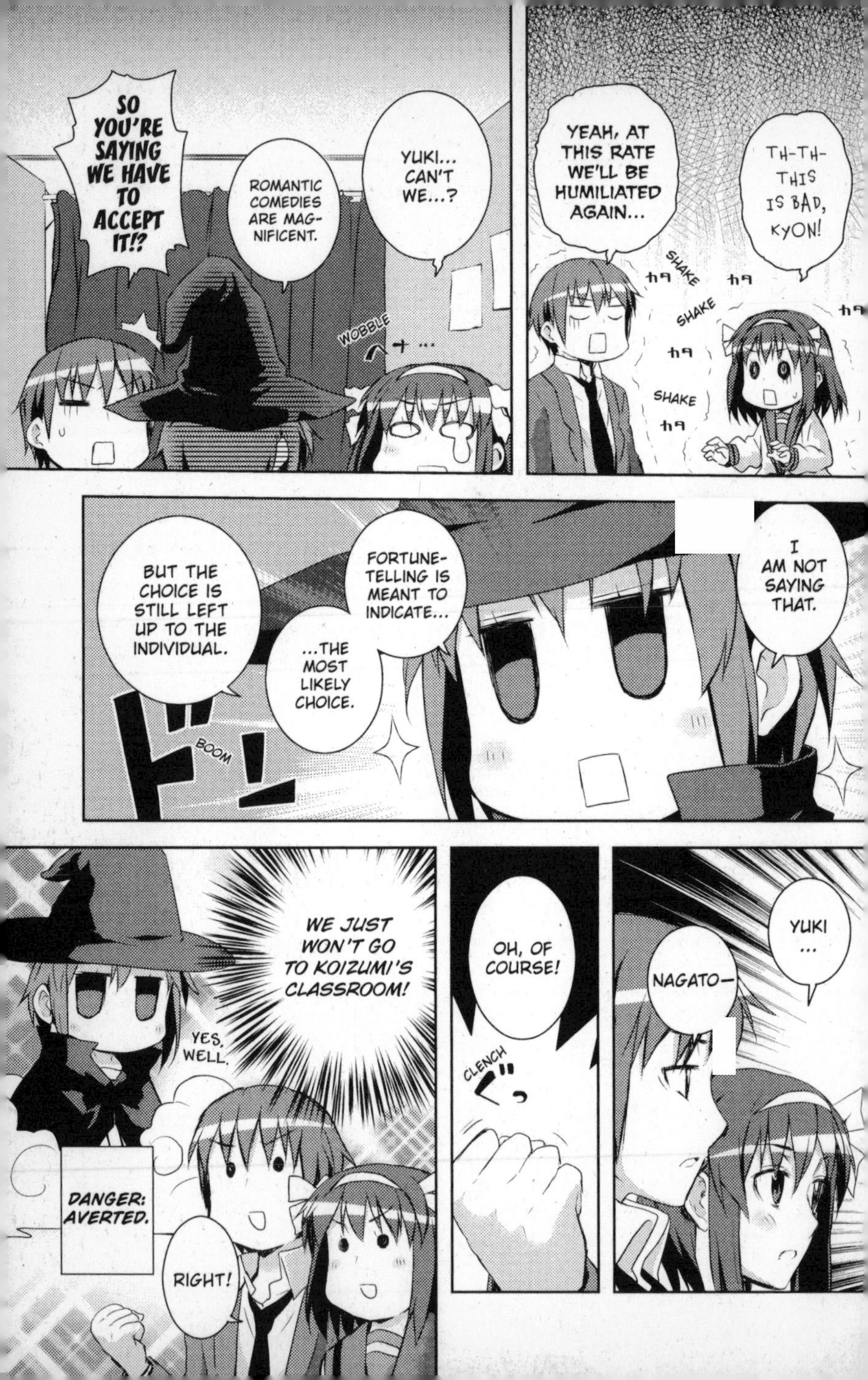
TH-TH-THIS IS BAD, KYON!
YEAH, AT THIS RATE WE'LL BE HUMILIATED AGAIN...
SHAKE
SHAKE
SHAKE
YUKI... CAN'T WE...?
ROMANTIC COMEDIES ARE MAG-NIFICENT.
SO YOU'RE SAYING WE HAVE TO ACCEPT IT!?
WOBBLE
I AM NOT SAYING THAT.
FORTUNE-TELLING IS MEANT TO INDICATE...
...THE MOST LIKELY CHOICE.
BUT THE CHOICE IS STILL LEFT UP TO THE INDIVIDUAL.
BOOM
YUKI...
NAGATO—
OH, OF COURSE!
CLENCH
WE JUST WON'T GO TO KOIZUMI'S CLASSROOM!
YES, WELL.
RIGHT!
DANGER: AVERTED.

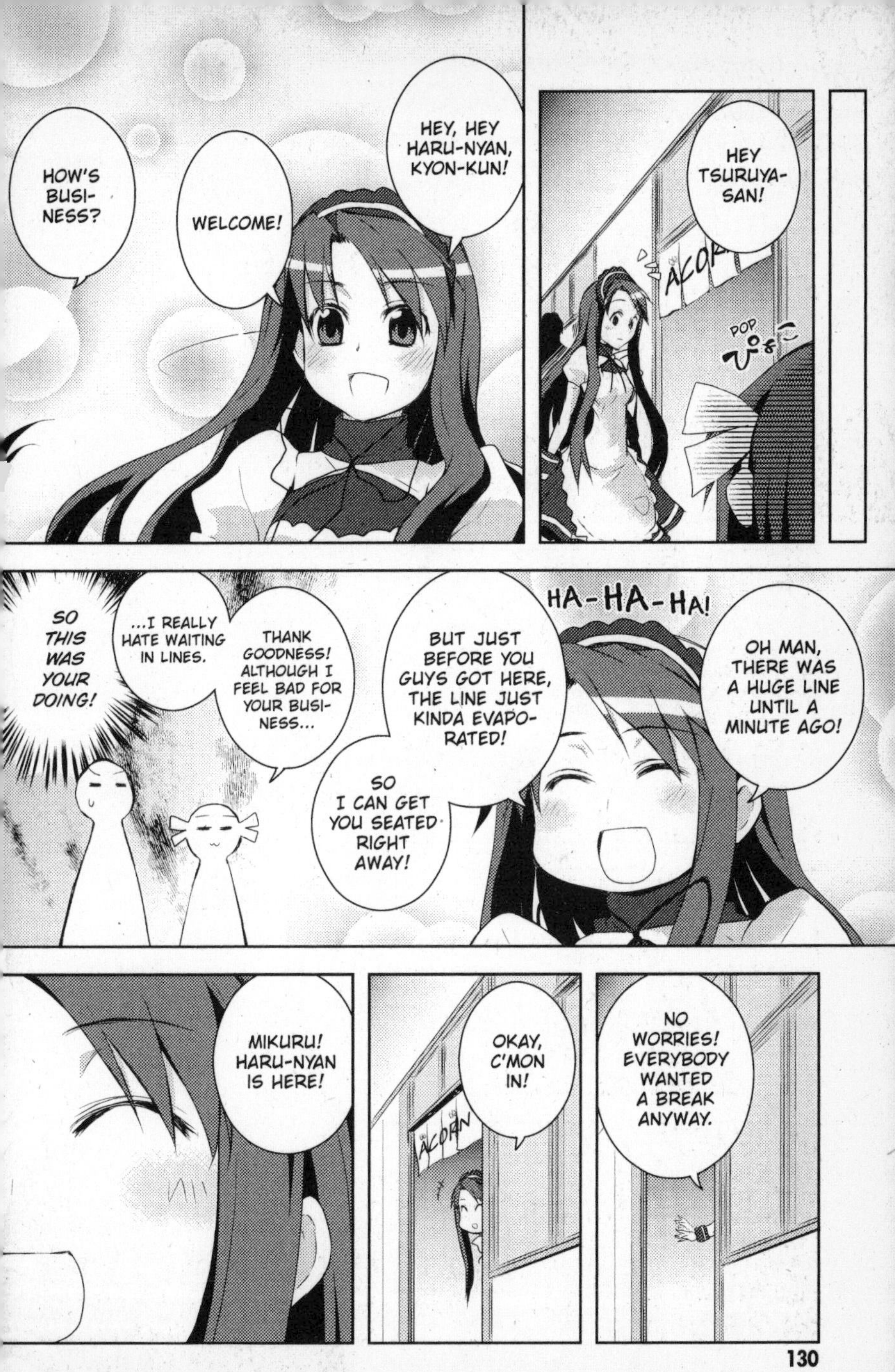

HEY TSURUYA-SAN!
ACORN
POP
HEY, HEY HARU-NYAN, KYON-KUN!
WELCOME!
HOW'S BUSINESS?
HA-HA-HA!
OH MAN, THERE WAS A HUGE LINE UNTIL A MINUTE AGO!
BUT JUST BEFORE YOU GUYS GOT HERE, THE LINE JUST KINDA EVAPORATED!
SO I CAN GET YOU SEATED RIGHT AWAY!
THANK GOODNESS! ALTHOUGH I FEEL BAD FOR YOUR BUSINESS...
...I REALLY HATE WAITING IN LINES.
SO THIS WAS YOUR DOING!
NO WORRIES! EVERYBODY WANTED A BREAK ANYWAY.
OKAY, C'MON IN!
ACORN
MIKURU! HARU-NYAN IS HERE!

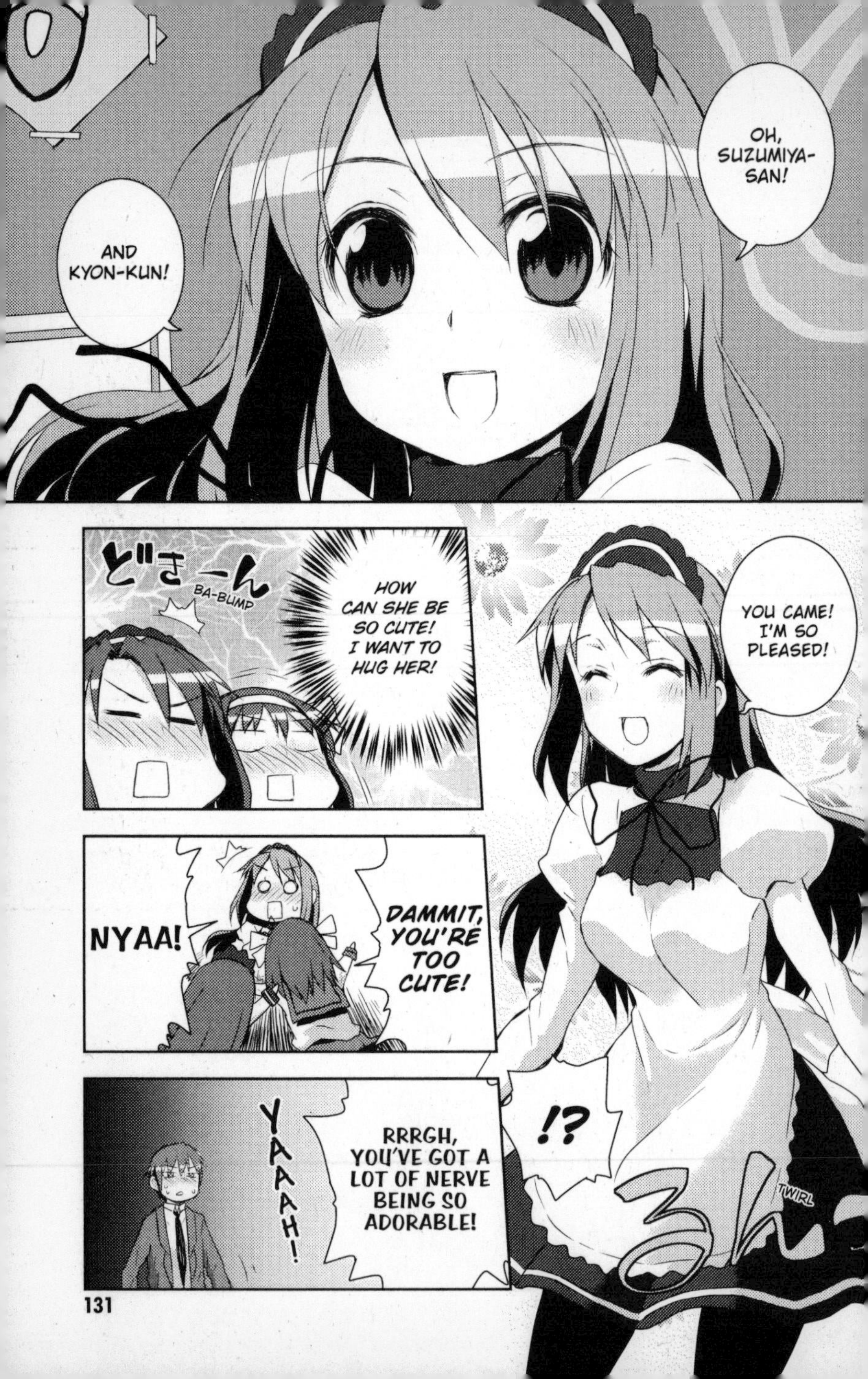
OH, SUZUMIYA-SAN!
AND KYON-KUN!
YOU CAME! I'M SO PLEASED!
TWIRL
どきーん
BA-BUMP
HOW CAN SHE BE SO CUTE! I WANT TO HUG HER!
DAMMIT, YOU'RE TOO CUTE!
NYAA!
!?
RRRGH, YOU'VE GOT A LOT OF NERVE BEING SO ADORABLE!
YAAAH!

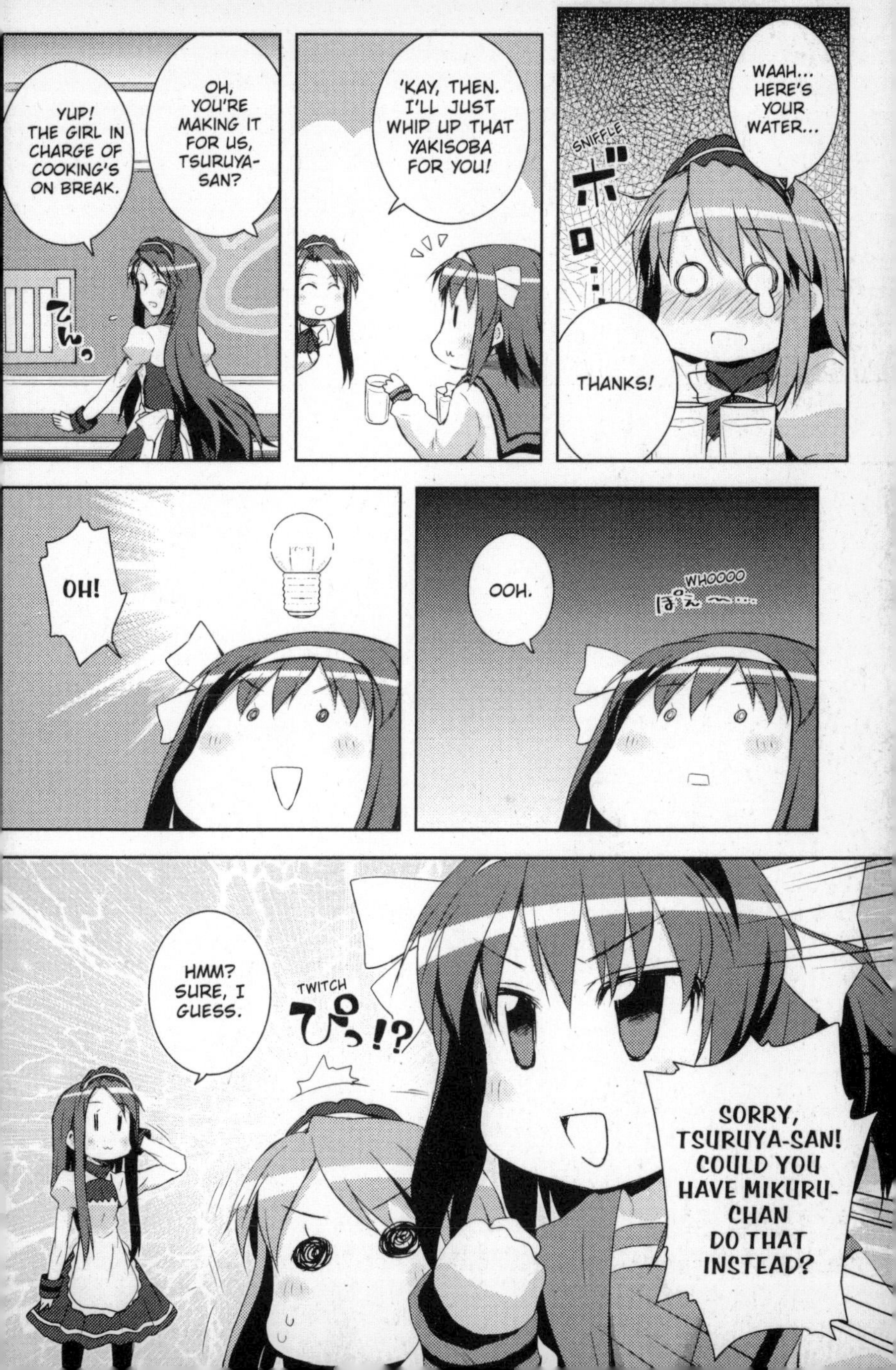
WAAH... HERE'S YOUR WATER...
SNIFFLE
ボロ…
THANKS!
'KAY, THEN. I'LL JUST WHIP UP THAT YAKISOBA FOR YOU!
OH, YOU'RE MAKING IT FOR US, TSURUYA-SAN?
YUP! THE GIRL IN CHARGE OF COOKING'S ON BREAK.
てんっ
WHOOOO
ぽえ〜…
OOH.
OH!
SORRY, TSURUYA-SAN! COULD YOU HAVE MIKURU-CHAN DO THAT INSTEAD?
TWITCH
ぴっ!?
HMM? SURE, I GUESS.

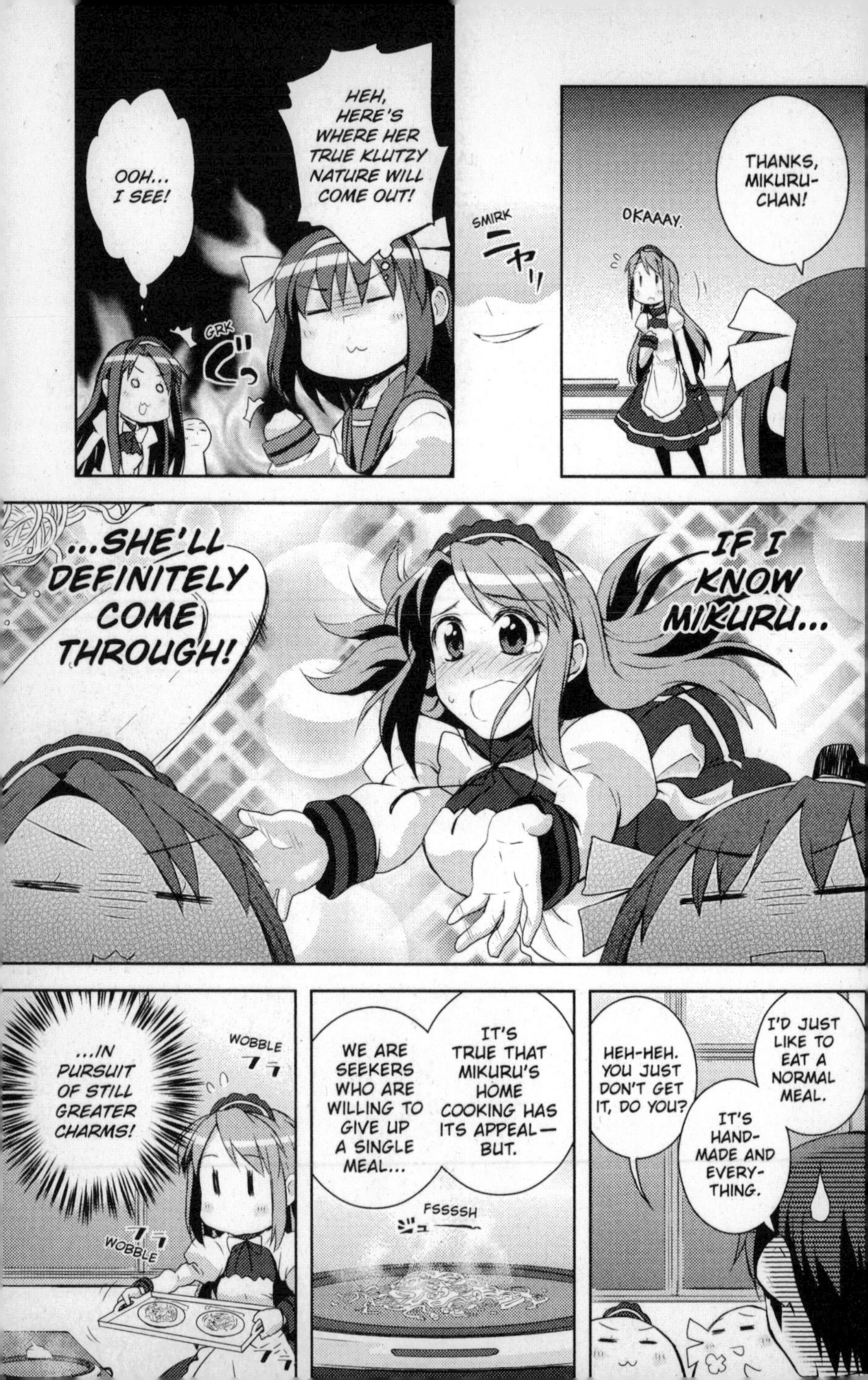
THANKS, MIKURU-CHAN!
OKAAAY.
SMIRK
HEH, HERE'S WHERE HER TRUE KLUTZY NATURE WILL COME OUT!
OOH... I SEE!
GRK
IF I KNOW MIKURU...
...SHE'LL DEFINITELY COME THROUGH!
I'D JUST LIKE TO EAT A NORMAL MEAL.
HEH-HEH. YOU JUST DON'T GET IT, DO YOU?
IT'S HAND-MADE AND EVERY-THING.
IT'S TRUE THAT MIKURU'S HOME COOKING HAS ITS APPEAL—BUT.
WE ARE SEEKERS WHO ARE WILLING TO GIVE UP A SINGLE MEAL...
FSSSSH
WOBBLE
...IN PURSUIT OF STILL GREATER CHARMS!
WOBBLE

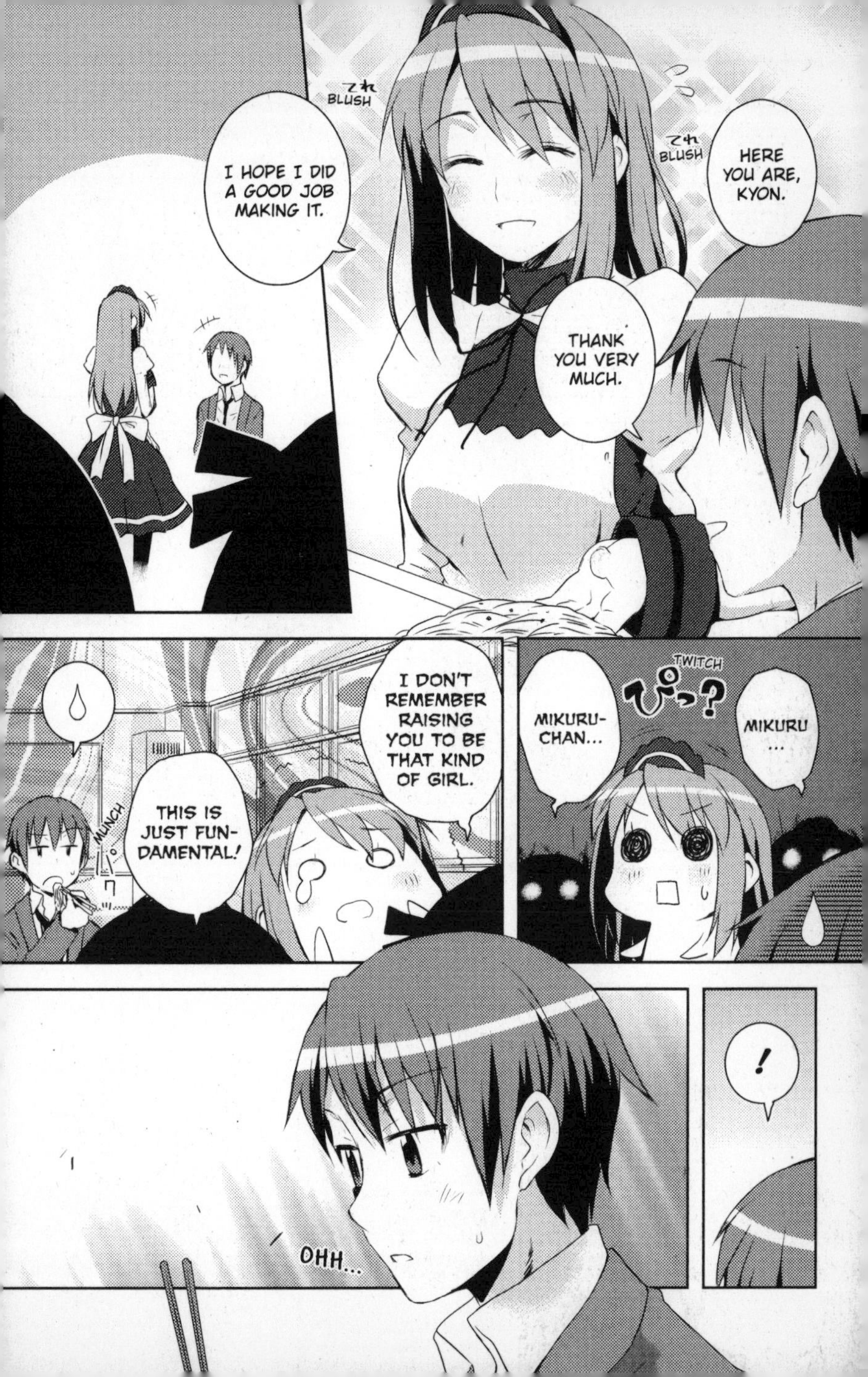
てれ
BLUSH
HERE YOU ARE, KYON.
THANK YOU VERY MUCH.
てれ
BLUSH
I HOPE I DID A GOOD JOB MAKING IT.
MIKURU...
TWITCH
MIKURU-CHAN...
I DON'T REMEMBER RAISING YOU TO BE THAT KIND OF GIRL.
THIS IS JUST FUN-DAMENTAL!
MUNCH
!
OHH...

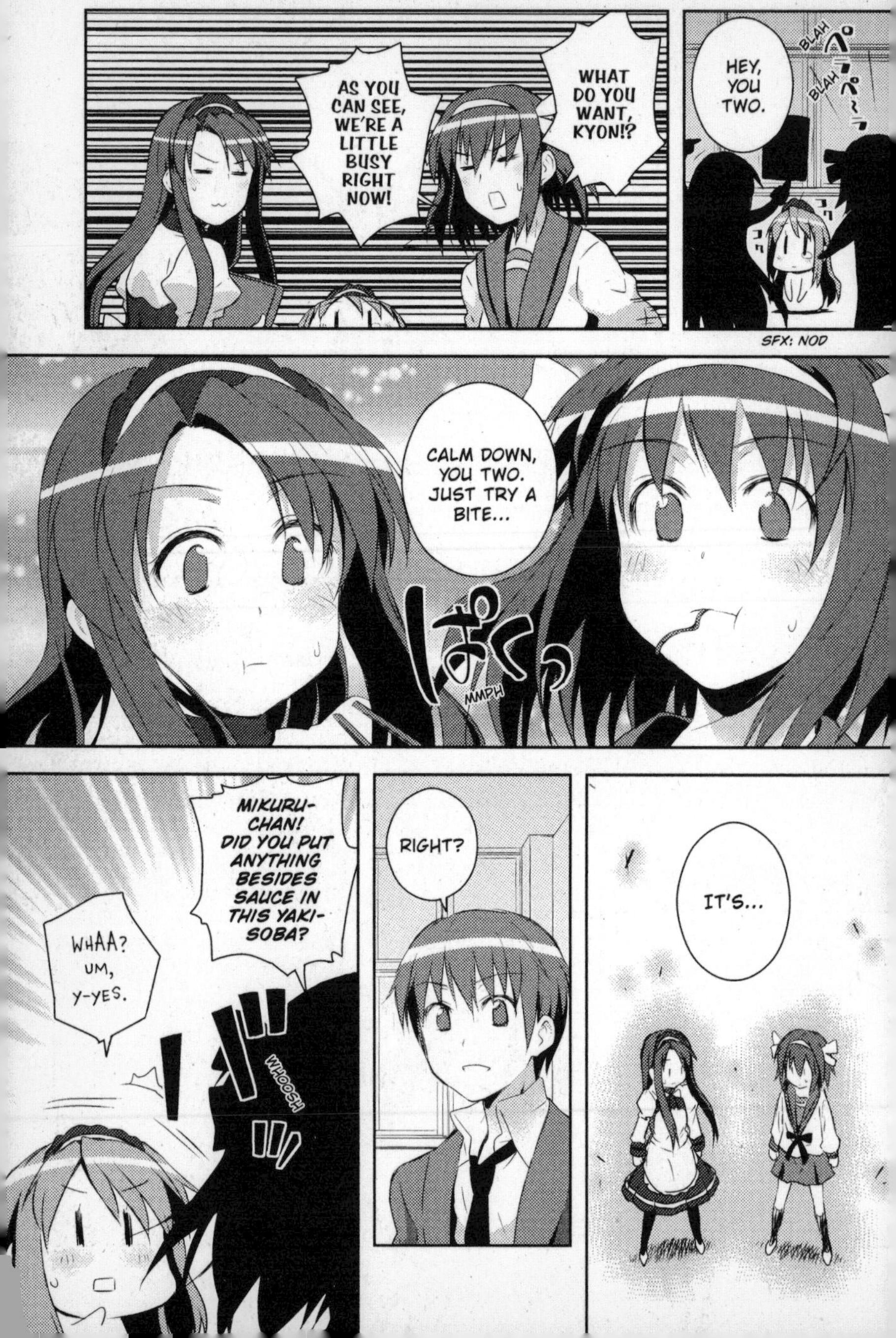
HEY, YOU TWO.
BLAH BLAH
SFX: NOD
WHAT DO YOU WANT, KYON!?
AS YOU CAN SEE, WE'RE A LITTLE BUSY RIGHT NOW!
CALM DOWN, YOU TWO. JUST TRY A BITE...
ぱくっ
MMPH
IT'S...
RIGHT?
MIKURU-CHAN! DID YOU PUT ANYTHING BESIDES SAUCE IN THIS YAKI-SOBA?
WHAA? UM, Y-YES.
WHOOSH

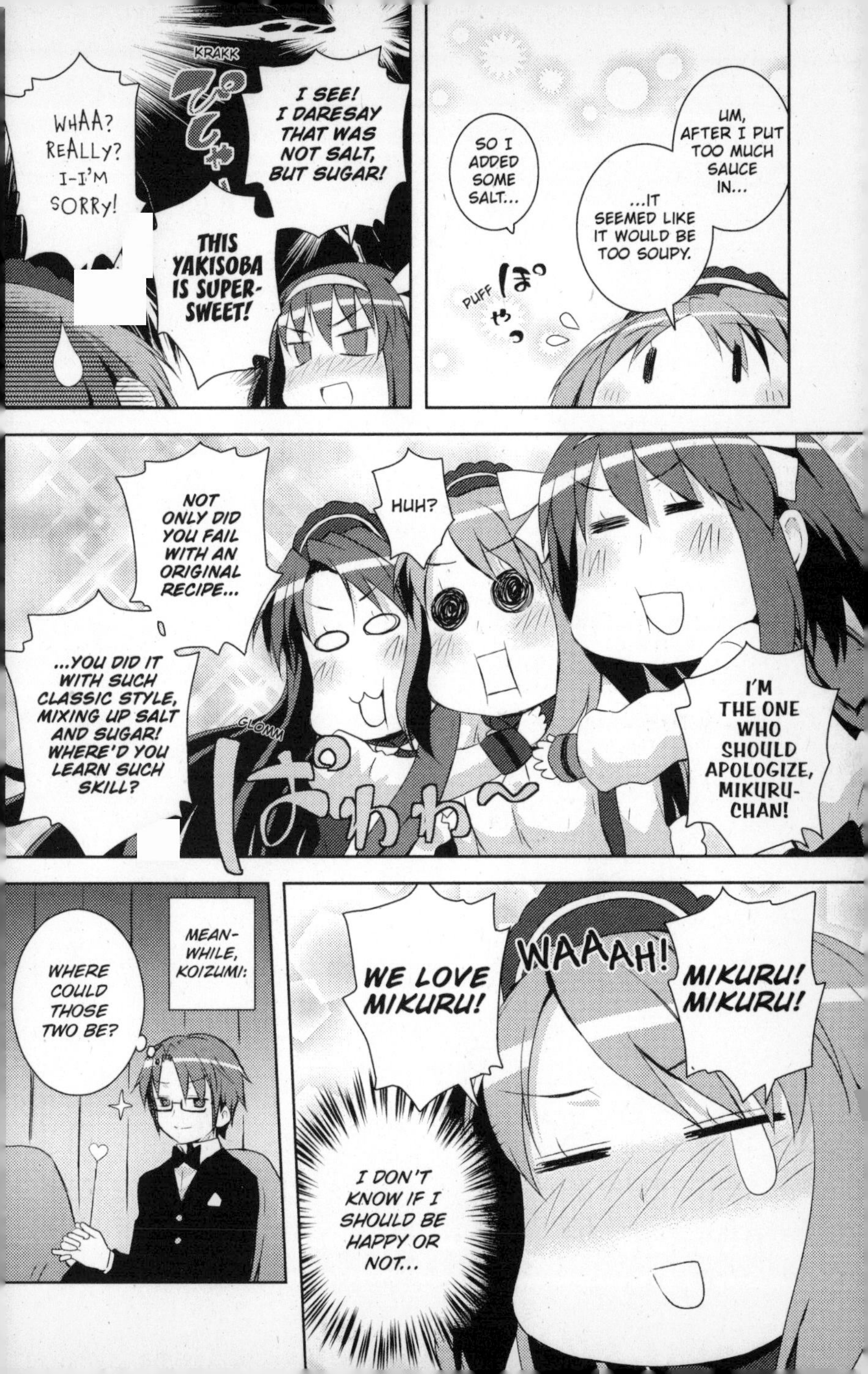
UM, AFTER I PUT TOO MUCH SAUCE IN...
...IT SEEMED LIKE IT WOULD BE TOO SOUPY.
SO I ADDED SOME SALT...
PUFF
ぽやっ
KRAKK
ぴしゃ
I SEE! I DARESAY THAT WAS NOT SALT, BUT SUGAR!
WHAA? REALLY? I-I'M SORRY!
THIS YAKISOBA IS SUPER-SWEET!
HUH?
NOT ONLY DID YOU FAIL WITH AN ORIGINAL RECIPE...
I'M THE ONE WHO SHOULD APOLOGIZE, MIKURU-CHAN!
...YOU DID IT WITH SUCH CLASSIC STYLE, MIXING UP SALT AND SUGAR! WHERE'D YOU LEARN SUCH SKILL?
GLOMM
おわわ～
MIKURU! MIKURU!
WAAAH!
WE LOVE MIKURU!
I DON'T KNOW IF I SHOULD BE HAPPY OR NOT...
MEAN-WHILE, KOIZUMI:
WHERE COULD THOSE TWO BE?

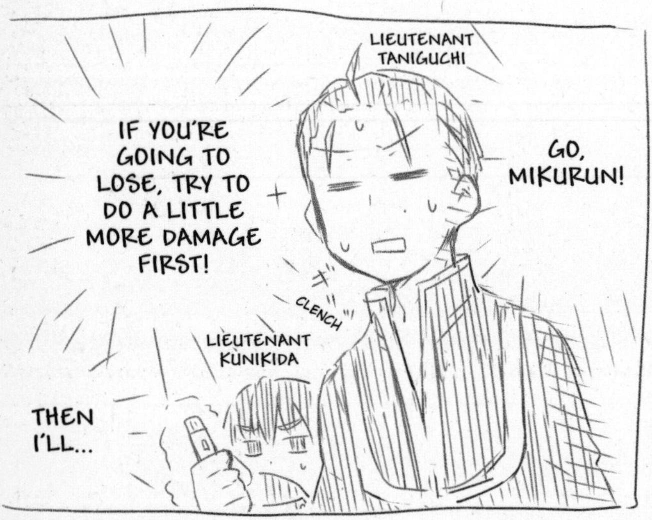
LIEUTENANT TANIGUCHI
GO, MIKURUN!
IF YOU'RE GOING TO LOSE, TRY TO DO A LITTLE MORE DAMAGE FIRST!
CLENCH
LIEUTENANT KUNIKIDA
THEN I'LL...

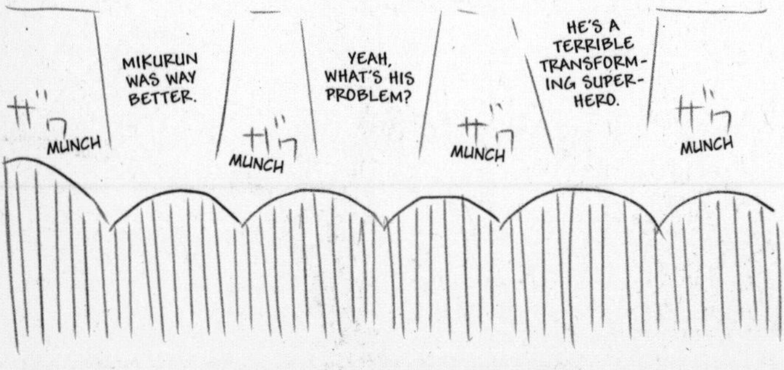
MUNCH
HE'S A TERRIBLE TRANSFORMING SUPERHERO.
MUNCH
YEAH, WHAT'S HIS PROBLEM?
MUNCH
MIKURUN WAS WAY BETTER.
MUNCH

THIS STORY RAN
IN ACE ASSAULT
MAGAZINE!

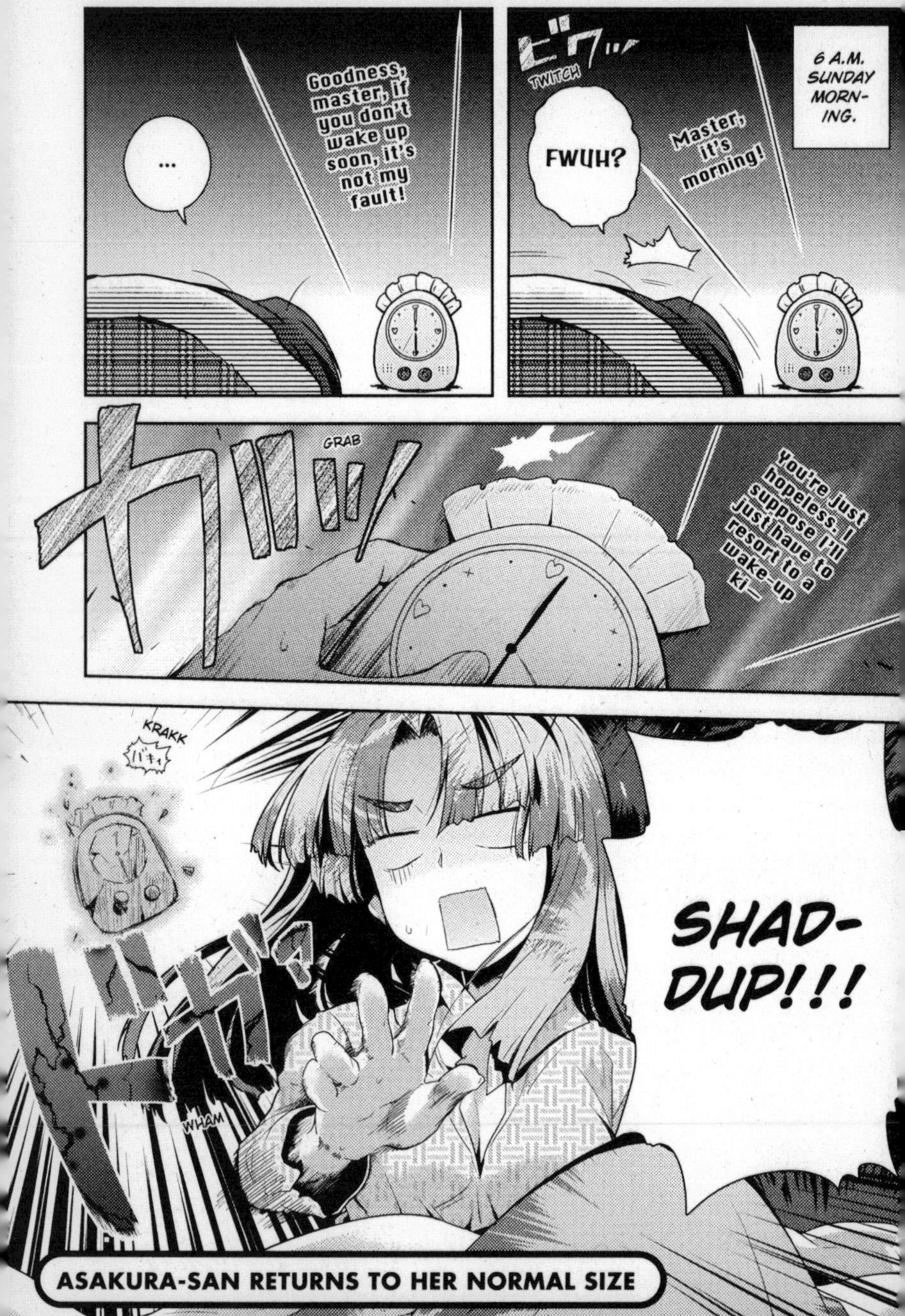
6 A.M. SUNDAY MORNING.
Master, it's morning!
FWUH?
ビクッ
TWITCH
Goodness, master, if you don't wake up soon, it's not my fault!
...
You're just hopeless. I suppose I'll just have to resort to a wake-up ki—
GRAB
KRAKK
バキッ
SHAD-DUP!!!
WHAM

ASAKURA-SAN RETURNS TO HER NORMAL SIZE

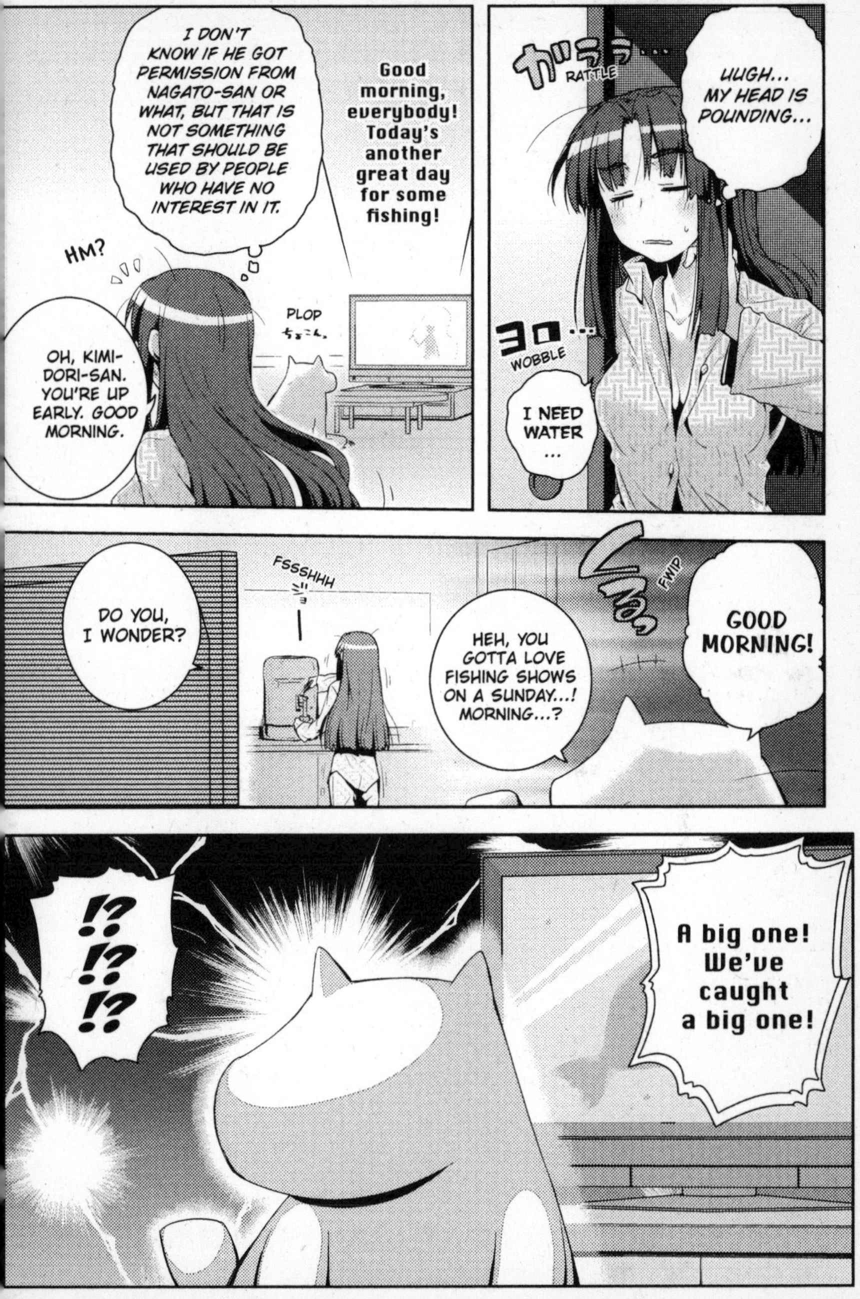
ガラララ…
RATTLE
UUGH... MY HEAD IS POUNDING...
ヨロ…
WOBBLE
I NEED WATER ...
Good morning, everybody! Today's another great day for some fishing!
I DON'T KNOW IF HE GOT PERMISSION FROM NAGATO-SAN OR WHAT, BUT THAT IS NOT SOMETHING THAT SHOULD BE USED BY PEOPLE WHO HAVE NO INTEREST IN IT.
HM?
PLOP
ちょこん
OH, KIMIDORI-SAN. YOU'RE UP EARLY. GOOD MORNING.
FWIP
GOOD MORNING!
HEH, YOU GOTTA LOVE FISHING SHOWS ON A SUNDAY...! MORNING...?
FSSSHHH
DO YOU, I WONDER?
A big one! We've caught a big one!
!?!?!?

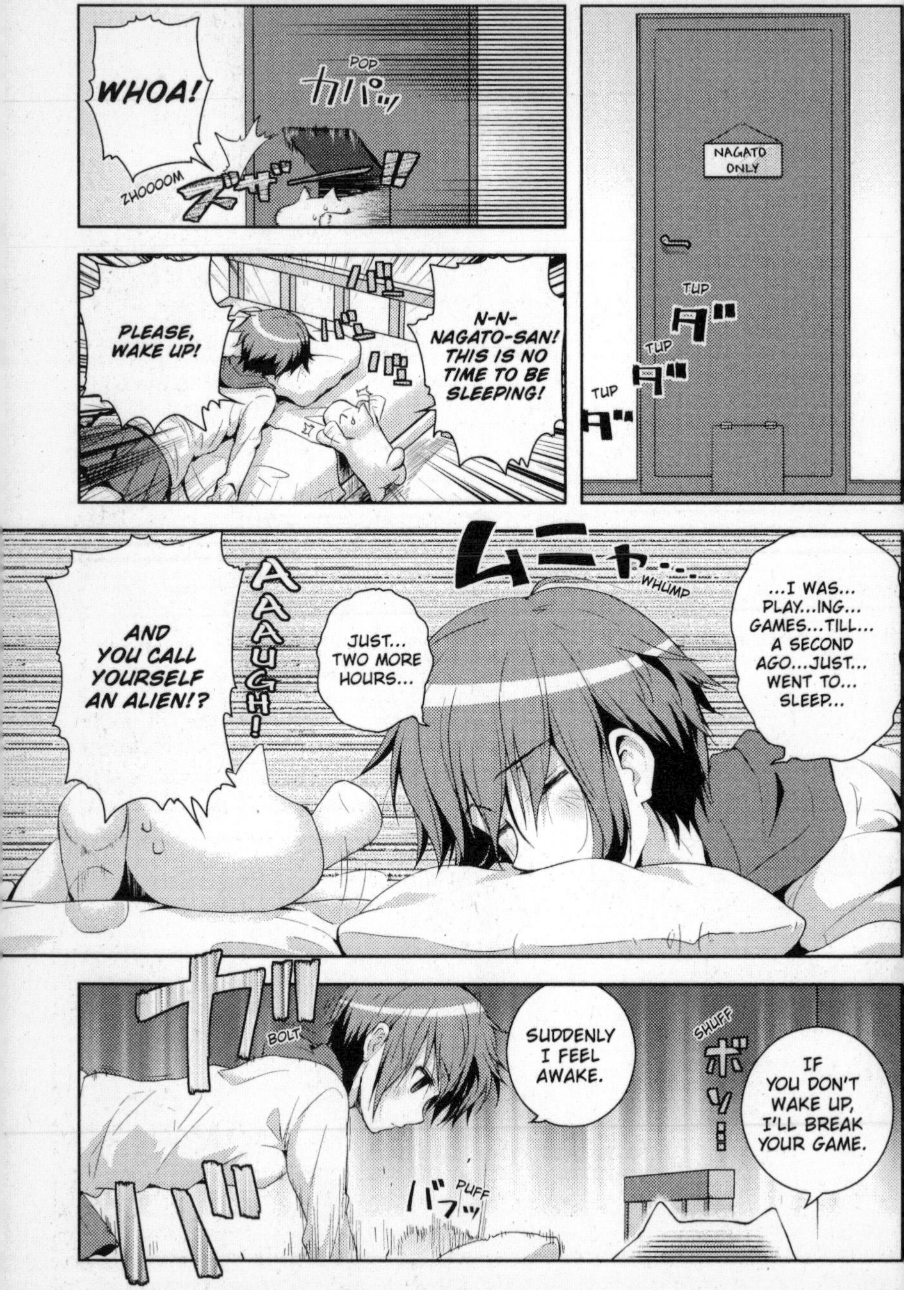
NAGATO ONLY
TUP
ダッ
TUP
ダッ
TUP
ダッ
POP
カパッ
WHOA!
ZHOOOOM
N-N-NAGATO-SAN! THIS IS NO TIME TO BE SLEEPING!
PLEASE, WAKE UP!
...I WAS... PLAY...ING... GAMES...TILL... A SECOND AGO...JUST... WENT TO... SLEEP...
ムニャ...
WHUMP
JUST... TWO MORE HOURS...
AAAAUGH!
AND YOU CALL YOURSELF AN ALIEN!?
IF YOU DON'T WAKE UP, I'LL BREAK YOUR GAME.
SHUFF
ボッ...
SUDDENLY I FEEL AWAKE.
PUFF
バフッ
BOLT

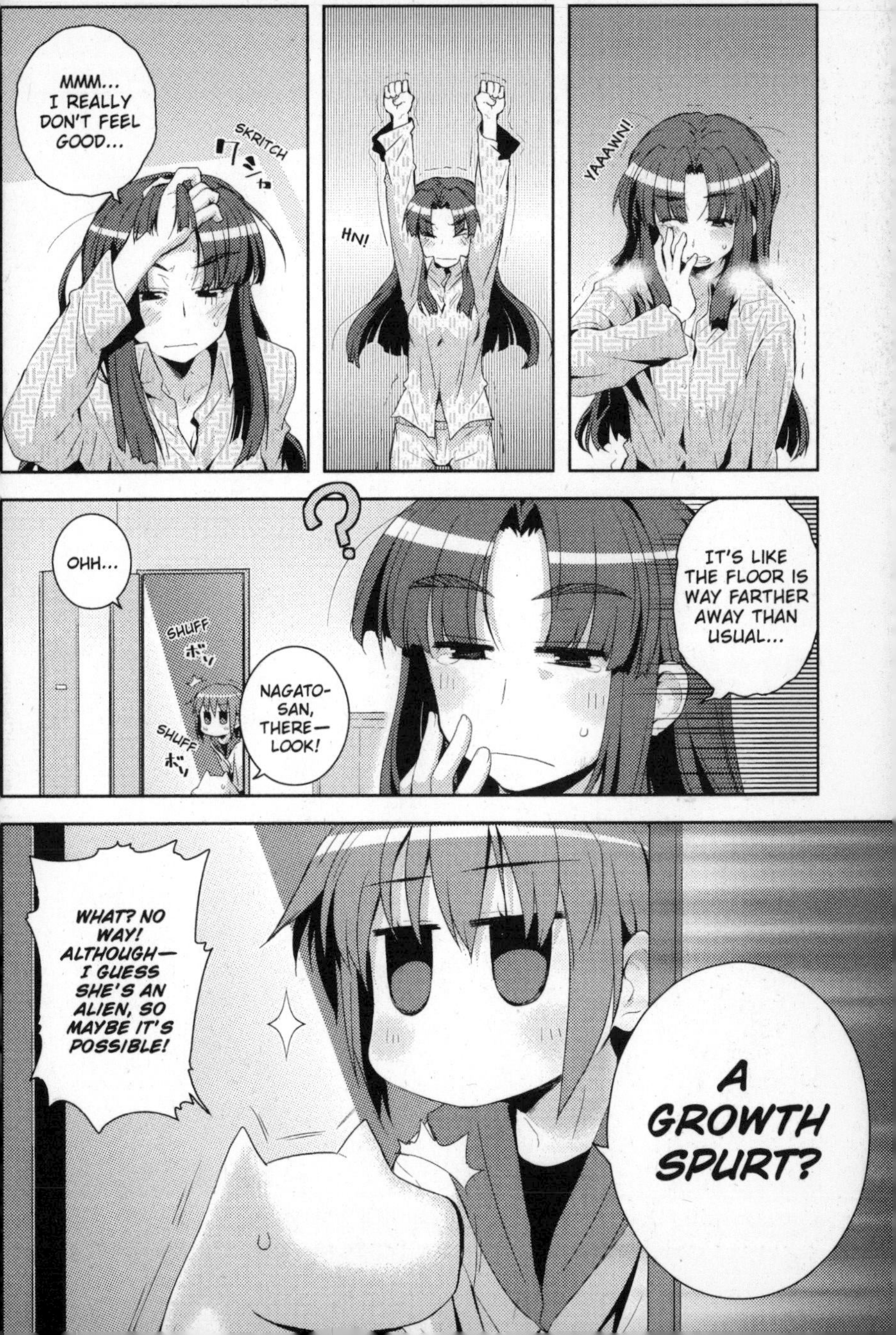
YAAAWN!
HN!
MMM... I REALLY DON'T FEEL GOOD...
SKRITCH
IT'S LIKE THE FLOOR IS WAY FARTHER AWAY THAN USUAL...
OHH...
SHUFF
NAGATO-SAN, THERE—LOOK!
SHUFF
A GROWTH SPURT?
WHAT? NO WAY! ALTHOUGH— I GUESS SHE'S AN ALIEN, SO MAYBE IT'S POSSIBLE!

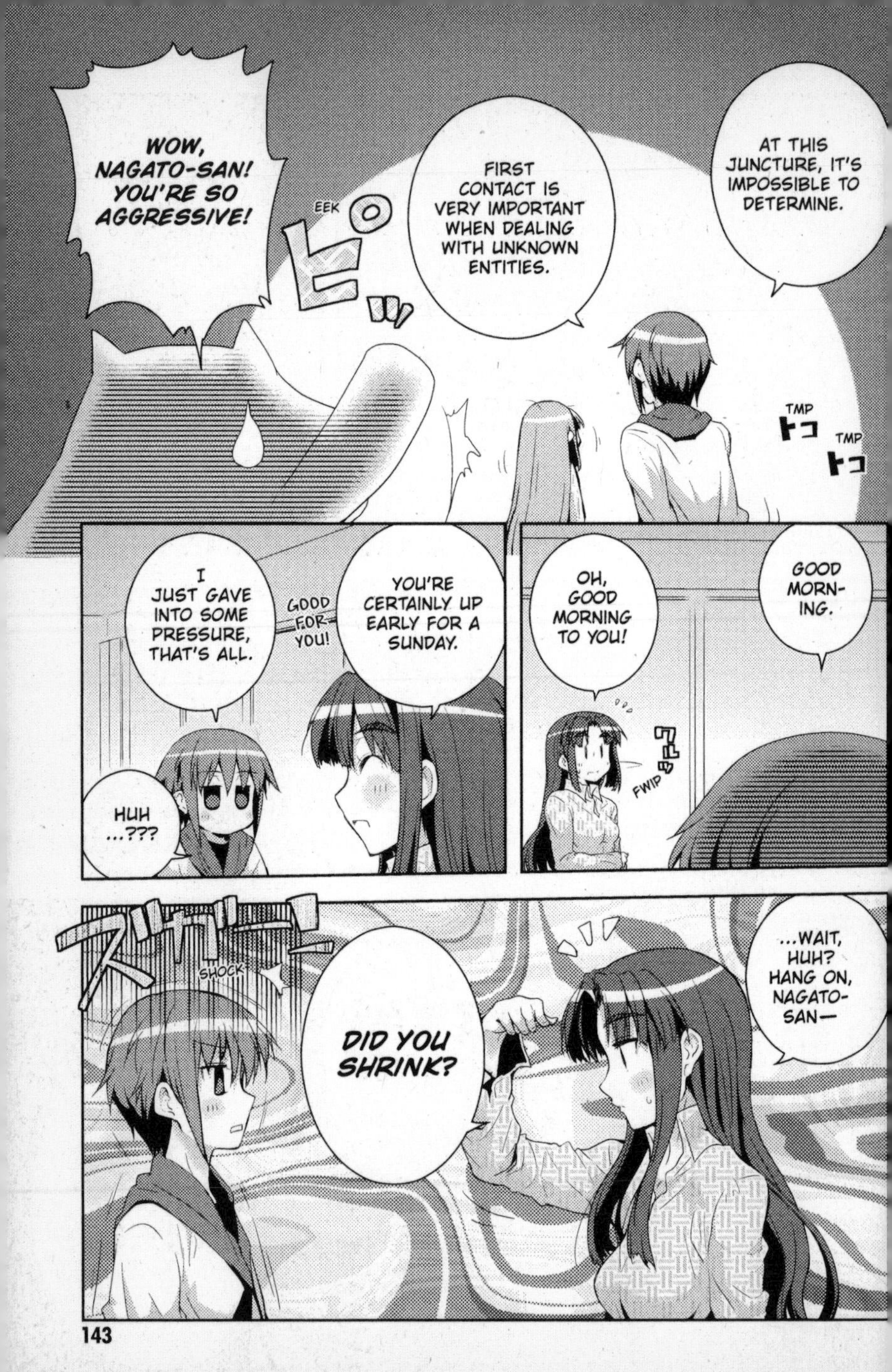
AT THIS JUNCTURE, IT'S IMPOSSIBLE TO DETERMINE.
TMP
TMP
FIRST CONTACT IS VERY IMPORTANT WHEN DEALING WITH UNKNOWN ENTITIES.
EEK
WOW, NAGATO-SAN! YOU'RE SO AGGRESSIVE!
GOOD MORN-ING.
OH, GOOD MORNING TO YOU!
FWIP
YOU'RE CERTAINLY UP EARLY FOR A SUNDAY.
GOOD FOR YOU!
I JUST GAVE INTO SOME PRESSURE, THAT'S ALL.
HUH ...???
...WAIT, HUH? HANG ON, NAGATO-SAN—
DID YOU SHRINK?
SHOCK

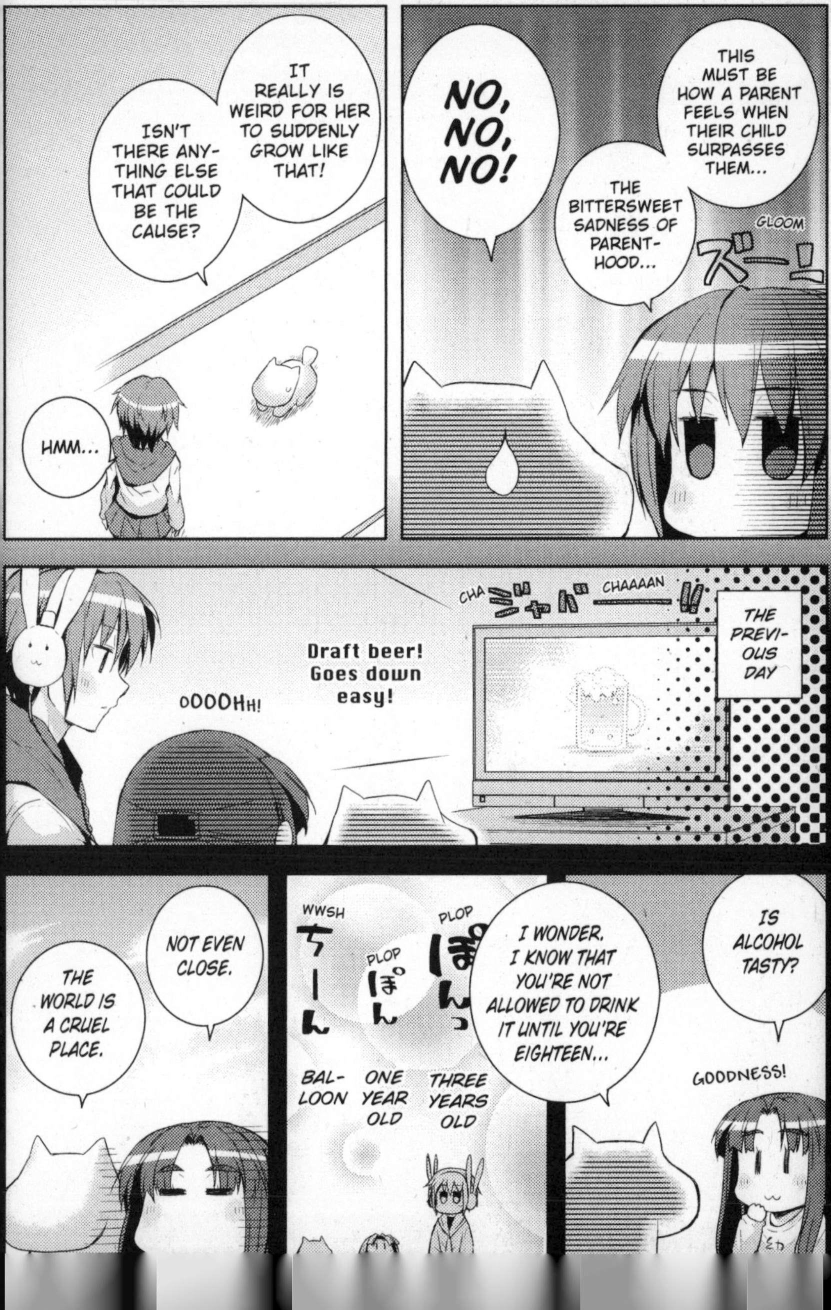
THIS MUST BE HOW A PARENT FEELS WHEN THEIR CHILD SURPASSES THEM...
THE BITTERSWEET SADNESS OF PARENTHOOD...
GLOOM
NO, NO, NO!
IT REALLY IS WEIRD FOR HER TO SUDDENLY GROW LIKE THAT!
ISN'T THERE ANYTHING ELSE THAT COULD BE THE CAUSE?
HMM...
THE PREVIOUS DAY
CHA
CHAAAAN
Draft beer! Goes down easy!
OOOOHH!
IS ALCOHOL TASTY?
GOODNESS!
I WONDER. I KNOW THAT YOU'RE NOT ALLOWED TO DRINK IT UNTIL YOU'RE EIGHTEEN...
PLOP
ぽんっ
PLOP
ぽん
WWSH
ち～ん
THREE YEARS OLD
ONE YEAR OLD
BALLOON
NOT EVEN CLOSE.
THE WORLD IS A CRUEL PLACE.

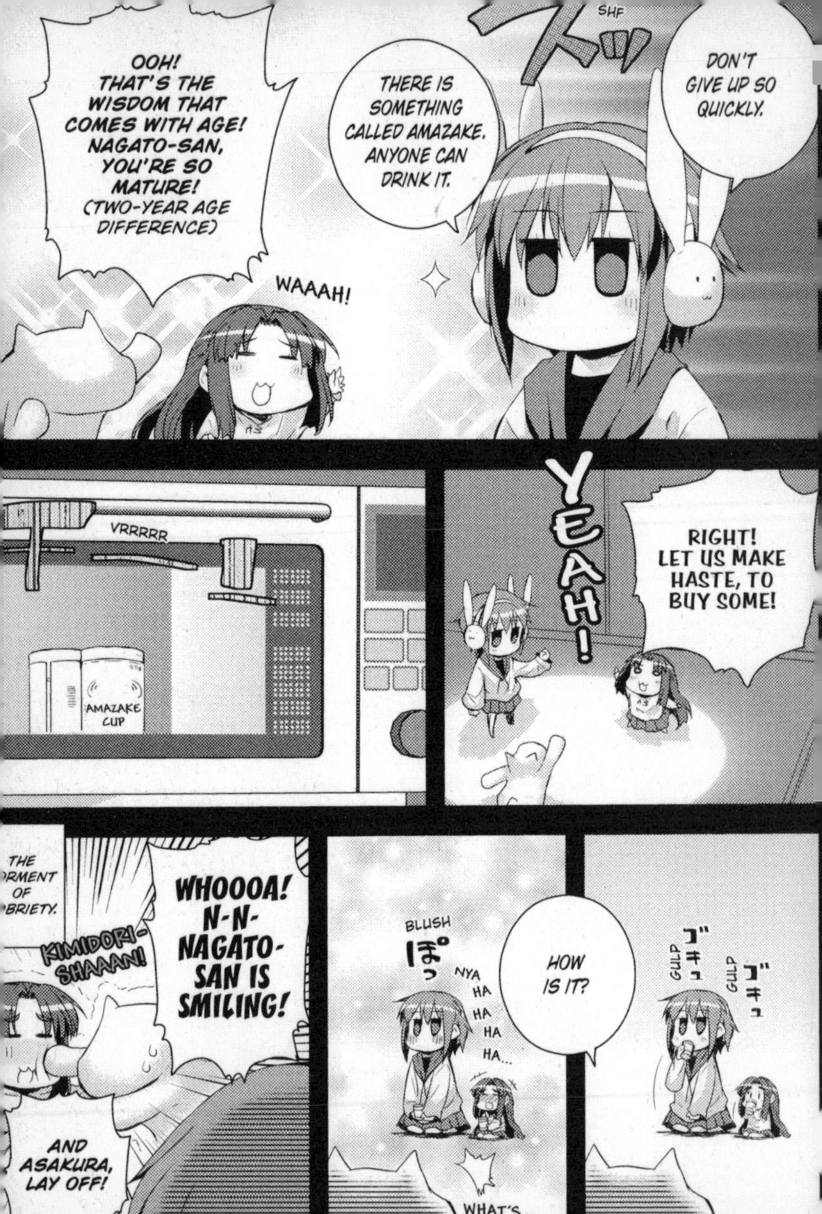
SHF
DON'T GIVE UP SO QUICKLY.
THERE IS SOMETHING CALLED AMAZAKE. ANYONE CAN DRINK IT.
OOH! THAT'S THE WISDOM THAT COMES WITH AGE! NAGATO-SAN, YOU'RE SO MATURE! (TWO-YEAR AGE DIFFERENCE)
WAAAH!
YEAH!
RIGHT! LET US MAKE HASTE, TO BUY SOME!
VRRRRR
AMAZAKE CUP
ゴキュ GULP
ゴキュ GULP
HOW IS IT?
BLUSH ぽっ
NYA HA HA HA HA...
WHAT'S THIS!?
WHOOOA! N-N-NAGATO-SAN IS SMILING!
KIMIDORI-SHAAAN!
AND ASAKURA, LAY OFF!

AKE, OR "SWEET SAKE," IS A KIND OF SWEET FERMENTED RICE WINE.

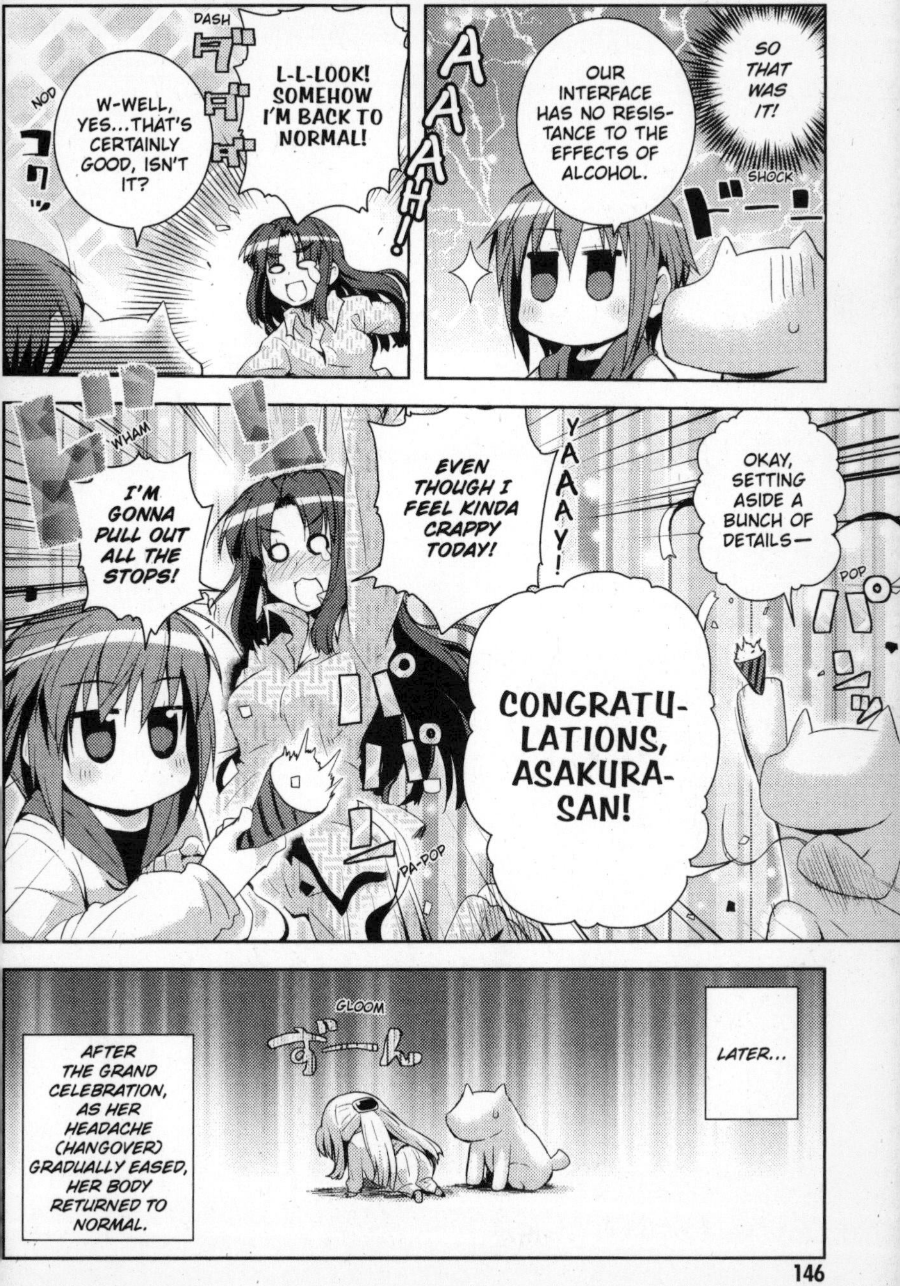

SO THAT WAS IT!
OUR INTERFACE HAS NO RESISTANCE TO THE EFFECTS OF ALCOHOL.
AAAH!
SHOCK
DASH
L-L-LOOK! SOMEHOW I'M BACK TO NORMAL!
W-WELL, YES...THAT'S CERTAINLY GOOD, ISN'T IT?
NOD
OKAY, SETTING ASIDE A BUNCH OF DETAILS—
POP
YAAAAY!
EVEN THOUGH I FEEL KINDA CRAPPY TODAY!
CONGRATULATIONS, ASAKURA-SAN!
WHAM
I'M GONNA PULL OUT ALL THE STOPS!
PA-POP
LATER...
GLOOM
AFTER THE GRAND CELEBRATION, AS HER HEADACHE (HANGOVER) GRADUALLY EASED, HER BODY RETURNED TO NORMAL.

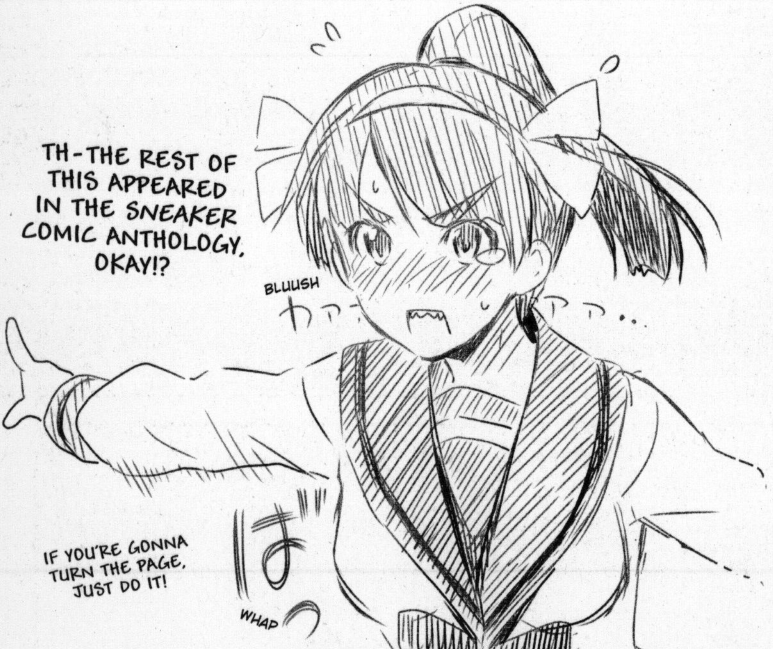
TH-THE REST OF THIS APPEARED IN THE SNEAKER COMIC ANTHOLOGY, OKAY!?
BLUUSH
IF YOU'RE GONNA TURN THE PAGE, JUST DO IT!
WHAP

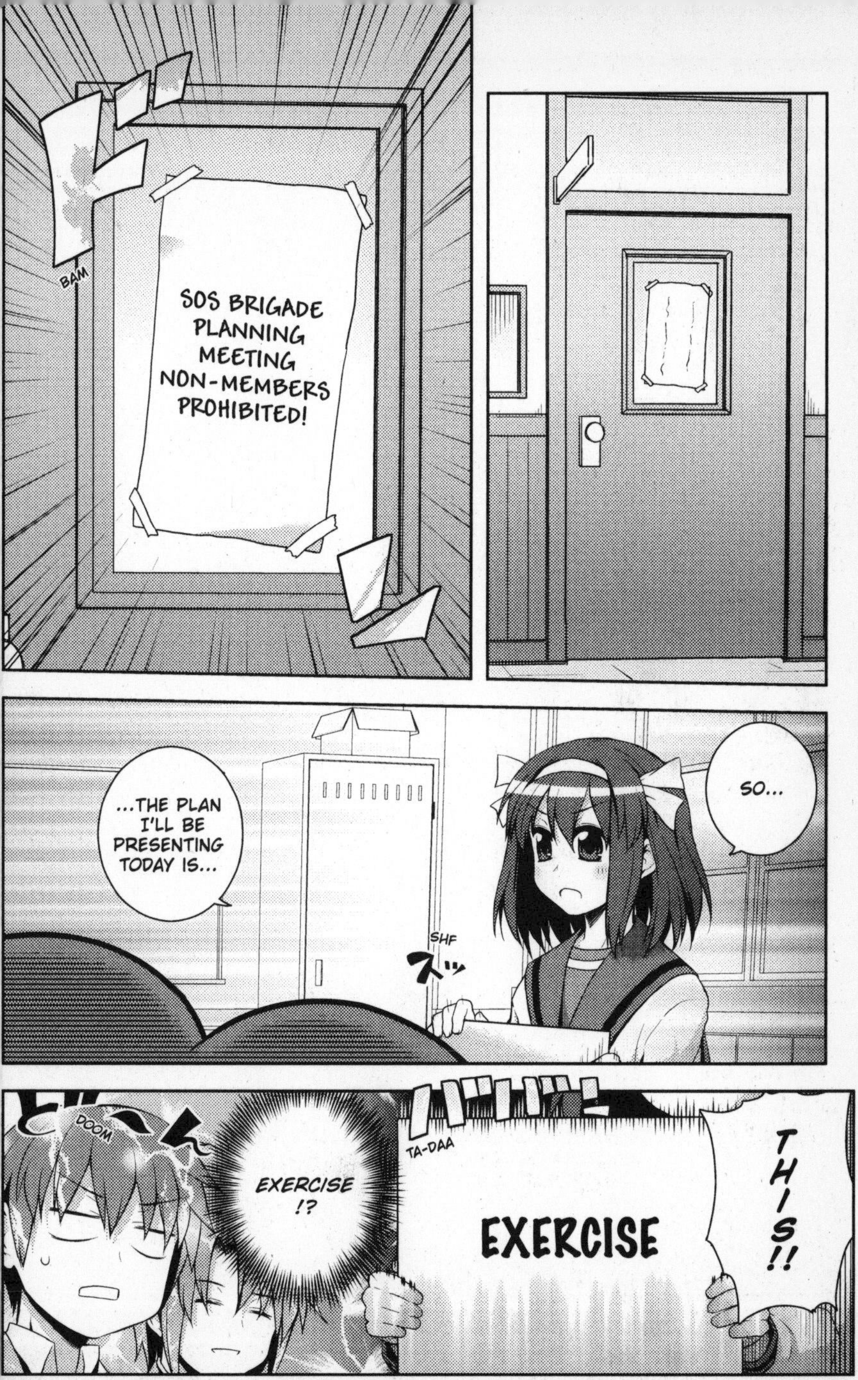
BAM
SOS BRIGADE PLANNING MEETING NON-MEMBERS PROHIBITED!
SO...
...THE PLAN I'LL BE PRESENTING TODAY IS...
SHF
TA-DAA
THIS!!
EXERCISE
DOOM
EXERCISE !?

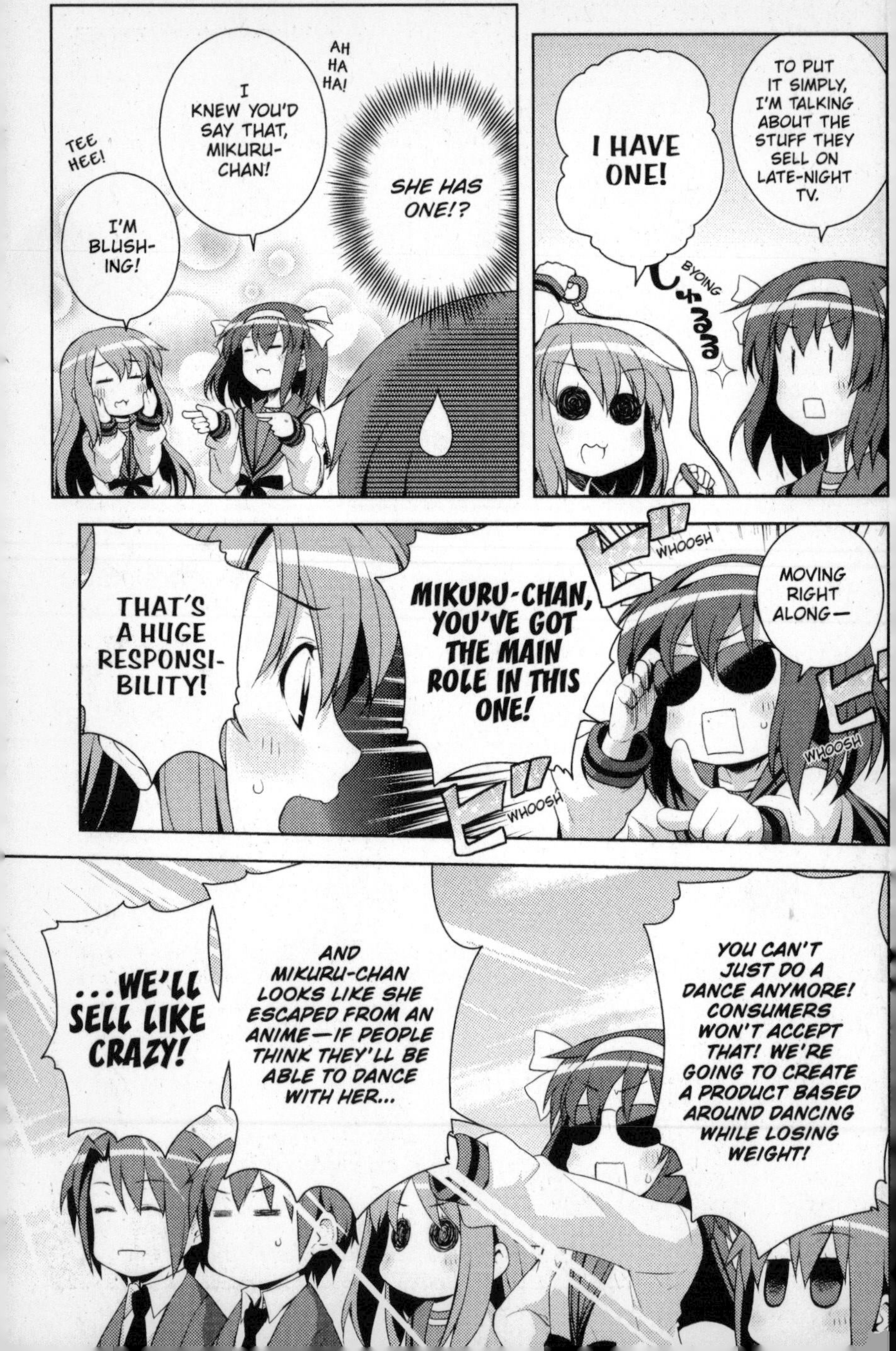
TO PUT IT SIMPLY, I'M TALKING ABOUT THE STUFF THEY SELL ON LATE-NIGHT TV.
I HAVE ONE!
BYOING
SHE HAS ONE!?
AH HA HA!
I KNEW YOU'D SAY THAT, MIKURU-CHAN!
TEE HEE!
I'M BLUSHING!
MOVING RIGHT ALONG—
WHOOSH
MIKURU-CHAN, YOU'VE GOT THE MAIN ROLE IN THIS ONE!
WHOOSH
WHOOSH
THAT'S A HUGE RESPONSIBILITY!
YOU CAN'T JUST DO A DANCE ANYMORE! CONSUMERS WON'T ACCEPT THAT! WE'RE GOING TO CREATE A PRODUCT BASED AROUND DANCING WHILE LOSING WEIGHT!
AND MIKURU-CHAN LOOKS LIKE SHE ESCAPED FROM AN ANIME—IF PEOPLE THINK THEY'LL BE ABLE TO DANCE WITH HER...
...WE'LL SELL LIKE CRAZY!

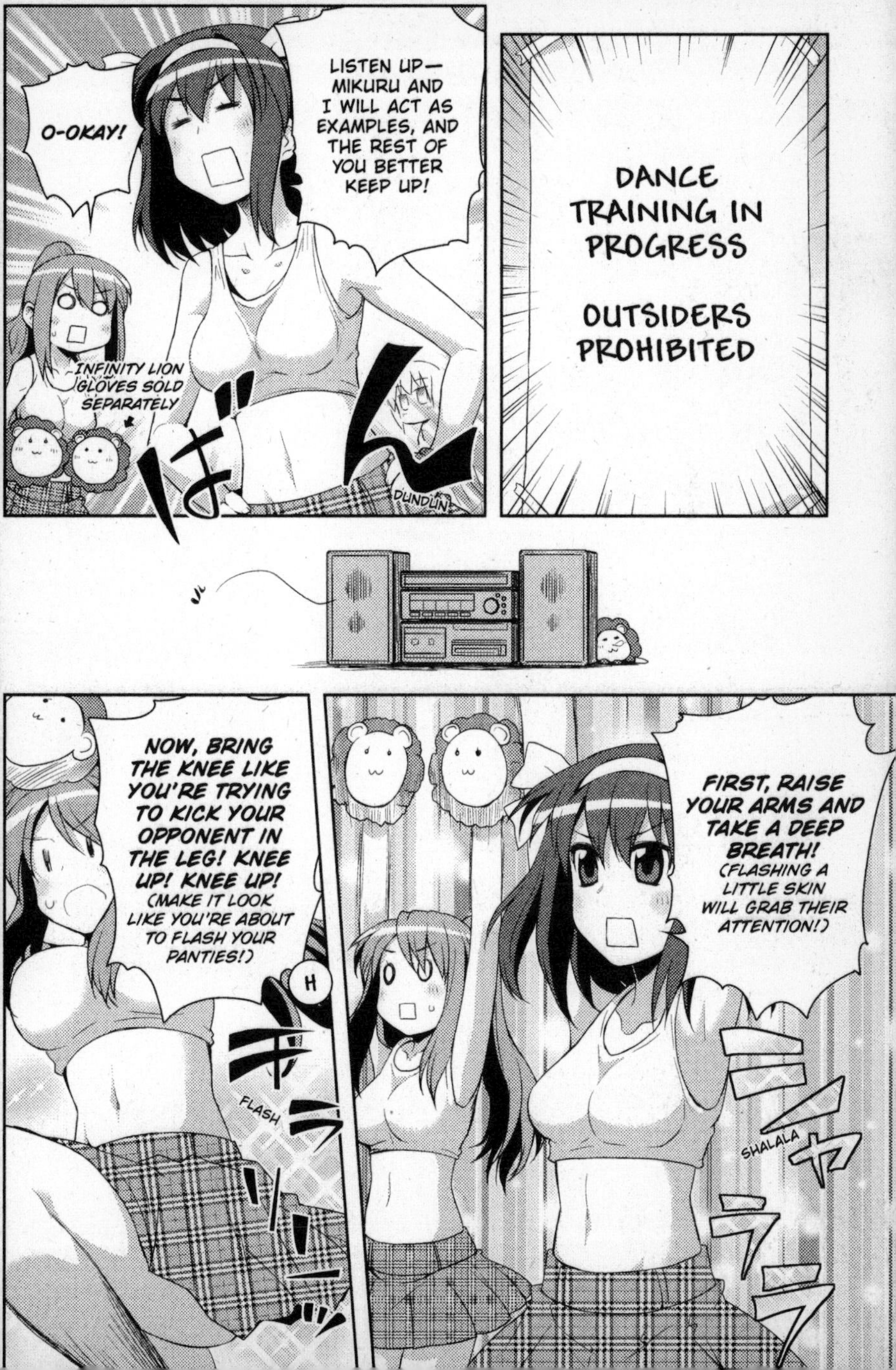
DANCE TRAINING IN PROGRESS
OUTSIDERS PROHIBITED
LISTEN UP— MIKURU AND I WILL ACT AS EXAMPLES, AND THE REST OF YOU BETTER KEEP UP!
O-OKAY!
INFINITY LION GLOVES SOLD SEPARATELY
DUNDUN
FIRST, RAISE YOUR ARMS AND TAKE A DEEP BREATH! (FLASHING A LITTLE SKIN WILL GRAB THEIR ATTENTION!)
SHALALA
NOW, BRING THE KNEE LIKE YOU'RE TRYING TO KICK YOUR OPPONENT IN THE LEG! KNEE UP! KNEE UP! (MAKE IT LOOK LIKE YOU'RE ABOUT TO FLASH YOUR PANTIES!)
H
FLASH

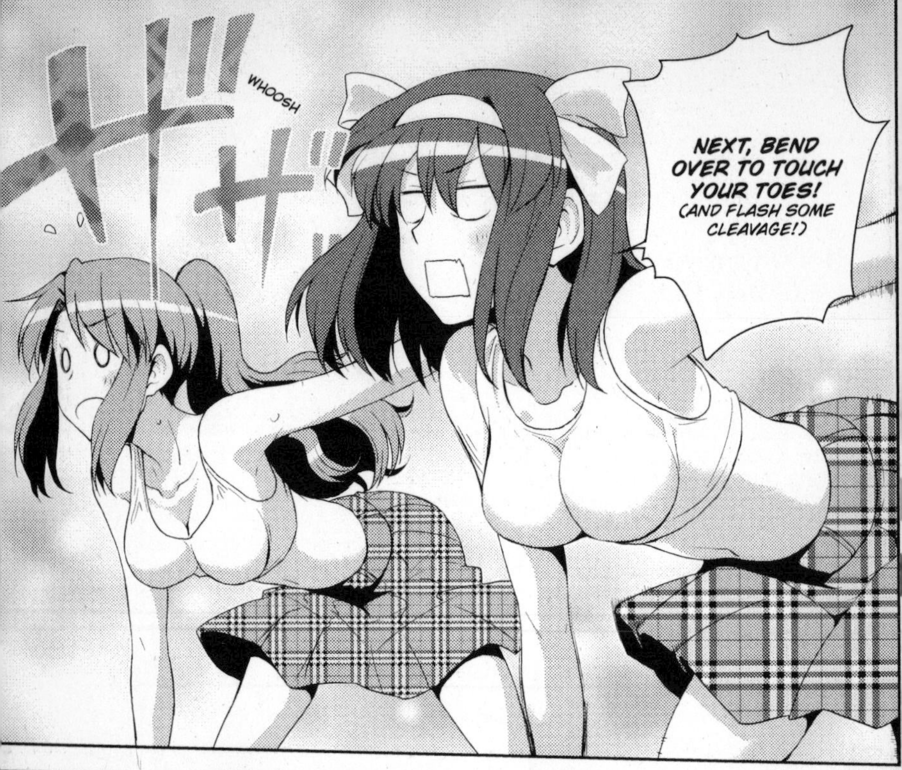
NEXT, BEND OVER TO TOUCH YOUR TOES!
(AND FLASH SOME CLEAVAGE!)
WHOOSH

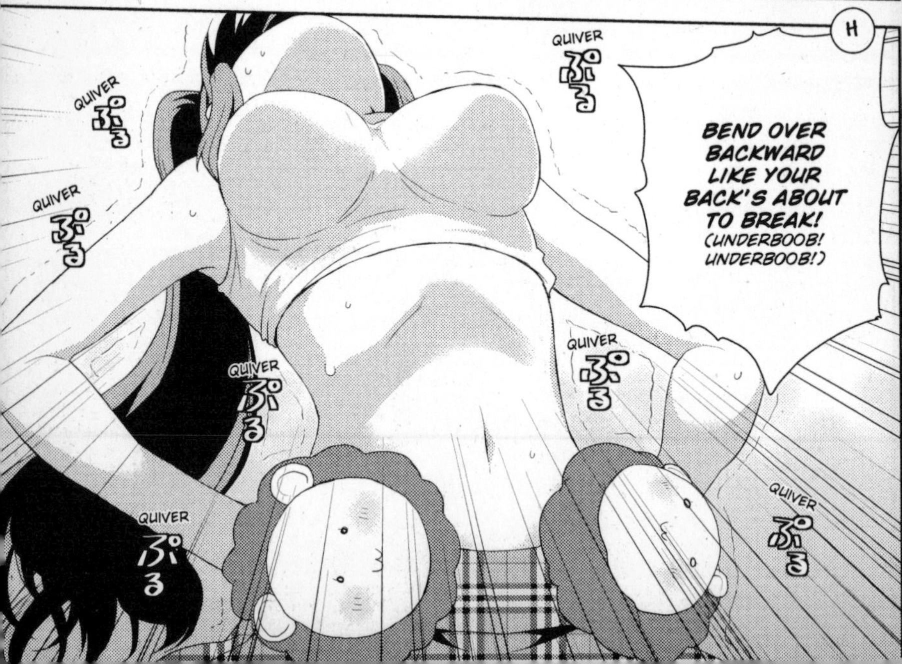
H
QUIVER
ぷる
BEND OVER BACKWARD LIKE YOUR BACK'S ABOUT TO BREAK!
(UNDERBOOB! UNDERBOOB!)
QUIVER
ぷる
QUIVER
ぷる
QUIVER
ぷる
QUIVER
ぷる
QUIVER
ぷる
QUIVER
ぷる

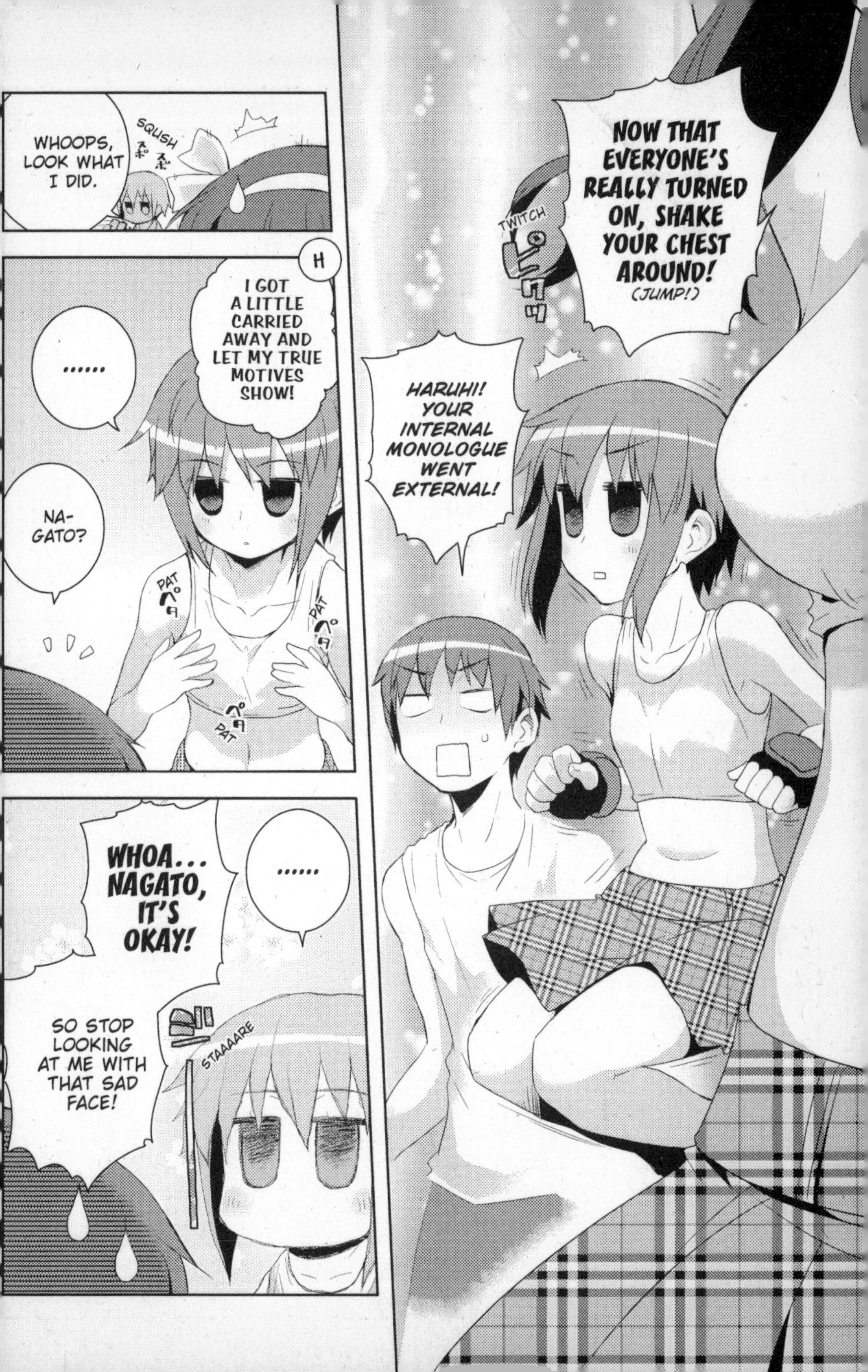
NOW THAT EVERYONE'S REALLY TURNED ON, SHAKE YOUR CHEST AROUND! (JUMP!)
TWITCH
HARUHI! YOUR INTERNAL MONOLOGUE WENT EXTERNAL!
SQUSH
WHOOPS, LOOK WHAT I DID.
H
I GOT A LITTLE CARRIED AWAY AND LET MY TRUE MOTIVES SHOW!
......
NA-GATO?
PAT
PAT
PAT
WHOA... NAGATO, IT'S OKAY!
......
STAAAARE
SO STOP LOOKING AT ME WITH THAT SAD FACE!

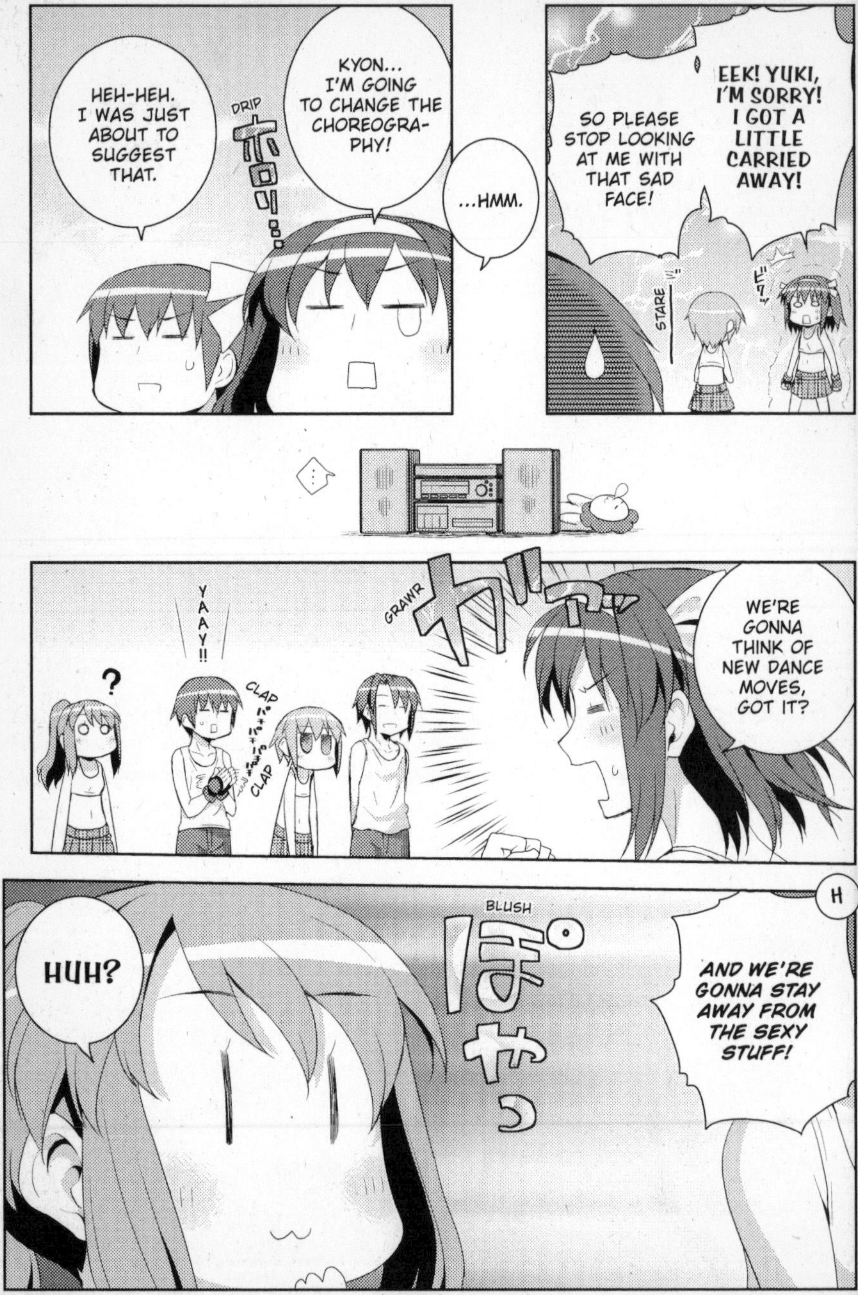
EEK! YUKI, I'M SORRY! I GOT A LITTLE CARRIED AWAY!
SO PLEASE STOP LOOKING AT ME WITH THAT SAD FACE!
STARE
KYON... I'M GOING TO CHANGE THE CHOREOGRA-PHY!
...HMM.
DRIP
HEH-HEH. I WAS JUST ABOUT TO SUGGEST THAT.
...
WE'RE GONNA THINK OF NEW DANCE MOVES, GOT IT?
GRAWR
YAAAY!!
CLAP
CLAP
?
H
AND WE'RE GONNA STAY AWAY FROM THE SEXY STUFF!
BLUSH
HUH?

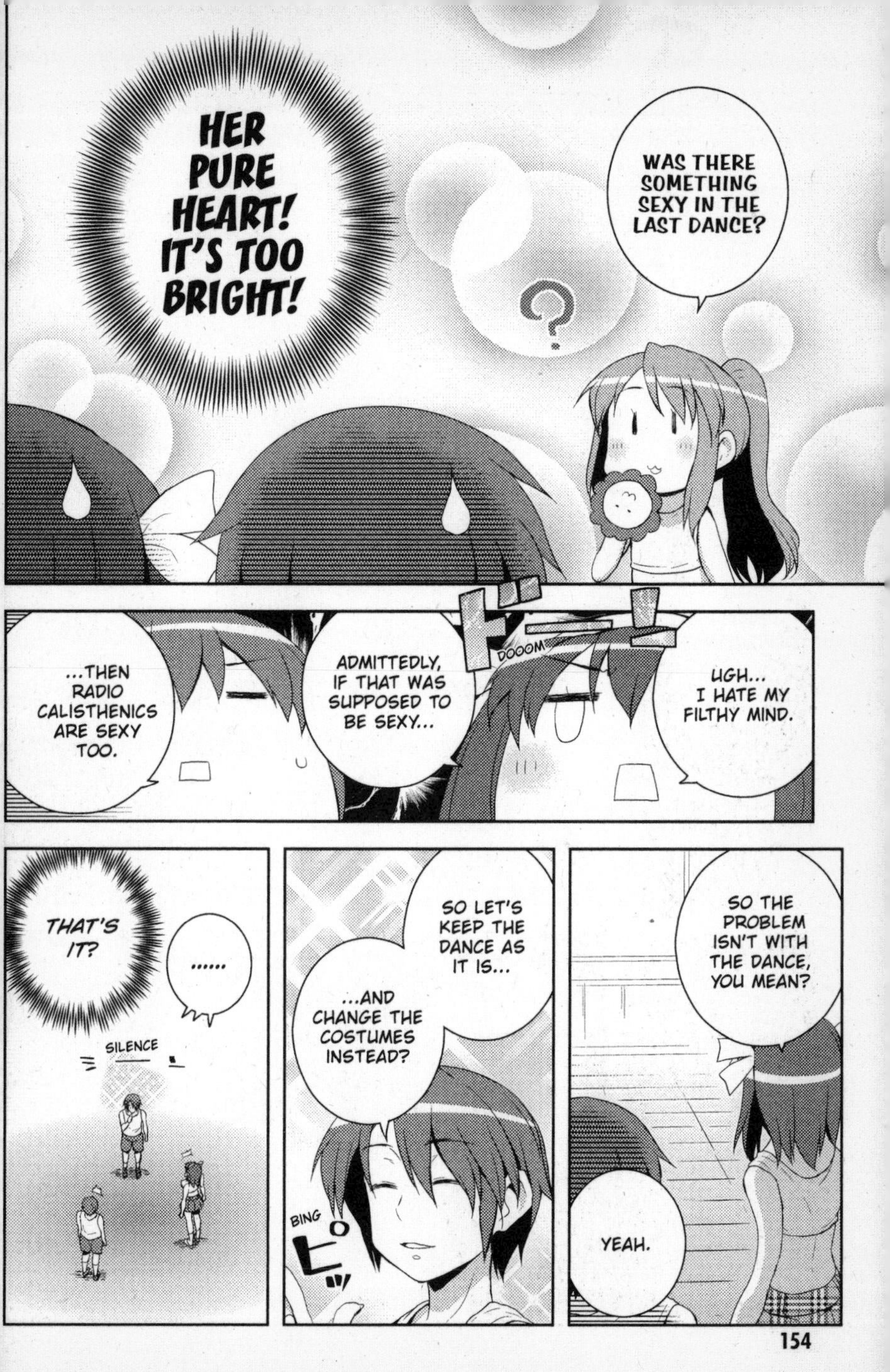
WAS THERE SOMETHING SEXY IN THE LAST DANCE?
HER PURE HEART! IT'S TOO BRIGHT!
DOOOM
UGH... I HATE MY FILTHY MIND.
ADMITTEDLY, IF THAT WAS SUPPOSED TO BE SEXY...
...THEN RADIO CALISTHENICS ARE SEXY TOO.
SO THE PROBLEM ISN'T WITH THE DANCE, YOU MEAN?
YEAH.
SO LET'S KEEP THE DANCE AS IT IS...
...AND CHANGE THE COSTUMES INSTEAD?
BING
......
THAT'S IT?
SILENCE

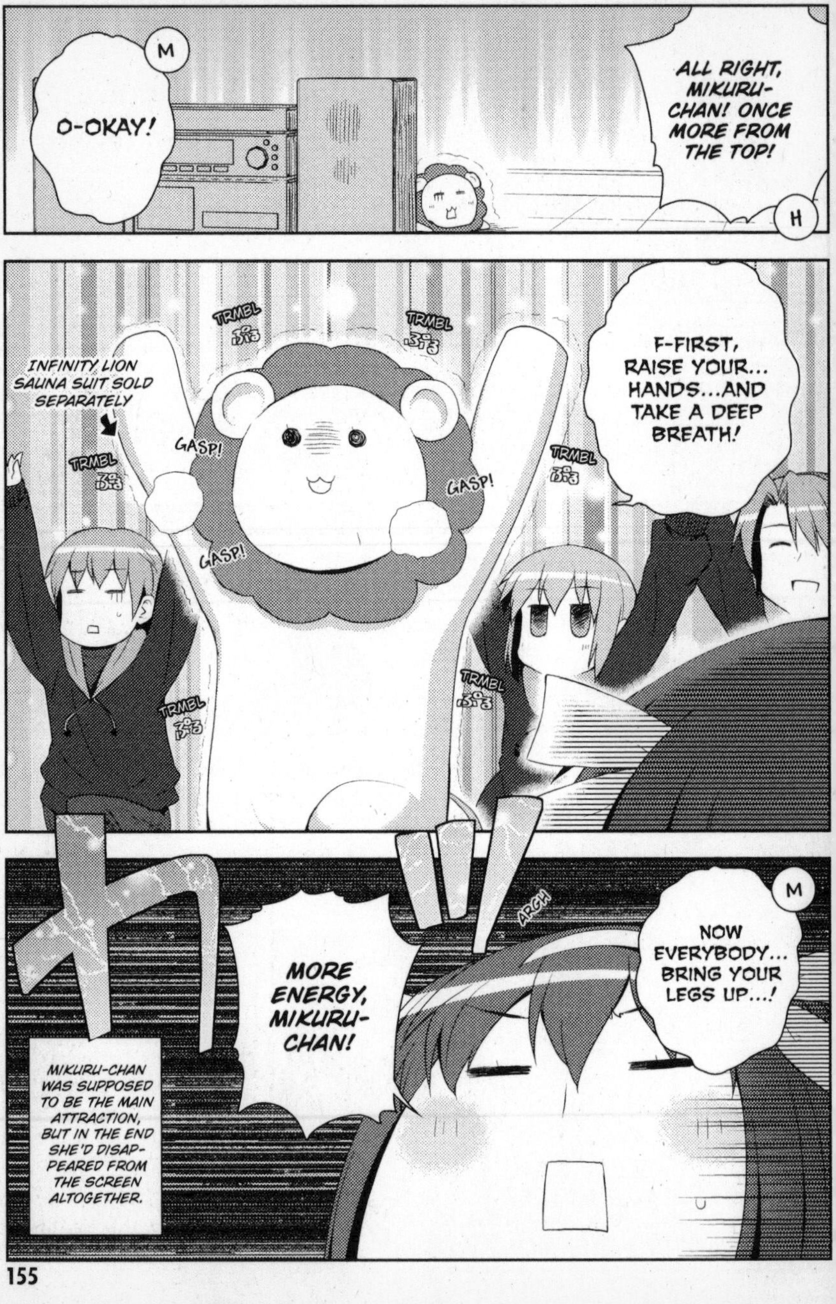
H
ALL RIGHT, MIKURU-CHAN! ONCE MORE FROM THE TOP!
M
O-OKAY!
F-FIRST, RAISE YOUR... HANDS...AND TAKE A DEEP BREATH!
TRMBL ぷる
TRMBL ぷる
GASP!
GASP!
GASP!
TRMBL ぷる
TRMBL ぷる
INFINITY LION SAUNA SUIT SOLD SEPARATELY
TRMBL ぷる
M
NOW EVERYBODY... BRING YOUR LEGS UP...!
ARGH
MORE ENERGY, MIKURU-CHAN!
MIKURU-CHAN WAS SUPPOSED TO BE THE MAIN ATTRACTION, BUT IN THE END SHE'D DISAP-PEARED FROM THE SCREEN ALTOGETHER.

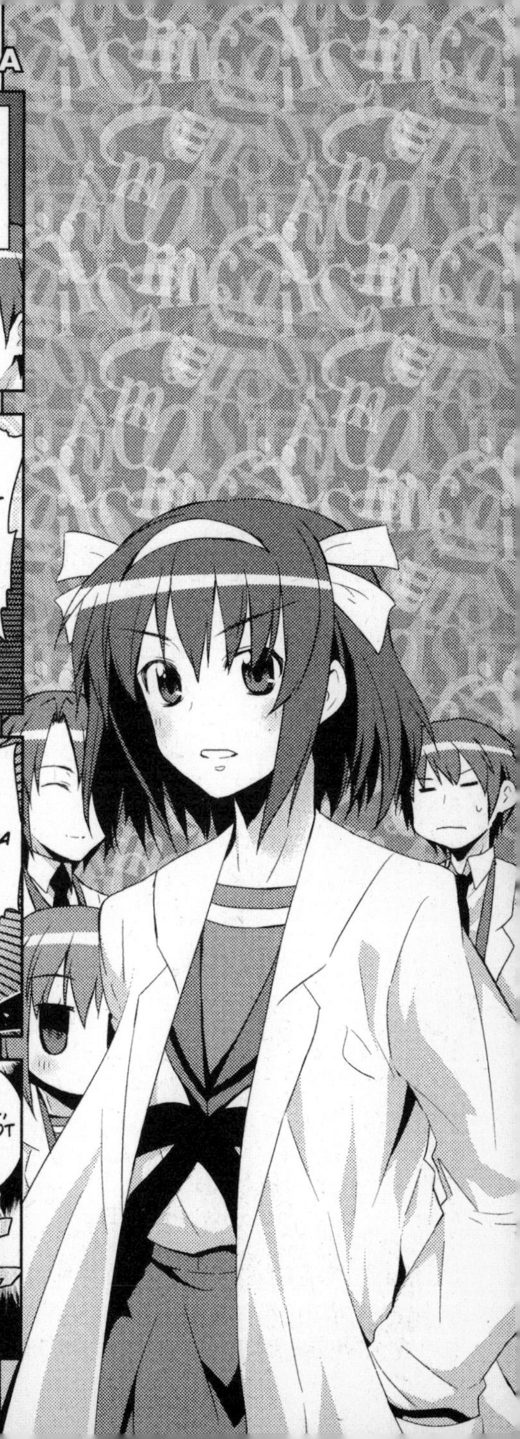

SUZUMIYA'S CRAZY IDEA

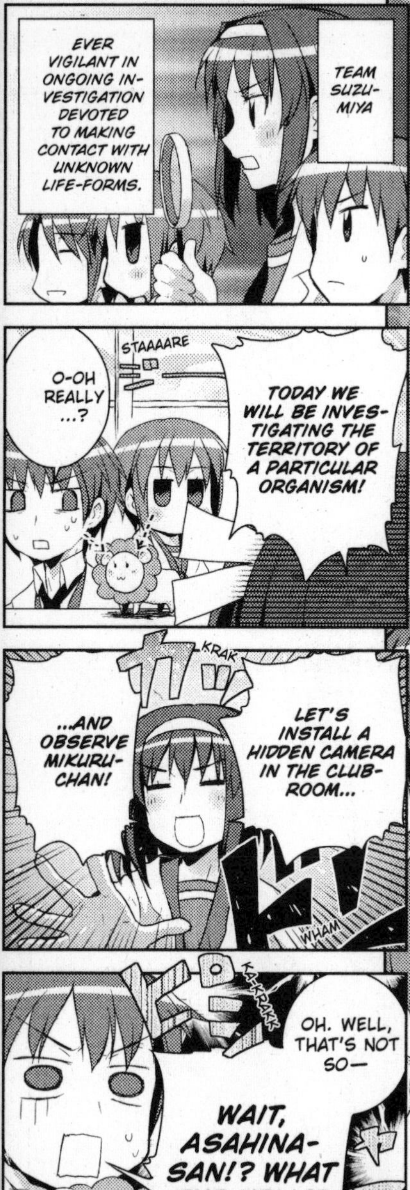
TEAM SUZUMIYA
EVER VIGILANT IN ONGOING INVESTIGATION DEVOTED TO MAKING CONTACT WITH UNKNOWN LIFE-FORMS.
TODAY WE WILL BE INVESTIGATING THE TERRITORY OF A PARTICULAR ORGANISM!
STAAAARE
O-OH REALLY ...?
KRAK
LET'S INSTALL A HIDDEN CAMERA IN THE CLUB-ROOM...
...AND OBSERVE MIKURU-CHAN!
WHAM
KA-KRAKK
OH. WELL, THAT'S NOT SO—
WAIT, ASAHINA-SAN!? WHAT THE HELL!?

COMMENCE INVESTIGATION

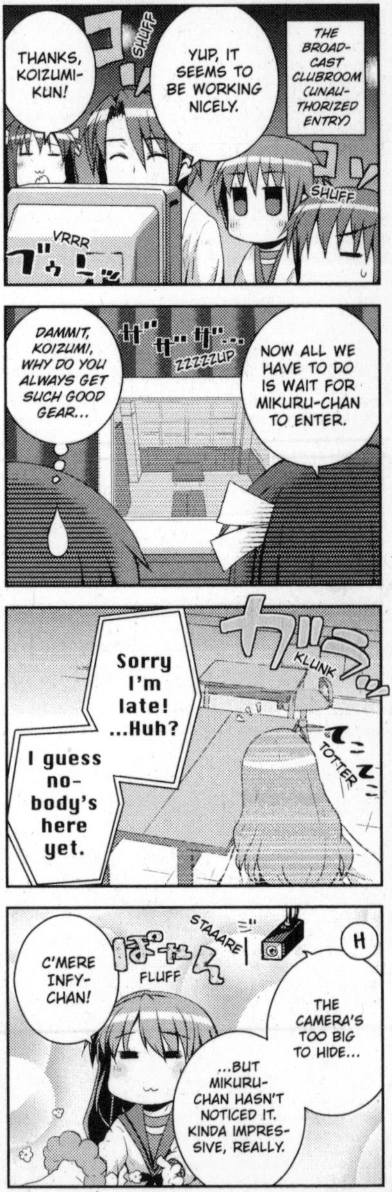
THE BROADCAST CLUBROOM (UNAUTHORIZED ENTRY)
YUP, IT SEEMS TO BE WORKING NICELY.
SHUFF
THANKS, KOIZUMI-KUN!
SHUFF
VRRR
NOW ALL WE HAVE TO DO IS WAIT FOR MIKURU-CHAN TO ENTER.
ZZZZZUP
DAMMIT, KOIZUMI, WHY DO YOU ALWAYS GET SUCH GOOD GEAR...
KLUNK
Sorry I'm late! ...Huh?
I guess nobody's here yet.
TOTTER
H
THE CAMERA'S TOO BIG TO HIDE...
...BUT MIKURU-CHAN HASN'T NOTICED IT. KINDA IMPRESSIVE, REALLY.
STAAARE
FLUFF
C'MERE INFY-CHAN!

MOVES

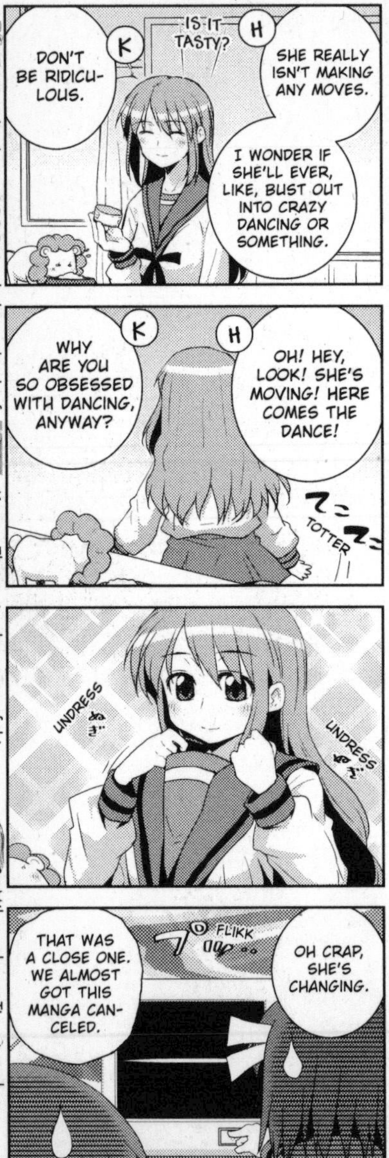
H
SHE REALLY ISN'T MAKING ANY MOVES.
I WONDER IF SHE'LL EVER, LIKE, BUST OUT INTO CRAZY DANCING OR SOMETHING.
IS IT TASTY?
K
DON'T BE RIDICULOUS.
H
OH! HEY, LOOK! SHE'S MOVING! HERE COMES THE DANCE!
K
WHY ARE YOU SO OBSESSED WITH DANCING, ANYWAY?
TOTTER
UNDRESS
UNDRESS
OH CRAP, SHE'S CHANGING.
FLIKK
THAT WAS A CLOSE ONE. WE ALMOST GOT THIS MANGA CANCELED.

•Haruhi-chan •SOS Brigade brigade chief. Attracts any abnormal phenomenon, no matter how minute.

•Kyon •The main character of this story. Keenly interested in the habitat of Mikuru-chan.

•Mikuru-chan •Time traveler. Evidently her wary nature is only skin-deep.

PROFESSIONAL

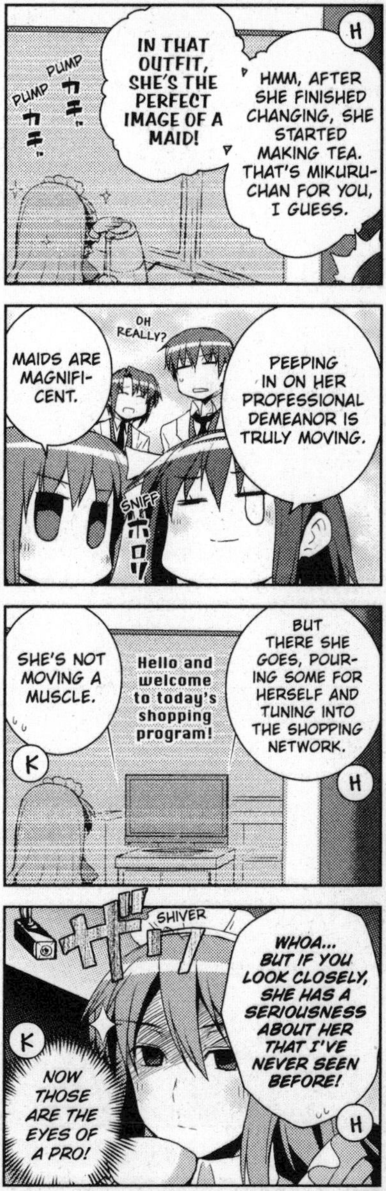
HMM, AFTER SHE FINISHED CHANGING, SHE STARTED MAKING TEA. THAT'S MIKURU-CHAN FOR YOU, I GUESS.
IN THAT OUTFIT, SHE'S THE PERFECT IMAGE OF A MAID!
PUMP
PUMP
PEEPING IN ON HER PROFESSIONAL DEMEANOR IS TRULY MOVING.
OH REALLY?
MAIDS ARE MAGNIFICENT.
SNIFF
BUT THERE SHE GOES, POURING SOME FOR HERSELF AND TUNING INTO THE SHOPPING NETWORK.
Hello and welcome to today's shopping program!
SHE'S NOT MOVING A MUSCLE.
SHIVER
WHOA... BUT IF YOU LOOK CLOSELY, SHE HAS A SERIOUSNESS ABOUT HER THAT I'VE NEVER SEEN BEFORE!
NOW THOSE ARE THE EYES OF A PRO!

SURPRISE

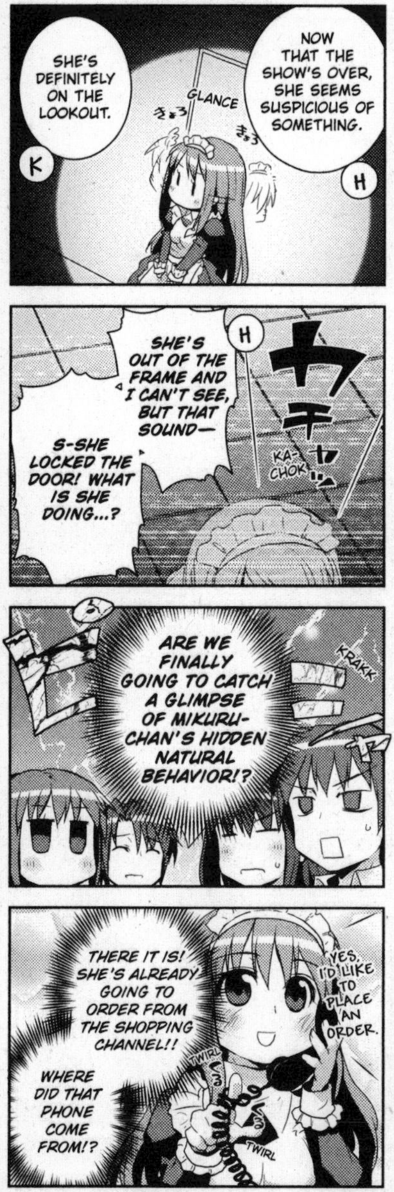
NOW THAT THE SHOW'S OVER, SHE SEEMS SUSPICIOUS OF SOMETHING.
GLANCE
SHE'S DEFINITELY ON THE LOOKOUT.
KA-CHOK
SHE'S OUT OF THE FRAME AND I CAN'T SEE, BUT THAT SOUND—
S-SHE LOCKED THE DOOR! WHAT IS SHE DOING...?
KRAKK
ARE WE FINALLY GOING TO CATCH A GLIMPSE OF MIKURU-CHAN'S HIDDEN NATURAL BEHAVIOR!?
YES, I'D LIKE TO PLACE AN ORDER.
THERE IT IS! SHE'S ALREADY GOING TO ORDER FROM THE SHOPPING CHANNEL!!
TWIRL
TWIRL
WHERE DID THAT PHONE COME FROM!?

•Nagato •An alien with a weakness for maids. Uses logic and force to overcome obstacles.

•Koizumi •Esper. Also adept at installing surveillance cameras?

•Infinity Lion •Alien life-form being cared for by Mikuru. Small, at the moment.

INVESTIGATION CONCLUDED

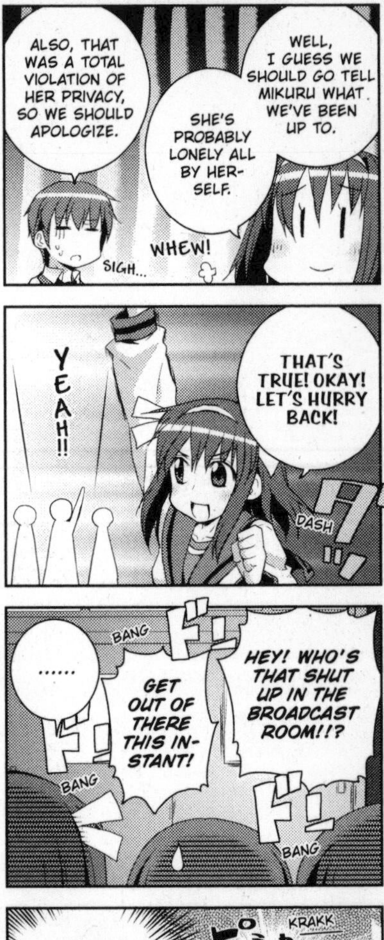
WELL, I GUESS WE SHOULD GO TELL MIKURU WHAT WE'VE BEEN UP TO.
SHE'S PROBABLY LONELY ALL BY HERSELF.
ALSO, THAT WAS A TOTAL VIOLATION OF HER PRIVACY, SO WE SHOULD APOLOGIZE.
WHEW!
SIGH...
THAT'S TRUE! OKAY! LET'S HURRY BACK!
DASH
YEAH!!
HEY! WHO'S THAT SHUT UP IN THE BROADCAST ROOM!!?
BANG
GET OUT OF THERE THIS INSTANT!
BANG
......
BANG
KRAKK
SORRY, MIKURU-CHAN! WE'RE GONNA BE A LITTLE LATE!

TEAM SUZUMIYA

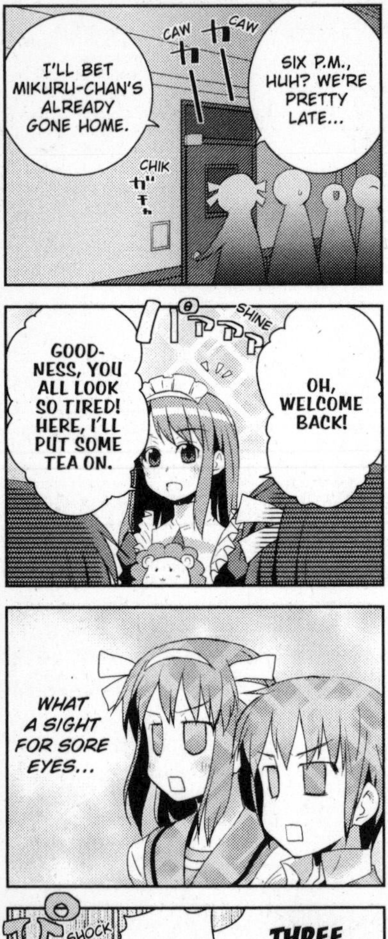
CAW
CAW
SIX P.M., HUH? WE'RE PRETTY LATE...
I'LL BET MIKURU-CHAN'S ALREADY GONE HOME.
CHIK
SHINE
OH, WELCOME BACK!
GOODNESS, YOU ALL LOOK SO TIRED! HERE, I'LL PUT SOME TEA ON.
WHAT A SIGHT FOR SORE EYES...
THREE CHEERS FOR MIKURU-CHAN, EVERYBODY!
YEAH!!!
SHOCK
WHY!?

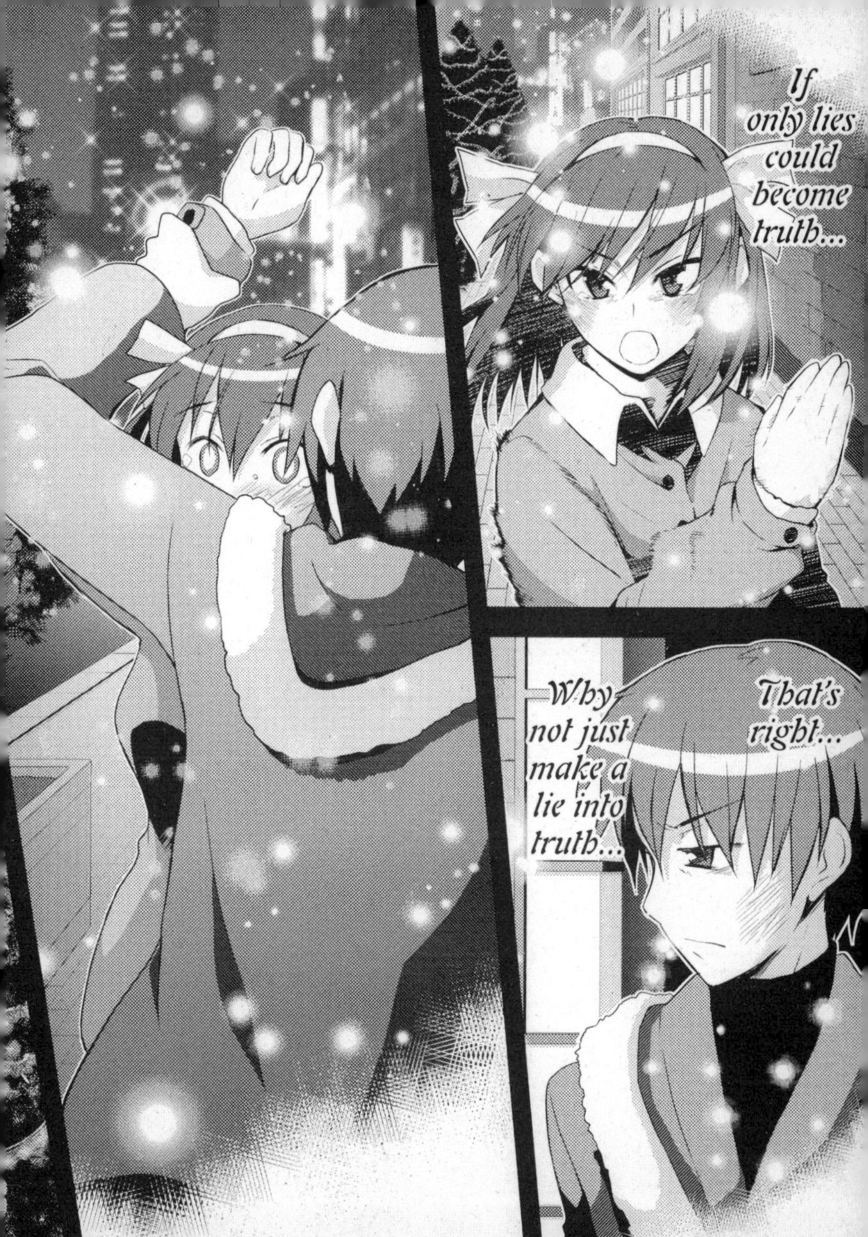
If only lies could become truth...
That's right...
Why not just make a lie into truth...

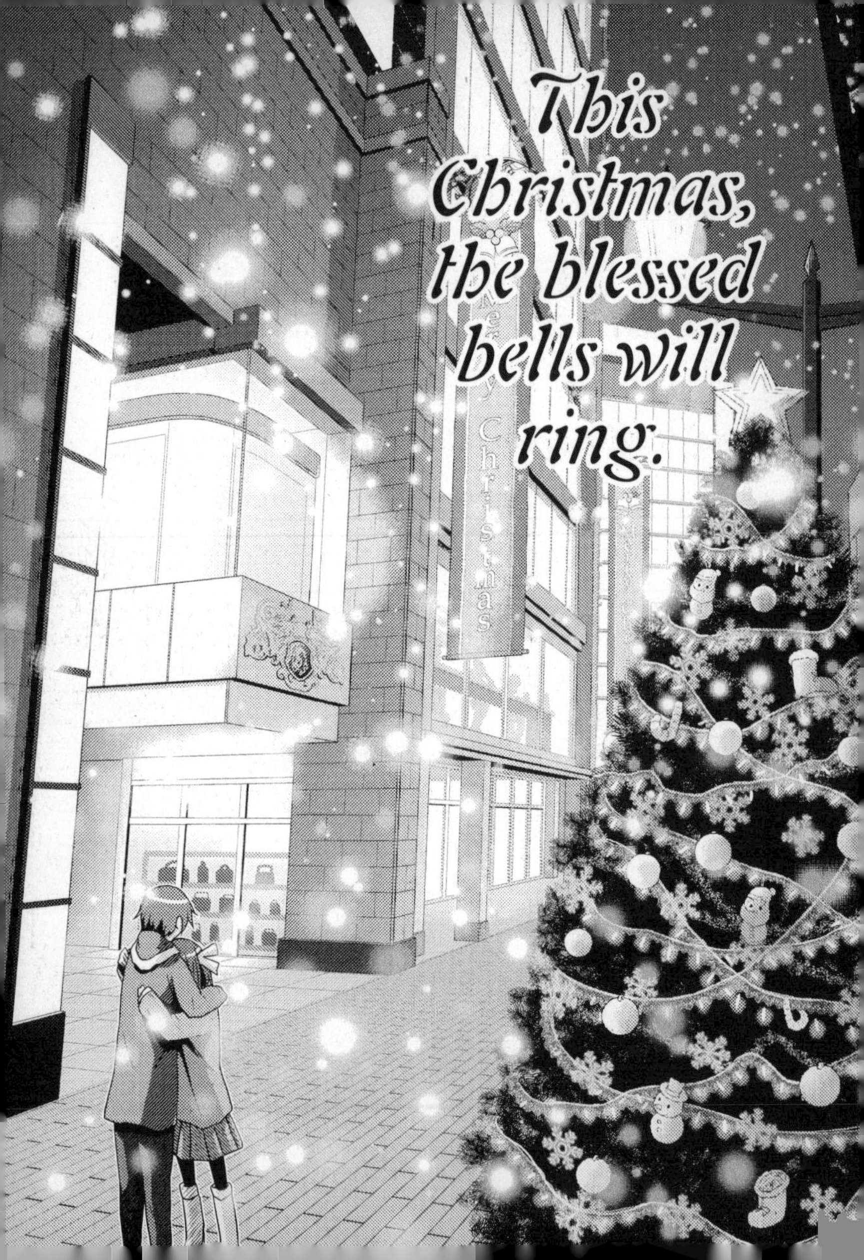
This Christmas, the blessed bells will ring.

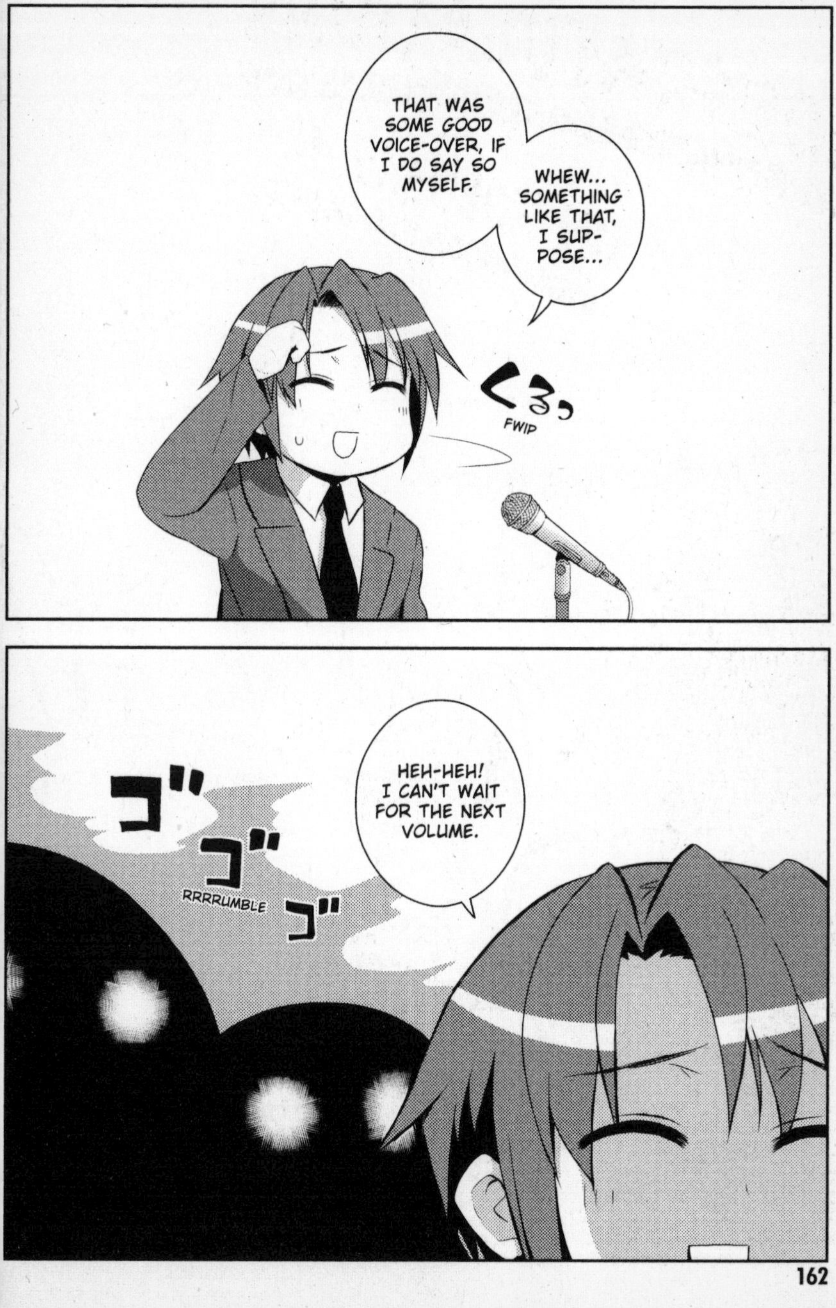
WHEW... SOMETHING LIKE THAT, I SUP-POSE...
THAT WAS SOME GOOD VOICE-OVER, IF I DO SAY SO MYSELF.
くるっ
FWIP
HEH-HEH! I CAN'T WAIT FOR THE NEXT VOLUME.
ゴゴゴ
RRRRUMBLE

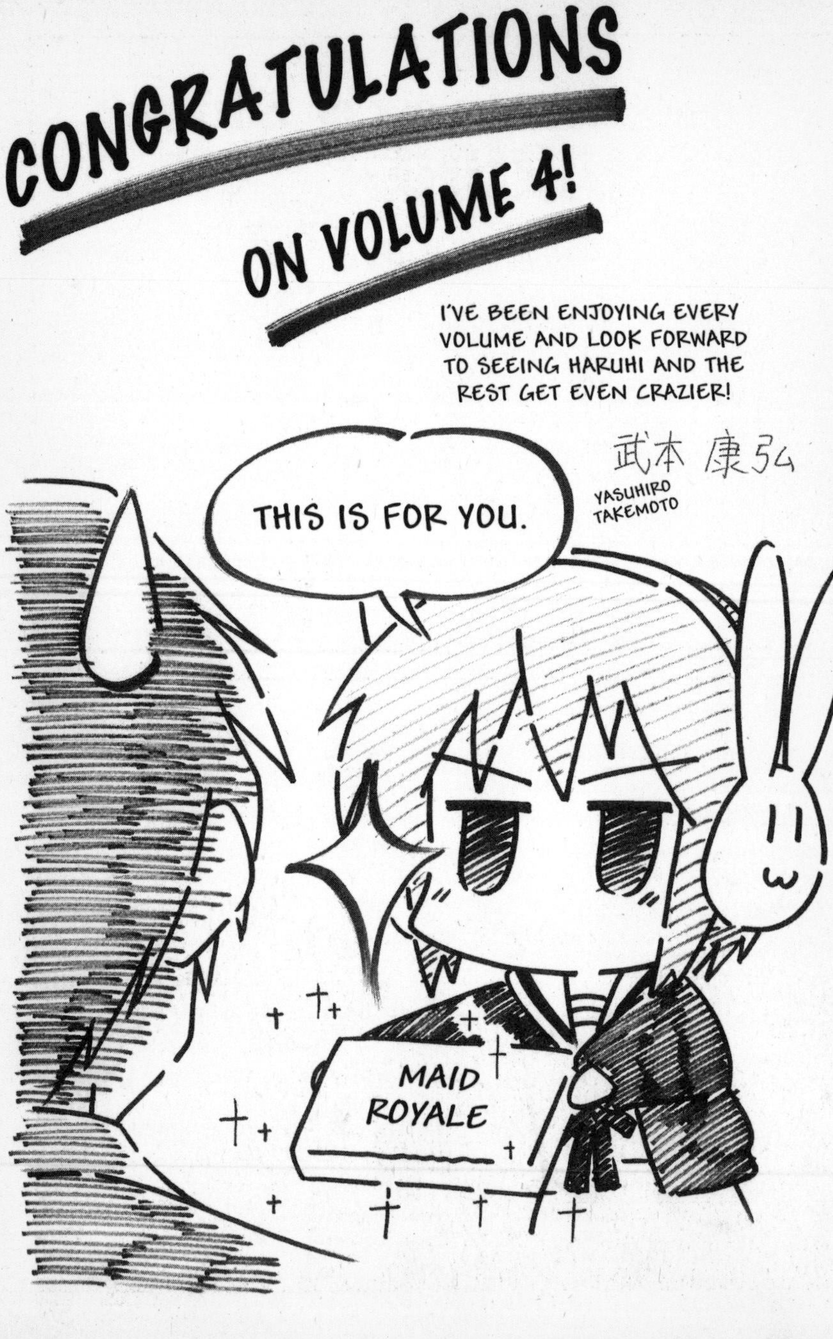
CONGRATULATIONS
ON VOLUME 4!
I'VE BEEN ENJOYING EVERY VOLUME AND LOOK FORWARD TO SEEING HARUHI AND THE REST GET EVEN CRAZIER!
武本 康弘
YASUHIRO TAKEMOTO
THIS IS FOR YOU.
MAID ROYALE

HRYA

THE MELANCHOLY OF SUZUMIYA
HARUHI-CHAN
④

Original Story: Nagaru Tanigawa
Manga: PUYO
Character Design: Noizi Ito

Translation: Paul Starr
Lettering: Hope Donovan

The Melancholy of Suzumiya Haruhi-chan Volume 4
© Nagaru TANIGAWA • Noizi ITO 2009 © PUYO 2009. First published in Japan in 2009
by KADOKAWA SHOTEN Co., Ltd., Tokyo. English translation rights arranged with
KADOKAWA SHOTEN Co., Ltd., Tokyo through TUTTLE-MORI AGENCY, INC., Tokyo.

English translation © 2011 by Hachette Book Group, Inc.

Yen Press
Hachette Book Group
237 Park Avenue, New York, NY 10017

www.HachetteBookGroup.com
www.YenPress.com

Yen Press is an imprint of Hachette Book Group, Inc.
The Yen Press name and logo are trademarks of Hachette Book Group, Inc.

First Yen Press Edition: November 2011

ISBN: 978-0-316-19577-5

10 9 8 7 6 5 4 3 2

BVG

Printed in the United States of America

D0106761